REVOLUTION OR DEATH

THE LIFE OF ELDRIDGE CLEAVER

JUSTIN GIFFORD

Lawrence Hill Books
Chicago

First edition
Published by Lawrence Hill Books
An imprint of Chicago Review Press Incorporated
814 North Franklin Street
Chicago, Illinois 60610
ISBN 978-1-61373-911-2

Library of Congress Cataloging-in-Publication Data
Names: Gifford, Justin, 1975- author.
Title: Revolution or death : the life of Eldridge Cleaver / Justin Gifford.

Other titles: Life of Eldridge Cleaver
Description: First edition. | Chicago : Lawrence Hill Books, [2020] | Includes index. | Summary: "The first trade biography of one of the most notorious black revolutionaries in history, exploring the audacious dreams and spiritual transformations of the eccentric radical and placing him squarely within the context of his changing times"—Provided by publisher.
Identifiers: LCCN 2020026189 (print) | LCCN 2020026190 (ebook) | ISBN 9781613739112 (cloth) | ISBN 9781613739129 (adobe pdf) | ISBN 9781613739136 (mobi) | ISBN 9781613739143 (epub)
Subjects: LCSH: Cleaver, Eldridge, 1935-1998. | African American political activists—Biography. | Political activists—United States—Biography. | African Americans—Politics and government—20th century. | United States—Race relations—History—20th century. | Black Panther Party.
Classification: LCC E185.97.C6 G54 2020 (print) | LCC E185.97.C6 (ebook) | DDC 323.092 [B]—dc23
LC record available at https://lccn.loc.gov/2020026189
LC ebook record available at https://lccn.loc.gov/2020026190

Interior design: Jonathan Hahn

Printed in the United States of America
5 4 3 2 1

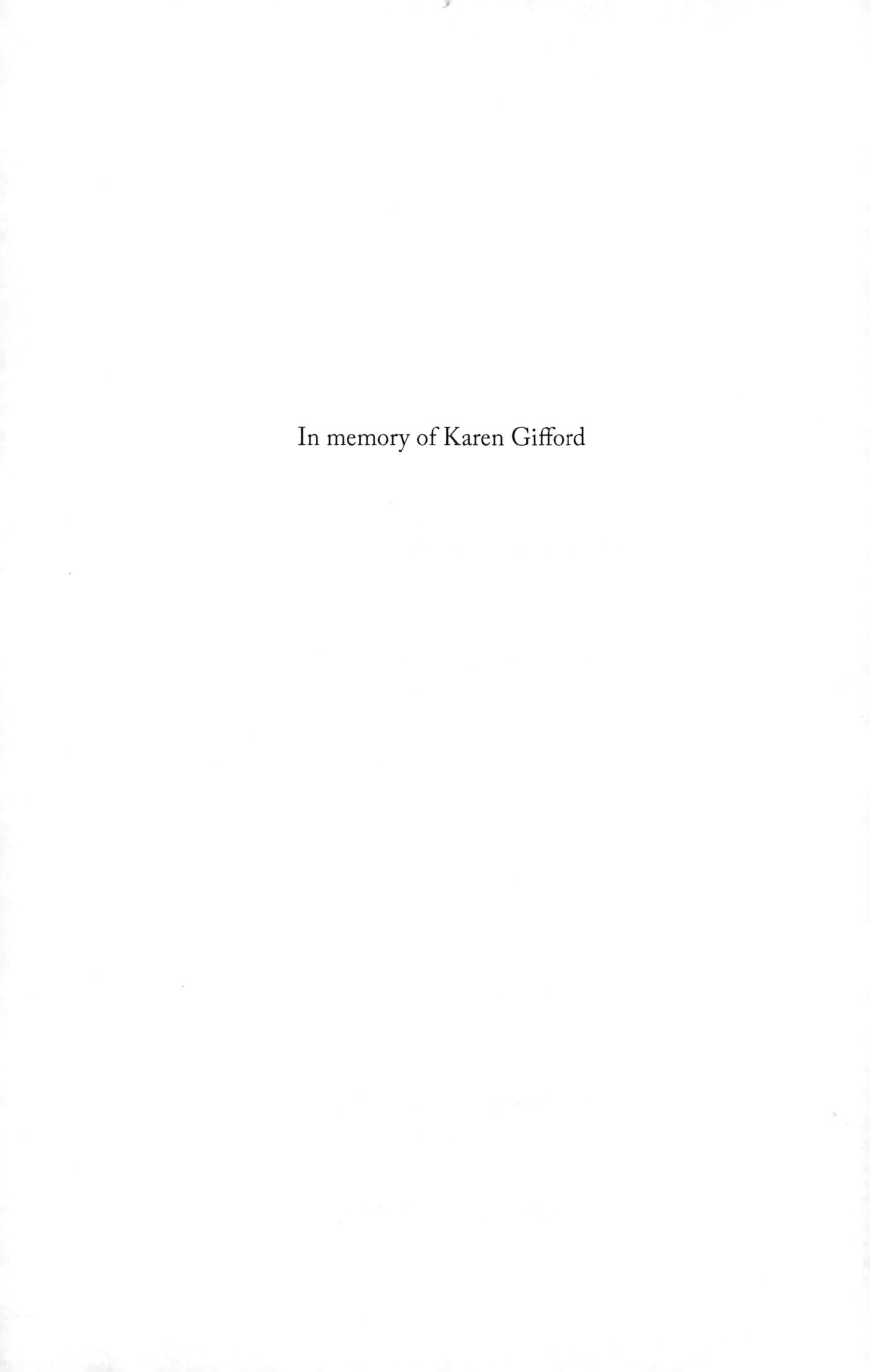

In memory of Karen Gifford

CONTENTS

PREFACE AND ACKNOWLEDGMENTS

When I first met Eldridge Cleaver's son Ahmad at a small café in Casablanca in the spring of 2018, he was carrying a small suitcase and a handmade beehive box. Ahmad, who was originally named Maceo after the Cuban revolutionary Antonio Maceo, was a beekeeper in Saudi Arabia. He had agreed to sit down with me for a series of interviews about his father on the condition that we meet in Casablanca. One hundred miles outside of the city there lived a master beekeeper who practiced ancient Berber methods, and she had agreed to train Ahmad. The beehive was a gift for his new mentor.

Ahmad arrived a few hours late. He apologized profusely and explained that the authorities always held him at the airport for hours to question him and search through his bags. "They think I am secretly another Eldridge Cleaver," he told me. "Now that we have been seen together, they will probably question you at the airport now too." He was right. When I later tried to fly out of the Casablanca airport, I was told there was a problem with my passport. I was taken to a small windowless room, where I was questioned in Arabic and French about I don't know what. At one point, an official came into the room and placed a pair of handcuffs on the desk where I was sitting. After an hour of interrogation, they stamped my passport and let me go.

Ahmad was hauling around his luggage because the hotel he had booked turned out to be a women's rooming house. He asked if he could stay with me. For the next week, we shared an apartment near the ocean overlooking the El Hank Cemetery. I interviewed him daily, and what emerged from our conversations about his father was the captivating story of a man who defied easy political or ideological categorization.

At the height of his fame, Cleaver led the Black Panther Party as a revolutionary activist, calling for the destruction of the United States government. Later, he became a neoconservative who voted for Ronald Reagan and praised the American military. He built an international coalition of radicals dedicated to overthrowing colonialism all over the world, and after he converted to Christianity, he aspired to become the "black Billy Graham" and bring a "spiritual revolution" to society. Over the course of his life, he was a Catholic, a Muslim, a born-again Christian, a Moonie, and a Mormon, though he never fully identified with any of these religious identities. Cleaver was a chameleon who adapted quickly to changing political and social circumstances. He was a man of seemingly irreconcilable contradictions, and these contradictions made me want to uncover his story and understand his life.

On my last day in Casablanca, Ahmad and I were walking through the Old Medina when he got a call from his mother, Kathleen Cleaver. He told her about my book and then handed me the phone. Kathleen was warm and effusive. We talked briefly, and she invited me to visit her at her home in Atlanta. She was willing to be interviewed, and, what's more, she had an entire attic full of Cleaver's papers that I could study.

Two weeks later, I arrived in Atlanta. Every morning over breakfast I interviewed Kathleen at her kitchen table. She spent hours telling stories of Cleaver, providing an intimate depiction of a deeply vulnerable and troubled man, one that defied the radical chic image he had cultivated as a Black Panther. In the afternoons, Kathleen allowed me to read through her archive. Dozens of boxes filled the attic, containing Kathleen's own journals and her memoir; stacks of letters from Cleaver's friends, lovers, and fans; his unpublished writings; prison and

FBI files; and even Cleaver's e-mails, which he had printed and saved like letters.

A few months later, Kathleen attended a funeral for Panther Elbert "Big Man" Howard in Oakland. She met me at the Bancroft Library at the University of California, Berkeley, which contains letters between her and Cleaver that are supposed to be sealed until 2025. Kathleen graciously gave me special permission to read through these letters, a heretofore unseen testimony of the political and personal struggles of the Cleavers from their days as Black Panthers to their time as exiles in Paris. Kathleen provided me with unprecedented access to her archives and was incredibly generous with her time. Cleaver's daughter, Joju, also spent hours telling me stories of her father, and she gave me important insights into his final years. If I am able to recount Cleaver's life successfully, it is because of his wonderful family.

I had originally started researching the life of Cleaver two years earlier, in 2016. I took a group of English literature graduate students on a trip to the Bancroft Library to study the archives of Bay Area activism. There, Theresa Salazar, a curator, introduced me to the newly processed Eldridge Cleaver papers. The archive consists of over thirty cartons of material, including reform-school and prison records, multiple unfinished novels, prison writings, personal letters, and materials from various political and religious organizations. It was an astonishing body of material, and I was surprised that no one had written a biography of Cleaver yet. For the next two summers, I studied the archive at the Bancroft, photographing tens of thousands of pages of material and building the foundation of Cleaver's biography.

I also tracked down Lani Kask, a former Berkeley PhD student and an English instructor at UC Berkeley who had written her dissertation about the love letters between Cleaver and his white lawyer, Beverly Axelrod. Lani was related to Axelrod by marriage, and back in the late 1990s she had planned to write a biography of her. She conducted interviews with Axelrod, Cleaver, and others and helped retrieve Cleaver's prison records from Sacramento. When I met her, she was just about to throw out all of her old Cleaver archives, and she generously handed them over to me instead. Lani has been invaluable to this project. She provided me with a unique collection of interviews, writings, and other materials; offered important insights through our many conversations; and gave feedback on my manuscript. We have Axelrod's indispensable perspective on a critical period in Cleaver's life, thanks to Lani's efforts to document and preserve history. She has indeed made much of this book possible.

After I received a Leon Levy Biography Fellowship at the City University of New York (CUNY) in 2017, I was able to enrich the project in significant ways. At the Arkansas State Archives in Little Rock, I uncovered tax and genealogical records that helped me reconstruct Cleaver's family history going back to slavery. I visited the Dr. Huey P. Newton Foundation Collection at Stanford University to view unpublished Panther writings about Cleaver, and I went to Texas A&M University, which houses Cleaver's personal writings that are missing from the Bancroft. At the National Archives and Records Administration, I examined declassified papers from the US consulate in Algeria, which reported on Cleaver's activities as a fugitive. I then traveled to Algiers, where I visited the Bibliothèque nationale d'Algérie and found critical information about Cleaver's time in North Africa.

The final pieces of Cleaver's life were located in France. French officials had been spying on him since he escaped the United States for Cuba in 1968. In 2018, I received a special derogation from the Préfecture de police to view seventy pages of classified Cleaver files. The police did not allow photography of the files, however, and I don't speak much French. At this time, I met Elaine (Klein) Mokhtefi, who had recently published a book about her experiences with Cleaver and the Black Panthers in the early 1970s. Elaine was kind enough to lend me her apartment in Paris so that I could visit the Préfecture de police. We developed a system for translation. I typed the original French documents on my laptop and then sent Elaine my files, which she translated from French into English. Through our system, I learned the extent of the international surveillance of Cleaver throughout his time abroad. I also traveled to the Centre des archives diplomatiques de Nantes in western France, which houses more files on the International Section of the Black Panther Party. Elaine was gracious enough to translate these for me as well, thus helping me uncover key information about Cleaver's life as a fugitive from the United States.

A number of people kindly agreed to be interviewed for this project, providing invaluable personal perspectives on Cleaver's life. Emory Douglas, Denise Oliver-Velez, and H. Bruce Franklin offered critical insights into Cleaver's life as a Panther, while Randy Rappaport and Alex Hing provided perspectives about his role as a quasi-dictatorial leader of the International Section. Marvin Jackmon knew Cleaver at a number of different points of his life—as inmate, Panther, preacher, and drug addict—and he gave some of the most perceptive interviews about his conflicting personalities. Cleaver's children Ahmad and Joju offered much-needed personal stories to balance those of Cleaver's very public life, and I thank them genuinely for their generosity and honesty. This book is dedicated to Ahmad Cleaver, who died suddenly in fall 2018, just months after I met him.

Thanks especially to the people who were closest to Cleaver—Kathleen Cleaver, Beverly Axelrod, and Elaine Mokhtefi—who provided this book with its most significant points of view on the complicated life of a complicated man. What emerges from the testimonies of Cleaver, Axelrod, and others is a picture of Cleaver as an abusive and emotionally distant individual who embodied some of the most toxic ideas about gender and sexuality in our culture. Their testimonies are difficult to read; they are full of explicit descriptions of emotional and physical violence. But by leaning into that difficulty, we gain a fuller and more truthful account of Cleaver's life and the world that made him. We can learn, for instance, that Cleaver became the successful writer and revolutionary he was precisely because of the influence that radical women—starting with his mother—had on him.

This book is the product of many people's generous contributions. I wrote the bulk of it with the support of my fellow Leon Levy writers: Eleanor Randolph, Lindsay Whalen, Bruce Weber, Aidan Levy, Thad Ziolkowski, and Kai Bird. They read various drafts of the book and, in the earliest stages of production, encouraged me with feedback.

Hayat Laouedj of the Bibliothèque nationale d'Algérie assisted me in my search for files in Algeria, patiently enduring my broken

French. Eric Lechevallier of the Centre des archives diplomatiques de Nantes was extraordinarily helpful in tracking down French documents dealing with Cleaver's activities in Algeria. David Fort and Haley Maynard of the National Archives and Records Administration at College Park were extremely gracious with their time, while John O'Connell of the President Gerald R. Ford library helped me dig up rare letters about Cleaver's return to the United States from exile. I am grateful to Jane Wilkerson at the Arkansas State Archives for helping me locate the tax records of Henry Cleaver, the owner of Cleaver's great grandfather. Thanks go to Jennifer Reibenspies-Stadler at the Cushing Memorial Library and Archives at Texas A&M for introducing me to some of the most extensive and interesting collections of Cleaver's papers. Thanks go, too, to the librarians at the Bibliothèque nationale de France, the Préfecture de police, the Schomburg Center for Research in Black Culture, the New York Public Library, the CUNY Graduate Center, and the Oakland Public Library for all of their assistance.

Alex Mendez did important translation work on the project, communicating with French archivists and translating documents. I thank Trey Bunn, the audiovisual conservator at Emory University Library, for digitizing some of Kathleen Cleaver's personal reel-to-reel tapes from the revolutionary era. Map librarians Glen Creason and Kelly Wallace from the Los Angeles Public Library found historic maps of Cleaver's Rose Hills neighborhood for me, which helped me locate his childhood home.

Ward Churchill read multiple copies of the book and gave invaluable feedback, which improved it immensely. He offered the necessary radical edge to the text. I need also to acknowledge Patrick Anderson, the most knowledgeable Cleaver scholar I know, for discussing the finer points of Cleaver's life and works over the years and improving my thinking. Matt Baker helped me with some of the earliest research on the book, uncovering genealogical records of Cleaver's family. The one and only Ed Mendez assembled all nine hundred endnotes, and he offered important feedback about the manuscript at critical junctures. I would also like to thank my literature students at the Northern

Nevada Correctional Center, who offered their unique ideas on Cleaver's life and writing from the inmate's perspective.

I owe a debt of gratitude to my agent and friend, Matthew Carnicelli, the greatest champion of my work. I would simply not have become a writer without his support over the past decade. I offer a special acknowledgement of appreciation to my editor, Yuval Taylor, who gave a sharp critical perspective and numerous helpful comments to shape this into a drastically better book. I need to acknowledge Karen Stanford, who read late drafts of the book and gave me many helpful suggestions. I want to express my affection for my close friends and family who offered encouragement throughout the book-writing process. Jessica Gifford, Johann Sehmsdorf, Patrick Walsh, Madeline Chaput, Scott Saul, Jim Webber, Cathy Chaput, and Lynda Olman are the most supportive people I have ever known. And finally, a word of love to Pardis, whose laughter changed my life.

Cleaver may seem a problematic choice for a biography. He was imprisoned for eleven years for possession of marijuana, assault with a deadly weapon, and assault with intent to kill. He was a violent man who used intimidation to frighten his enemies and coerce everyone else. As a Panther, he threatened the United States government with insurrection, and after spending seven years in exile, he appeared to sell out his political ideals to save himself when he returned home. He died nearly forgotten in 1998.

But *Revolution or Death* is a different kind of biography: It is not a celebration of a life. It is a nuanced and vivid history of a troubled man who survived by any means necessary. Reading about Cleaver's strange and often surprising life, readers will both admire his bravery in the fight for racial justice and recoil at his disturbing behavior. Most of all, *Revolution or Death* provides readers with a searing portrait of one of the most inscrutable men of the twentieth century. We cannot understand the story of modern America—with all of its racist violence and struggles for radical egalitarianism—without understanding the story of Eldridge Cleaver.

PROLOGUE

ESCAPE (1968)

In December 1968, Eldridge Cleaver was on the run. In the spring, he had led some Black Panthers in an armed assault against Oakland police officers in response to the assassination of Martin Luther King. Cleaver hoped he could spark a guerrilla war across the United States. Several officers were wounded in the ninety-minute shootout, and seventeen-year-old Panther Bobby Hutton was killed by the cops. Cleaver was shot in the foot during the siege and severely beaten after he was taken into custody. He was released on $50,000 bail in June, but then a higher court ordered him to return on November 27. He never showed. Cleaver had spent nearly half of his life in reform schools and prisons and had only recently been released from the California prison system for assault with intent to murder. He could never go back to jail, no matter what the cost. On December 10, the FBI issued a warrant for his arrest and warned that he "has engaged police officers in a gun battle in the past. Consider armed and extremely dangerous." Hundreds of Cleaver supporters held candlelight vigils outside his home, while college students around Berkeley hung signs in their windows reading, ELDRIDGE CLEAVER WELCOME HERE.

Months before his escape, Cleaver had concocted a number of wild schemes to avoid going back to prison. He considered riding horseback through the Rockies and then into Canada. He thought about hijacking a plane from LAX and flying to Cuba. He even pondered shooting it out with the police. He had picked Merritt College as the site of his last stand. Located in the heart of Oakland's black community, Merritt had emerged in the 1960s as the Bay Area's most important educational institution supporting black activism.[1] It served Oakland's working- and middle-class black population, and it had one of the first black studies programs in the country. It was also the alma mater of Black Panther founders Huey Newton and Bobby Seale, who had inspired Cleaver to take up the struggle against the white power structure. Merritt College was ground zero of black political and educational activism in the East Bay. For Cleaver, it was the ideal place for his final showdown with the so-called pigs.

Merritt was also built like a fortress, with stone walls and a three-story tower that could be used as a sniper's perch. Cleaver knew from his time in prison that with a large enough field of vision and sufficient firepower, he could outlast the cops for some time. "Of course [the police] could take it," a Panther and Vietnam veteran told Cleaver, "but it would take a full-scale invasion with some heavy artillery. It would take tanks and some very big guns. If properly defended, then the pigs would have no choice but to leave it or raze it to the ground." Cleaver planned to die a martyr and inspire his Panther comrades. He obtained blueprints of the campus. He mapped underground tunnels as well as plumbing and electrical lines. He created a list of supplies he would need, including everything from gas masks to Band-Aids. He even enlisted Bunchy Carter—a friend from Soledad State Prison and founding member of the Los Angeles chapter of the Panthers—to help him amass an arsenal for the showdown. As November 27 approached, Cleaver prepared himself for the end: "I was going to call a press conference the morning of the 27th at Merritt College, setting forth my reasons for refusing to surrender to the pigs, and calling the people to be witnesses to whatever happened."[2]

In the end, Panther Minister of Defense Huey Newton, who was in prison on a murder charge, ordered Cleaver to flee to Cuba, not only to avoid unnecessary bloodshed but also to follow through with another plan. In summer 1968, Cleaver and a delegation had met with Cuban officials at the United Nations. Cuba promised to provide him with training facilities for guerrilla warfare. Cleaver could later sneak back into the United States and use the Appalachian Mountains as a base to carry out maneuvers against police units. The plan was part of Cleaver's larger vision to free black America by driving out the occupying white police force. It had worked in places like Algeria, and Cleaver hoped to make it work in the United States.

On November 26, the day before he was supposed to return to jail, Cleaver escaped from San Francisco. Outside his home, protesters held up signs that read, KEEP ELDRIDGE FREE while uniformed and plainclothes policemen milled about. Cleaver enlisted a friend named Ralph Smith, who looked a bit like him, to act as a double to fool the police. He slipped out the back door of his house with $15,000 in royalty payments from his recent bestseller *Soul on Ice*, and he jumped over the fence where a car was waiting to take him away. Cleaver enlisted the help of a San Francisco acting troupe to escape. The actors covered his face in stage makeup to make him look old and put him in a wheelchair. Then one of the actresses dressed up as a nurse to push him through the airport. As a final touch, the troupe outfitted him with a fake colostomy bag so that nobody would get too close. He then got on a plane heading for John F. Kennedy International Airport in New York.

Standing over six feet tall and built like Muhammad Ali, he was nervous about passengers recognizing him. About halfway through the flight, the makeup started to melt, giving him a ghoulish appearance. But no one paid too much attention to a sick old man, and he made it to New York without incident. From there, he crossed into Canada and made his way to Montreal, where he stowed away on a freighter heading for Cuba. "I am on my way to exile. Exile!" Cleaver wrote in his journal aboard the ship with a mix of excitement and melancholy. "Behind me, I leave everything: wife, family, friends, the struggle of my people for their liberation, the American revolution."[3]

As the minister of information for the Black Panther Party (BPP) and the flamboyant author of the bestselling *Soul on Ice*, Cleaver was the group's fiercest spokesman and advocate for armed revolution. He helped build the Panther organization from the ground up with Seale and Newton. With his impassioned speeches, Cleaver created meaningful alliances with white radicals, and he inspired thousands to join the cause of black liberation. Along with revolutionary artist Emory Douglas, Cleaver was much of the creative force behind the highly successful *Black Panther* newspaper, the economic and literary engine for the party. He was uncompromising in his vision for overturning the white capitalist order in America. When the dream of a nonviolent social transformation of American society died with the assassination of Martin Luther King, Cleaver was prepared to incite guerrilla warfare to destroy Babylon, his pejorative name for America. As he said in a speech at the height of his influence, "Instead of submitting to this any longer, we would rather provoke a situation that will gut this country, that will lay waste to the cities, that will disrupt the economy to such an extent that the enemies of America can come in and pick the gold out of the teeth of these Babylonian pigs."[4] Cleaver thrilled and outraged audiences. He sprinkled his speeches with enough *motherfuckers* to scandalize the average listener. He challenged Governor Ronald Reagan to a duel to the death—with pistols or marshmallows. He ran for president of the United States under the leftist Peace and Freedom Party, and he promised to bulldoze the White House if elected.

The Black Panther Party represented the vanguard of black radicalism in the late 1960s. Founded by two Oakland college students, Bobby Seale and Huey Newton, the party drew from the ideas of Malcolm X and Frantz Fanon to create a new kind of black political organization. The party argued that black communities were internal colonies within a larger white imperialist nation and that the police was an occupying force. It enlisted "brothers on the block" while preaching a doctrine of armed self-defense and forming patrols to combat police brutality. The gun was a recruitment tool to organize black discontent into a coherent political movement. The Panthers created a Ten-Point Program, which they published in each issue of the *Black Panther*. Among their demands were equal protection under the law, an end to police brutality, exemption from military service, and affordable housing. The program concluded, "We want land, bread, housing, education, clothing, justice and peace." With Cleaver as their spokesmen, the Panthers caught the imagination of African Americans across the United States. In the late 1960s, over sixty Panther chapters were established, with thousands of members willing to coordinate community programs and bear arms in the revolutionary struggle. Throughout this era, the Panthers forged political alliances with white radicals and black nationalist organizations within the United States, as well as with countries engaged in struggles against colonial rule across the globe, including Cuba, Algeria, Vietnam, North Korea, and the Congo.

Because of the Panthers' success, they became the target of FBI Director J. Edgar Hoover's COINTELPRO (Counter Intelligence Program), a clandestine government operation that sought to disrupt and neutralize "black nationalist hate groups" like the Black Panthers. The federal agency successfully created factionalism between the Panthers and other black organizations by planting informants within the party, forging letters to create conflict among party leaders, and encouraging Panthers to commit acts of violence. Although the FBI had initially targeted civil rights organizations like the Southern Christian Leadership Conference (SCLC) and the Student Nonviolent Coordinating Committee (SNCC), by fall 1968 it had turned its attention to the Panthers, characterizing the organization as "the greatest threat to the internal security of the country."

The FBI had been shadowing Cleaver since late 1967, and throughout 1968 he was one of its key targets. In a February memo from the San Francisco FBI field office, the director reported with some alarm, "Cleaver has demonstrated a propensity for violence and holds a position of leadership with the BPPSD, which threatens guerrilla warfare, the burning of cities and revolution."[5] Following Cleaver's shootout with the cops, the FBI placed him on its Agitator Index and labeled him "armed and dangerous."[6] He was followed everywhere by the FBI and the Oakland police. California governor Ronald Reagan perhaps best summed up the prevailing attitude toward Cleaver. When Cleaver was invited to lecture at Berkeley in fall 1968, Reagan responded, "If Eldridge Cleaver is allowed to teach our children, they may come home one night and slit our throats." By the time he slipped police surveillance at his house in late November and escaped the country, Cleaver was considered by many the most dangerous man in America.

The two-week trip down the East Coast to Cuba was difficult. The Saint Lawrence River was so choked with ice that the crewmen had to use an icebreaker to get to the sea. They dropped anchor a number of times to wait out the storm. While he sat bobbing in the ocean waves, Cleaver was gripped by the fear that the FBI or CIA would torpedo the boat out of the water. He was forced to stay hidden in the cabin of a Cuban sailor. It was a tiny room with two small beds and a little table between them. Cleaver was not allowed to leave his room. He was given a box full of canned and packaged food—condensed milk, tuna, beans, and a stack of chocolate bars—and was told he would have to survive the entire trip on it. He also had to cram his giant frame into a closet anytime someone knocked on the door. American agents were everywhere, he was told, and he had to remain hidden. It was suffocating and claustrophobic in the tiny closet. "It was not long before I began to feel like a jack-in-the box," Cleaver wrote in his journal. "The knocks on the door became so frequent that every time I turned around I found myself inside that closet. Sometimes I would remain in the closet for over an hour."[7]

There was no going back to America now. Cleaver had started a gunfight with the Oakland police, and he was in open rebellion against the American government. During the decade he had spent in prison, Cleaver had studied a range of thinkers, from political philosophers Thomas Paine and Karl Marx to radical intellectuals W. E. B. Du Bois and Che Guevara. In fact, one of Cleaver's greatest talents was that he was able to immerse himself in a range of intellectual traditions and adopt different kinds of vocabularies, rhetoric, and ideologies. All of this intensive studying led him to one simple conclusion: the system of capitalism and its agents preyed upon black people and therefore had to be destroyed. There was no compromise—it was revolution or death. Writing about his final meeting with his parole officer, Cleaver reflected, "I would always think to myself: here is this chump, a descendant of the kidnappers and enslavers of my ancestors, sitting before me, looking me in my eyes, trying to show me the point as to why I should not be working to smash this evil system! All of that is now over. It should be clear, even to parole officers that I repudiate America The Ugly, in toto, and my every effort is to destroy it, so that out of its ashes America the beautiful can be born."[8]

A few minutes after midnight on Christmas, the steamer entered Havana Harbor. As Cleaver waited for the ship to dock, he was unsure what part he would play in the coming upheaval. Cuba, with its long history of slave revolts and revolution, seemed to him the ideal place to organize black resistance against white America. "The very name, *Cuba,* was full of molasses and blood, machetes and screams in the night," wrote Cleaver, seeing the shoreline for the first time. Yet beneath the layers of bravado, there was another Cleaver, one who was suspicious of the fantasy that Cuba was a Communist utopia. Rumors circulated about rampant racial discrimination against black people throughout Cuba, and Castro was still a relatively unknown quantity in the struggle for black American liberation. Cleaver would have to see for himself. He was now a deserter and a man without a country, and as the uncertainty pressed upon him, he admitted, "I was full of trepidation as that boat pulled into the Havana harbor."[9]

1

SLAVERY AND THE AMERICAN SOUTH (1838–1944)

The story of Eldridge Cleaver's life begins with the story of slavery in the United States. Cleaver had always believed his ancestors could be traced back to Jefferson Davis, the Southern senator who became president of the Confederate States of American during the Civil War. But this was a family myth, told and retold by his mother Thelma over meals and at gatherings. It was a story that Cleaver himself perpetuated over the course of his life. Although future documents may reveal undiscovered connections between the Cleaver and Davis families, there is no current evidence that they are related. Cleaver's true lineage is at once more modest and heroic than he knew. Over generations, his ancestors escaped slavery, gained literacy, and pursed artistic expression to overcome segregation. The Cleaver family's struggle for freedom anticipated Cleaver's own journey, and to understand his life as an activist, artist, and preacher, we must first understand his family history.

On June 3, 1838, Cleaver's great-grandfather Edwin arrived by steamer at the Port of Mobile in Alabama. Edwin was a ten-year-old slave, standing four feet tall and listed as "Black" on the manifest. He was accompanied by a seventeen-year-old young woman named Mary, who was listed as "Yellow." They had both been purchased in New Orleans by Henry Cleaver, a white farmer from Missouri who was ambitious to make his fortune in cotton.[1] Since the international slave trade had been outlawed since 1807, Edwin and Mary were not imported from Africa. They were most likely from a state like Virginia or Georgia, where the cotton industry was in decline because of overworked soil. Like many aspiring plantation owners, Henry decided to buy children in order to save money. He planned to breed them when they reached adulthood, to create a family workforce for his plantation.

Edwin and Mary were just two of the thousands of slaves auctioned off each week in New Orleans, the largest slave-trading city in America. During the first half of the nineteenth century, nearly a million slaves were taken to New Orleans—mostly by slave traders—via railway, stagecoach, ship, or foot, in the largest forced migration in American history.[2]

From New Orleans, Edwin and Mary were taken to Mobile, Alabama's largest slave-trade center and second only to New Orleans in the Gulf Coast region. Mobile was one of America's wealthiest and most cosmopolitan cities. To Edwin and Mary, it must have been a bewildering place, an incongruous mixture of white wealth and black misery. Grand hotels and palatial Greek Revival homes lined the streets, while affluent white people visited theaters, which offered everything from *Macbeth* to minstrel shows. Tourists from all over the world came to Mobile to see its opulence. In the mid-nineteenth century, Alabama was the US cotton kingdom, and Mobile was its gateway.

Edwin and Mary were transported by boat up the Alabama River to Henry Cleaver's plantation in Lowndes County, the center of Alabama slave society. By the time Edwin arrived, the last of the

Cherokees and other native tribes were being forced west of the Mississippi River along the Trail of Tears under the Indian Removal Act of 1830, signed by President Andrew Jackson. White planters had made a frenzied bid for the five million acres of ceded territory between the mountains to the north and the coast to the south, known as the Black Belt. Rivaled only by the California Gold Rush, Alabama Fever was the largest land grab in American history. Cotton was the everyman's crop. It grew quickly in the dark, fecund soil. Countless pioneers and plantation owners like Henry Cleaver came to Alabama to cash in on the booming trade. With enough forced labor and stolen land, there was no limit to the amount of money a white man could make.

Henry had come to Alabama with his brother William in 1826 from Missouri to make a living in cotton farming. The brothers were frontiersmen and self-styled Southern gentlemen. With an inheritance they received from their father, they bought slaves, cleared land, and started farming cotton. Henry married and built a home. The Cleaver brothers planted corn and other crops, but it was slave-based cotton farming where the money was to be made.

Edwin's life as a slave under the system was a brutal one. As a child, he picked cotton, fed the livestock, stoked fires, and fetched water. As he grew into a young man, he became responsible for clearing trees, chopping wood, plowing fields, ginning cotton, and bagging it for sale. Each slave picked between two hundred to three hundred pounds a day during the harvest season. Slaves worked from sunup until sundown and sometimes up to eighteen hours a day. They were not allowed to own property or pets or leave the plantation without a written pass, and state law forbade them from learning to read or write.[3]

On his five-hundred-acre plantation, Henry accumulated handsome sums of money off the backs of slave labor. He purchased more slaves with the profits and expanded his holdings, all while looking west to even greater opportunities. In 1844, the Cleaver brothers set off in covered wagons with their families and slaves, traveling five hundred miles west to Arkansas. No one knows why the brothers gave up a stable life in Alabama for the uncertainty of the West. It might have simply been a matter of money. Land in Arkansas was cheap, and with its alluvial plains and waterways for transportation, the state was emerging as another booming cotton market. It was a harrowing journey. Spanish conquistador Hernando de Soto had died either here or in neighboring Louisiana three centuries earlier on an ill-fated expedition searching for gold. With its pine forests and swampy lowlands, Arkansas was still a wilderness in the mid-nineteenth century. West of the Mississippi, there wasn't even a marked trail. Edwin and his fellow slaves drove the livestock across a disorienting frontier of heavy woodlands and crisscrossing streams. They blazed trails through dense thickets with axes and waded through the swamps that spotted the landscape. They were among Arkansas's first pioneers, forced to brave the harsh landscape to make a new home out west.

The Cleaver brothers and their slaves settled in Camden—Arkansas's second-largest city at the time—along the Ouachita River. It was a shrewd choice, as the river was becoming a major transportation hub on the way to New Orleans. The Cleaver brothers purchased a square mile of land a few miles west of Camden. Edwin and the other slaves were set to work clearing the boggy marshes for a plantation and slave cabins. It was exhausting and tedious labor, made more difficult because they were low on food that first winter of 1844.

After the plantation was firmly established, Edwin and other slaves were tasked with the grueling work of harvesting cotton. After picking a few hundred pounds each day, they processed it in their cabins at night. In its raw form, cotton is full of seeds, which have to be removed painstakingly by hand unless ginned. On Henry Cleaver's plantation, "there were cotton gins, but not enough to separate all the lint from the seeds. Slaves had to work in their cabins at night, pulling the locks apart, putting the seeds in one pile, the lint in another. When a slave had filled his shoe with seeds so that he could not get his foot in it he was allowed to quit for the night."[4]

Over the next fifteen years, Henry and William made a small fortune from the cotton trade. In 1846, the brothers owned seven slaves, who worked 720 acres. Just a year later, Henry and William owned sixteen slaves. By 1853, just seven years after their arrival, they owned twenty-nine slaves working over one thousand acres.[5] The 1850s was an era of high cotton prices and good weather, and the Cleavers continued to build their fortune. In 1856, William died and left his slaves to his brother. By the eve of the Civil War, Henry Cleaver was a member of the elite class of planters.[6]

Despite the hardships that Edwin and the other slaves faced, they still found ways to survive. Family life was very important. In 1860, there were a total of twenty-six slaves on the plantation: four adult couples and eighteen children.[7] Edwin married a woman from the plantation named Charlotte, and she gave birth to a girl named Eliza, as well as two boys, Milton and Redman. Although slave marriages were not recognized by state law, many slave owners encouraged monogamous family units. Henry Cleaver sanctioned these slave marriages, not only because it increased the value of his property but also because he believed that it discouraged slaves from running away.

In 1862, Union troops marched into Arkansas, heralding the end of slavery and the collapse of the Cleaver plantation. Thousands of slaves joined the Union as the army made its way through the state, abandoning plantations and enlisting in black infantry regiments. On January 1, 1863, Abraham Lincoln's Emancipation Proclamation took effect, freeing slaves in states that were rebelling against the federal government, which inspired even more black men to join the Union encampments springing up all over Arkansas. The Union set up one such encampment in Camden, right near the Cleaver plantation. As Union forces plundered plantations and burned crops, erstwhile slave owners abandoned their lands and left the state, sometimes taking their slaves with them. Texas was the most common destination for slave owners who did not want their slaves to end up in Union hands. Half of Arkansas's 110,000 slaves ended up in the Lone Star State by the end of the Civil War. As news of the Emancipation Proclamation spread across Arkansas, Henry took most of his slaves and fled to Waco, Texas. Here he reportedly gave each of them one hundred dollars and set them free.[8]

Edwin, Charlotte, and their children were not among those who traveled to Texas. They may have been left behind, though it is more likely that they escaped and sought protection from soldiers as the

Union marched into town. After the war was over, Edwin and Charlotte reemerged in Camden, where they would live out the rest of their lives as free people.

For the white Cleaver family, it was the end of an era. Henry's son William, a Confederate soldier, was killed out west in the New Mexico Campaign, as the Confederates sought to take control of the gold and silver supplies funding the Union. Henry Cleaver himself died in his sister's home in Waco not long after his arrival. The slave system that had brought him so much wealth and his slaves so much misery was now in ruins. But for Edwin, Charlotte, and their children, Eliza, Milton, and Redman, it was a time of liberation.

In 1865, following the end of the Civil War, Charlotte gave birth to a son named Henry, who would become Eldridge Cleaver's grandfather. Why they named him after their former master is unknown. Following emancipation, many slaves adopted new names reflecting their break from their former masters and as an assertion of their free status. Edwin shortened his name to Ned, though he and the rest of the family kept the last name Cleaver. Many other slaves across the South kept their master's surname as well, not out of any affection for the master, but because in small communities like Camden they would have been known by census takers, government officials, and potential employers by that surname. This would have been common in Camden, where the Freedmen's Bureau set up an office to help newly freed slaves settle in the postemancipation South. Charlotte's son Henry was the first African American Cleaver child born free from slavery.

Although slavery was destroyed at the end of the Civil War, the postbellum South started reinstituting many of the same economic practices and social structures that had characterized slavery. Forced bondage had been outlawed by the Thirteenth Amendment, but many large landowners still wielded massive power in this new America. Farm tenancy or sharecropping soon replaced slavery, as white people refused to sell property to black people or to advance them credit. In this arrangement, sharecroppers made contracts with plantation owners to work in the fields for a share of the harvest. African Americans were completely dependent on the fairness of white people, and this led to the exploitation of sharecroppers. White employers underreported the size of the crop, lied about their accounts, and cheated former slaves, most of who could neither read nor write. They also used every form of intimidation to keep them working, including whippings.[9] After slavery, sharecropping quickly emerged as the new economic system of the South.

With a growing family and few options, Ned and Charlotte found work in the fields from which they had just been liberated. In 1867, with the aid of the Freedmen's Bureau, they negotiated a labor contract with a white plantation owner named Eliza A. McElrath, a neighbor of their former master. Some parts of the contract were typical of the period. McElrath agreed to provide "good and sufficient quarters and full teams and feed for same and implements to make a crop." In exchange, Ned and Charlotte promised to "labor faithfully." Other sections were reminiscent of slavery. They had to "be at work at one half hour by the sun on each and every working day (unless prevented by sickness) and labor until sunset." They were allowed two hours of rest starting at noon in the hot summer months, but only one hour of rest at noon in spring, autumn, and winter. In addition to picking, ginning, and packing the cotton, they had to consent to "labor at all times under the exclusive direction and control" of Eliza McElrath.[10] Ned and Eliza also had to promise not to leave the plantation without permission, or they would have to pay a dollar fine. Such indentured servitude tethered Ned and Charlotte to Camden and the sharecropping system for the rest of their lives.

Despite the legacies of slavery, Henry Cleaver grew up in a world that witnessed dramatic new opportunities for black people. The period of Reconstruction (1865–1877) was a brief moment of black political power and social progress. Following ratification of the Fourteenth and Fifteenth Amendments, which bestowed citizenship and voting rights on black men, nearly two thousand African Americans were voted into local, state, and national office. In Arkansas, legislation was passed that banned discrimination on railroads, street cars, stagecoaches, hotels, and saloons.[11] But it was the creation of formal education that was probably the single most significant development in the postslave society. Most southern states had once enacted legislation that made it illegal to teach a slave to read, and therefore literacy was seen as a pathway to freedom by many enslaved people. After the war, black citizens themselves created and ran schools out of churches, old buildings, or people's homes. As one Freedmen's Bureau agent in Arkansas reported, "The desire for education is unabated, and is so strong among some as to be deemed by some as excessive, amounting almost to a passion."[12] Despite having few resources, African Americans funded one-third of the costs for setting up these new schools and invented black public education in the South.[13]

For the Cleaver family, education was supremely important. Ned could both read and write at a time when 90 percent of the adult black population in the South was illiterate.[14] Henry attended school in Camden and learned the value of education from his parents. As a teenager, he took a job as a lumberjack in the emerging timber industry, which had been expanding as railway lines replaced rivers as the main transportation in the area. The lumberjack was a more specialized worker than the sharecropper, and it was therefore a highly coveted job among black people. As an adult, he became a Methodist circuit preacher who had no established church but traveled to neighboring counties to preach at picnics and revival meetings. By the time Henry was in his forties, he had saved enough money to buy a farm in Bradley, a small community not too far from Camden. He built a cabin in middle of the property, grew cotton around it, raised hogs and chickens, and hunted rabbits. With the little money he had left, he purchased a typewriter, a testimony to all that he had achieved as the son of former slaves. It was the Cleaver family's prized possession.

The turn of the twentieth century witnessed more dramatic transformations in black life, as African Americans began leaving the rural South for urban centers. The rising tide of white violence and the failure of Reconstruction to produce lasting legal and economic equality for African Americans encouraged many of them to abandon their homelands. During World War I, many southern black people boarded trains and moved north to cities like New York and Chicago, while others simply walked off sharecropping farms and headed to the closest urban center. It was a movement that would eventually become known as the Great Migration, and by the time it subsided in the 1970s, six million African Americans had made the pilgrimage out of the feudal South searching for a better existence. Like other black families in this era, Henry Cleaver and his new wife, Laurah, were swept up in these transformations.

In 1900, Laurah gave birth to a son named Leroy, who would eventually become Eldridge Cleaver's father. Throughout his childhood and teens, Leroy worked on his father Henry's farm along with his many brothers and sisters. When he was eighteen, he followed in Henry's footsteps and took a job as a lumberjack at Eagle Lumber Company just outside Camden. But he was restless. Like many of the young men who worked in the fields and the sawmills around Camden, Leroy dreamed of moving to the city.

Leroy set his sights on Little Rock, which had emerged as the black cultural center of Arkansas. Following the Civil War, the federal army set up a log cabin shantytown for runaway slaves next to the city's graveyard. During Reconstruction, African Americans came to Little Rock in droves, settling near downtown, between Capitol Avenue and Twelfth Street west of Main Street. What started as a small settlement grew into a city within a city, especially along Ninth Street. A number of black churches anchored this African American community, none more significant than the Bethel African Methodist Episcopal (AME) Church. Located at the corner of Ninth and Broadway, it became the spiritual and political center of black Little Rock. The church held classes in its basement to increase literacy among former slaves and their descendants, raised funds for social movements such as the Back-to-Africa Movement, and even started a college for black students.

As legalized segregation—also known as Jim Crow—became the law of the land following *Plessy v. Ferguson*, the black community in Little Rock evolved to meet the needs of its citizens. In the early twentieth century, dozens of small businesses sprang up throughout the neighborhood, including grocers, blacksmiths, shoe repairmen, tailors, and jewelers. Black barbershops, such the Deluxe Barbershop, became the heart and soul of black Little Rock, places where people could gossip and argue about politics over games of dominoes or checkers.[15] Men could have their hair conked—straightened with lye—while women could have their eyebrows groomed and their hair styled. Ninth Street boasted its own black hotels, while a number of restaurants served southern delicacies to black customers. Rough-and-ready hot dog and barbeque stands dotted Ninth Street, and at all times of the day or night the smells of soul food—pork chops, chitterlings, southern fried chicken, and goose-liver sandwiches—wafted through the streets.[16]

There was also a grittier side to the Line, so-called because Ninth Street marked the boundary separating white and black Little Rock. Bootleggers peddled their wares up and down the block, and violent fights broke out. Black Little Rock had its share of pool rooms, saloons, and juke joints, where musicians played to diverse black crowds. In the absence of parks and other places of entertainment available to black people, these establishments provided some of the few places where African Americans were welcome. As a Little Rock Vice Commission report about pool rooms put it, "Large crowds lounge about, tell smooty jokes, and sometimes quarrel. These places are also used as half-way houses to the saloons, where beer is carried by minors and distributed freely. The pool rooms are visited occasionally by women, who are instrumental in carrying beer to the pool rooms."[17]

The nightclubs along the Line were part of what became known as the Chitlin' Circuit, a loose collection of cabarets and dance halls across the South and Midwest where black actors, musicians, and comics entertained black audiences. Like the African American delicacy made of pig intestines for which it was named, the Chitlin' Circuit was considered by white people to be a space for cultural refuse. But for black audiences and artists who were shut out of other entertainment venues, the Chitlin' Circuit was at first a necessity and then a source of great pride.[18]

Leroy was drawn to the Line, and at the age of twenty, he left his father's farm to make a life in the city. After a brief stint as an elevator operator in Hot Springs, he moved on to Little Rock in the early 1920s.[19] Leroy was a talented piano player, and he hoped to make it as a blues musician in the nightclub scene. How he learned to play the piano growing up on a cotton farm isn't entirely clear. Leroy often traveled with his father to various religious gatherings where gospel music was played. Both gospel and the blues derive from African American spirituals, mournful songs sung by slaves that expressed suffering and sometimes coded messages of escape. Because blues and gospel are both grounded in similar black experiences, rhythms, and tonal idioms, it is likely that Leroy picked up the blues through gospel. In Little Rock, he met a white singer named Dick Powell, and they played clubs together until the mid-1920s, when Powell left Little Rock to sing and play banjo in a Kentucky orchestra before eventually pursuing a successful career as a film star. Leroy kept playing music in the clubs along Ninth Street, but the pay was low and the work irregular. When the Little Rock Boys Club opened in downtown in 1930, he took a job as a janitor there, which he would hold for the next decade.[20] Leroy, like many black people, faced extreme prejudice in the job industry. African Americans made up 25 percent of the city's population, and yet most were employed in what were known as "Negro jobs."[21]

In the mid-1920s, Leroy met Thelma Robinson, his future wife and mother of Eldridge Cleaver. Her grandparents, Preston Robinson and Eliza Means, had moved to Little Rock in the 1890s from Malvern, a railroad stop fifty miles southwest of the city. The Robinsons aspired to black middle-class status. Thelma's grandfather started off as a cook and lived in the heart of Little Rock's black district at 520 West Sixth Street. Her father, Henry Robinson, had worked his way up through a series of jobs, first as a driver for grocer J. M. Critz and Sons, then as a porter, and finally as a shipping clerk.[22] Henry was successful enough that he and his wife Hattie purchased a small home at 2929 Short Ringo Street around 1910. In the mid-1920s, they moved just a few blocks away to 3101 S. State Street.[23] The location was in a developing black neighborhood about a mile and a half south of Ninth Street, a lower middle-class district full of modest bungalows and shaded by giant trees.

Like Leroy, Thelma came from a religious family. Henry Robinson was the respected minister of the St. Andrews AME Church, a southside branch of the original Ninth Street Bethel AME Church. This was no small achievement, given the stature of the AME church among black people across the South. For over one hundred years, the AME church had been the central spiritual and political institution in the lives of black people. Founded at the end of the eighteenth century after white Methodists had refused to integrate church seating, the African Methodist Episcopal Church emerged as an important institution that promoted social uplift for slaves. AME church leaders boycotted the purchase of slave-created goods and raised funds to purchase slaves in order to set them free.[24] Denmark Vesey famously used the AME church as a forum to organize the slave revolts of 1822. Because the AME church gave slaves an organization to assert their humanity and rally against their oppression, it was largely outlawed in Southern states. Following the end of slavery, AME churches reemerged all over the South as the first institutions to provide former slaves with a sense of shared belonging. In Little Rock, the AME church provided the religious and social foundation for the growing black community, first along Ninth Street, and then, thanks to Henry Robinson, on the southside.

When Thelma and Leroy decided to get married, the Robinson family at first objected to it. After all, Leroy was a honky-tonk piano player and a janitor with an eighth-grade education. His father, Henry Cleaver, was a circuit preacher, which Henry Robinson considered a less than prestigious position. The Robinsons, by contrast, were part of Little Rock's small but emerging black middle class, with a religious and educational pedigree. According to Cleaver, they considered themselves to be "a great tribe of Mulattos, proud of their gray blue eyes and pointed noses."[25] In January 1926, Thelma got pregnant with her first child, Wilhelmina, and, over the protests of her father, she and

Leroy got married that same year. For a while, they lived in the Robinson household until they could save up enough money to rent their own home. Thelma worked as a maid in a doctor's office, while Leroy worked as a janitor and played in piano bars downtown.

On August 31, 1935, Thelma gave birth to Leroy Eldridge Cleaver. It had been an unseasonably chilly summer in central Arkansas that year, a small mercy for a region usually bathed in subtropical heat and sweltering humidity. They named their firstborn son Leroy after his father. As an adult, Cleaver would identify by his middle name Eldridge, an Anglo-Saxon moniker nearly a thousand years old meaning "noble ruler." Depending on one's view of his many conflicting identities—criminal, Nation of Islam leader, Black Panther, international revolutionary, and born-again Christian conservative—this name was either prophetic or deeply ironic.

After Cleaver's birth, Leroy, Thelma, and their growing family moved to 2106 S. Park Street in South Little Rock, about a mile and a half from Thelma's parents. The house was modest and shaded by oak trees, but it also had a large backyard covered in dark clay where the children chased lizards, trapped bumble bees in jars, and played in the "gooey muck."[26] Thelma stressed the importance of reading and education. Cleaver remembered, "Getting an education was a religion in our house. Mother was the high priestess of its doctrine. According to her, the worst thing in life was to miss an education. It was worse than going to hell!"[27] Thelma taught her children to read, and she even gave them books for birthdays. It was more than just a matter of self-improvement. Both the Robinsons and the Cleavers believed that access to formal education was the most powerful weapon in the fight for black liberation. Thelma herself was a high school graduate with aspirations to become a schoolteacher. This was brave, given the obstacles that black people faced long before the Little Rock Nine. In the mid-1920s, Arkansas's school system was the most poorly funded in America, and black schools received less than half the share of state funding they were promised.[28] Furthermore, because black schools symbolized upward mobility for segregated black individuals, white people often tried to destroy them. In 1929, Gibbs High School in

Little Rock, which Thelma had attended, was set on fire twice in a period of two weeks by arsonists.[29]

Thelma was also devoutly religious, and she imparted her beliefs to her children. She made them say their prayers before bed. She also took her children to church regularly, and she hoped that her young son Eldridge might follow in her own father's footsteps and become a preacher. This was the beginning of the conflict between his parents. "I don't want my boy to be no jack legged preacher," his father used to say.[30] Leroy himself was an atheist, and he told his kids with some harshness, "There ain't no God, and I'm the only Santa Claus you ever gonna see."[31]

Leroy's violence toward his family grew over time. He played the piano clubs at night, and he spent what little money he made on shoes and flamboyant suits. Thelma would often intercept him when he got a paycheck to keep him from buying more clothes. He became an alcoholic and an abusive husband. Occasionally, he came home from work and slapped Thelma around. One night, he completely lost control. Cleaver remembered, "Daddy took an axe and chopped up his piano. Then he broke everything in the house made of glass, starting with all the dishes. He smashed the glass covers on the pictures hanging on the walls. One corner of our living room was like a family shrine, whose focus was my parents' wedding photo on the wall. Hanging around this photo, and on little whatnot shelves on either side, were our treasured family photos and memorabilia."[32] Leroy destroyed this shrine as well as anything of value that evening with the ax, and it created an unbridgeable gulf between him and the rest of the family.

Leroy and Thelma fought constantly. Leroy assaulted his wife, and she threw household items at him to defend herself. They accused one another of infidelity and perversions. On Saturdays he would come home drunk and beat up Thelma. The kids tried to stop him, but he was too strong. "There was screaming and the thunder of our feet and bodies scuffling around as we all joined in the melee. It was everybody against Daddy, and we'd all hit him as hard as we could, trying to make him stop hitting mother."[33] Cleaver's desire to protect his mother became one of the driving forces of his young life, taking on Oedipal proportions. As he wrote in his prison journal years later, "For years I was driven by the monomaniacal passion to grow up and become large enough to contest my father and take his life."[34]

Cleaver's parents separated for short periods, during which he and his siblings were sent to the Robinson grandparents. These estrangements were deeply unsettling for Cleaver, and they would drive him to a life of crime during his teenage years. Leroy and Thelma were going to file for divorce as early as 1942, but before they could split, an incident would send them fleeing the South for their lives.[35]

Leroy had wanted to move out of the South for some time. He made under $800 a year, even after ten years as a janitor.[36] In the early 1940s, he got a job as a Pullman porter, which was one of the most prestigious jobs a black man could get. Following the Civil War, George Pullman had invented a new kind of luxury travel for the white middle class with the creation of the Pullman sleeping railroad car. He hired black men to serve customers who traveled in cars with plush carpets, walnut furniture, and fine fabrics. Working conditions for porters were extremely difficult. They were expected to be perfect servants, attending to every whim of white travelers, and their earnings consisted in large part of meager tips. They worked long hours, sometimes up to twenty per day. By the 1920s, as train travel became the dominant mode of transportation in the modern era, Pullman became the largest employer of African Americans in the country. Pullman porters contributed to the growing black middle class. In 1925, they formed the Brotherhood of Sleeping Car Porters, the first black union in America and the precursor to civil rights organizations. By 1937, the union finalized a deal with the Pullman company, paving the way for black organized labor and collective bargaining. When Leroy took a job with the Pullman company a few years later, he was extremely proud. Although he traveled away from home for weeks at a time, he made about $100 a month. With tips, he sometimes doubled that wage.

Leroy's job could not have come soon enough. One rainy day, when Cleaver was about nine, he was walking with his father along a wooden sidewalk in downtown Little Rock, the streets covered in mud. Two white men approached with their arms spread wide, screaming at Leroy, "Get off the walkway, Nigger!" Leroy was dressed in a pair of his newest shoes, and he refused to move off of the sidewalk into the mud. Cleaver remembered the incident years later: "So then those guys pushed my father. And so my father, his right foot went off the sidewalk into the mud, and he bounded back up on the walkway. So these guys tell him again to get off the walkway, and so the guy went to push my father again—and then he started screaming. And then I could see what was happening. He got his arm back, and it was all cut up. My father wiped a knife on the guy."[37] Leroy told his son to run straight home and not to stop for anything. A half an hour later, Leroy arrived home. He hastily packed a bag and left aboard the next train out of town. Before he left, he promised to find them a home outside of the South. The police showed up soon afterward with a warrant for his arrest, but he was already long gone.

Leroy was wise to run, as black men had been lynched in Arkansas for far less serious offenses. Even Little Rock, a cosmopolitan city compared to much of rural Arkansas, saw its share of white violence. In 1927, a mob of a few thousand white people rioted in downtown Little Rock and burned the body of John Carter on the main street of the black business district. He had been accused of attacking two white women. The mob shot him two hundred times, strapped him to the hood of a car, and drove him through the streets for hours. At Ninth and Broadway, the heart of the black community, they made a bonfire with pews from AME Bethel Church in front of the Mosaic Templar building and threw him into the pyre. For the rest of the evening, white mobs marauded through the African American community, threatening and attacking black residents. Ku Klux Klansmen rode their horses up and down Ninth Street challenging any black resident to show his or her face. Following that incident, over a thousand black residents fled Little Rock, and many businesses closed and left Little Rock for good, including drug stores, laundries, and a photography shop.[38] Although this was one of Arkansas's last lynchings, its specter haunted the black community in Little Rock for decades.

After Leroy left, Thelma and the five children hid out on Henry Cleaver's farm. This was a moment of real happiness for Cleaver.

Temporarily free from the violence of his father, he settled into the daily rhythms of his grandfather's farm. After school, he spent the afternoons doing chores. He fed the chickens and slopped the pigs. Grandpa Henry taught him how to shoot a .22-caliber rifle. Cleaver used to take his grandfather's Collie, Shep, on hunting excursions for rabbits for the stew his grandfather made. "He would make a big soupy stew, a real yummy chicken type stew, and he called it 'Dandy Funk' because he'd put in something of everything [that] you would have in your kitchen. It would be the kind of thing that people fill and keep going. They have some places where they have kettles that have been going for twenty-five or thirty years."[39] It was one of those rare periods of Cleaver's childhood that he remembered with true happiness. "These were the days of kissing the earth, of touching and smelling wild things growing, of running barefoot through cotton fields, of fishing in rivers and dragging in crawdad holes, of watching Grandpa and his friends slaughter hogs, of later sneaking in the smokehouse and licking the salty smoked hams hanging there. Thus I spent the time waiting for my father to send for us."[40]

2

PHOENIX AND THE WEST (1944–1945)

When Eldridge Cleaver was nine years old, his mother Thelma gathered up her five children and boarded a train for Phoenix, Arizona. Leroy had gone ahead to set up a home, and they would have to make the five-day trip alone. Thelma was pregnant with her sixth child, and the trip was exhausting for her. However, like the thousands of black migrants who were leaving the South each week, she hoped that the move would provide a better life for her children. It was the height of the Great Migration, and African Americans were heading to sprawling industrial cities like Detroit, Chicago, and Los Angeles, as well as smaller urban areas like Oakland, Milwaukee, and Phoenix. These migrants left their homes for many reasons. Factories paid more than double the wage of sharecropping, and cities offered more social freedoms. For many black people, the world out west offered better jobs, better homes, and a broader range of civil rights. As one booster organization brochure advertised, Phoenix promised to be a "city where diligence and industry will bring you the best of the worldly goods."[1]

Cleaver was at first thrilled to ride the train. He and his siblings had only ever played in the mud or chased rabbits in the cotton fields surrounding their grandfather's farm. "At first, at least for the children it had been fun," Cleaver recalled, "full of mystery, adventure, and excitement which overwhelmed them simply because there was nothing in their past experience to which such a huge event could be compared."[2] The novelty wore off after a few days. The cabins were crowded with people, and in the summer heat, they filled with suffocating air. The ride was interminable. No direct route ran from Little Rock to Phoenix, so the party had to change trains a number of times. Cleaver passed the time sitting at the window and watching the landscape fly by. "[I]t was punishment and pain to sit there. It was no longer fun, there was nothing exciting and everyone was anxious and would be glad when it was all over."[3] Worse yet, the Cleavers ran out of food halfway through the trip. Leroy was supposed to make an arrangement with the porters, but there had been some mix-up. With two days to go before they would reach Phoenix, they were starving. It was the first time Cleaver felt "how hateful hunger can be."[4]

They finally arrived at Union Station in Phoenix, disheveled and hungry after the long journey. Leroy came to get them in a pickup truck, and when Cleaver saw his father, he felt a sense of dread. The months he spent away from his father were the happiest of his life. Now that they were together again, he wondered how long it would be until the beatings started. As they drove down the street toward the black section of Phoenix, Cleaver suddenly felt that "all had been lost for some time now."[5]

Arizona had been a destination for black migrants since the end of the Civil War. Ex-slaves, Buffalo Soldiers, cowboys, and miners had all journeyed to the desert territory for the freedom promised by the western frontier. Black sharecroppers poured into the state following the completion of the Theodore Roosevelt Dam in 1911, which provided the irrigation technology to expand the cotton market across the Southwest. By the early twentieth century, two recognizable black communities started to emerge in south Phoenix. One was alongside the railroad tracks between Central Avenue and Twelfth Street, and the other was south of the tracks along Buckeye Road. These sections were segregated geographically, socially, and economically from the rest of the city. Banks refused to give mortgages to black people for homes in white neighborhoods, and real estate agents rejected black customers who tried to move north across the railroad tracks. Housing covenants or deed restrictions also barred black persons and other minorities from buying property in the lily-white northside.

Despite the promises of a more egalitarian society out west, extreme racism pervaded Phoenix life in the 1940s. Black people were mostly barred from public life. Jim Crow laws kept them out of white restaurants, theaters, hospitals, hotels, swimming pools, and cemeteries. School segregation was legalized in Arizona in 1909, and although the policy was not adopted in the majority of the state, it was in Phoenix. White people earned double what black people made, as most Africans Americans were forced into low-wage, unskilled jobs.[6] By the 1920s, the Ku Klux Klan had established a presence in Phoenix, reflecting a national trend of resurgent white nationalism and violence. The KKK's membership in Phoenix included the county sheriff, mayor, and publisher of the *Arizona Gazette*. Most black people lived in deplorable housing run by unscrupulous white landlords. Half of the African American population lived in homes without running water, and most structures were dilapidated or deteriorating.[7] The federal government characterized Phoenix—with its high rates of disease, inadequate housing, and lack of health-care facilities—as the worst slum in America.[8]

The Cleaver family settled in the middle of Phoenix's red-light district, known as "the bucket of blood" because of the stabbings and shootings that occurred there. Cleaver's first exposure to crime both frightened and fascinated him. He often slept outside because of the suffocating heat, and while there he witnessed the sights and sounds of the red-light district. "Whorehouses, gambling joints, and bars lined both sides of the road," he later wrote. "After dark, especially on weekends, Buckeye Road would be all lit up, creating quite a spectacle to watch when we slept outside. Music blasted loudly from the jukeboxes, making you feel right there instead of a couple hundred yards away. People danced in the streets, shouted, laughed and whooped it up."[9]

Cleaver found it difficult to adapt to this strange new place. The family lived in a rectangular house indistinguishable from the others lining Buckeye Road. Behind the house was just empty desert. The heat was overpowering, radiating in waves from the caliche soil. Cleaver stopped running around barefooted because it blistered his soles. On the first day of school, the air was so stifling in the school that "the only thing I learned in that class was how to breathe hot air without fainting."[10]

At home, the relationship between Thelma and Leroy deteriorated even further. With the birth of their sixth child, Claudette, Leroy became paranoid and dangerous. He insisted that Claudette did not look anything like him and was the child of another man. He drank and beat Thelma. In one of Cleaver's unpublished journals, he blamed his father for all the pain the family suffered. "He had brought this poison with him, instilled it in the house he acquired, so that when his family walked into the house, the terror was already there waiting for them, to resume its insidious and omnivorous growth, which in its relentless and inexorable progress devoured all warmth and security in the family."[11] While Leroy was on the road, Cleaver was at ease. He helped his mother around the house, kept his younger siblings in line, and read voraciously. But when his father came back and the fighting started again, Cleaver became increasingly disturbed. His parents fought loudly, violently, and, sometimes, publicly. As Cleaver recalled, "The most embarrassing thing I remember was one day being out in the street playing marbles with my friends, when my mother ran by, my father chasing her."

Cleaver started to act more rebelliously. He stopped cooperating with his father, refusing to do even the most basic tasks around the house. He started staying out beyond his eight o'clock curfew, even though he knew he would be beaten. "I didn't have anything to do, but still I would just sit outside and wait until it was long past eight o'clock before I would go inside where there would be a tough spanking waiting for me. That's how I handled the bitter feelings I had for my father."[12] Cleaver also sought refuge in a gang of neighborhood boys a little older than himself. "I found for the first time a place for myself outside our home. Nothing at home attracted me to stick around. I wanted to get as far away from my sisters and brothers as possible, and when Daddy came home, I wanted to be around as little as possible. Each morning I hit the streets at the same time as the sun, returning a little sad each evening at sundown."[13]

This brotherhood provided Cleaver with his first sense of belonging beyond his family, and he would seek out this kind of comradeship throughout his life. Cleaver was a strong athlete, and he quickly learned how to swim, play football, and run track. He hung out at the YMCA and the pool, both of which were segregated in Phoenix. The older boys taught him the sweet science of boxing, and he took to it immediately. At the gym, the boys were allowed to box in the ring after the adults were finished. "We'd dress up just like big boxers, put on boxing gloves just like theirs. They taught us how to block punches, jab, and connect with a strong right hand. Soon we were putting on exhibitions between fights once each week, to the delight of the crowds that screamed for blood."[14] It was during one of these sports exhibitions that Cleaver had his first interaction with white people and racism. As he remembered, "It was a public sports contest run for us by white people, and they made a big thing of announcing that there would be prizes for running and jumping and other sports. Prizes are exciting to little kids, and we ran our hearts out. The prize was a piece of watermelon. For really the first time I understood what white people expected of us."[15]

With his new friends, Cleaver got into all sorts of petty trouble. They all lived close to the railroad tracks, and as the trains passed by, they stole fruit from the open cars. "Watermelons, cantaloupes, and other fruits and vegetables were shipped by train through Phoenix. On any given day, hundreds of boxcars heavily laden with such goodies passed through the train station in a monotonous convoy. We'd sneak up into the staging areas of the train yard, pick the type of fruit or melons we wanted today, then eat them until our bellies about popped open."[16]

Cleaver and his friends were also ambitious to make some money. They constructed handmade shoeshine boxes and wandered the outskirts of downtown hoping to catch customers. Cleaver's father forbade it, telling him, "Ain't no son of mine gonna shine no damn shoes."[17] But Cleaver kept at it, drawn in by the promise of quick cash. One day, the boys headed into the center of the downtown area in the hope of finding customers. They were immediately picked up by the police. "Suddenly about five big burly white cops came from out of nowhere and swooped down upon us. In no time, they had confiscated our shine boxes, loaded us in the back seat of the patrol car, and sped away to the police station. We were terrified."[18]

Cleaver and his friends were locked in a holding cell for a few hours and then taken to a squad room. The police handed Cleaver and his friends blue-and-gold shoeshine boxes and explained that there was a new arrangement. "We were free to shine shoes in the downtown area any time, as long as we used one of these blue and gold shine boxes. The boxes belonged to the police. The fee was twenty-five cents a day. They supplied all the polish and saddlesoap free. All we had to do was come in, check out a shine box, shine shoes, and bring the box back when we were finished—dropping off the rental fee, of course."[19] At first it sounded like a good deal to Cleaver. After a few days, he realized that, after he paid the police, he didn't have enough money to go to the movies. It was Cleaver's first interaction with the police, and he learned how they exploited black people. It was a lesson he would never forget.

Cleaver's experiment shining shoes did not last too much longer. One day, Leroy caught him downtown shining a man's shoes and became so angry he threatened to break his son's neck. Leroy had worked in menial jobs as a janitor or waiter his entire life, and he wanted to make sure that his son did not do the same. For all of his abuse, Leroy did want a better life for his son. Cleaver agreed to stop, and he looked back on this incident as a critical turning point. As he remarked later, "To this day I've never looked upon shining shoes as one of the choices open to me."[20]

Not long after this, Leroy and Thelma announced that they were moving the family to Los Angeles. Cleaver was thrilled. California was a place of opportunity and hope. Perhaps this was the chance the family had been waiting for. The Cleavers boarded a train one more time and headed west to the end of the line.

3

LOS ANGELES AND THE GREAT MIGRATION (1945–1949)

Eldridge Cleaver and his family arrived at Los Angeles's Union Station in summer 1945. The scene was vibrant and bustling: as many as six thousand black migrants came through Union Station every month looking for jobs in the recently desegregated war industries.[1] In 1941, civil rights activist A. Philip Randolph—who had helped negotiate the union contract for the Brotherhood of Sleeping Car Porters—threatened President Roosevelt that he would organize a march on Washington of one hundred thousand people if Roosevelt didn't end prejudiced hiring practices. As a result, President Roosevelt issued Executive Order 8802, which banned racial discrimination in federal agencies engaged in war-related work. In Los Angeles—the second largest industrial economy behind Detroit—steel, shipbuilding, and automobile plants were repurposed for wartime production, and factory jobs were suddenly made available to African Americans on an unprecedented scale. Two hundred thousand black people came to Los Angeles in the next decade. It was a time of optimism and prosperity for black migrants, probably the greatest since emancipation.

The Cleavers moved into a rooming house a mile south of downtown on the corner of Newton Street and S. Central Avenue. African Americans had been racially segregated in that area of South Central Los Angeles since they started arriving during World War I. During the 1920s, the Ku Klux Klan threatened violence against any black family that tried to move outside South Central. White Angelenos also employed restrictive covenants and block restrictions to keep African Americans contained within this firm geographical boundary south of downtown.[2] The housing conditions were crowded and chaotic. At the rooming house where Cleaver lived, people sometimes slept in shifts because of the shortage of beds. As he remembered it, "Everyone was always running through the house screaming and cursing. The rooms were separated by curtains slung across the doors. You might be eating and a woman would run through naked and screaming, a man running behind her with a long knife in hand."[3]

For the impressionable Cleaver, life along the "Stem," as S. Central Avenue was called, was exciting. Across the street sat the Newton Street Police Station. Fistfights regularly broke out between the cops and lawbreakers out front, while screams and laughter could be heard coming from inside all day or night. Cleaver loved to walk up and down the street, taking in the sights and sounds. "It was like a parade or carnival. Cars filled with black, brown and yellow faces drove up and down the Stem, music blasting from their radios. Jukeboxes blasted different songs back to back. You could never be beyond the sound of music, black voices screaming out the blue funk of black lives."[4] Along the Stem, African Americans owned their own restaurants, pool halls, liquor stores, and hotels. The barbershops and beauty shops that lined S. Central Avenue were like small theaters, where barbers, hairdressers, and patrons passionately discussed politics, sports, and other topics of the day. The street boasted some of the best gospel, blues, and R&B acts in the country at places like the Downbeat Club, the Last Word, the Plantation Club, and the Casablanca. The elegant Dunbar Hotel, located on Forty-Second Street and S. Central Avenue, was a hub for the nation's leading black luminaries. Entertainers and intellectuals like W. E. B. Du Bois, James Weldon Johnson, and Josephine Baker all stayed there. It was one of the finest hotels for black people in the country, decorated in a bold, modern style that featured expensive furnishings, tapestries, and an elegant chandelier.[5]

In this new and thrilling world, Cleaver became immersed in music and film. His older sister, Wilhelmina, got a job at Club Alabam, the most opulent after-hours nightclub along the Stem. Located right next to the Dunbar Hotel, the Alabam featured replica palm trees and a shimmering curtain. Black and white audiences dressed in their finest formal wear and furs to see the likes of Charles Mingus, Charlie Parker, and T-Bone Walker. On Sundays, the Cleaver family went to the Rosebud Theater or the Jinx Theater to see the latest comedies and romances. Sometimes Leroy splurged and took them to the Lincoln Theater, also known as the "West Coast Apollo." Designed in the Moorish Revival architectural style, with honeycomb archways and soaring spire facades, the Lincoln looked like an ancient temple transported from a bygone era. It had a massive stage and orchestra pit, and it featured everything from vaudeville and talent shows to live theater, film, and concerts. Musical legends like Duke Ellington and Billie Holiday played to packed houses of over two thousand people here. At an early age, Cleaver found the world of black art, and it inspired a lifelong passion for learning and expression.

After a few months, Thelma finally convinced Leroy that the family needed to get away from the Stem. They moved to 3720 Reicker Avenue in Rose Hills. It was a Chicano neighborhood on the far northeast side of Los Angeles, nestled in the foothills of Pasadena. Rose Hills was a unique enclave, a semirural hamlet mostly separated from Los Angeles's concrete sprawl. It was hilly and crisscrossed by dirt roads and makeshift staircases. After a heavy rain, the entire village was thick with mud. Shacks and lean-tos dotted the rural landscape, while goats, chickens, and livestock wandered along the roads. Much like S. Central Avenue, Rose Hills was the product of white segregation. During World War I, Mexican laborers had begun crossing the border into California in larger numbers. Some had been driven out of Mexico by the violent revolution taking place. Others came looking for work in California's growing agricultural industry. Like the African Americans who migrated to Los Angeles, Mexican Americans were largely shut out of white neighborhoods through restrictive covenants, block associations, and white violence. Many Mexicans settled in the semirural slums along California's ditch banks. Los Angeles's Rose Hills neighborhood emerged as a makeshift community, an area so geographically and socially marginal in Los Angeles that it showed up on few maps.

As a migrant from the South, Cleaver at first had difficulty assimilating into this environment. He was still a southerner in his speech and affect. With his telltale drawl, he used the word *yonder* to describe distance and said *chunk* instead of throw. The neighborhood kids teased him harshly for it. But Cleaver knew how to box, and he earned their respect with his fists. "I had to fight them to prove I was human," Cleaver later remembered. "When they saw that I knew how to bloody their noses, they showed me their teeth in smiles."[6] After Cleaver made friends, Rose Hills became a sanctuary. It reminded him of his grandfather's farm in Arkansas. He scoured the hillsides surrounding Rose Hill looking for arrowheads left behind by the Tongva tribe that had lived there thousands of years before. He and his friends made slingshots from the rubber tubes they rummaged from derelict cars, and they stalked doves and quail. In the summers, they collected "wild walnuts from the trees, and there were wild peaches, apricots, pears, figs, loquats and quince."[7] When Cleaver was incarcerated decades later, he wrote a romantic ode to Rose Hills:

No smog in Rose Hills
Far from the industrial heart of Los Angeles
A forgotten hamlet
A peaceful spot

Site of home
Ours a jealous love of our sacred ground
We were bound to each other
With what pride we owned the land
We knew Rose Hill as our own
We'd bow down on hands and knees to kiss our dirt.[8]

For Cleaver, Rose Hills was a kind of utopia. It was, as he remarked later, "in that sacred sense of roots and soil and soul, Home."[9]

Cleaver's early teenage years in Rose Hills were the last happy moments of his young life. He was a member of the Boys and Girls Club and a dutiful Catholic. He said his rosary and regularly attended confession and catechism. At Abraham Lincoln High School, he wasn't the best student in the class, preferring athletics to history and English, but that wasn't unusual for a kid his age. He liked reading adventure stories for fun, and he loved going to the movies, especially romantic pictures. Cleaver was a curious explorer. He loved to wander all over Los Angeles. He walked to school in Lincoln Heights, dances at Ramona Gardens housing project, movies in El Sereno, the swimming pool near Elysian Park, and the Boys Club at Five Points. "I liked to walk anywhere," he later mused. "I liked hiking up into the hills near our neighborhood as well as I liked walking along the streets, on the sidewalks. I was broadminded in that sense—and I truly enjoyed it all equally. To be moving, going someplace, is what counted with me, seeing things."[10] Cleaver was also dutiful to his mother, making sure that his brothers obeyed her and completed their chores.[11] Her teaching credentials from Arkansas did not transfer to California, so she was forced to become a janitor at Lincoln High. Even though Cleaver was somewhat embarrassed by this, he helped her regularly. "I think I distinguished myself in this regard, that I was always trying to be helpful to her, used to go help her clean up those school rooms, but I was so slow that I used to slow her down."[12]

Leroy grew more violent during this period. He still beat up Thelma when he got drunk, and now he increasingly turned his violence on his oldest son. As Cleaver recalled it, "Every night, I would come home late. And every night my father would beat me. As time went by, the beatings became more severe. At the same time, I was growing bigger and stronger, and the beatings began to hurt me less and less. My feelings, my pride, my sense of dignity and worth, suffered more than I did physically."[13] Cleaver found solace in the woods surrounding Rose Hills. "I liked to go up into the Hills because up there, away from everyone, the fighting of my mother and father, there was peace and communion with the universe. The wind would roll over the hills . . . a rabbit breaking from behind a bush, the snakes, the birds, the sky, the vast distances, the long, clear scenic views, an airplane so high up, one could hardly see it, unbelievably high. Freedom, absence of restraint, the amorality of the hills, the law of survival."[14]

As the situation at home worsened, Cleaver started to fantasize about killing his father. Then, after one particular severe beating, he decided that he had had enough. "It seemed the logical, inevitable conclusion of the collision course we were on," he confessed later. "I had a knife and had locked my mind on the idea that when my father hit me again, I was going to plunge it into his heart. I knew that I would do it. Everything had been building to this point. I was ready."[15]

Cleaver never got his chance. One day, Leroy simply abandoned the family, boarding a train to Chicago and not returning home. He moved in with his two brothers and his father, Henry, who had recently moved to Chicago. Leroy started working as a maître d' at the Palmer House in the Loop and continued working on the train between Chicago and Los Angeles. He occasionally called and sent letters to his children.

For Cleaver, this was the final betrayal. He had been the victim of Leroy's abuse for years, and now he would never have the opportunity to get revenge. He was maddened by it, and he focused his rage on the world around him. "It turned all of the children against father and made me, in particular, very angry with him. I wanted to grow up, big and tall like he was, so I could pay him back for what he had done to our home. And with that kind of rebellion in my heart, I started to rebel against everything and everybody that tried to instill discipline in me."[16]

After his father left, Cleaver became drawn to Los Angeles gang life, particularly the Pachuco gang of Rose Hills. The Pachucos were US-born Mexican Americans caught between the culture of their migrant parents and an American society that rejected them. They developed a distinctive style of dress—zoot suits (long coats, wide lapels, and pegged trousers)—and they developed their own distinctive slang. The zoot suit, which was worn by both Latinos and black people as a form of rebellion against American racism, became a symbol of protest. The Pachucos emerged as a Chicano subculture at a time when Mexican Americans were discriminated against in every aspect of Los Angeles life. For instance, the Pachucos became the focus of anti-Mexican public hysteria in Los Angeles during the 1940s. In the Sleepy Lagoon trial of 1942, nearly two dozen Pachucos were prosecuted for a murder they didn't commit. Their convictions rested in large part on so-called expert testimony that claimed youths of Mexican descent were biologically inclined to commit violent acts. Racism toward Pachucos exploded on the streets during the Zoot Suit Riots of 1943 in Los Angeles. During World War II, cloth was being rationed for the war effort, and zoot-suited youngsters with their flamboyant ensembles were viewed as unpatriotic by white individuals. In the summer of 1943, white servicemen roamed the Los Angeles streets hunting for youths wearing the suits. Chanting inflammatory slogans like "They raped our wives!" the servicemen attacked black and Chicano men, tearing off their clothes and beating them. White crowds cheered, and policemen stood idly by as they attacked both zoot-suiters and innocent bystanders who were black or Mexican.

Cleaver admired the defiance and chic of the Pachucos. They feared no one, and they had enviable swagger. "The Pachucos let their hair grow long, combing it in a distinctive style called the duck tail. They wore zoot suits and shiny shoes and carried razors, knives, and guns. Each Pachuco stood on his own reputation. Reputation was an active category, and one had to have exploits to one's credit, scalps to display, to add content and luster to one's name. Strength was admired and life was a trial by fire. Insult or injury could only be met by retaliation and revenge. The vendetta was a way of life."[17] Cleaver started hanging out with them. He didn't have a zoot suit, but his sister Wilhelmina bought him a blue drape suit, a subtler version of the zoot with a full chest, tapered sleeves, and a suppressed waist. For Cleaver, putting on the suit was a transformation into manhood. "I put on my drape suit and walked up and down the sidewalk all day showing myself in the full pride of a boy no longer too young, a young man coming into being."[18] Cleaver also had his hair conked—or straightened with hot lye—mimicking the modernist stylings of black performers like Nat King Cole and Duke Ellington. He began to adopt a posture of macho coolness to deal with the pressures of family and social life, as these subcultures provided him with the dignity he could find nowhere else. The Pachucos were in many ways the precursor to the Black Panthers Cleaver would join two decades later.

Cleaver identified with the Chicanos because they were not only tough but also a bit reckless. "They were like me," Cleaver remembered, "wild, crazy, didn't give a damn. We were happy together."[19] With Leroy gone, Cleaver grew more and more violent. "When my mother or older sisters tried to discipline me, I just gave them a lot of back talk. If they tried to spank me, I would do like I had seen my father do and beat them up."[20] At the age of twelve, Cleaver started getting into trouble with his friends. They vandalized school buildings, broke into an athletic shed and stole all of the equipment, took food out of the cafeteria, and turned on the kitchen burners. When the fixtures around the stove caught fire, they ran. The next morning, Cleaver was arrested for three instances of burglary and seven instances of malicious mischief. In April 1948, he was placed in a junior forestry camp maintained by the Los Angeles County Probation Department at Mount Baldy. He lasted seven weeks there before he was kicked out. According to officials, he was such a "disturbing and disruptive influence" that the camp supervisors demanded that he be removed. According to reports, "At camp he was disobedient, fought with other boys, and appeared totally unamenable to their discipline."[21]

During this time, Cleaver's troubled relationship to young women emerged. It started when he felt the first stirrings of desire for a classmate named Mildred Ortega. "She was the most beautiful girl I'd ever seen. Her skin was white as milk and she had long black hair. She was very delicate, very feminine—even at that titless, shapeless age."[22] When Cleaver professed his love, she rejected him. This shocked and humiliated him, and he insulted her with a barrage of slurs. The teacher overheard him, and, as he remembered it, she slapped him across the face and called him a "black nigger." This painful episode had deep and lasting consequences for Cleaver's relationship to women. He was attracted to light-skinned women but felt he was scorned for being too black. From this young age, Cleaver began to cultivate a violent attitude toward women, one born out of fear of rejection for his black skin. As Cleaver wrote about Ortega later, "My feeling for her was no longer the warm desire of the lover. What I felt for her was the lust/hatred of the rapist."[23]

Cleaver became predatory toward women. His remembrances read like a long list of aggressive sexual conquests. There was Fruitie, whose "teeth looked like they had been shaken up in the cup of two hands and then tossed in her mouth all at once, sticking out in whatever way they landed. Kissing her was like trying to kiss a cactus apple." There was Carolyn. Cleaver bragged that he "felt her up in the swimming pool in El Sarreno [*sic*]. Little bitch thought she was hot shit." Cleaver and his friends created a system for stalking young girls. "We had a regular circuit, a territory we'd patrol. Frank had a natural genius for sniffing out choice broads whose parents kept them hidden away from the evils of the world—from horny cats like us. We'd drive down weird streets, spot the girls peeping out at us from behind huge bushes in their yards, through knot-holes in tall fences, behind curtains drawn all over dark windows."[24]

Cleaver also became a more practiced thief. He and his friends started small, ripping off fruit from a delivery man's truck. They snuck dollars out of the register at the Lincoln Park Speedway, and they prowled neighborhoods surrounding Rose Hills at night looking for things to steal. "I would commit all kinds of little burglaries. You might leave your child's bicycle out one night and the next morning find it gone. That would be me."[25] They stashed their stolen goods in an abandoned church in Rose Hills. "The church became our spot. It had a cellar and an attic. It was truly our Heaven and hell. We fucked in the attic and hid our stolen goods. This became the den of us thieves, our lair."[26] Cleaver started breaking into people's homes and taking larger risks. His increased recklessness was partly born of a growing resentment toward authority, especially white society. As he remembered it decades later, "I progressed from vandalism to more serious crimes: real burglaries and robberies. All the time I was developing in my mind and in my heart, real hatred, first of all, for those white people whom I considered responsible for the things in society I didn't like. I had a particular attitude toward policemen, political leaders, school officials and I really didn't have much respect for preachers."[27]

At fourteen, Cleaver was arrested for a series of crimes, including burglarizing a housing authority building, stealing money from a truck, and committing a series of other "depredations." In December 1949, he appeared in juvenile court for his crimes. The court was harsh, sentencing him to sixteen months at the Fred C. Nelles School for Boys.[28] It was the beginning of his decades-long encounter with imprisonment and institutionalization.

4

REFORM SCHOOL (1950–1954)

In 1891, the Whittier State School (later renamed the Fred C. Nelles School for Boys) opened as a rehabilitative institution for juvenile delinquents. The school adopted a military-style approach to reform. Cadets remained silent during meals and work and while marching from place to place. Administrators and staff inflicted physical pain to manage misbehavior. Guards whipped wards with leather straps or rubber tubes and then locked them in solitary cells without food or water. Runaways were fitted with an iron ankle weight, known as the "Oregon Boot," which weighed up to twenty-five pounds and sometimes cut to the bone.[1]

In the years just prior to Cleaver's arrival, the California juvenile system had replaced physical punishment with psychological testing, medical diagnosis, and behavior modification. Through the efforts of reformer Fred C. Nelles, the school drew upon emerging fields of sociology, eugenics, criminology, and psychiatry to address juvenile punishment. These new forms of rehabilitation, based on quasi-scientific determinism, had devastating consequences for young men of color. Nelles adopted standardized intelligence testing to place pupils on a scale that ran from "feebleminded" to "superior." Because the tests did not account for things like cultural background, bilingualism, class, or racial identity, African Americans and Chicanos were often categorized as feebleminded. Such pupils were deemed unassimilable to society and a danger to normal family structure. Large numbers of African Americans and Mexican Americans were confined, quarantined, segregated, sent to insane asylums, and sometimes even sterilized.[2]

Cleaver arrived at the Fred C. Nelles School for Boys on January 10, 1950.[3] It marked a major turning point in his life, as it was his first real exposure to institutionalization. He was admitted through the main administration building and then taken to the infirmary, where he was examined and quarantined for a few days. He took a series of aptitude tests to determine his placement in the school. Finally, he was assigned a cottage, where he lived dormitory style with other boys. Cleaver did his best to adapt to the discipline at the school—or at least he pretended to adapt. He was assigned jobs in the laundry and in the kitchen, and he managed them with mixed success. "His adjustment was marginal to excellent," one school report stated. "Subject in many ways impressing supervisors with his capacity to act maturely, but with an inability to maintain that level of adjustment."[4]

On the surface, Cleaver was a model cadet, going out of his way to show officials that he was compliant. But beneath this, he distrusted authority and was loyal only to his gang of peers. Cleaver started smoking marijuana, which some of the other had boys snuck into the school.[5] Smoking weed gave him a feeling of calmness that he had never felt before. It made him feel "complete," as he put it.[6] When he was finally paroled in May 1951 at the age of fifteen, Cleaver had been anything but reformed. He decided to enter the marijuana trade.

Cleaver went back to a life of crime. He broke curfew and stopped going to school. He also hooked up with a Chicano friend who had connections in the drug trade. "I went with him to his oldest brother's house, and his older brother turned over the family business to him, and he did it verbally, and he gave him two great big navy duffle bags. One of them was full of money. The other one was full of marijuana."[7] This proved lucrative, as the Mexicans in Rose Hills sold marijuana only to other Mexicans. As Cleaver put it, "There was a time when niggers and honkies couldn't even buy dope from the Mexicans. The Mexicans were the only ones who had it, and they would only sell it to other Mexicans. We changed that, Chester, Nelson and me, and we flooded L.A. with weed. That shit did not sit still. It was a fast moving commodity."[8] Cleaver bought larger and larger quantities of marijuana, sometimes by the pound, stashing it in the abandoned church near his home. "I knew every crack and cranny of it, the little secret tunnels underground. That was always my stashing secret, and I used to run that way to get away from the pigs."[9]

Cleaver was soon making enough money to explore more of Los Angeles. He bought a car, even though he didn't have a license, and his gang drove all over. They went to the Floral Drive-In, a Spanish-language movie theater where cars lined up around the block on Saturday nights to find the choicest spots. They hung out at the Zenda Ballroom, a formerly all-white music venue that started opening its doors to Chicanos and black people in the early 1950s. Every day they smoked marijuana from their stash, and sometimes they took "yellow jackets," barbiturates that brought on trancelike states. They drove through the streets with hundreds of dollars in their pockets, searching for prostitutes, and, at least once, they drove to Tijuana to visit a bordello. Cleaver liked the excitement and danger of sleeping with prostitutes, though there were consequences. On one occasion, he contracted gonorrhea, and on another, according to prison records, he picked up "lice from a prostitute, who granted him sexual favors in exchange for marijuana."[10]

It was not too long before Cleaver's recklessness caught up with him. On Halloween night in 1952, he was arrested for delinquency and possession of marijuana. He was convicted for selling three marijuana cigarettes and breaking his parole. In December, Cleaver was sentenced to a year at the Preston School of Industry, the most notorious reform school in California.

On January 16, 1953, Cleaver arrived at Preston, located in Ione, California. It was an intimidating, Dickensian place, with a reputation for breaking young men deemed unmanageable at Nelles. It focused on rigid discipline of the boys. The main school building was an imposing Romanesque building—known by many as simply "the castle"—with high arched windows and a spired clock tower. It was like something out of a gothic movie. Opened in 1894, it was originally organized as a military school with students divided up into companies and housed in large dormitories. In its early history, Preston used physical punishment. Boys were struck with table-tennis paddles soaked in water or even locked in the castle tower for ten days at a time. The wards were beaten with whips for the smallest infraction, and guards were allowed to shoot at escapees at their discretion.

By the time Cleaver got there, the school had abandoned physical punishment, though a heavy emphasis on discipline remained. Disruptive pupils were isolated and forced to observe an all-day silence, and sometimes they were held in rooms without furniture. Runaways and homosexuals were placed in the segregation unit, which was surrounded by a thirteen-foot-tall wire fence. The administration tried to use social engineering as a method of reform, introducing psychiatric treatment and vocational training to the program. There was an increased emphasis on personal cleanliness and strong educational and counseling programs. Nevertheless, many of the boys called Preston a concentration camp.[11]

Preston was indeed a harsher environment than Nelles. Upon entering the school, Cleaver was stripped and dunked into the "plunge pool," which was filled with toxic chemicals to treat boys for crabs, lice, or scabies. He was given a close-cropped haircut and issued a Sunday uniform and a pair of Sunday oxfords, two pairs of work clothes, two pairs of underwear and socks, two pairs of work shoes, and two nightgowns. He wrote his name in each item of clothing, which supervisors inspected each week before laundry pickup. Cleaver had a locker, which had to be organized just so: Sunday cap on the top shelf, toilet articles and clean socks on the second, books stacked neatly on the bottom, and towels hung on the double hook near the front. The school placed him in a company of about fifty boys.

Cleaver's schedule was relentless. Wards awoke at 5:55 AM and, after a quick breakfast, assembled on the grounds to work at a trade for four hours. After a brief lunch, they would return to trade work or academic classes for another three hours. (Cleaver worked at tailor shop for his vocational assignment.) Army drills and athletics were sprinkled in throughout the day. The young men were allowed one hour of recreation in the afternoon and then one at supper. After supper, there were two hours of reading before lights-out at 9:00 PM. Sunday was a day of rest.[12] All of these activities were performed in silence under the strict supervision of officials. According to a Preston training handbook, "boys are to be on silence when entering the buildings, during the toilet lines, when washing, bathing, and changing clothing, or when any business of the company is being transacted."[13]

Cleaver took to the school's program of reform with mixed success. According to staff reports, he was at first "mature, orderly, friendly, and [a] leader for all races." He and his father started up a friendly correspondence, and Leroy even sent his son money from time to time. However, Cleaver could not hide what officials called his "thinly veiled hostility toward authority figures." He was written up for a variety of infractions, and he complained about his work detail and assignments. He boasted to the other boys that he could get them marijuana after they left Preston, and he tried to manipulate the system. As one official reported, "He did little to hide his feelings about work or training, and was frank enough to say that his only reason for insisting on State clothing was so that he could pawn it. This appears more a gesture of defiance than anything else, since subject had approximately $50.00 in saving, most of which had been sent by his father." Officials blamed Cleaver's home life for his troubles. One report summed it up: "Subject is the product of a broken home, but the consequences of the family difficulties resulted in no particular economic insecurity. Instead, Subject suffered from anxiety whenever the family would break temporarily and for many years there was a conflict of loyalties, Subject having a great deal of affection (although not with[out] some hostility) for both parents."[14]

At Preston, Cleaver became even further enmeshed in gang culture. The school was divided up into cliques, each with a clear hierarchy of "straights" on the top and "punks" on the bottom. Straights projected an outward compliance with the rules but enforced the code of the streets among their peers. Fighting ability, athleticism, criminal behavior, and aggressive conduct toward girls all contributed to a student's reputation within these cliques.[15] Drug use was also a fast way to establish a rep. "There's no hope without dope" was a common saying among the young men. Tattling, backing down from fights, and cooperating too readily with staff made one a punk. The code was made up of a few simple rules:

Stick to your own race or group most of the time.
Fight if you are called out.
Don't mess up too much, causing trouble for the company.
Don't fink on anyone, under any conditions.
Don't be "kissy"; don't volunteer any more than you have to.
Go along with the guys, even if it's wrong.[16]

The complex social order required a careful balance of subscribing to the group without sabotaging one's progress toward release. Straights were leaders and had the respect of their peers, while punks were ejected from the group, pressured into sex acts, or "rat-packed" (beaten) by a gang of boys. In this hierarchy, Cleaver emerged as a straight. He was smart. At eighteen, he cut a striking figure at six-foot-two, 187 pounds. He was a skilled boxer and had dealt marijuana. He had run with the notorious Pachuco gang, and he had had sex with girls. In the hierarchy of the juvenile-justice system, Cleaver was a leader among his peers.

In December 1953, Cleaver was paroled from Preston, and he moved in with his sister Helen Jones, at 4033 Trinity Street in East Los Angeles. She was married to a man who owned a rug-cleaning service. According to Cleaver, she was an aspiring member of the black bourgeoisie and an "undercover square." He tried to find work, but nothing interested him. He told his mother that he was going to join the army, but it was a half-hearted promise.

Cleaver went back to peddling weed in Rose Hills almost immediately, buying and selling it in huge quantities. On February 13, 1954, police officers were staked out in Rose Hills after they received multiple complaints of drug dealing in the area. From their cruiser, they watched Cleaver enter an abandoned house at 4439 Florizel Street, carrying three large paper sacks in his hand. They followed him into the house where they discovered him standing next to a secret compartment in the wall. "The bags that the defendant had been carrying," reported the officers, "contained several smaller sacks which contained marijuana. The total weight of the sacks found in the possession of the defendant was approximately four pounds."[17] Four pounds was a considerable amount of marijuana, worth $400 to $500 if sold in smaller quantities on the street. This put Cleaver in the category of drug dealer, and since he was now an adult, he could get up to ten years of hard time in prison.

Cleaver at first insisted on his innocence. According to the police, he "put on an act of righteous indignation" that was designed "to impress his mother and police."[18] Cleaver insisted, "I was on my way to see a girlfriend and went in there to get out of the rain. I had gotten off the bus and was a half a block from the girlfriend's house."[19] Cleaver also claimed that the police were particularly aggressive. "I was inside the house for about a minute when a man ran in from the rear of the house with a gun in his hand. He called out for me not to move or he would shoot. He then called to another man that came through the front door."[20] When it became clear that he would be convicted, he switched tactics and tried to play the part of a penitent young man. As he said in his court statement, "I feel that I was a fool to yield to temptation, however that is in the past now and all I can do now, is to prepare myself while I am in custody, so that when I am released I will know better than to try and make fast and easy money."[21]

A number of people tried to come to Cleaver's aid. His parole officer, R. Richardson, claimed that he was too young and intelligent for prison. He recommended that Cleaver be sent back to reform school at Deuel Vocation Institution. His older sister Wilhelmina also came to his defense, claiming that he was "easily led" by peer pressure and that he was essentially a good man. "Leroy is a victim of temptation, as might well be any one of us. Whenever a child is exposed to poverty, he never forgets it. . . . After he completes his routine of discipline, I am sure that he will become an honorable citizen."[22] His mother, ever Cleaver's greatest defender, claimed that he had committed no crime. "In my opinion I don't believe he was guilty. According to law I believe he had a fair trial, but I think there were some evidence that could have been anyone's marijuana in that abandon house. I think the circumstantial evidence is the cause. I believe he would have admitted it to me."[23]

The court didn't buy it. Cleaver had already been arrested fifteen times for his crimes, which included malicious mischief, curfew violations, truancy, burglary, vandalism, and possession of narcotics.[24] He pled not guilty at his arraignment on March 8, 1954, and his trial was set for April 2. After a monthlong trial, a jury found him guilty. Keeping up a tough exterior, Cleaver claimed that he didn't want to go back to reform school anyway. He stated that he would rather go to the state prison where he would be among "men."[25] On June 18, 1954, the court sentenced him to six months to ten years in the Soledad State Prison. Cleaver later reflected that his imprisonment was the beginning of his political awakening. "My early years were outlaw years, full of vandalism and petty crimes and so forth, so that before beginning to view things in a political perspective I was very hostile to the situation I found myself in. This included the political system, except that I didn't relate to it in any political sense. I was just hostile."[26]

A decade in the California prison system would transform Cleaver from a petty criminal into one of the most important radical activists of the black power era.

5

SOLEDAD PRISON (1954–1957)

In June 1954, Eldridge Cleaver boarded a bus and rode three hundred miles up Highway 101 to Soledad Prison. It was California's newest prison, nestled in the Salinas valley in America's agricultural heartland. Soledad was a monument to California's new rehabilitation-based approach to incarceration. The walls were composed of fencing rather than granite, so that inmates could look out at the alfalfa fields checkering the landscape and the rolling green hills beyond. John Steinbeck had immortalized this place in *Of Mice and Men*, writing, "A few miles south of Soledad, the Salinas River drops in close to the hillside bank and runs deep and green. The water is warm too, for it has slipped twinkling over the yellow sands in the sunlight before reaching the narrow pool." Soledad officials saw the "valley of the world" as the perfect place for a prison. The natural beauty there would transform inmates into productive citizens.

Soledad's interior design was also informed by the philosophy of rehabilitation. In the old prison model, known as the Auburn model, prisoners worked, ate, and lived in complete silence. They were marched in formation and isolated in solitary confinement at night. By contrast, Soledad was designed to be a self-contained city that facilitated the humane treatment of inmates. In the main building was a long corridor flanked by cell block wings. The cell blocks consisted of three tiers, each made up of a row of back-to-back cells connected by a catwalk. Each prisoner had his own cell, which was equipped with its own radio and earphones. Medium-security inmates even had keys to their own cells. The prison had a hospital, a dining hall, a chapel, a kitchen, an auditorium, vocational work spaces, and classrooms. Common rooms contained televisions and board games, and a gym was filled with sports equipment and weights.

Soledad Prison was symbolic of the changes sweeping through the prison system following the California Reorganization Act of 1943. After World War II, state officials reformed the entire structure of sentencing and incarceration in California. People who were convicted of a crime were now given indeterminate sentences. Parole boards were instituted to monitor progress and determine when inmates were ready to reenter society. Psychologists and religious staff supervised them and made recommendations for parole. Convicts no longer broke rocks in a quarry as punishment for their crimes. They attended liberal arts classes and studied trades like landscaping, welding, gardening, cooking, or printing. Fastidious records were kept of their progress in education and vocational classes. A new vocabulary was even invented to give an air of scientific authority to the enterprise. Guards were now called "correctional officers," while prisoners were referred to as "inmates." Prisons themselves were renamed "correctional facilities," while the isolation cells were now called "adjustment centers" or "segregation units." Soledad placed tremendous faith in principles of reform and rehabilitation in managing America's growing prison crisis.[1]

Cleaver was subjected to the standard battery of medical, psychological, and vocational examinations. His psychological evaluation found that he had no psychological abnormalities, but it concluded,

"He has a quite passive approach to life, tends to take things as they come." His social evaluation report agreed with this assessment, stating, "While he gives the impression of a serious youth, with a sincere desire to be co-operative and useful, nevertheless he recognizes that he is poorly motivated toward any program of work or self-improvement." Experts blamed his attitudes on his "broken home" as well as his resentment toward his father. They characterized Cleaver as antisocial and hostile toward authority but believed he could be rehabilitated through vocational and educational training. "His greatest handicaps—passivity to the point of inertia and inaccessibility to normal motivation—can be remedied only by clinically oriented procedures."[2] In his vocational examinations, Cleaver scored average on spatial visualization and manual dexterity and low on mental ability and mechanical comprehension.[3] During the test for shop class, he successfully built a coffee table with another inmate, showing promise as a student. However, the vocational staff judged him to be too shy and unmotivated to stick with the training.[4] Cleaver expressed interest in pursuing music, social services, sales, or following in his father's footsteps as a Pullman porter. Prison officials assigned him to wait tables and work in the bakery.

Cleaver quickly adjusted to prison life. In November 1954, he enrolled in a high school equivalency program, and he earned average grades in the first few months. He was also promoted from waiter to machine operator in the clothing factory. He was bitter to find himself in prison and adopted an iconoclastic stance toward the world. As he remembered it, "I attacked all forms of piety, loyalty, and sentiment: marriage, love, God, patriotism, the Constitution, the founding fathers, law, concepts of right-wrong-good-evil, all forms of ritualized behavior." He fell in with a like-minded group of inmates that formed a clique. "We cursed everything American," Cleaver once said of himself and his fellow prisoners, "including baseball and hot dogs."[5]

Cleaver's aggressive stance got him into trouble in early 1955. According to reports, "Cleaver stated that he had become friendly with inmate Thomas after his arrival at this Institution and that Thomas had been doing his clothes for him. He said that there was a very close relationship between the two of them. About three weeks ago he decided to break off this relationship and have nothing to do with Thomas. Since that time, he claimed that Thomas has been sending him threatening notes."[6] On the morning of February 4, 1955, Cleaver was exiting the mess hall when Thomas approached him and told him, "Quit messing around with me." Who threw the first punch is unclear, but by the time the guards arrived on the scene, the situation had escalated into a fistfight. It ended when Thomas tried to hit Cleaver with a metal lunch tray. He missed and hit one of the guards instead. Cleaver was sentenced to twenty-nine days in isolation for disorderly conduct, and the Adult Authority also put off possibility of parole for an extra six months.[7]

Isolation was the darker side of Soledad's reformist vision. Located in the prison's notorious O Wing, isolation cells were used to deal with Soledad's most troublesome prisoners. They were about six-by-eight feet, surrounded on three sides by concrete. Floor-to-ceiling bars were covered in a heavy steel mesh. There were no windows, furniture, or lights. Food trays were passed through a three-by-ten-inch slot. Prisoners in isolation slept on the floor on a thin mat. The toilets consisted of a circular hole in the concrete floor, which only the guard could flush from outside the cell.[8] While in isolation, Cleaver thought seriously about his next move: "I made a little decision for myself that when I got out of solitary confinement I would quit wasting my time and become a little more serious, and I would read more and study more and try to get some fat on my head."[9]

Cleaver emerged from that dark, windowless room with a new perspective about his incarceration. He knew that many prisoners improved their bodies with weights in prison, or they played checkers to pass the time. He decided to improve his mind. Remembering the lessons of his mother, he turned to books.

A number of prisoners at Soledad were known for their intelligence. One man named Pontifelt introduced prisoners to the classics of literature and philosophy. Pontifelt had been in Soledad for twelve years, and he informally taught younger inmates. As Cleaver remembered it, "We used to go down to the library on Saturday and sit around and listen to him talk. He was very knowledgeable about the philosophers, and he would talk about them and tell us how we were very stupid and didn't know what was going on in the world, and that the only way that we could save ourselves was to read these books and to gain this knowledge."[10] Cleaver had always loved reading adventure novels. But Pontifelt challenged him to engage with literature in a way that did more than entertain him. He persuaded Cleaver to awaken his political consciousness.

At the beginning, Cleaver's studies were haphazard. He checked out books on American history, but he didn't know what he was looking for. In summer 1955, he requested permission from the superintendent of prison education to buy his first book in prison, a Webster's collegiate dictionary, to aid him in his lessons.[11] Cleaver also debated John Hall, a man many considered the most well-read man in the prison. One day, after besting Cleaver in every debate, Hall gave him a copy of Karl Marx and Friedrich Engels's pamphlet *The Communist Manifesto*. As Cleaver remembered it, "I took the book back to my cell and stayed up all night, reading it all the way through. When I finished, I felt I had received a great revelation about what was really going on. All those ideas I had been studying and groping with seemed to fall into a pattern. All the feelings I had of rebellion and hatred were justified by this document."

Reading Marx provided Cleaver with his first grounding in political philosophy. He was particularly drawn to Marx's notion that society is the product of class struggles between the bourgeoisie and the working class. The bourgeoisie exploits the labor power of the proletariat, and only violent revolution will reshape the foundational economic and social structures. Cleaver saw himself as a proletarian in the heroic struggle against American capitalism. "I was no longer a criminal, but a revolutionary in support of a noble cause. I used the remainder of my time in prison to train myself for the day when I would get out, when I intended to apply the principles of the communist revolution."[12]

Cleaver expanded his understanding of political philosophy in a number of ways. He studied Vladimir Lenin's theories about the revolutionary vanguard party. In Lenin's view, the vanguard party provides the working class with the education and political consciousness to establish a socialist state. Cleaver later adapted this idea to apply to the Black Panther Party, which he believed to be the vanguard party for black people. Under Marxist-Leninist theory, colonies were the front line in the struggle against Western hegemony and imperialism, a philosophy that would later inform Cleaver's political relationships with third-world countries. Taken together, Marxist philosophies provided the groundwork for Cleaver's developing radical thinking throughout his time as an activist.

Cleaver was also interested in Sergey Nechayev's foundational revolutionary manifesto, *Catechism of a Revolutionary*. Cleaver admired the central message, that the revolutionary is an expendable mercenary in the struggle against capitalism. He often liked to quote the book's opening lines: "The revolutionary is a doomed man. He has no private interests, no affairs, sentiments, ties, property nor even a name of his own. His entire being is devoured by one purpose, one thought, one passion—the revolution." *Catechism* went further than Marxism in advocating for the destruction of institutions. Its central message of anarchy appealed to the destructive impulses that had been brewing inside Cleaver since his teenage years. He liked to think of himself as a doomed and heroic man in the struggle against society, and *Catechism* gave him the language to express this.

Cleaver spent all of his free time in the library, reading the classics. He became fascinated with Niccolò Machiavelli, the Italian Renaissance philosopher whose cynical theories of political duplicity confirmed Cleaver's deepest suspicions about the corruptness of authority. He read Enlightenment thinkers Thomas Hobbes and Jean-Jacques Rousseau, who explained how social contracts bind individuals and societies together. Voltaire and Thomas Paine provided Cleaver with attacks on organized religion, while Ralph Waldo Emerson's essay "Self-Reliance" gave him rationales for his own nonconformist behavior. Taken together, Marxism, transcendentalism, and Enlightenment writing provided Cleaver with a radical new worldview, a cornerstone for his developing revolutionary consciousness and his future work as a writer and race leader.

During this first year in prison, Cleaver paid close attention to the burgeoning civil rights movement. Only a month before he came to Soledad, the Supreme Court had voted unanimously to desegregate public schools in the *Brown v. Board of Education* decision. The case overturned "separate but equal" policies sanctioned by *Plessy v. Ferguson* and signaled the end of legal Jim Crow. Like all the black prisoners at Soledad, Cleaver watched these developments closely on television and in the newspapers, and they inspired him to explore his own black identity for the first time. "The controversy awakened me to my position in America," Cleaver wrote later, "and I began to form a concept of what it meant to [be] black in white America."[13]

Cleaver again turned to the library for guidance. He started by reading the biographies of early race leaders his mother had praised: W. E. B. Du Bois, Booker T. Washington, and Walter White. He studied the histories of National Association for the Advancement of Colored People (NAACP) and the Niagara Movement, the first civil rights organizations in America. He read books about the history of black voter suppression, the struggles between the KKK and black communities, and separate-but-equal policies during Jim Crow. Through Cleaver's study of the history of black civil rights, he gained a painful awareness of the long history of black people's suffering in America. It enraged him.

Cleaver's growing racial consciousness led to confrontations with prison officials. Like many inmates, he occasionally ingested mace—a cooking spice that doubles as a psychotropic drug—as a distraction from the pressures of prison life. In July 1955, he took too much of it and overdosed. As the guard reported it, "I found the inmate in a highly emotional state, claiming that his heart was hurting him and that he was afraid that he might die if left alone in his cell."[14] Cleaver was worried they might find out about the mace, so he began a fake rant about white racism to throw off suspicion. However, it backfired. What started off as a form of playacting turned into a real breakdown. "I started yelling about racism in the jail, about a white conspiracy to keep blacks down. The white guards and the hospital attendants freaked out, and locked me up in a padded cell. By that time I had really bugged out. One attendant took notes, wrote down all my attacks on the white race and their oppression of Negroes. When Monday morning came, I was on the psychiatrist's list."[15]

The psychiatrist told him that his rant was connected to his hatred of his mother. Cleaver felt that this was a deflection of real issues of racism in the United States. As he remembered, "What revolted me about him was that he had heard me denouncing the whites, that each time he interviewed me he deliberately guided the conversation back to my family life, to my childhood. That in itself was all right, but he deliberately blocked all my attempts to bring out the racial question, and he made it clear that he was not interested in my attitude toward whites."[16] The psychiatrist's prognosis that Cleaver's mother was to blame for his criminality anticipated the infamous Moynihan Report, which was released ten years later. It argued that single black mothers, and not institutional racism, were to blame for the racial crisis in America. During his incarceration, prison officials subjected Cleaver to this narrative that his mother was to blame again and again. It was one of the main reasons he remained openly hostile to their opinions throughout his time in prison.

Cleaver did not fare well at his first parole hearing in August 1955. In his written request for release, he told officials rather blandly, "I agree to conduct my future in an acceptable manner. I would like to say that I am ready to go home, but since you gentlemen were hired to decide when I am ready, I will only say that I wish to go home and that I believe I am ready to go home."[17] His test scores measuring progress were the lowest scores an inmate could receive. In his vocational progress, he received a score of "poor" for morale, perseverance, technical knowledge, and human understanding. Cleaver did attend high school classes and church, and he received average grades in the clothing factory. Nevertheless, officials viewed Cleaver as a problem case. The parole board reported that he had not accepted responsibility for his crimes or gained insight into his problems. In the written comments, officials wrote simply: "Made poor impression. Minimized his delinquency." Cleaver's first parole request was denied. He would have to spend at least another year in Soledad.[18]

In the same month that Cleaver went up for parole, the mutilated body of fourteen-year-old Emmett Till was pulled from the Tallahatchie River in Mississippi. He had allegedly flirted with a white woman, Carolyn Bryant, and for this, he had been kidnapped by two white men and beaten beyond recognition. (In an interview with a historian six decades later, Bryant admitted she had lied about Till flirting with her.) A fan from a cotton gin, weighing seventy-five pounds, had been tied around Till's neck with barbed wire, and he had been dropped into the river. When he was finally pulled from the water four days later, he was so badly mutilated that he had to be identified by the ring that he wore. Till's mother, Mamie Bradley, insisted on an open casket so that the public could bear witness to the brutality of the crime against her son. "Let the world see what I have seen," she said. The world did see. Ten thousand people came out to pay their respects at Till's funeral, and the photos of his body circulated widely after they were published in the African American weekly *Jet*. Till's horrific death provoked such outrage that it helped galvanize the burgeoning civil rights movement.

Till was just the latest victim in a long line of lynchings that went back to the 1880s. Since Reconstruction, over three thousand black people had been killed by groups like the KKK in an effort to maintain white supremacy. Victims were beaten, hung, and set on fire, and sometimes their dead bodies were photographed for postcards sold as souvenirs. In many cases, the lynch mob used the myth of the black rapist to justify the murder of black people. Some of the largest massacres in American history started with the rumor of a black man making advances toward a white woman. In Tulsa in 1921, for example, white people murdered almost three hundred black people and burned thirty-five blocks to the ground after a young black man named Dick Rowland supposedly flirted with a white woman in an elevator. Two years later, the all-black town of Rosewood, Florida, was destroyed and many of its residents lynched after unsubstantiated reports circulated of a black man raping a white woman. In many places across the South, these killings were sanctioned or at the very least ignored. The two white men accused of Till's murder, J. W. Milam and Roy Bryant, were acquitted by a jury of white men only weeks after the body was found. A few months later, they even admitted their crimes in *Look* (with a condensed version of the article appearing in *Reader's Digest* soon thereafter) and went unpunished.

Cleaver was disturbed by the brutality of the crime against Till. However, he was more unsettled by his mixed feelings toward Carolyn Bryant—the woman who had falsely accused Till. When he saw her picture, he realized, "I felt that tension in the center of my chest I experienced when a woman appeals to me. I was disgusted and angry with myself. Here was a woman who had caused the death of a black, possibly because, when he looked at her, he also felt the same tensions of lust and probably for the same general reasons that I felt them. It was all unacceptable to me." Although Cleaver had cultivated a subversive stance toward all things American, he was embarrassed to discover that he was still attracted to light-skinned women. He found this intolerable, and he decided to root out and destroy his desire for white women. "I flew into a rage at myself, at America, at white women, at the history that had placed those tensions of lust and desire in my chest."[19]

Cleaver discussed this topic with fellow black inmates, who expressed a preference for white women as well. He theorized that that they were all brainwashed by "the white race's standards of beauty." They all preferred white women, not because white women were more attractive, but because they had been indoctrinated to think whiteness was more beautiful. Cleaver reached much the same conclusions that famed sociologists Kenneth and Mamie Clark had reached in their doll experiment. In their study, African American children were shown a black doll and a white doll and asked to identify the "nice" doll and the "bad" doll. The children overwhelmingly preferred the white doll. The Clarks argued that this illustrated how deeply ingrained white standards of beauty were in American society and how damaging they were to psyches of black people. Their study became one of the key pieces of evidence used in the *Brown v. Board of Education* case to desegregate schools. Cleaver turned to literature once more to rid himself of his attraction to whiteness. "It intensified my frustrations to know that I was indoctrinated to see the white woman as more beautiful than my own black woman. It drove me into books seeking light on the subject. In Richard Wright's *Native Son*, I found Bigger Thomas and a keen insight into the problem."[20]

The publication of *Native Son* in 1940 transformed the discussion of race in America. Famous literary critic Irving Howe once said, "The day *Native Son* appeared American culture was changed forever. Richard Wright's novel brought out into the open, as no one ever had before, the hatred, fear, and violence that have crippled and may yet destroy our culture."[21] *Native Son* is the story of a black chauffeur named Bigger Thomas who accidentally kills the white daughter of a prominent Chicago real estate investor for whom he works. The murder triggers a citywide hunt for Bigger and whips up public fears about an accused black rapist on this loose. The novel—which draws on realist literary techniques and a Marxist vision of the world—indicts white American society for the way that it criminalizes black men as rapists. Cleaver was deeply moved by Wright's unapologetically bleak vision of American society, and he identified with Bigger, the black outlaw and antihero of the novel. Cleaver began to develop his own theories about the significance of the black outlaw figure in combating ideologies of whiteness. As he mused in his notebooks, "It seems to me that a black heroic fictional figure in America must of necessity be a prisoner or at least an Outlaw. He must be in total rebellion against the white man's system."[22] Wright's novel taught Cleaver that the black rapist was the most feared and rebellious symbol in a white society. Cleaver decided to embody that fearful symbol as his protest against white America. "Somehow I arrived at the conclusion that, as a matter of principle, it was of paramount importance for me to have an antagonistic, ruthless attitude toward white women."[23] By physically assaulting white women, Cleaver believed he was taking up a radical political position against a system that lynched black men. In his perverse logic, becoming the rapist was a way for him to challenge white supremacy.

Throughout 1956, Cleaver tried to be a model prisoner, with mixed success. He enrolled in a welding class in late August but was dropped from it only three months later. As the teacher reported, "Student did not even try even though he was given every opportunity."[24] He did better at academic subjects. He took high school courses and earned a B-minus average. His teachers remarked that he was cooperative, had a good attitude, and worked hard at his subjects. He earned A's in geography and mathematics and B's in biology, bookkeeping, and typing.[25] He also enrolled in an elementary shorthand course, a correspondence class in which he excelled. In his free time, he boxed and wrote letters to his family.

Cleaver still occasionally struggled with his anger. On April 2, 1956, he got into a fight with a fellow inmate named Jackson. During a game of dominos, they started to argue and Cleaver began calling Jackson dirty names. As Jackson got up to fight, Cleaver punched him. The fight got so intense that both Jackson and Cleaver ignored orders by the guards to stop. At one moment, Cleaver lost control. As officer K. D. Britt reported, "During the fight I saw inmate Cleaver break a pane of glass in one of the windows in the day room with his fist."[26] For this fight and the destruction of property, Cleaver was given five days in isolation.

In August 1956, Cleaver went up for parole once more and was optimistic about his chances this time. He had performed well in his academic coursework and his work assignments. He promised officials to move in with his mother, avoid prior associates, and take a job working in a hardware store. His ultimate plan, he told them, was to attend Compton Junior College to pursue an electronic engineering degree and then transfer to a four-year college. In his statement to officials, he appeared genuinely reformed: "I sincerely believe that I am ready and able to take my place in society as a productive, law-abiding, acceptable citizen. Looking back upon the distance between my present self and the Leroy Cleaver that I was upon my arrival at prison, I cannot reconcile the two personalities. I cannot say that I am glad that I came to prison, but to be truthful, I must say that I have gained something that I could not have gotten had I remained on the streets, especially the road I was traveling. I have, among other things, educated myself to a degree."[27]

The parole board was not entirely sure Cleaver was ready for release. "Inmate has a tendency to minimize his difficulties and appears to accept little responsibility for his recent disciplinary," wrote Robert Davidson, his correctional classification officer. "Prognosis unpredictable at this time."[28] Despite its misgivings, however, the parole board decided to let Cleaver go. It seemed that he had benefited at least somewhat from the programs of the prison.

Cleaver's real education, though, had taken place in the solitude of his cell. Reading widely from Western philosophical and American literary traditions, Cleaver had started to cultivate a rebellious, antisocial identity. He was convinced that the rapist was the ultimate black American outlaw, and he wanted to test his theories on the streets. As soon as he got his release notice, he dropped out of his high school classes. As his final gesture of rebellion, he shaved his head with a razor just days before his release, which was against prison policy.

On the afternoon of December 3, 1956, Cleaver boarded a Greyhound bus heading for Los Angeles. He had earned just twenty dollars during his thirty-two months of incarceration, and after buying his bus ticket, he had seven dollars in his pocket. He arrived in Los Angeles and moved into his mother's house at 1277 W. Twenty-Fifth Street, southwest of downtown and about three miles from where the Cleavers had first settled along S. Central Avenue. It was a burgeoning new black neighborhood. After the Supreme Court decision *Shelley v. Kraemer* had made it illegal to enforce racially restrictive covenants in 1948, African Americans started moving in large numbers into the area west of downtown, known as West Adams district. Thelma lived in a little bungalow on a quiet street just off Adams. She really hoped that now that her son was free he would turn his life around. She helped him as much as she could, giving him a room and cooking him three meals a day.

Cleaver seemed sincere about making a new life for himself. He met with his parole officer and filled out his reports on time. His officer reported that Cleaver was "courteous and attentive." He promised officials that he would "complete his parole successfully for his mother's sake" and that he would "not to use or sell marijuana." Cleaver searched for regular employment, though he found it difficult to find work as an ex-con. He took a job cleaning carpets at Jones's Rug Cleaning Service, which was owned by his brother-in-law. His sister Helen drove him to the shop in Pasadena every morning, and he earned fifteen dollars a day.[29] It was labor-intensive and dirty work, and he quit after just two weeks. From there, he bounced around from job to job. He took a position as a stock clerk at the Coast Distribution Company earning fifty dollars a week, which he held until the middle of January 1957. For the next three months he worked at the Los Angeles County Heart Association as a stock clerk for fifty-five dollars a week. In March, he was fired after he lacerated the back of his right hand and it got badly infected. When his hand healed, he took a job as a loader on a junk truck for a man named Robert Hale for fourteen dollars a day. He hated this job, feeling that it was beneath him. Finally, he worked for Giant Rug Cleaning Company starting in November 1957. "His employment record has not been too good," reported his parole officer, "and it is felt that this is due to the fact that subject has a rather high opinion of himself and considers many jobs to be too menial for him." Overall, Cleaver's parole officer felt that his prognosis for staying out of prison was not good: "subject is resentful of the fact that he is on parole and is latently hostile."[30]

Cleaver tried to enroll in Los Angeles City College to study economics, but he lacked both credentials and money to get in. He briefly turned to the idea of pimping his girlfriend Eddice Pickens to make enough money, but he ultimately rejected this idea. "My sole purpose in getting this girl was to turn her out," Cleaver later admitted, "to make a prostitute of her, and to be her pimp." Cleaver wore her down with psychological manipulation and emotional abuse. He set up a pad in a rooming house for her to turn tricks, but when it came time to take her there, something inside prevented him. "I couldn't do it. I have always hated pimps and was unable to become one. This made me sick of myself and I considered myself weak." Cleaver decided he couldn't become a pimp because he didn't hate black women enough to do it.

"I realized that I would have had to really hate a woman in order to be her pimp. I remember knowing with conviction, that I could have very easily pimped a white woman, but I didn't have the heart to pimp a black woman."[31]

But while Cleaver did not pimp black women, he did sexually assault them in his bid to become an outlaw rapist. As he famously wrote in his confessional, *Soul on Ice*, "I became a rapist. To refine my technique and modus operandi, I started out by practicing on black girls in the ghetto. When I considered myself smooth enough, I crossed the tracks and sought out white prey. I did this consciously, deliberately, willfully, methodically—though looking back I see that I was in a frantic, wild and completely abandoned frame of mind."[32] Cleaver spent his Saturday nights robbing men and raping young women. He was chillingly calculated about these crimes. He carried with him a pistol and two six-foot-long strips of clothesline rolled neatly into separate coils. He took everything out of his pockets and left his watch and ring at home so nothing would be left behind for police to find. He made sure to wear clothes with no buttons. He stalked white couples parked in cars or entering cheap hotels. He preferred these people because they were often cheating on their spouses and were less likely to report the crime.

Cleaver wrote about these rapes later in salacious detail in his unpublished prison manuscripts. In his "Book of a Rapist," Cleaver presents his crimes as part of a grand literary and political project. As he announces in the opening line, "My magnum opus. Prodigious task! To capture the prototype of the American Negro rapist."[33] Part manifesto, part pornographic novel, Cleaver's story presents the rapist as the ultimate iconoclast, whose sexual violence is an attack on white society. The rapist is "beyond the white man's law, beyond the white man's power, beyond his authority, beyond his dictates and standards."[34] The particulars of the story are shocking. Cleaver's alter ego, named Stacy, parks outside of a motel and waits for a white couple to enter a room. As they do so, he takes them by surprise and forces them into the motel at gunpoint. He ties the man's feet and hands with the rope. He commands the woman to sit on the bed and tells her, "Yes I am going to hurt you, but not with this gun."[35] When the woman starts to cry, Stacy is brutal, taking delight in her fear: "Go ahead and cry, you white bitch."[36] He strips her naked and rapes her, which Cleaver describes in page after page of pornographic detail. But what is particularly unnerving about the story is not just these explicit descriptions but also Cleaver's fantasy that the woman enjoys being raped. When she recoils from him, he "fucked her savagely and relentless, but with a deft touch, a sure touch, as if he were a burglar who knew every possible combination of a lock." At the conclusion of the story, the woman climaxes despite herself, which Cleaver describes as "divesting herself of a burden."[37] Cleaver's writings reveal his brutality as a young man, but also a self-serving fantasy—by portraying his victims as wanting to be brutalized and raped, it absolved him from any responsibility or guilt. Although he would disavow this behavior later in his book *Soul on Ice*, for a brief period Cleaver saw rape as an effective political strategy to combat white supremacy.

Cleaver's experiment as an outlaw rapist came to an end on the night of November 3, 1957. According to police reports, at about two in the morning, Cleaver approached a parked car sitting on Miramar Street near Grand Avenue in Los Angeles, with two college students, Clifford James Barnett and Sheila McGrath, sitting inside. Wearing a hat to cover his eyes and having turned his collar up to shield his face, Cleaver tapped on the driver-side window with his pistol and demanded they let him in. He squeezed in beside Barnett in the front seat and ordered them not to look at his face. He made McGrath get into the backseat while he bound Barnett's hands with scotch tape. Cleaver then crawled into the backseat and ordered McGrath to take off her coat. When she refused, he struck her on the side of the head with the pistol. He repeatedly ordered her to take off her clothes, and each time she refused, he hit her with his gun. Barnett managed to free himself, and, after a struggle, Cleaver struck him in the back of the head with the butt of his gun and ran. As Barnett gave chase in his car, Cleaver shot wildly over his shoulder. At least one of the bullets struck the car.[38] A marine named Norris Wallery witnessed the commotion from across the street and started honking his horn to attract attention. Cleaver turned and fired two shots at Wallery and his girlfriend, Marianne Scott. Another man named James Davis also noticed Cleaver running down the street. He gave chase, and Cleaver squeezed off a couple shots at him. He finally reached his car, started it up, and drove off. He was in such a panic, however, that he crashed into a parked car just down the block. When the police arrived, he was still standing there, inspecting the damage.[39]

At the scene, the police officers ran a make on Cleaver's car and found out he had a record from marijuana sales. At that point, they tried to beat a confession out of him. "The police pounced upon petitioner and began to get rough with him, twisting his arms and punching him in the stomach and beating him about the body with black jacks and night sticks and slapping his face."[40] When a crowd gathered, Cleaver called out to them for help, at which point the police hauled him off to the Central Police Station. He was handcuffed to the table in the interrogation room and slapped around more by officers. He was not read his Miranda rights. He was charged with five counts of assault with intent to commit murder, one count of assault with the intent to commit rape, and two counts of assault with a deadly weapon.

Cleaver was railroaded by the court system. His trial began on February 3, 1958, and lasted five days. The prosecution rested its case on the witness testimony and the fact that the police had found tape in Cleaver's car that matched the tape from the holdup. The prosecutor never introduced any tape into evidence, nor did he produce any testimony from the police that proved they had found tape in Cleaver's car. The pistol was never entered into evidence either, and its existence was never proven. Therefore, it came down to Cleaver's word against the witnesses'. Even this part of the prosecutor's case was a bit shaky. When Sheila McGrath was asked to identify her attacker, she was unable to do so until the prosecutor called for a recess, coached her briefly, and then put her back on the stand.

Through it all, Cleaver maintained his innocence. He claimed that he had also been parked on that street with his girlfriend Eddice Pickens when he heard a horn and shots fired. He claimed that he was trying to save himself and girlfriend by fleeing the scene, and that is when he crashed his car. In court, he stated, "I can't say that these things did not happen, but I do maintain that I am not the person that committed the acts. At the time that the shooting took place, I was in the area, accompanied by my girlfriend. I attribute my being here today to these factors: my financial inability to hire a competent attorney, the fact that I had a prior felony conviction, the failure on the part of my attorney to use my witness, my own ignorance which had the same effect as indifference, topped by a very able prosecuting attorney."[41] By Friday at 4:00 PM, the jury had still not come to a decision. The judge, in an attempt to bring the trial to a close quickly, threatened to sequester them. He told them that if they "had not found a verdict by 4:30 p.m., he would turn them over to the Sheriff and have them locked up in a Hotel over the weekend, until the following MONDAY MORNING."[42] Even though the jury had previously been gridlocked on Cleaver's case for six hours, they deliberated for ten short minutes before returning to court with a verdict of "guilty." On February 7, 1958, Cleaver was convicted of two counts of assault with a deadly weapon and three counts of assault with intent to commit murder. He was sentenced to six months to fourteen years at San Quentin Prison.

6

SAN QUENTIN PRISON (1958–1963)

When gold was discovered by accident in the American River in 1848, it triggered the largest migration in United States history to that point. In just one year, eighty thousand people flocked to the Sierra foothills in search of their fortune. These pioneers were a mixed group: middle-class men from the East Coast, immigrants fleeing the political upheavals of Europe, Mexican prospectors, sex workers, Chinese laborers, formerly enslaved African Americans, and ex-cons. Gold-mining towns sprung up all over the Sierras, and San Francisco emerged as a thriving port city on the West Coast. Migrants established shantytowns across the steep slopes of San Francisco, with gambling halls, saloons, and opium dens dotting the landscape. It was a dangerous and sometimes lawless place. Prostitution, theft, and public drunkenness were everyday realities, and duels to the death were not uncommon. Mob justice was the order of the day. White mobs lynched Mexicans, Chileans, and other "foreigners" with impunity in disputes over land and property. The majority of California's indigenous population was wiped out by settlers seeking gold.

In 1852, California officials created the first prison to deal with the growing crime in the state. They dragged a military brig named the *Waban* across the San Francisco Bay and dropped it on an isolated hook of land called Point Quentin. The wooden ship became California's first state prison, and it housed thieves, prostitutes, and murderers. A permanent cell block was constructed just a few years later, which had both a hospital and a dungeon. The stone building contained forty-eight cells, each with a giant iron door fitted with a judas hole for air and light. Inmates slept on wooden bunks and shared a night bucket as a toilet. Misbehaving inmates were flogged with rawhide or hung up by their wrists with a derrick. The worst offenders were given a "shower"; that is, hung upside-down naked and sprayed in the mouth and on the genitals with a high-pressure hose.[1] Disobedient inmates were forced to stand in four-hour shifts on two-foot spots painted on the floor in a row of cells called "Siberia." Those inmates were allowed a two-minute bathroom break in the morning and a two-minute break in the afternoon. If they were unable to stand at attention, they were flogged with rubber hoses or truncheons.[2]

Cleaver entered San Quentin at a moment of tremendous change in the prison system. At the center of this transformation was Clinton Duffy, a progressive who served as warden to San Quentin from 1940 to 1952. Duffy was the spokesman of an enlightened generation of penal administrators who believed that behavior modification through education, job training, sports, religious practice, and reading could transform convicts. Duffy saw San Quentin as "a huge, modern laboratory for the study of criminals and crime" and himself as its lead scientist.[3] He completely transformed San Quentin. He got rid of the draconian punishments as well as physical torture. He painted over the circles in the cells in Siberia, and he had the iron doors of the dungeon cells removed from their hinges. He hired a team of specialists—psychologists, sociologists, religious leaders, and doctors—believing that their expertise would revolutionize incarceration at San Quentin.

Under this new regime, radical forms of observation and scrutiny were adopted to manage inmates. Group therapy and bibliotherapy (reading literary classics to help treat disorders) became common rehabilitation practice. Teams of doctors probed and documented all aspects of a prisoner's life in search of the causes of his criminal behavior. Guards routinely ransacked prisoner cells, looking for magazines, personal writings, and books that might indicate rebellious thinking or plans for escape. Library records were scrutinized, and everyone on staff was charged with rooting out anything insurrectionary. Prison officials read every piece of mail coming in or out of the prison in order to keep tabs on prisoners' thinking and any potentially subversive activities.[4] As Duffy explained, "We keep a careful record of every letter written or received by the inmates, and our censors read every line. This is a prodigious book keeping job, but in the long run it benefits the men themselves. Letters are clues to a man's thinking and emotions—they show progress or despair; they reveal an unreported illness, a family crisis that has affected a man's behavior, or even evidence that may be vital to his chances for parole."[5] San Quentin's approach represented a new form of punishment, where quasi-scientific scrutiny and surveillance replaced physical cruelty as the primary method of control.

San Quentin is a hauntingly beautiful place. Perched atop a windswept peninsula overlooking the San Francisco Bay, the five-story stone structure towers above the water like a medieval castle. Neatly manicured lawns and gardens surround the prison, the work of the well-behaved inmates temporarily allowed past the gate.

When Cleaver arrived in early 1958, he knew San Quentin's history and reputation, and he was afraid. Later, he remembered his arrival:

> The first time I was driven, amongst a Greyhound Bus full of prisoners in chains, into the gates of San Quentin, I along with every other prisoner on that bus who was going to that prison for the first time, was wired up. The other cats on the bus, who had already gone through it all years before, played it cool. But we had our faces glued to the windows, taking a

> long last look at the outside world. The bus stopped, between the double fence outside the main gate of the wall, and then we were plunged, with the finality of the beat of a drum, which was your heart, into what we knew was a maneater, a pool of terror, and a battleground. Many who went into those walls, came out feet first, and years later.[6]

Cleaver was taken to the Reception and Guidance Center, where he was processed and given the usual barrage of tests. He was searched for weapons and contraband, and his ears, nose, armpits, and rectum were thoroughly inspected. After Cleaver showered, prison officials issued him prison clothes, in addition to toothpaste, a toothbrush, socks, and tobacco. In the following weeks, sociologists, doctors, psychiatrists, religious leaders, and teachers questioned him, and Cleaver took a range of tests. On the intelligence test, he scored a low average. He did fair or poor in general memory, counting, and reading retention, and Cleaver was characterized as only "fairly articulate" and "fairly introspective."[7] In his Readmission Clinical Report, officials noted that Cleaver denied wrongdoing and he focused on the technical details of the case. "Inmate claims he was mistakenly identified, denies criminal responsibility, and maintains very tight defenses." Officials concurred with earlier diagnoses from Soledad that Cleaver was "quite passive in his approach to life," but they now admitted, "Inmate is capable of extremely aggressive activity, and it can be observed that during his previous term, he exhibited traits of violence."[8]

Cleaver's psychiatric tests also diagnosed that he was passive and perhaps even suffered from gender confusion from being raised by a single mother. "Psychosexual development here is not too clear," read his psychological evaluation, "but test results suggest that he has become somewhat overidentified with the passive, feminine approach to life." Overall, psychiatrists judged that "he had some underlying hostility toward authority, a fairly close identification with a delinquent value system." They predicted that because of his passive nature, however, he would be an unproblematic inmate. "Cleaver will make a very conforming adjustment, accepting supervision in a mild and placid manner," the psychological report concluded. "As noted above, there are no indications of excessive impulsivity, and thus he need not be considered a serious escape risk."[9]

Cleaver started looking immediately for any way out of San Quentin. He had learned from his time in Soledad that the quickest pathway to freedom within the parole system was to participate in educational and vocational programs and to avoid disciplinary write-ups. Securing parole depended on the support of prison psychologists, educators, and therapists, and Cleaver vowed to win them over. He started taking classes in July 1958, and he impressed his teachers with his diligence and focus. In accounting and bookkeeping, he earned nearly perfect scores, while in US and world history, he earned a B average. His teachers were all pleased with his determination. "Cleaver worked as hard as anyone in the class. He deserves to be complimented upon his effort," wrote one teacher.[10] They all agreed he was "serious and determined."[11] Cleaver started up his obsessive reading schedule again. He always checked out the maximum quota of five books each trip, and he even surreptitiously took books out of the library. At one point, he was caught stealing a copy of *Moby Dick*.[12]

Cleaver also repudiated his former identity as a sexual predator. He enrolled in group psychotherapy in September 1958, and he told the prison psychiatrist that he felt guilt over his multiple acts of sexual assault.[13] Following his failed experiment as an outlaw rapist, Cleaver no longer viewed this as a viable political strategy but rather an immoral action. As he wrote later in *Soul on Ice*, "After I returned to prison, I took a long look at myself, and for the first time in my life, admitted that I was wrong, that I had gone astray—astray not so much from the white man's law as from being human, civilized—for I could not approve the act of rape."[14]

Cleaver studied other ways to get out of San Quentin. He started preliminary research on his case, looking for ways to overturn the decision. He was inspired by fellow inmate Caryl Chessman, also known as the Red Light Bandit. Chessman's case was similar to Cleaver's. In the late 1940s, he had committed a series of robberies, kidnappings, and rapes, and under an unusual application of the law, he was sentenced to death, even though his offences were not capital crimes. Chessman acted as his own attorney for the next twelve years, challenging his conviction. He taught himself the law in the prison library and filed dozens of writs and appeals. Because the legal resources in the library were so limited, he purchased his own law books and became an amateur legal councilor, offering help to other men on death row. He exploited every possible loophole in the case against him, claiming the stenographer had not properly recorded the case, he was the victim of mistaken identity, his confession was coerced, and his sentence was unfair.

Chessman also wrote a series of bestselling books about his experience, which he had smuggled out of San Quentin for publication. These included *Cell 2455, Death Row: A Condemned Man's Own Story; Trial by Ordeal; The Face of Justice;* and *The Kid Was a Killer*. These books inflamed the public debate about the death penalty, and they earned Chessman the support of figures such as Aldous Huxley, Norman Mailer, and Eleanor Roosevelt. Through his relentless public campaigning, Chessman got eight stays of execution. He also led some of the first organized prison strikes at San Quentin, demanding better treatment for prisoners. San Quentin officials would eventually execute him on May 2, 1960, and although he never secured his freedom, he inspired a whole generation of amateur jailhouse lawyers, especially Cleaver. "Even though Chessman was executed in the end," he wrote later, "to convicts he became a powerful symbol of resourcefulness, defiance, and the will to fight for one's life and freedom."[15]

Chessman provided Cleaver with a model to challenge his incarceration. Gaining knowledge of the law was the first step. Cleaver started teaching himself the basics at the library, which was run by the ambitious and energetic bibliophile Herman Spector. Like Duffy, Spector saw the library as a central part of the prison's mission to reform prisoner behavior. He was an eccentric who read journals in his field and took classes in criminology, psychology, and social work.[16] He wrote for numerous periodicals and served as assistant managing editor of *Prison World*. At San Quentin, he created a vast library of thirty-three thousand books, which was well used.[17] In the year Cleaver arrived, 90 percent of inmates used the library, checking out about one hundred books per man per year.[18] Spector kept meticulous data concerning the reading habits of the men, and he closely monitored the purchase of books. He was eager to test his idea that classic literature—such as *The Iliad* and *The Odyssey*—could transform convicts.

Spector kept tight control over the law books, and Cleaver initially had a hard time gaining access to the Legal Library. On October 6, 1958, he complained to officials, "I must have the use of the Legal Library if I am to competently pursue the disposition of my case. I am under the impression that I have a right to use the Legal Library and under the impression the Librarian's actions seem somewhat arbitrary and improper."[19] When he was finally granted access, Cleaver read widely, studying cases similar to his own and teaching himself how to write legal petitions and writs. On March 29, 1959, he contacted the prison education department to request permission to receive a portable typewriter from his mother. "I am striving to develop skill in the art of writing and a typewriter would facilitate this effort beyond measure. Also it would aid me with correspondence courses and school work generally. I am quite serious in making this request and I pledge myself to scrupulously comply with all rules and regulations concerning the matter."[20] Cleaver received the typewriter in late April 1959.

Armed with his amateur knowledge of the law, Cleaver started reaching out to attorneys to help him with his case. He wrote to a lawyer in Los Angeles named Harold Ackerman to obtain aid in filing an appeal. In a rambling fifteen-page letter, Cleaver cited dozens of cases—including Chessman's—to argue that his own case should be overturned. He lobbied for his innocence based on everything from his attorney's incompetence to a lack of physical evidence introduced by the prosecutor. Cleaver also argued that McGrath had been coached by the prosecutor to finger him as the culprit.[21] In his response to Cleaver, Ackerman explained that none of this mattered because he had not filed an appeal immediately after the verdict. "Certainly at this late date it would be difficult if not impossible to explain your lack of diligence in failing to pursue some legal remedy, hence I must regretfully inform you that despite whatever validity there may be to your contentions, you just waited too long to do something about it."[22]

Cleaver tried to find other ways out of San Quentin. He campaigned to get transferred to Chino to be closer to his family. On July 5, 1959, he wrote to the prison's classification committee, arguing that the long journey from Los Angeles put a strain on his family.[23] Less than two weeks later, he wrote again. "My mother is rather aged, and it is very difficult for her to make the trip up here, also the financial requirements work a great hardship upon her and any of the other members of my family when they make the trip."[24] A week later, Cleaver's sister Wilhelmina wrote to the warden to request a transfer on his behalf. "I, his sister, and his mother are employed by the Los Angeles City Schools, and are only able to visit him once a year, which I believe, is not helping the progress of his rehabilitation."[25] Cleaver's request was denied.

Cleaver also enlisted the help of his therapist, Dr. Carr, to help him get a transfer to Vacaville, where there were more advanced therapy programs. From Dr. Carr's therapy sessions, Cleaver had gained insight into his psychological motivations for his crimes. As he said in a letter to the classification committee, "Mr. Carr, my Group Therapist, is helping me probe into my background in an effort to make me more aware of what makes me tick—my motivations and so forth, and I feel that I am deriving from all this a knowledge of myself that is my only hope of achieving a future worthy of the name."[26] Carr believed Cleaver was making great progress and encouraged him to apply for the transfer. On November 4, 1959, Cleaver wrote officials an impassioned letter requesting a change. "As sullied as my past is, I am only twenty four years of age at the present time, and I think I know myself well enough to say that, with certain radical changes in several of my personality traits and in a few of my response approaches to social situations, if I can accomplish this, then I can go back to the streets with a reasonable hope of not falling back upon the deadly treadmill of criminality."[27] On the bottom of this letter, Dr. Carr wrote, "He is well motivated for more intensive exposure to psychotherapy—such as is available at CMF."[28] On December 6, 1959, the chief psychiatrist Dr. David Schmidt approved the transfer, stating that Cleaver had made considerable progress and would benefit from more therapy.[29] It appeared that Cleaver might be transferred as early as Christmas. But then on December 9, 1959, he received a notice from CMF denying his request because Vacaville was at capacity and had a long waiting list.

As Cleaver's parole hearing drew near in spring 1960, he felt pulled in two distinct directions. On one hand, he tried to perform well in his classes and keep a clean record. In his annual evaluation of February 1960, officials noted that Cleaver was doing very well in his high school equivalency classes, earning a B-minus average and the praise of his teachers. "A superior student, studies hard," wrote one teacher on his parole report.[30] On the other hand, Cleaver was starting to develop a literary voice, one he felt could serve his race in the civil rights movement. As officials stated in his annual psychiatric summary, "Although he still feels oppressed, he has been able to sublimate his hostile and rebellious acting out with socially acceptable writing. His sole interest is in writing which again creates further problems due to the frustrations present in a writing career. Due to his prior nervous disorder, if his work for the freedom of the oppressed Negro fails, he could easily have another relapse. Also, his test IG is low average and a more realistic planning might be needed." Doctors thought that Cleaver was not smart enough to develop a career as a writer and leader of his race. With somewhat racist overtones, they concluded that "Mr. Cleaver is a tall sleepy eyed Negro who presents himself as an individual who is dissatisfied and confused about his social role."[31] They diagnosed Cleaver with "sociopathic orientation" as well as "schizoid and autistic ideation." On March 15 the board denied him parole, stating that he could benefit from more psychiatric help managing his expectations.

Following his parole rejection in spring 1960, Cleaver redoubled his efforts to become a model prisoner. Except for his failed heist of *Moby Dick* from the prison library, Cleaver had managed to stay out of trouble for the two years in San Quentin. He earned good grades in his classes, and his teachers praised him as hardworking and intelligent. Cleaver also continued his intensive study of books, and in March 1960, he wrote a letter to the job assignment lieutenant asking to work in the prison library. "I am something of a bibliophile," Cleaver wrote enthusiastically, "and I have no doubts that I will find the work personally satisfying, for I have an ardent desire to learn all that I can about books. Also, I do a little writing and I am sure that the atmosphere of the library will inspire me."[32] There was a long waiting list of prisoners who wanted to work in the library, so Cleaver was denied. However, for his good behavior in his first two years, his custody was reduced to minimum security, and he was transferred to the "honor wing" in West Block in spring 1960.

Honor wing was a real privilege for Cleaver. He got a larger cell, more access to TV, and less surveillance of his movements. He was given the job of key man on the West Block, which allowed him to let prisoners in and out of cells on his tier. Cleaver used the prized job as an opportunity to make himself into a banker in the underground economy. In San Quentin, prisoners bought and sold everything, using cigarettes as the unit of exchange. Cleaver heisted baked goods from the kitchen, and he opened a profitable trading circuit. He later wrote, "Nothing could happen on my tier unless I got a piece of the action. I sold candy, cigarettes, sandwiches, loaned cigarettes at the going rate of two packs for three in return, ran errands from cell to cell for the prisoners who lived on my tier, brought them hot water, sold them clean sheets, socks, towels, blankets, or anything else that was available. If a prisoner on my tier wanted to spend some time alone and undisturbed with his lover, I could arrange it. It was a juice job and the tier tender was the connection man."[33]

Cleaver kept close company with a clique of "sharks," who helped him collect debts. They were some of the toughest men in San Quentin. As Cleaver described them, "Otis was brutal as an ax, and Tree Top was worse than the razor blades he was rumored to favor. Otis would walk right up to your face, and then pull out a pipe and knock you in the head with it, or stab you, or catch you locked in your cell and toss in a firebomb on you, whatever he thought you deserved."[34] Cleaver himself was a violent character in the prison, a persona he had cultivated from his days in reform school and Soledad. Although he projected an image of compliance to prison officials, Cleaver lived by the convict code. In San Quentin he had a cell partner who was a jazz musician. At one point a conflict emerged between them, and the guy challenged Cleaver to a fight. Cleaver responded, "I'm going to cut off two fingers from each of your hands so that you can't play the piano and cut off your lips and the tip of your tongue so that you can't sing."[35]

Cleaver used his position of power to exploit smaller, weaker prisoners for sex. Sexual abuse was part of the social hierarchy where Cleaver had been incarcerated, and he had always been on top of that hierarchy. Although he would later become known for his homophobia following the publication of *Soul on Ice*, Cleaver had sexual relationships with men throughout his life. His latent homosexuality and his rampant homophobia were two sides of the same coin. As he told his lawyer Beverly Axelrod years later, he didn't think there was anything unusual about this as long as he was the dominant partner: "I do not like to have sexual relationships with men. Homosexuality, to me, is more futile than beating my meat. I have had sexual relations with men while I've been in prison; I have had them suck my dick and I've fucked them in their asses. That's as far as I've ever gone. It seemed to me that I could go that far and still remain a man. If I were to let someone fuck me in my ass or were I to suck some man's dick, I would not respect myself as a man or even consider myself a man."[36]

Cleaver later wrote about these sexual experiences in prison in "Ahmen's Jacket," an unpublished prison memoir in the form of a novel. At the center of the narrative is Little Jesus, an upstanding Christian who is so bourgeois, Cleaver reports, he "would make Booker T. Washington leap with joy in his grave."[37] Wrongfully convicted for purse-snatching and abandoned by his wife and family, Little Jesus is isolated in the prison and thus a target for the predatory Cleaver. Standing in line for the shower one night, Cleaver sees Little Jesus naked and gets turned on. "He had a nice smooth ass, that stood up and out just like the nice, smooth, brown ass of a nice smooth brown girl. He did not like to stand naked in a crowd like that. And niggers were cold blooded. Everybody would check out Little Jesus's ass, on the serious side, and it was made absolutely clear that a whole lot of cats wanted to fuck him in his ass."[38] Cleaver begins to hatch a plan to have sex with Little Jesus.

For weeks, Cleaver stalks Little Jesus. "When I looked at him," Cleaver wrote, "I told him with my eyes that I wanted to lay him down, and plunge myself inside him. I began to see a certain hint of terror in Little Jesus's eyes, as though he was recoiling from me when I would look him dead in his eyes. At the same time, I could see a certain accommodation to whatever terror lurked inside him, and something brazen, coquettish, and burning with a thousand tongues of fire, all in his eyes, and by the hint of shame that gave a virgin's tautness to his mouth, his lips, and to the quivering smile that danced on his face."[39] Cleaver makes his intentions known to Little Jesus, who agrees to have sex with him, afraid what might happen if he refuses. One Saturday, they sneak away to the Guardian Chapel. They find a secluded spot between the pews, and Cleaver becomes excited. "Maybe I am a dirty dog, but I was happy, because I was ready to deflower a virgin and bust my nuts. The proposition was that I was going to down Little Jesus, and I would still be a man, but Little Jesus was going to be slain."[40] Cleaver didn't provide any further details in his memoir, though the meaning here is clear. Inside the prison, Cleaver targeted and exploited people weaker than him for his own sexual satisfaction and sense of power. According to Cleaver's logic, by dominating Little Jesus he could have sex with a man while still feeling like his masculinity remained intact. He used sexual dominance to try to resolve the contradiction between his homophobia and his same-sex desire, a pattern that would define his relationship to homosexuality for the rest of his life.

Throughout 1960, Cleaver focused his energy on building a case for his parole. He maintained a clean record with no infractions. As key man on West Block, he was dependable and well liked by many guards and inmates alike.[41] He continued his work in group therapy; by all accounts, Cleaver was making headway.[42] Most notable, he had become more disciplined in his behavior. Doctors noted that he had "developed excellent controls over his reactions so that he does not act-out in the destructive manner he formerly had."[43] He maintained strong connections to his mother and Wilhelmina through letters and occasional visits. In his conversations with his therapist as well as prison officials, Cleaver expressed a desire to attend college and study both creative writing and the social sciences.[44]

Cleaver's job as the key man gave him time to study and improve his writing. He devoured Gunnar Myrdal's classic study of race relations, *An American Dilemma*; E. Franklin Frazier's important work of sociology, *Black Bourgeoisie*; and multiple volumes on Eastern religion and philosophy. He even started trying to publish some poetry. In early May 1960, he sent fourteen pages of poems to *Poetry* magazine in Chicago. They had names like "Image of the 20th Century," "Prince of Purple Hearts," and "Confemale Confusion."[45] The following week, he sent the poem "Nymph in Tyranny's Temple, Unmoved" to *Ebony* magazine.[46] He also sent out his first essay, titled "As Crinkly as Yours" to the *Negro History Bulletin*. It was a polemic against the way black people internalized white standards of beauty. The piece would become his first published writing.

In spring 1961, it appeared officials might grant Cleaver parole. He had made good progress in the programs, and he now freely admitted his guilt for his crimes of attempted rape and assault with a deadly weapon. However, officials did not believe that he had yet fully come to terms with his wrongdoings, and they wanted to keep him for further treatment. "Current psychological test indicated that the Subject continues to manifest a very high degree of sociopathic orientation and psychosexual confusion in his personality structure. His ideation is noticeably schizoid and he continues to have severe passive-dependent needs which he has yet to recognize or deal with effectively."[47] On top of this, officials felt that Cleaver's plans for becoming a writer were unrealistic. "The Subject's release plans are rather indefinite, but he entertains the rather impractical notion of working at an unskilled job so that he can attend school in order to study such subjects as economics, the social sciences and pursue his desires to be a writer."[48] They recommended keeping him for another year of observation and treatment.

After his third board appearance, Cleaver began to have serious doubts that his good-behavior approach was going to get him out of prison.

He had followed all their rules, had made good-faith efforts in group therapy and classes, and by all appearances had been a model prisoner. Cleaver was furious that his years of work had come to nothing. At this point he became radicalized by the philosophies of Malcolm X and the Nation of Islam. Cleaver had first seen Malcolm X in a 1959 documentary called *The Hate That Hate Produced* and was drawn to the minister's message that "by nature, the white man is evil." It reflected his own experience in prison. He felt a strong connection to Malcolm X, because he had once been a criminal who had educated himself while incarcerated at Leavenworth Federal Penitentiary. Now Malcolm X was a national figure, speaking out defiantly against the white man. He was the kind of race leader Cleaver's mother wanted him to be, and he looked to Malcolm X as a source of inspiration in his own transformation from prisoner to political figure.

With Malcolm X as its spokesperson, the Nation of Islam had been growing within America's prisons throughout the 1950s and exploded after the broadcast of *The Hate That Hate Produced.* Preaching doctrines of black separatism, the Nation of Islam provided black prisoners with a sense of radical acceptance and shared black identity in the face of white oppression. It was a deeply political organization. Since religious freedom was protected under the Constitution, the Muslim inmates across the country had filed hundreds of legal challenges to protest mistreatment while practicing their religion.[49] They won the right to hold religious services, wear religious medals, and practice their religion freely without punishment. In the late 1950s and early 1960s, the Nation of Islam was the most significant source of African American militancy within America's prisons. Cleaver wasn't a true believer in the Nation of the Islam. He didn't entirely buy its mysticism, including the fable that a black scientist named Yakub created the white race six thousand years ago. But he was attracted to the political and cultural power of the organization, and he was determined to use the religion to protest the conditions at San Quentin.

Soon after his parole rejection in 1961, Cleaver and his fellow Muslims performed their first act of civil disobedience. They staged a hunger strike and sent a letter to San Francisco attorney Willie Brown informing him of their protest. On April 11, 1961, the officer on duty noticed that Cleaver was not attending to his duties as key man. When the officer questioned Cleaver, he told him: "I am on a hunger strike, have been for the past 1½ days, this hunger strike will continue, I am involved with thirteen other inmates." It was the first time Cleaver had broken the rules in three years, and it clearly disturbed officials, who referred to his group as a "Muslim cult."[50] Cleaver was given six days in isolation for the offense. After so many years of good behavior, it was unsettling for him to be back in solitary. "For the briefest moment I felt like yelling out for help," Cleaver remembered, "and it seemed that in no circumstances would I be able to endure that cell."[51] However, by the next morning, Cleaver had regained his composure. When prison officials interviewed him, they reported, "His general demeanor throughout the interview was quiet and unemotional. Even his complaints were given in a flat, undemonstrative tone."[52]

Over the next few months, the conflict between Cleaver and prison officials escalated. In July, Cleaver applied for a job in the education department but was refused for being a Muslim. "Race superiority and Racial hatred has no place in a department where there are several inmate employees assigned who have a daily work load to complete," read his rejection slip.[53] Cleaver retaliated by printing up speeches by Elijah Muhammad at the print shop and distributing them throughout the prison. He also wrote essays about the Nation of Islam and circulated them among Muslim readers. Prison officials responded by confiscating his materials. On September 1, 1961, during a routine inspection, guards found his various papers and charged him with the possession of contraband as well as the "misuse of state property."[54] Cleaver complained to the officer in the file room that the manuscripts were priceless, and he demanded to have them back. "Concerning the five (5) manuscripts which were seized from my cell on a 'shakedown', I estimate conservatively that they were worth no less than $10,000 to me. Each of them were composed in a fleeting moment of inspiration and they cannot be replaced. The only possible satisfaction that San Quentin could grant me for destroying my property is the amount mentioned above or an equivalent value."[55] Cleaver's request for $10,000 for his manuscripts may have just been a ploy to provoke officials, but it also revealed how important his writing had become to him. Now more than just a hobby, his writing was central to his identity and his struggle for survival at San Quentin.

As the conflict between Cleaver and the prison intensified, he became more desperate to get out of San Quentin. On December 19, 1961, he wrote his mother, begging for her help. "I HAVE ABSOLUTELY NO HOPE OF COMING HOME NEXT YEAR," he wrote, "OR THE NEXT OR THE NEXT OR THE NEXT OR THE NEXT." He pleaded with her to get him a lawyer. "California does not recognize Muslims, but regards them as a trouble-making element that needs to be controlled, and therefore those Muslims who are in jail—as far as California is concerned—may as well be kept there."[56] Cleaver renewed his attempts to get transferred. Just after the New Year in 1962, he wrote the associate warden: "I urgently need a change of environment and a change of associates. During my long stay here in San Quentin, my life has fallen into a pattern and taken on a tone which it never had before I came here."[57] After a week with no reply, he wrote again on January 11: "I have been in San Quentin for nearly four years now and with no disrespect intended, I have really had enough of San Quentin. I have become lost in this prison, like being sucked down to the bottom of a deep pit of quicksand."[58] Cleaver was in fact so desperate to get out that when he was asked where he would like to be transferred, he wrote, "Anywhere."[59]

Cleaver was again denied parole in the spring of 1962. His annual psychiatric evaluation predictably blamed his membership in the Nation of Islam for his lack of "direction or particular aim."[60] Doctors also targeted Cleaver's father Leroy for his son's crimes. "Subject's need for positive father image is apparent. His need for a father image, to imitate, and his profound feelings of inadequacy, probably caused him to accept the Muslim beliefs."[61] Spouting armchair Freudian psychology, the doctors again criticized Cleaver's family structure for his criminal deviancy and radical beliefs. Additionally, they believed that, even though he readily admitted to his crimes, he was not sincerely remorseful. As his psychiatric report stated, "His current psychological tests reflect his continued state of confusion and indicate that he is using neurotic defense mechanisms as a means of avoiding his real, underlying problems. He continues to be somewhat hedonistic, manifests psychosexual confusion and despite his verbalizations, continues to project the blame for his difficulties onto others." Doctors labeled him "emotionally unstable" and again recommended vocational training opportunities to address his difficulties.[62] "S[ubject] needs more insight into his problems. Should use institutional programs and become active member of group therapy class. S[ubject] should learn to [get] along [with] people."[63]

Cleaver became angrier than ever. He had been attending the programs, and they had gotten him nowhere. In open rebellion of the prison's recommendations, Cleaver decided to do the opposite of what they suggested. He stopped going to group therapy after attending it for three and a half years, and he quit showing up to his print trade. He was fired for poor attendance.

Following the parole rejection, Cleaver redirected his energies toward writing and activism. The aforementioned publication of his first piece of writing, "As Crinkly as Yours," in the *Negro History Bulletin* fueled his hope that he could use his literary skills to change society. Cleaver embarked on an aggressive letter-writing campaign to challenge the discrimination against Muslims in San Quentin. On May 17, 1962, he wrote to the director of corrections, Walter Dunbar. Citing multiple sections of the Constitution, he demanded that the prison recognize the Nation of Islam as a religion and that ministers be allowed to conduct ceremonies. He also asked the prison provide a mosque for worshippers.[64] A few days later, Cleaver wrote to civil rights lawyer Charles Geary to request his services on behalf of Muslim prisoners. His early letters were esoteric and overwritten, but in them are the beginnings of Eldridge Cleaver the fiery orator. Cleaver wrote to Geary, "Because of your proven legal perspicacity and the assiduous fidelity you have evinced to your clients, I beseech you to accept this case, a 'Civil Rights Suit'. There is no nebulosity of legal rights involved—it is an inherent right ukased by our creator and given an imprimatur by the Constitution of the United States."[65] Cleaver also wrote Governor Edmund Brown, employing similarly obscure language to criticize the administration for instituting "onerous mechanisms to illegally extirpate an unalienable tenet of Democracy—Religious Freedom." The letter was signed by thirty-eight prisoners, and it was sprinkled with quotes from Albert Einstein, a Supreme Court justice, and the UN General Assembly.[66] These letters expressed Cleaver's enthusiasm for new vocabularies and news ideas, as well as his growing facility and fascination with language and the law as a tool for protest.

By late summer 1962, Cleaver had become a significant leader of the San Quentin Muslims. Going by the name of "Christian Seekers," Cleaver and other Muslims held prayer services in the Protestant Chapel. After prison officials broke up these meetings, the Christian Seekers congregated in the lower yard of the prison on Sundays. These meetings were held in secret and kept quiet by inmates. However, administrators had a spy on the inside named Freeman. He told officials in early August 1962 that the Christian Seekers were "radically dangerous Muslim inmates who were again attempting to stir up the Negro Muslim population to perform acts of violence against the institution, and the white race in general."[67] The administration was alarmed, and it increased surveillance of the group. One official who observed a prayer meeting noted that the men appeared "spellbound" by the incantations of the minister.[68] He said the preacher implored the group "in a highly emotional manner, gesticulating wildly with his arms and exhorting the group with typical Muslim phraseology. The group was responding in unison and with great fervor. At that moment the situation was highly charged with emotion."[69] Witnessing this scene, the guard told the Muslims to disperse. After they refused to disband, ten more guards were called to the scene. Cleaver and the Muslims scattered, telling the correctional officers that they "could expect a battle in which Muslims would give up their lives."[70] The sergeant who filed the report concluded that a "dangerous and explosive situation could result from men in this irrational state."[71]

Cleaver worried about a crackdown on the Muslims. The day after the confrontation in the yard, he wrote his mother, asking her to find him a lawyer. "Absolutely no word from lawyer. Situation has become desperate. Must have Legal Aid immediately. Send FBI to see me—QUICK!"[72] Prison officials wasted no time squelching the religious gatherings of Cleaver and the other Muslims. On August 10, 1962, they were rousted from their cells and placed in segregation for their participation in an illegal assembly. The segregation area was where unruly prisoners were locked in solitary cells for a month, sometimes longer. Here the Muslims were brutally tortured by correctional officers. As Cleaver described it, they "were handcuffed, beaten and kicked, then had thick beards scraped off with a dull razor blade without the use of soap and water—this was very painful, and it was criminal."[73] A few days later, Cleaver was tried before the disciplinary committee. The official charge was "leading inmate groups in airing complaints and agitating racial and religious problems leading to violence."[74] He got twenty-nine days in segregation.

Cleaver was incensed. He felt that it was a direct infringement of his Constitutional right to the freedom of religion. He wrote letters to the warden, the director of corrections, and anyone else who would listen. He wrote to the director of corrections, "This letter is written to you in protest of the savage, dehumanizing treatment which we, the Muslims, are and have been the victims of here at San Quentin. How long do you think you can get away with this? Don't you know that we will not rest until justice is done to our Persecutors? The time is gone forever when the white man could treat the black man like a piece of personal property!"[75] Cleaver's complaints were dismissed. Weeks went by, and then months. Cleaver and the other Muslims were subject to all kinds of abuse. He wrote to Dunbar to complain. "Here we are kept locked in cells perpetually, allowed to come out only for meals, showers, and one (1) hour exercise each day. We are constantly made the object of harassment, threats, all manner of petty, vicious maneuvers, at the hands of correctional officers."[76] In late September, Cleaver tried to hire two lawyers, Loren Miller and Earl Broady, to help him with his case. One of the guards stopped his mail from being delivered, and he was informed that he had no right to correspond with a lawyer.[77] As officials explained, "The letter in the envelope was refused by the Warden because of gross misstatements and innuendos that amount to falsehoods. In other words, it does not stick to true facts."[78] Cleaver shot back in response, "The right of prison officials to inspect communications between prisoners and their attorneys should not be used unnecessarily to delay communications to attorneys or the courts."[79]

Throughout the fall, the small war between the prisoners and the administration intensified. The Muslims were constantly harassed by guards, who did not even attempt to conceal their disdain for them. They delayed Cleaver's letters from his family, and they blocked his letters to them altogether. In response, Cleaver led small tactical protests against the guards. On October 4, 1962, he and four other inmates started a disturbance in segregation block, yelling slurs at guards and chanting Muslim phrases. They called guards "white beasts" and claimed that "all personnel employed by the Department of Corrections are Homosexuals and thieves." Cleaver was cited for "creating a disturbance and using obscene language toward the officials of the institution."[80] Two weeks later, the guards ransacked Cleaver's cell in the middle of the night, taking his medicine for the skin disease neurodermatitis and confiscating speeches by Elijah Muhammad, religious literature, and newspaper articles. They took all legal materials, letters from court clerks, legal motions, and writs of habeas corpus, as well as personal papers and old letters. Most important, they impounded his creative work, including an essay he had been working on for the *Nation*, "America's Debt to Elijah Muhammad."[81]

The administration closely studied Cleaver's writings and determined he was a dangerous presence in the prison. As the warden remembered it later, "I have read a lot of Cleaver's material. I had a stack of it that high [six inches] on my desk at one time. He was a prolific writer. Christ, he turned out that stuff by the ream. At the time the Black Muslims were writing and all this writing I had was racist as hell, talking about white honkies and death to the white man and that sort of thing. . . . A lot of it was this typical convict jargon about the oppressed and the—I consider it garbage, the words of a diseased mind."[82]

On October 19, 1962, officials reported that Cleaver was a threat to the stability of the prison population. "Since assignment on B Section he has continued his pattern of harassing inmates and personnel alike by vocal and other means. He is a prolific writer and bombards everyone [with] documents that are filled with threats and misstatements, lies and innuendos."[83] Officials considered him a rabble-rouser who might start a riot in the prison and pondered sending him to the correctional training facility so that the San Quentin prisoners might be "adequately controlled," but they ultimately decided against it because the facility already had a high ratio of Muslims.[84]

Cleaver continued to challenge officials in person and in his writings. In a November letter confiscated by officials, Cleaver referred to the warden as a "beast." On another occasion, he tried to incite inmates to defy authorities and commit acts of violence.[85] When prison officials asked him if he would like to be returned to general population, he stated that "it would be only with the proviso that he might assemble groups of his 'brothers' and attempt to lead them in their religious meetings."[86] In December, Cleaver and a Muslim preacher named Doctor were called before Associate Warden Louis S. Nelson for a meeting. Before the meeting started, Doctor starting calling the associate warden names like "beast," "slavemaster," and "white dog." The warden was so angry that he took Doctor by the arm and threw him out of his office. Cleaver threatened the warden with legal action, and he was taken away by correctional officers.[87]

Cleaver believed he had found his political calling. His challenge to prison authorities with his fellow Muslims was the first time he had worked together with black men for the cause of racial justice. As he remembered later, "Slowly, I was boring my way deeper and deeper into prison. At the time, I didn't care if I lived or died. The important thing was that I was standing up with my black brothers against the white system and white people who were crushing us. I was filled with a pride, a power, and a sense of direction I had never known before."[88] Cleaver knew that he had probably lost his chance for parole, but for the moment, he didn't care. He was the leader of a cause for racial uplift and social justice. It would make his mother proud.

The conflict between the administration and the Muslims turned deadly early in 1963. On February 15, violence broke out between black and white prisoners in the yard of the adjustment center. During the mayhem, Cleaver's cellmate Booker T. Johnson, also known as Booker X, was shot and killed by white guards. Many Muslims, including Cleaver, believed it was a politically motivated assassination to quell black activism. Sixty Muslims gathered the next day to protest and make demands for freedom of religion. Associate Warden Nelson dismissed their demands and characterized prisoner behavior as a "state of insurrection."

Cleaver immediately took up the leadership role left open by Booker X's death and worked hard to solidify the organization. He led Muslim rituals in the segregation yard and met with a lawyer to discuss what legal action might be taken on behalf of Booker X.[89] He kept the brotherhood disciplined so that it did not initiate any violence.[90] Prison officials worried that Cleaver's power was becoming too great. "Subject has inherited the mantle of the 'Muslim' sect and is attempting by means of letters to intimidate staff including the Warden to accede to his demands," one report stated. "For a long time he has been the spokesman for the group as an articulate leader who is now the accepted minister. No one of the group will do anything without his permission."[91]

When Cleaver came up for parole again in spring 1963, he tried to characterize his relationship to the Muslims as a positive form of rehabilitation. On March 9, 1963, he wrote to the parole-board members, "The truth is that I was born onto the wrong path. I grew up, developed, and lived all my life on the wrong path—the path of crime, violence, vice, and sex."[92] Cleaver claimed that he was transformed when he met the Muslims. "Islam, the teachings of the most Honorable Elijah Muhammad, has changed all of that because now I have a language—a system of symbols and definitions—that enables me to understand and discuss my problems. I have been given a perspective on life where before there was only Chaos and confusion."[93] Prison officials agreed that Cleaver had made some progress toward parole, particularly with his education. Early in 1963, his essay "A Prisoner Cell Can't Contain Us" was published in a collection by librarian Herman Spector. "Your views on reading are interesting," Spector wrote to Cleaver. "Your answer was a constructive and meaningful affirmation of the values of reading."[94] The associate warden was also pleased and wrote to Cleaver directly: "I am particularly impressed with your discussion of the universality of man, and the fact that one man is of equal value with every other man."[95] Cleaver was awarded a copy of the collection and a small cash royalty. Cleaver wrote the warden and asked if a copy could be sent to his mother.[96]

But Cleaver's association with the Muslims doomed all chances of parole in 1963. Officials reported that Cleaver remained antagonistic, pensive, and reluctant to divulge anything. They felt that whatever progress he had made in San Quentin had "soon deteriorated when he became involved in Muslim activities." Cleaver was openly critical of the white race, and he vocalized his criticisms every chance he got. One report stated, "There appears little doubt as to his growing overt hostility toward authority, particularly the Caucasian element. He vehemently projects the blame for his many misdeeds upon the 'white man' as a result of his being 'kidnapped' from Africa and upsetting their cultural balance."[97] The prison doctors didn't even bother to write up a new psychiatric report. Head psychiatrist Dr. David Schmidt just used a copy of the 1962 report. The 1963 report simply repeated earlier diagnoses: Cleaver suffered from psychosexual confusion and an emotionally unstable personality. The parole board predictably decided that he would benefit from further vocational programming.[98]

By May 1963, Cleaver had been held in segregation for nine months. He lived in fear for his life after the death of Booker X. In one of his unpublished manuscripts, he explained, "I was worried about getting killed, soon, or being blown into a form of oblivion by what the prison psychiatrists called Electro-psychotherapy. We called it Shock Treatments. The head psych at San Quentin, Dr. Schmidt, had told me that he was going to recommend, and see to it that I received, Shock Treatments. I was, he told me, a dangerous sociopath. He was, I told him, a white devil."[99] Cleaver claimed that after he refused electroshock therapy, he was set up by prison guards to be killed by a rival gang of prisoners. In his time at San Quentin, he had seen stabbings, and Molotov cocktails tossed by prisoners through the bars of a cell. He was always on guard and always kept a blanket nearby in his cell to smother a fire. One night, a dozen Chicano prisoners suddenly cornered Cleaver in his cell. He had to fight for his life. As he later told it, "The rattling of the bars, the war cries and screams, the sound of the deadly struggle, and the scent of blood lasted about ten minutes. My lip was bleeding, my left eye was out of focus, and all along my arms were scratches where the Mexicans dug my flesh trying to pull me through the door of my cell."[100]

A few days later on June 18, 1963, he received notice that he was being transferred to Folsom Prison.[101] Officials had grown wary of Cleaver's influence among the Muslims, so they decided to send him to a prison where he had no clout. Cleaver had been held in segregation for almost a year, and he had survived. It was a small triumph. "From the San Quentin Adjustment Center, I was transported to Folsom Prison, and placed in the Folsom Adjustment Center. I lay in my cell licking my wounds, but I was also savoring my victory. For I had gotten kicked out of San Quentin, and regardless of what happened to me now, I had survived San Quentin."[102]

7

FOLSOM PRISON (1963–1965)

In 1880, California opened Folsom State Prison, its second prison. Inmates constructed the cell blocks and walls from 150,000 tons of granite they mined from local quarries. The walls were built thirty feet high and buried fifteen feet below the ground to prevent inmates from escaping. The prison was perched on a bluff overlooking the American River, and with its copper guard tower and stone archways, it looked like an ancient battlement.

Over the course of the twentieth century, Folsom grew into a self-contained city. It had a dam and powerhouse, a chapel, a hospital, dining and recreation facilities, massive cell blocks, a sewage disposal plant, and even a locomotive to haul supplies. In the early days, discipline at Folsom was handled much like it was at San Quentin. Inmates were locked in cells behind iron doors with three-by-ten-inch slots. The cells contained no restroom facility, electricity, or water system. Punishments for misbehaving prisoners were severe. Guards carried lead-tipped canes, which they used to dole out physical abuse swiftly and silently. Prisoners who tried to escape were fitted with the Oregon boot, while others who broke the rules were straightjacketed in a lung-compressing apparatus known as "Susie's corset."[1]

By the 1940s, Folsom, alongside other California prisons, had abandoned these practices. In the age of rehabilitation, isolation and behavior modification were used to punish inmates. Unmanageable prisoners were held in the adjustment center, also known as isolation, until they were deemed ready to reenter general population. When Cleaver arrived at Folsom prison at the end of June 1963, officials put him there.

The adjustment center at Folsom was a prison within a prison. Inmate cells were made of three windowless concrete walls and a metal door. Inmates spent twenty-three hours a day in their cells, and they slept on thin mats on the floor. For entertainment, inmates were given a bible to read. Within this dreary environment, Cleaver decided to change tactics to get out of prison. He was not known as a Muslim leader in Folsom, so he decided to distance himself from the organization. He was still loyal to Malcolm X, who had given him a voice to challenge white supremacy within the prison system. But he decided to stop organizing demonstrations and to go back to being a model prisoner. He hoped that in this new environment, he might be given a clean slate.

When Cleaver first appeared before the disciplinary committee, he asked to be released into the general population. He promised to behave and to conform with prison rules. The committee decided to keep him in isolation. "In view of recent disciplinary problems and poor institutional reputation, however, it is the Committee's conclusion that a period in the Adjustment Center to test the sincerity of his general attitude and to observe behavior is a reasonable prerequisite to trial in general population."[2] They would revisit his case in ninety days. Cleaver wanted desperately to get out of the adjustment center, so he remained an obedient prisoner. Three weeks later, the adjustment center officials reported Cleaver had "behaved in a compliant, cooperative manner" and recommended he be released to the general population.[3]

The disciplinary committee still considered him a risk, however, and kept him in the adjustment center for the full three months.

At the beginning of fall 1963, Cleaver was finally released into the general population. He was given a small single cell, containing only a bed, a cold-water sink, a plywood table, a shelf, and a toilet. The door was a steel slab containing fifty-eight holes in it for air and a slot five inches long. Cleaver decorated the cell with framed pictures of Malcolm X, Patrice Lumumba, W. E. B. Du Bois, Norman Mailer, and one—turned upside down—of Lyndon Johnson.

He quickly got into the prison routine. He woke by 5:30 and performed exercises in the nude for a half an hour—knee bends, butterflies, toe touches, squats, and windmills. At morning roll call, the tier man came by and poured hot water into Cleaver's one-gallon bucket so that he could take a "bird bath" before breakfast. He was given back his typewriter, and sometimes in these early hours, he wrote letters to his family before the 7:30 breakfast. Whites, blacks, and Chicanos all sat at racially segregated tables in the dining hall during every meal. After breakfast, Cleaver worked for three hours in the bakery, and, in his spare time, he sometimes lifted weights or played chess. On a radio in his cell, he listened to jazz or country and western music, which he called Okee music.[4] Like most convicts at Folsom, Cleaver spent seventeen hours a day in his cell. But for him it was an opportunity to read and write. He felt safe in the solitude.

In this environment, Cleaver felt a renewed hope in his chances at parole. Although his records had followed him from San Quentin, he was determined to change his reputation at Folsom. Cleaver worked hard in the bakery, and he received As from his teacher for his skill level and attitude. In his annual psychiatric review in November 1963, staff psychiatrist William C. Keating argued on Cleaver's behalf, stating that he had made substantial progress toward accepting responsibility for his crimes. "In fairness to the subject he freely admits that his intention was to commit rape by force, that this was an acting out mechanism partially against his own feelings of sexual inadequacy and partly out of his total feeling of frustration because of his racial and cultural handicap. He clearly recognizes the malevolence of his action, accepts responsibility for it and indicates that, although some acting out may be appropriate, his particular choice was completely inappropriate and unacceptable."

Keating even went so far as to credit Cleaver's positive changes with his participation in the Muslim movement. He took issue with San Quentin officials, who believed the Nation of Islam was inherently subversive. "I do not agree with this position, but neither do I agree with the Muslim movement, but then I don't agree with Democrats and still there might be some good come out of people actively in participation in the Democratic Party politics." Keating suggested that Cleaver's participation in the Muslim movement had given him language and ideas to deal with his racial frustration. Keating diagnosed Cleaver with a "sociopathic personality" but concluded somewhat optimistically, "Although he is somewhat hedonistic and manifests psychosexual conclusions, and does tend to project [to] some extent, he has developed some insight."[5]

The parole board did not believe Cleaver had made significant progress, and they rejected his bid for parole in November 1963. They were disappointed that Cleaver did not take a more enthusiastic interest in vocational baking, as they believed that occupational training was critical to prisoner rehabilitation. "It is doubtful he will attempt to utilize whatever gains could be accrued through the Vocational Baking Program he is now undertaking, as he states he feel[s] his services in other areas can be better utilized." They worried that Cleaver had only learned to ventriloquize the language of reform, and that he was still a Muslim sympathizer. "He verbalizes quite freely but there is little indication of significant growth in his personality structure. His hostility is hidden behind a well-controlled façade and has been diverted into Muslim channels."[6]

At Cleaver's hearing, officials told him that he would most likely serve out the entirety of his remaining sentence. At that moment, Cleaver finally realized that no amount of good behavior or vocational training was going to get him out of prison. As he reflected later, "The Adult Authority's threat of seven more years in prison, following the San Quentin guard's attempt to set me up for the kill, and Dr. Schmidt's threat of Shock Treatments, destroyed my ability to escape the present by dreaming of the day when the intolerable situation would become a faded memory."[7] Cleaver had gone up for parole five times, and no matter what he said or did, he always ended up back in his cell. He would have to fight this battle with the prison system through other means. "Clearly, there were only two ways out: to be let out, or to break out. I was going out one way or the other," Cleaver decided, "and it wasn't going to take seven more years." As always, he looked to the library for answers.

At the beginning of 1964, Cleaver started revisiting his case. On January 8, 1964, he wrote to the county clerk of Los Angeles, William Sharp, to obtain transcripts of his trial. He requested everything from opening statements to the exchanges between the judge and lawyers to the final announcement by the jury.[8] Cleaver also began teaching himself more of the fundamentals of the law by reading three books: *The California Penal Code*, *California Criminal Procedure*, and *California Rules of Evidence*. He sent out a flurry of letters to law journals seeking advice. On January 27, 1964, he wrote to the *Howard Law Review* to ask which textbook would help him prepare briefs, particularly a writ of habeas corpus.[9] Four days later, he wrote to the *DePaul Law Review* to request a copy of the current issue because it contained an article about disparities in prison sentences.[10] He wrote to West Publishing Company to request court cases having to do with parole sentencing, and he bought a stack of law books from the Legal Bookstore in Los Angeles—*California Criminal Evidence*, *Criminal Law*, *Criminal Procedure*, *Summary of the Law of Searches and Seizures and the Exclusionary Rule*, *Black's Law Dictionary*, and *Clarke's Criminal Trial Practice*.[11] Finally, he wrote the Supreme Court of California to ask for a copy of the rules of the court.[12]

Cleaver spent a year intensely studying his case. When he found that the Folsom Law Library did not have books he needed, he wrote to state librarian Carmen Leigh to complain: "My difficulties lie in the fact that I am unable to obtain the law books which I urgently and desperately need. The so-called Law Library here at Folsom is disgustingly and woefully inadequate, containing only a sad assortment of dog-eared tomes."[13] Cleaver read legal books and studied court cases that resembled his own. He taught himself to draw up petitions and joined a clique of like-minded "jailhouse lawyers" hell-bent on overturning their cases. He wrote to the dean at Howard University to ask about applying to law school,[14] and he wrote to both the Berkeley Law School and the UCLA Law School asking how to compose a writ of error coram noblis and a writ of habeas corpus.[15]

Cleaver felt empowered learning the law. He was beginning to understand the structures that had been controlling his life for a decade. "Court room proceedings had always seemed like a lot of mysterious incomprehensible hocus pocus, if not just plain bullshit, which I found bewildering and from which I was always anxious to escape. Now I was learning something of the history, principles, and structures of the law, how it moved, and how it had been used successfully by people in circumstances more desperate than my own."[16]

Even with his interest in the law, Cleaver did not ignore his literary and political education. He created vast bibliographies with dozens of titles. Every time he finished a book, he circled the title in red. Cleaver was broad-minded in his study of literary classics, reading Mark Twain, William Faulkner, and Ernest Hemingway alongside LeRoi Jones, Lorraine Hansberry, Claude McKay, and Langston Hughes. He deepened his understanding of black history, studying everything from Virginia's earliest slave laws to the slave insurrections of Denmark Vesey and Nat Turner. He read American sociology, including E. Franklin Frazier's important chronicle of the black church, W. E. B. Du Bois's groundbreaking study *Black Reconstruction in America*, and Howard Zinn's revisionist history of the American South. He studied a wide variety of revolutionary writers, such as Frantz Fanon, Che Guevara, Mao Tse-tung, and Fidel Castro. He read the biographies of comedian Dick Gregory, sociologist Horace Cayton, and pamphleteer Harriet Beecher Stowe. He kept up with a number of journals and magazines, including *Encounter*, the *New African*, *Freedomways*,

Commentary, *Harper's Bazaar*, the *Realist*, and *Maghreb Digest*. He subscribed to *Negro Digest* and *Ebony* when he found out the library did not carry them.

Cleaver remained a model inmate during this year. By the fall of 1964, he had logged two thousand total hours in the bake shop; his instructor praised him, saying he did "well on any job assigned to him."[17] In his psychiatric evaluation, his psychiatrist Dr. Wright wrote that Cleaver had been "more conforming" and "reasonable in his attitude." He felt that Cleaver had adjusted to prison life and made no difficulties for prison officials. Wright concluded, "He has received maximum benefits from incarceration, with some improvement. This is in view of some conformity to institutional system for the past year."[18]

But when Cleaver came up for parole again in November 1964, officials still did not believe he had made any progress. As one official reported, "He sits in chair with military bearing and replies to questions politely, but one senses a controlled surliness and hostility under his veneer of control."[19] Officials believed that while Cleaver had made gains from an academic and vocational point of view, they saw him as hostile. "Cleaver is intelligent, well controlled," the parole board concluded, "but still considerably disturbed and impresses the undersigned as capable of extreme violence."[20] Cleaver's bid for parole was again rejected.

Throughout 1964, Cleaver worked away on the foundational essays that would compose his most influential work, *Soul on Ice*. From the practical side, he wanted to sell the book and make enough money to hire a lawyer. From the artistic side, he wanted his essays to offer incisive social criticism following in the tradition of W. E. B. Du Bois's *The Souls of Black Folk* and James Baldwin's *The Fire Next Time*. But most important, Cleaver set out to write *Soul on Ice* in order to save himself existentially. He saw his writing as a form of rehabilitation from his days as a violent rapist, and he also saw it as a productive way to express his rage at white America.

One of Cleaver's main contributions to the conversation about race in the United States was his theory that racial conflict was essentially a psychosexual phenomenon. In his first articles, "Allegory of the Black Eunuchs," "The Primeval Mitosis," "Convalescence," and "To All Black Women, From All Black Men," Cleaver laid out his vision of sexual and racial mysticism through four basic American types. There is the Omnipotent Administrator (the white man with state power), the Ultrafeminine (the white woman), the Supermasculine Menial (black man with bodily power), and the Amazon (black woman forced into domestic labor). Taken together, Cleaver's essays put forth his emerging philosophy that racial struggle is an expression of gender identity and sexual desire. In his formulation, the white Omnipotent Administrator manages society by conditioning black men to desire white women, while prohibiting sexual contact between them. The white man also expresses his dominance by exploiting those beneath him on the social ladder. This casts black women into the simultaneous role of domestic household laborer and sex object. Cleaver believed that social change could occur if black men and black women worked together to combat their pregiven roles. As he wrote at the end of "The Primeval Mitosis," black people "are the wealth of a nation, an abundant supply of unexhausted, underessenced human raw material upon which the future of the society depends and with which, through the implacable march of history to an ever broader base of democracy and equality, the society will renew and transform itself."[21]

In late December 1964, Cleaver gave his essay collection the provocative title, *White Woman, Black Man*. He tried to send out his manuscript to the publisher G. P. Putnam's Sons, but it was rejected by Associate Warden Walter Craven. As Craven informed him, "This will not be allowed out of the prison because it contains a racist interpretation of history."[22] In mid-March, guards went through Cleaver's cell and confiscated a three-ring binder of materials that he had been using to brainstorm ideas for his book. Officials deemed the stories in the notebook "obscene."[23] Cleaver was placed in detention, and his notebook was kept by the disciplinary committee.[24]

Cleaver was at first outraged with these blatant acts of censorship.

Then he had an idea. "I was also happy, because their act of administrative censorship gave me a weapon with which to fight them. They were wrong, as prison officials, for not even allowing my manuscript to leave the prison." He filed a civil suit in US court against the California Department of Corrections, protesting prison censorship. He just needed a competent lawyer to help him with his case. "Those who are responsible for administering the prisons always have many things to hide, and are therefore basically hostile to all public scrutiny; the last thing they wanted to see was a crusade mounted against them by a lawyer. So [what] I needed above all else was a lawyer."[25] Cleaver got a hold of the California Bar Association's list of names and addresses of its members. He wrote to a few lawyers every day for several months, explaining his case and offering his manuscript as payment. Only a few lawyers wrote him back. None took him up on his offer. After a few months, Cleaver had written hundreds of letters with no success.

Cleaver was increasingly frustrated until one day he came across a copy of the *Sun-Reporter*, a weekly black newspaper based in San Francisco. On the cover was a story about workers organizing sit-ins to protest discriminatory hiring policies at a luxury hotel. In one photo, a white lawyer named Beverly Axelrod was exiting the Hall of Justice with one of her black clients. Cleaver suddenly conceived of a different strategy. He decided to approach Axelrod from a romantic angle. "Perhaps, just perhaps, hers might be the soul of a woman adrift, who was open to something new and off the beaten track. There might be a thirsty taste for adventure somewhere inside her."[26] Cleaver was desperate, so he decided to try to seduce Axelrod. He was entirely aware of what he was doing. He justified it by telling himself that it was a matter of survival. "I had to get something together that would touch Beverly's heart. If not her heart, then her body. I very precisely was not aiming at her mind. . . . I was aiming at her soul."[27]

Beverly Axelrod was born Beverly Diana Jarrett on March 3, 1924. Her parents, Jerry Jarrett and May Resnick, were Russian Jews; the family name had been shortened from Jaretsky after immigration to America. Axelrod's father was a traveling salesman, and between 1929 and 1936, the family moved to Toledo, Detroit, Houston, New

Orleans, Chicago, Highland Park, Atlantic City, Brooklyn, and the Bronx. Throughout Axelrod's childhood, her parents hid the fact that they were Jewish from her until someone called her a "dirty kike" at school. The family was poor, and from an early age, she prepared the family budget and tracked down grocery specials. As a teenager, Axelrod was an adventurous soul with a passion for education. She hitchhiked across the country to California, where she attended Santa Monica Junior College, UCLA, and Berkeley. After she completed her undergraduate work at Berkeley in 1943, she rode her bike across the country and took a job at a tax office in New York. In 1946, she entered Brooklyn College to pursue a law degree. She was one of only two female students in a class of two hundred people.

Axelrod wanted to practice law in California after she finished law school, so she moved to San Francisco in the early 1950s. She started a law practice with an African American lawyer named John Bussey in the Fillmore District. As Axelrod remembered it, "I was known as the first black woman lawyer in San Francisco. Nobody could imagine I was anything but black since I was on Fillmore Street and John Bussey was my partner."[28] Axelrod gained a reputation as a brilliant trial lawyer and activist. She was president of the NAACP chapter in Modesto, a lawyer for Cesar Chavez and the United Farm Workers Organizing Committee, council for people facing housing discrimination, and the lawyer for Jerry Rubin before the House Un-American Activities Committee. Although she never drank, she chain-smoked Parliaments. She threw wild parties and had torrid affairs with men, both black and white. "I wasn't any great beauty," Axelrod once said, "but what I had that other women didn't have, and used, was intellect. Mine was, so I thought, unusual for a woman. I played it to the hilt. I had the feeling that any man I wanted to be involved with, barring the fact that he was madly in love with someone, I could get to be interested in me."[29] At one point during her correspondence with Cleaver, Axelrod bragged that she had had thirty-seven lovers.

Cleaver sent his first letter to Axelrod on May 26, 1965. He kept it formal and polite, but he also tried to entice her with details of his book. He recounted the history of his incarceration, his membership in the Nation of Islam, and the injustices he faced as a writer. He explained that his book had been censored, and he pleaded for her assistance in getting his book published. "The title of my book is: WHITE WOMAN, BLACK MAN. I know the associations which that title has in the American mind. But I believe that we are living in a time when certain things must be openly discussed if we as a nation are ever going to resolve some of our historic problems."[30]

Cleaver was uneasy after he sent the letter. Axelrod might just toss it, as many lawyers had done before. A guard might steal it, or it could be intercepted and placed in his file by an administrator. Cleaver knew that if he could just communicate with her, Axelrod was his best hope for early parole. "I wanted to wire her up, get her involved with me through whatever opening I saw, because she was qualified to get me out of prison, and I knew it."[31]

Axelrod received letters from inmates all the time, but Cleaver's letter impressed her with the power of the writing. "It was clear, and cogent," she remembered, "and it sounded as though there was something that could be done."[32] Axelrod was struck by his "political purity," and she felt he might even fulfill the void left behind by Malcolm X's death. After this one letter, she began formulating the rough outline of a plan for both publishing his manuscript and getting him parole. "He'd been a rambunctious prisoner," Axelrod recounted, "politicking inside the system, so he hadn't endeared himself to parole authorities or to the jailers."[33] Instead of trying to challenge the prison censorship directly, she decided to sneak Cleaver's book out of the prison herself. She felt she could find a publisher through her contacts at the leftist magazine *Ramparts*. Perhaps with enough public attention, she could get him paroled. On June 4, she sent Cleaver a letter that simply read, "I am quite interested in the matters which you brought up in the letter, and I hope to be able to visit you shortly to discuss them further."[34]

Cleaver and Axelrod met for the first time at Folsom soon thereafter. The prison set up a glass box in the warden's office where they could talk and be observed. Cleaver had not been this close to a woman in five years, and her perfume almost knocked him out. Over the course of a few hours, Cleaver told her about his case and his writing. Axelrod listened intently and took pages of notes. At the end of the conversation, he slipped her his book, which he had hidden in a folder full of legal papers.

Cleaver was ecstatic that their plan had worked. In his first letter to her after their visit, he could hardly contain his excitement. "You will forgive if I confess that for a couple of days following your visit my head was swimming, and I was in a euphoric state of excitation which neither sleep nor wakefulness could dispel."[35] In their correspondence over the next few months, Cleaver tried to woo Axelrod. He told her of his childhood, he confessed his crimes, and he discussed his philosophies on writing. He sent her poems, and he talked endlessly about his love of literature. He mailed miniessays about a range of topics, including his self-education, Malcolm X, and Watts. Much of this material would make it into *Soul on Ice*.

Soon Cleaver began pushing their discussions into romantic territory. After Axelrod wore a pink dress to a visit one day, he wrote, "All I can see in my mind's eye is a swirling dazzling image of your pink dress and the matching ribbon in your hair." After that, he started calling her Portia, the beautiful heroine from Shakespeare's *The Merchant of Venice*.[36] Officials sensed the personal overtones of Cleaver's letters and blocked their delivery, telling him, "Confine the contents to legal business *only*." Cleaver was angered by this, perhaps fearing his plan to seduce Axelrod might be foiled. He wrote the warden to complain. "I am greatly distressed by this, as it seems to me, arbitrary and unwarranted proscription of the scope of my correspondence with my attorney. There was nothing in my letter which could remotely be construed as breaching the security of Folsom Prison. There was nothing offensive or odious in my letter and nothing I said could have done anybody any harm. Therefore I can only interpret the action of returning my letter as needless, unjustified, calculated harassment." He concluded, "As long as I am not breaching the security of this Prison or violating the Law, it is nobody's business what I say to my attorney—or how I say it."[37]

Axelrod went to work right away getting Cleaver's book published. She passed his essays and letters along to Ed Keating, the cofounder and editor of *Ramparts*. Keating was the right recipient for Cleaver's work. As a literary critic, he preferred the protest-oriented literature of Richard Wright over the modernist aesthetics of Ralph Ellison and James Baldwin. He once wrote to Arthur Barron, "I have never been that mad over *Invisible Man*, and would use instead Richard Wright's books, like *Native Son*, a masterpiece of our literature, or *Black Boy*, that gives the feeling of the South, of the haunted Negro consciousness."[38] Cleaver, for Keating, was the perfect heir to Wright. After he read Cleaver's work, he wrote to literary critic Max Geismar to share his enthusiasm. He felt that even though Cleaver needed some polish, he was nothing short of a genius. "I am convinced that we have her[e] an instance of raw talent that could be developed. For example, his letters, which are naturally less self-conscious than his creative writing, are absolute masterpieces. His insight into the Black Muslims and into Malcolm X are particularly incisive. I believe there are moments when he writes magnificently, and I also believe that there are moments when he falters badly."[39]

Keating sent Cleaver comments for revisions in September 1965, and Cleaver was grateful for the suggestions. "I consider myself something of your protégé and I accept your editing with an eye to improving and developing whatever skill and talent I may possess. This means everything to me, as I'm sure you can appreciate."[40] Cleaver wrote out a page of comments of his own, defending certain creative choices and specific vocabulary. He felt a growing sense of confidence in his writing, and he felt himself being pulled in two distinct directions. He told Keating, "I vacillate between writing and revolutionary politics. I swing easily between the two and am fascinated by both. In either one, you have to bet your life."[41]

Throughout the fall, the relationship between Cleaver and Axelrod grew more personal. Although Cleaver had started off with the plan to deceive Axelrod, he found himself developing feelings for her. During an interview years later, he said, "I used to love that Beverly Axelrod. Man, if somebody said something about Beverly Axelrod when I was in Folsom Prison, I'd throw his ass off the fifteenth tier. There were a lot of Muslims who didn't like it either. I'd tell them, Kiss my ass, blackass niggers."[42] In letters to Axelrod, he admitted that he had been trying to deceive her initially. "I have tried to mislead you. I am not humble at all. I have no humility, and I do not fear you in the least. If I pretend to be shy, if I appear to hesitate, it is only a sham to deceive. By playing the humble part, I sucker my fellowmen in, and seduce them of their trust. And then, if it suits my advantage, I lower the boom—mercilessly."[43]

None of this mattered to Axelrod, who had already fallen in love with him. "I accept you," she wrote back. "I know you little and I know you much, whichever way it goes, I accept you."[44] She was optimistic. "I know you will not hurt me. Your hatred is large, but not nearly so vast as you sometimes imagine; it can be used, but it can also be soothed and softened." Axelrod believed that she was the one who could sooth Cleaver's anger. She recognized that this was a dangerous belief. She admitted, "I'm not strong enough to take the safest course, which would be to not widen the subject matter of our correspondence."[45]

Cleaver wrote more explicitly intimate letters to Axelrod. He told her about homosexual relationships he had while in prison, and he admitted that he had had wet dreams about her in his bunk. He wrote sexually explicit descriptions of his fantasies about her, which somehow got past the censors: "I want to freak off with you, to have an orgy with you. I want to eat you up, caress and suck your tits, suck your pussy, lick your crack, to lash your clitoris into submission with the tip of my tongue. I want to kiss your right arm. I want to fuck you. I want to fuck you in your ass. I want you to suck my Rod. I want to come in your pussy, to come in your mouth, to come in your ass." He attempted to tantalize her with his past as a rapist, telling her, "There was a time when, if I had wanted to communicate this message to you, I would have had to lie in wait, on some dark night, in the blackest part of the night, and raped you—ravished you. Devoured you. Chewed your flesh, drank your blood."[46]

But Cleaver felt deeply ambivalent using these tactics of sexual explicitness to seduce Axelrod. A few days after he sent her the previous letter, he wrote her again, embarrassed. "Do you know what it is that I have written above? It is an act of Rape. After you have read it, it will be the same as though I had Raped you. I am appalled by the violence, by the rage, and by the cruelty of my sexuality. I urge myself to say that I am not like that at all—but of course I am."[47]

Through the fall of 1965, Cleaver's feelings deepened. He was grateful to her for trying to publish his manuscript and secure him parole. He was romantically and sexually attracted to her as well. But beyond these things, Cleaver appreciated Axelrod because he could talk to her about everything from the writings of James Joyce and Oscar Wilde to the political conflict between India and Pakistan. At one point, Cleaver excitedly wrote to her:

> It must be something special to be able to tour the Kama Sutra, discuss Alinsky, Shakespeare, Fanon, Henry Miller, John Coltrane—or [jazz musician] John Handy! (Grrrr!)—DuBois, Malcolm X, Mario Savio, Marx[,] Mao, James Baldwin, Le Roi Jones, Fidel, John Brown, Lenin, Governor Brown, Governor Faubus, LBJ, Governor Wallace, Goldwater, Warren Heinze [probably Warden Heinze, head of Folsom Prison], Chief [of the LAPD] Parker, J. Edgar Hoover, and Constitutional Law—all with the same fascinating woman! That's too good to be true.[48]

Axelrod developed her own deep feelings toward Cleaver as well. She admitted in one letter to him, "The public Beverly Axelrod is aggressive, strong, dynamic, self-assured, sophisticated, self-reliant. I am none of those, though I can wear the masks whenever I choose."[49] Over time, she revealed more about her personal life. She told him that she had been married twice and had a son from each marriage. She filled him in about the details of her everyday domestic existence: going to work, attending protest rallies, cooking dinners for her children, painting her living room, and playing solitaire. She admitted that she was falling in love with him and was letting her guard down. "I am no longer a critic, just a woman warm in the glow of having received reassurance that she is not alone in her feelings." Axelrod was acutely aware of the problematic nature of the relationship. At one point, she quipped, "God, can you imagine what a psychiatrist would do with us?" She believed they would survive as a couple. She just insisted that upon his release, Cleaver sleep with "at least 20 other women first" so that she would know it was not his celibacy driving their relationship.[50]

As the relationship between Axelrod and Cleaver intensified, they began taking greater risks. On September 21, 1965, during a visit, Axelrod slipped some poetry, pamphlets, and books into a folder and gave it to Cleaver. He was caught by the guard, and the materials were confiscated. At his hearing, Cleaver tried to deflect blame away from Axelrod by taking full responsibility for the infraction, and he was given five days in isolation and thirty days probation.[51] The next day he destroyed all of Axelrod's letters to keep them from falling into officials' hands. "I've removed Portia's letters from the planet earth," Cleaver announced to her grandly, "storing them up where neither thieves, moths, nor rust can touch them." Axelrod was devastated by the news that he had been caught. She felt that she had put his parole at risk, but Cleaver was upbeat. He wrote her from isolation, "The next time I see you I will—shall—tell you that I love you."

By this point, Cleaver was completely committed to a relationship with Axelrod. He told her he wanted her to have his baby, and that she had changed his perspective on everything. "When I was a Black Muslim I wanted two things: to marry a jet-black woman and to see America destroyed, brought low, humiliated. Now I am no longer a Black Muslim and I want to see America saved—but changed!—and I'm in love with a white woman. It seems natural, mathematical."[52]

Throughout the fall, their passion for one another grew. As a gesture of her love, Axelrod promised to remain celibate until Cleaver got out of prison. "But for now, I will be faithful to you. No man will touch me until you do. I want to suffer with you, I want to leave the burning desire unfulfilled, as yours has to be, with no substitute, no way of easing that component of us which is lust. I want to agonize with you, and I want you to know it, that what you are feeling I feel too."[53] Their exchanges took on new familiarity, as they joked over how to best raise Axelrod's mischievous son, Doug. She affectionately called Cleaver "My Sartre," while he called her "Simone de Beauvoir." They developed a secret code in their letters to bypass the eyes of the censors, which they called the "Cyclops." Cleaver wrote to her, "But the real important thing that I am keeping my eye and ear on, is that we are developing our own private language which, so full of meaning for us, must be, I hope, opaque for others—meaning Cyclops. The vitality of a developing language is a sign of life."[54] Axelrod even started signing her letters "Your Ogre," the name that Cleaver had given white women in his book.

As their relationship intensified, prison officials tried to figure out how to handle it. At one point, the warden wrote to the director of corrections to solicit advice: "Mrs. Axelrod currently visits Cleaver under the guise of attorney-client relationship although we know by Cleaver's letters that there is a full-fledged romance underway which has gotten to the point (in their most recent 'conference') of knee rubbing and little-finger holding."[55] The prison created a system that allowed Axelrod to occupy dual roles as partner and lawyer. As Axelrod remembered it, "We finally worked out a deal where I agreed that I was personally involved with him, and yet I was also his lawyer. I would go in as his lawyer and into the lawyer's conference room and they wouldn't search me, and I'd go in with my briefcase and so forth and then I would notify him when the legal portion was over. When the legal portion was over, I would then come out, then they would search me, and then I would go into the visiting room, and we would have personal visits."[56] During these sessions, Cleaver and Axelrod would sometimes spend as much as five hours together, talking of his case, the book, radical politics, and love.

Letters of support for Cleaver started pouring in from all sorts of intellectuals and politicians, including Max Geismar, Norman Mailer, John Howard Griffin, Norman Podhoretz of *Commentary*, Fred Jordan of Grove Press, a correspondent for the *Baltimore Afro-American* named William Worthy, California congressman Phillip Burton, California assemblyman Willie Brown, and Alex Haley. In his letter of support, Keating stated that he felt "Mr. Cleaver has the potential to become one of this country's most important writers,"[57] while Norman Mailer said, "He is a very talented man and might in a period of time, emerge as one of the more important writers in America."[58]

John Howard Griffin was particularly impressed by Cleaver, writing, "I volunteered the honest opinion that he was superbly gifted. In a long career of reading manuscript materials, I have never encountered such immediately recognizable gifts. Mr. Cleaver has an original and brilliant ability to articulate complex truths. I believe that with some nurturing of these talents, Mr. Cleaver should become a major writer on the American scene."[59]

Cleaver was startled by the praise. Suddenly, the enormity of writing more chapters of a book weighed on him—he was terrified. In one of his private journals, Cleaver reflected, "I should be grinding them out. And I have not hit a single lick. I don't even have any real ideas on what to write about. The things that I do have stacked out will not come alive. I need something to grasp hold of me and then I will be able to compose." Now that it looked like he might publish, he was worried that he did not have enough to say. "I've fallen into a hip brogue that is not really me. I think I must fake stronger and smile less. And talk slowly with an intellectual air. But such is not me. I only want to be myself."[60] Cleaver suddenly became gripped by an uncontrollable dread. He wrote to Axelrod about this: "I am beset by a million fears that something is going to go wrong, somehow, to keep us from our happiness. At times, I fear that I will be killed before I can leave Folsom; and at other times I fear contracting a fatal disease. At this very moment, and for a couple of days now, I have been consumed by the fear that, unknown to me, I may have a disease in my sexual apparatus which at any moment may erupt into the final stages which if they do not leave me dead will leave me unsuited to consummate our love."[61]

In November 1965, Cleaver went up for parole once again. His whole family was rooting for him. Even his father sent him encouraging words. "I hope you will just as soon as you are free, head right to Chicago. I do think it that would be better," he wrote. "I will have the money there waiting for you to come. I would be much pleased. Don't worry about the snow, we have big overcoats & boots (smile)."[62] Cleaver wrote to his mother with qualified hope that he might make parole this time. He felt that if he were freed from prison, it would be because of Axelrod's efforts. "She is Beverly to me and not only do I want her to be Beverly to you," Cleaver wrote, "I want you to accept her as your daughter because she is going to be my wife."[63] In private, Cleaver reflected on his original plan to use Axelrod to get himself out of prison. It all seemed distasteful to him now. "It would be a simple thing to throw her over once I get out of here and made use of her to get on my feet. But I do not approve of such ruthlessness to innocent people and their feelings. It is not my desire to inflict pain on people. If Beverly will have me, I am hers. It is the right thing for me to do, and if it seems to contradict other things which I have in mind, then will just have to stand."[64]

At his parole hearing, Cleaver was rejected. Even though he had performed well in his classes, been involved in the Gavel Club, and worked hard in the bakery vocation, officials still didn't believe he was sufficiently remorseful. As they put it, "It would appear he has an 'ax to grind' and he wants to be released as a result of some ulterior motivation." Prison officials did not make clear what Cleaver's "ulterior motivation" beyond getting out of prison might be, but they concluded the report, "[Cleaver] is an impulsive person and it would be difficult to predict what he might do in a given situation."[65]

Cleaver was surprisingly unperturbed by the news. This was not just because he had come to expect these rejections but also because he was thrilled that so many from the literary world had written on his behalf. Just a few weeks after his parole hearing, Cleaver wrote excitedly to his brother Theophilus, "Beverly went all out to help me get a parole this time. I sent her some of my manuscripts and she cut into some of the top figures in the field of literature and they dug my writing and came to my aid."[66]

8

CALIFORNIA MEN'S COLONY AND SOLEDAD PRISON (1965–1966)

The same day that Cleaver was denied parole, prison officials informed him that he was being transferred to the California Men's Colony (CMC) in San Luis Obispo. Cleaver was immediately suspicious. A few years earlier, he would have seen this as a victory. But now he suspected that they were moving him to disrupt his relationship with Axelrod. On the morning of December 13, 1965, he was loaded on a prison bus and driven to CMC.

When it first opened in 1954, CMC was billed as "a new kind of correctional facility." Designed for older prisoners, it featured dormitory-style housing, counseling services, and exercise programs for the aged. CMC was considered an "open" prison, and it focused on rehabilitation programs, religious fellowship, and education. As Cleaver remembered it, "It incorporated in its architecture and technology a paternalistic, liberal penology with the eternal goal of re-ordering human behavior. The staff of the prison were gloatingly proud of their new play-pretty, and they wanted the convicts to appreciate it also. As I was being processed into the prison, a staff member said to me, 'Cleaver, forget everything you've been through in Folsom and Q. CMC East is different.'"[1]

CMC had been built to feel more like a college campus than a prison. It was separated into four quads and contained an isolation unit, a library, a gym, and a hospital. At orientation, inmates were told that they were part of a grand experiment in progress and that CMC did not incarcerate prisoners but rather "confined them while rehabilitating them." Cleaver later remembered, "The visiting room was as plush and smooth as the lobby of a large hotel, and there was a special section of small rooms where attorneys were allowed to visit in private with their clients."[2] Guards were kept mostly out of sight, and the prison depended on surveillance technology to monitor prisoners. "Instead of sullen-faced guards patrolling on foot and walking the cat-walk with rifles on shoulders and pistols on hips, watching you, breathing down your neck, your every movement was monitored by closed circuit TV cameras. Instead of rude guards walking up and listening to what you were talking about, the whole joint was lousy with hidden microphones. I have never seen any convicts so paranoid, so reduced to psychological terror, as those I found in CMC East."[3] An air of total paranoia hung over the place. Guards called inmates "sir" and "mister" to their faces, but with an air of contempt and mockery.

Despite CMC's challenges, Cleaver hoped that this new atmosphere might provide a place to finish his manuscript. Only a few days after he arrived, he wrote to Ed Keating. "My feeling at the moment is that I may be able to get a little writing done in this environment, because it is quiet and peaceful, and one can be alone with one's thoughts in a way that I've never experienced before in any other prison."[4]

The tranquility did not last long, however, as officials were monitoring Cleaver's movements closely. Two days after Christmas, a guard named T. L. Michaud seized a story that Cleaver was writing called

"Maxine's Legs." The story contained a number of four-letter words, and Michaud deemed it "lewd and lascivious." Cleaver was hauled before the disciplinary committee, where he was questioned and then given a "warning and a reprimand." His story was put with his other confiscated property to be returned to him on the day of his release from prison.[5] Cleaver wrote Keating a few days later, expressing his frustration with the censorship of his material. "I hate to suppress my true feelings when talking to another man and I have to do this because I have no patience at all with the whole idea of Censorship."[6]

The guards enacted other forms of subtle warfare on Cleaver as well. One held his letters from Axelrod all day long, even though he could have handed them over at any time. Other officials rejected letters he tried to send out, stating that they were full of inappropriate language. Nevertheless, the relationship between Cleaver and Axelrod deepened. On January 1, 1966, Cleaver wrote her a poem called "To My Love on New Year's Day," in which he half-seriously called her a "White Witch" and a "Bloodletting Ogre":

> A billion years of murdered blood are in her kisses
> Her lips stain mine with blood
> Her fingers streak my skin with scarlet streaks.
> Her rich perfume cannot hide the stench of corpses.

At the end of the poem, he admitted "I love her. / Loathsome, craven-hearted coward that I am."[7] The next day a guard had to separate them when he found them rubbing knees during a meeting.[8]

A few days later, Cleaver received a notice that he was being transferred back to Soledad. According to officials, he was being moved because he was a "trouble maker."[9] Cleaver was working in the bakery when two guards came in to inform him of the move. He was given no time to pack up his belongings, and the only items he could take with him were those already on his person. He was forced to leave behind his typewriter, books, and manuscripts. He wasn't even allowed to grab his toothbrush. He was simply marched by two guards out to the front gates, where he was strip-searched and then tossed onto a Greyhound bus. When Cleaver complained, one guard responded, "Tell it to your lawyer, sir." All the guards laughed.[10]

Cleaver arrived back in Soledad in January 1966, nine years after he had been released the first time. A lot had changed. He had been a young man when he first came to Soledad, and now he was an emerging writer with radical ideas. He was the target of prison officials both because of his personal relationship to his lawyer and because of his past affiliations with the Muslims. During processing, they pestered him about his connection to Axelrod, accusing him of blackmailing and intimidating her. They refused to give him back his property, because they believed that he might have Muslim propaganda among his papers. Cleaver asked to be assigned to the print shop for his vocational assignment, but they put him in the mess hall. It was one of the least desirable jobs in the prison. Cleaver was irritated but not surprised by the treatment. As he complained to Axelrod in a letter, "I am sick and tired of being kicked around by the whim of one or two lower echelon officials. There is absolutely no justification for me to be denied a job opening for which I am qualified simply because of my past affiliation with the Black Muslims."[11]

Cleaver was soon moved out of the adjustment center and into general population. He was given his own cell on the Freeway, the ground floor of the Y Wing. The Freeway was barely a cut above the adjustment center. Inmates had fewer privileges here, and they were held in their cells longer than other prisoners. The Freeway was full of dangerous men: radical Muslims, neo-Nazis, and KKK members. Cleaver was harassed in both small and big ways by officials. The guards regularly searched his cell, pretending to look for weapons, but really just pestering him. Administrators blocked Cleaver from sending an essay called "Lazarus Come Forth" to Ed Keating for review. Cleaver's essay outlined the contributions of radical black leaders like W. E. B. Du Bois, Marcus Garvey, and Paul Robeson, and it celebrated Muhammad Ali as a defiant symbol of black masculinity and militancy. As Cleaver wrote, "Muhammad Ali is the first 'free' champion ever to confront white America. In the context of boxing, he is a genuine revolutionary, the black Fidel Castro of boxing."[12] Officials kept the essay from going out because they found this "offensive to race, nationality, religious faith, political parties, etc."[13]

Cleaver soon found an outlet to politicize and organize black prisoners when he joined an African history and culture class in early February. Sponsored by a black guard named Sidney Waldron, it was the first class of its type in the country. It was packed every week, and Cleaver decided it was the perfect place to raise the revolutionary consciousness of his fellow inmates. Following Frantz Fanon, Cleaver believed that the lumpen—the criminals and nonpolitical members of the working class—could be the vanguard of the revolution if properly educated. The first time he attended the class, Cleaver decided to test this theory on his classmates. "We must use the time we have in prison to prepare ourselves for the war which is raging outside," he told the class. "We must organize ourselves inside into an invincible force. Once we achieve an adequate degree of organizational power, we will be able to tear down the walls and set all our people free!"[14]

Cleaver got an enthusiastic response, so he began attending the class every week and spreading a message of revolution. He was a megalomaniac, believing that he was the only one suited to lead the struggle for black freedom in the prison. But he had the intellectual background and the leadership experience to educate the other men. Cleaver provided a political education grounded in Marx, Mao, Guevara, Fanon, and C. L. R. James. As he taught the history of slavery, black insurrection, abolitionism, and Reconstruction, his influence grew as mentor and teacher. He gave a copy of Malcolm X's autobiography to enlist a new inmate named "Killer" Wells, and he befriended another young inmate named Byron Booth, who would later join him in exile. "My best friends are Murderers," he told Axelrod in a letter. "Rapists. Armed Robbers. ADWs [assault with a deadly weapon]. The Hatchet Men who could not contain their violence—the wretched of the earth."[15] Cleaver knew that this was a risky strategy. Not even Karl Marx himself had believed the lumpen could be organized for the purposes of revolution. But as he explained to Axelrod, he had a plan to educate black men behind bars the way that he had educated himself. He would turn the American prison system's wretched of the earth into enlightened revolutionaries. "The ideal of our class is to awaken every black inmate to his identity, his historical roots, and his responsibilities to himself, his loved ones, and to the progress of his race which, seen in its true light, inevitably counteracts all doctrines of racism and teaches the universality of mankind and the oneness of human aspiration."[16]

The class also gave Cleaver an opportunity to teach the philosophies of Malcolm X, who had split from the Nation of Islam before his death in 1965. Cleaver felt it was his job to organize Malcolm's followers and oppose the Nation of Islam, which had a large presence in the class. He had a master plan. "We also believed that, scattered throughout the United States, there were pockets of Malcolm's followers who would remain faithful to his ideas. We therefore saw it as our task to keep Malcolm's ideas alive, to further develop them, and once we were out of prison, to seek out Malcolm's followers, unite with them, and put his ideas into practice by in fact founding and building the Organization of Afro American Unity. This became the goal and dedication of the African History and Culture Class."[17] Cleaver felt that Muslims were straightjacketing people with their religious beliefs, and he believed that the black people could only be radicalized through Malcolm X's secular approach.

Cleaver joined forces with Alprentice "Bunchy" Carter, the former captain of the Soledad Muslims. Bunchy had been a leader of the notorious Slauson street gang in Los Angeles and had earned the nickname "Mayor of the Ghetto." Together, Cleaver and Carter wrested control of the African history and culture class away from the Muslims. They planned a vigil for February 21, 1966, the anniversary of Malcolm's death. The Muslims in the class objected and refused to show up to the ceremony. Cleaver and the other Malcolm followers held impromptu elections and replaced all the Muslim leadership who held control of the class. Seven of the eight executive board members were replaced with Malcolm sympathizers, while Cleaver was elected president. Cleaver and Bunchy instituted new reading groups, which they named after African peoples: Zulu, Yoruba, Mandingo, Fulani, Kikuyu, and Maasai. The class invited speakers, including African American studies professor J. Herman Blake, publishers of the radical magazine *Black Dialogue*, and representatives from the San Francisco Negro Historical and Cultural Society. Under Cleaver's influence, the class soon became so popular that the group had to move it from a classroom to the library. He was turning prison into a space for political education. He remembered later, "It became our Holy Cause, to get ourselves properly organized while in prison, and prepare ourselves on all levels to go outside and go to war, because we understood precisely that we had been at war already for hundreds of years."[18]

Cleaver relentlessly pursued his education at Soledad. He read constantly: Ken Kesey's *One Flew over the Cuckoo's Nest*, Sylvia Plath's *Ariel*, and Simone de Beauvoir's *The Prime of Life*, in addition to works by Albert Camus and D. H. Lawrence. While he didn't like the impenetrable prose of *Jude the Obscure* or the fantastical world of *The Lord of the Rings*, he loved T. S. Eliot's modernist masterpiece *The Waste Land*. Cleaver studied books about Africa, including the histories of the Zulu nation and W. E. B. Du Bois's *The World and Africa*. He described his passion about Africa: "I have a deep and abiding interest in the study of the history of peoples of African descent—in fact, the problems confronting these people is my one consuming interests."[19] He read volumes of Marxist theory and admitted to Axelrod that Fyodor Dostoyevsky had become his favorite author.

In mid-March 1966, he enrolled in a creative writing course taught by a white man named Salisby. Cleaver described him to Axelrod as "a 'live wire' type cat and he is down with literature, etc., and creates a very stimulating atmosphere."[20] The course was organized around writing exercises and workshops. On Thursdays, students read a work and offered a reading response. Cleaver enjoyed the format, and he wrote papers on LeRoi Jones, Norman Mailer, and Aldous Huxley. He received As on everything. From Salisby, Cleaver learned new principles of exposition, ones that would help strengthen his writing skills. Cleaver gleaned three main ideas: "1. From observation and reflection on the subject-structure, abstract a principle that epitomizes it. 2. State this principle as the brisk, punchy sentence of the opening paragraph. 3. Give a graphic, moving panoramic description of the subject-structure."[21]

Cleaver drew from Salisby's instruction to compose a wide range of essays. In one, he criticized the prison library for having so few books by black authors,[22] and in another, he argued for the symbolic significance of jazz in America. In "The Roots of Identity," Cleaver provided a history of early civil rights pioneers, such as Henry Sylvester Williams, a Trinidadian writer who organized the first Pan-African Conference, and Alexander Walters, a civil rights leader who organized the National Afro-American Council to protest lynching.[23] He traced the origins of black protest against white supremacy, including the Niagara Falls Convention, the creation of the NAACP, and Marcus Garvey's back-to-Africa movement. He wrote a number of essays about Marxism, including one that explored how Thomas Hobbes, John Locke, and Adam Smith contributed to our understanding of capitalism. Cleaver also wrote a speculative essay about the world in the year 2000. "All capitalists will be dead," he wrote hopefully. "All Europeans will have returned to Europe. All black men will have returned to Africa. America will belong to the Indians."[24] Cleaver dreamed there would be full employment and access to global travel and that workers would own the means of production.

One of Cleaver's best works was an impassioned review of Kwame Nkrumah's book, *Neo-Colonialism: The Last Stage of Imperialism*. In it, Cleaver attempted to expand his international perspective, thinking about the relationships among revolutionary leaders from across the globe. He wrote,

> He is to the black man as Lenin was to the Whites, Mao was to the yellow, even though the three Giants are in harmony and their thought represents a continuous chain coming down from the great original work of Marx. The mark of their authenticity is that they are all there in harmony. This completes the circle: a great man from each race has arisen to

> certify the radical truth of Marx and the need for Socialism in which the salvation of humanity lies. The universal scope of his concern encompasses the whole black race and goes beyond to embrace all mankind.[25]

This essay represented the beginning of Cleaver's attempt to think about class and race as intersecting issues in the international context, an idea that would inform his work as the leader of the International Section of the Black Panther Party later. Salisby liked Cleaver's analysis so much that he urged Cleaver to polish it up and have it published.[26]

Cleaver channeled his creativity in various directions, including working on more fiction. He composed a new outline for "Maxine's Legs," his story of a college dropout who becomes a drug dealer. He wrote a vignette about a man named John, a childhood friend who was considered the "best walker in our clique," who walked along Los Angeles's streets, dancing and teaching others how to "walk hip."[27] He wrote a handful of poems, as well as a play called *Rigor Mortis*, about two Muslims who stand up to a white nationalist. He created an outline titled "Blood Money," which Cleaver billed as "a short story built around the incident of a brother selling his blood and his reluctant partner about to do it but his woman begging him not to." In this story, two partners try to make some money selling blood only to realize that the white nurses at the hospital are actually vampires.[28] In a tragic story called "Stacy," Cleaver told the tale of a young man put away in prison. He pines for the love of his life, Tina, but he does not send her letters because the separation is too painful. Finally, one day, he sends her a valentine. By then, she has married, and when her husband discovers the valentine, he is enraged. He punches her in her pregnant belly so hard that she hemorrhages and dies.[29] Finally, Cleaver composed a masterful short work about his childhood in Rose Hills, called *The Flashlight.* It would win the prestigious O. Henry Award for best short story within just a few years.

Cleaver cultivated relationships with the white intellectuals who supported him. In February 1966, Max Geismar offered to write an introduction for *Soul on Ice.* Ed Keating visited him often and convinced officials to allow Cleaver to send out the essay on Muhammad Ali, even though the librarian said it was "reeking with hate."[30] Keating informed Cleaver that *Ramparts* would be publishing his essay on James Baldwin, "Notes on a Native Son," in June. Given the essay's explicit homophobia, Cleaver anticipated criticisms of his work. He sent his responses to Axelrod. He defended himself, saying that he was "not a bigot in the sense of wanting to see all homosexuals burnt at the stake or confined." But he claimed that homosexuality would ruin society. "Gay is not the way" asserted Cleaver, and he believed his views were supported by science. "If you follow their ideas to a logical conclusion, we would have a world wherein everything is bisexual, or, perhaps, homosexual, with the procreative function divorced from sex and with test tube babies relied upon to keep up the population. That's where it leads to."[31]

Cleaver started a correspondence with Norman Mailer, though he was still starstruck that one of his favorite authors was interested in his work. "I also register here my still-surprised pleasure over your very encouraging remarks on my writing. Knowing you, I can stash blind faith that you mean what you said. I'm trying, for the sake of America's mutilated, knick-knack crotch—i.e. my own—to drain the spring water of an unsimpering prose from the mute stone of my prison cell."[32] Cleaver also corresponded with John Howard Griffin, whose controversial book *Black Like Me* recounted his journey through the South dressed up in blackface. Cleaver was almost fawning in his appreciation for Griffin, writing, "I am most gratified and encouraged by your response to my present writings and potential as an American writer. This is my single ambition in life and to receive encouragement from you and other noteworthy persons whose opinions can be taken to heart, has had a salutary effect upon me and caused me to redouble my efforts and dedication."[33]

For his continued good behavior, Cleaver was moved to the Super Honor Wing in spring 1966. Because they were the most well behaved, inmates here got their own keys, which allowed them to move in and out of their cells at will. The lights stayed on twenty-four hours per day, so they could read or write as much they wanted. Cleaver liked his new home. It was more peaceful, and he could get more work done here.

Cleaver turned his attention to completing the remaining sections of *Soul on Ice*. He stopped going to dining hall for breakfast, which added three hours per day to his writing routine. He finished "The White Race and Its Heroes," his call of support for white radicalism in America; "Rallying Around the Flag," his assessment of black revolution in the post–civil rights era; "The Black Man's Stake in Vietnam," his reading of the racial politics of America's unpopular war; and "Domestic Law and International Order," his critique of the modern police state. Taken together with his earlier articles on racial mysticism, his essays "Notes on a Native Son" and "Lazarus, Come Forth," and his letters to Axelrod, Cleaver had nearly completed his book.

Throughout the spring of 1966, Axelrod and Cleaver grew ever closer. Axelrod never missed a weekly visit, and she had matching religious jewelry made for them. It was the only kind that inmates were allowed to wear. He wore a medal with the inscription BE WITH GOD on it, and she wore a matching ring with the same inscription.[34] The *BE* represented the combination of their initials. Axelrod also sent him a record player on Valentine's Day along with records by John Coltrane, Miles Davis, and Charles Mingus. He had never heard Coltrane's music before, and it floored him. "Coltrane is about to blow a hole in my head! Mercy."[35] Axelrod continued to hunt down job offers for Cleaver from a number of people, including Fred Jordan of Grove Press and Reverend Cecil Williams of the Glide Urban Center.[36] Cleaver and Axelrod's letters at this time were filled with hundreds of statements of "I love you." Cleaver even wrote bad poetry to her on her birthday. In "To a Nomad," he wrote, "Now we are One; our search is done— / Is it meant to be? / On March 3, 1966, Beverly, my love / I say you are ALL to me."[37]

Their physical relationship also grew more intense. As Axelrod remembered it, "Our relationship was more and more personal; we would sneak in sexual stuff while we were visiting. I wouldn't wear pants, and he would— You know, whatever he could."[38] These sexual interactions occurred with more frequency. After one particularly intense meeting, Axelrod wrote Cleaver, "Our Wednesday visit was powerful, I still feel you touching me, I'm still trembling, and it's too much to be afterglow."[39] The guards monitored this behavior more closely. In one custody and general report, a correctional officer noted, "I observed Cleaver's visitor (attorney) kissing his hand and arm across the table at which they were sitting. She started by kissing his hand continued all the way up close to his elbow."[40] They attempted to put a stop to it. During one visit, a guard ordered Cleaver to sit across from Axelrod at the table. In response, Cleaver "picked up a 'reserved' sign that was on top of the table, and like a spoiled child, slammed it against the floor. This was done hard enough to attract the attention of all the people present in the visiting as well as in the waiting room."[41]

By the summer of 1966, Cleaver and Axelrod were deep in a romantic relationship. Cleaver opened his letters with greetings like, "My Magnificent Queen: Excuse me if I sound like a silly schoolboy because that is exactly how I feel. I love you so!"[42] He ended each letter with "I kiss my medal for you," referring to the jewelry they both wore. Axelrod continued to send him records by Billie Holiday, Wayne Shorter, Johnny Cash, Miles Davis, and Archie Shepp, which Cleaver played for fellow inmates. "Today was wonderful," he wrote to Axelrod. "I took my record player out in the yard and we all dug the sides and shot the breeze; the breeze was really blowing, too and I got a great kick out of it."[43] They talked about engagement rings and marriage often, and Cleaver started referring to her as his wife. They contemplated getting married inside the prison.

Cleaver even proposed that his mother and father meet Axelrod at the prison. Thelma was too afraid to fly, but Leroy came from Chicago. Cleaver hadn't seen his father in ten years, and he hardly recognized the man in front of him. "I was appalled at what time had done to his body. He was still a giant, but now a skinny one, who had all but lost his struggle with the force of gravity, which was pulling him towards the ground. His shoulders seemed heavy with the weight of about sixty-five years."[44] The reunion dissolved all of Cleaver's rage. As he wrote in his journal after their meeting, "For years I was driven by the monomaniacal passion to grow up and become large enough to contest my father and take his life. At what point I outgrew this youthful preoccupation—or indeed, whether or not I ever really outgrew it—is hard to say. The salient factor, however, is that as I write this my father still lives and I have never made an attempt upon his life. We are buddies now. He is a spry old man of 66 and I, his oldest son, am 30 years old and a prisoner of the California Department of Corrections."[45]

Over the course of the summer, Cleaver began to feel a rising confidence that he would be released at the next parole hearing in November. He made lists of things he wanted to buy: a turtleneck sweater, a polished turkey bone for his hair, and a dog. He liked German shepherds and Dobermans, but he wanted a saluki most of all. He fantasized about traveling across Europe and China and perhaps making enough money to settle on a Greek Island or someplace in Africa. "One thing I'd like to do, in my travels, is go into a remote rural area of Africa where there are only black people and stay for at least six months. Without reading any newspapers or magazines, no listening to radios, TV etc. Not even looking at any pictures or signboards, no posters or anything. To see no white faces, and hopefully no brown ones. Only the black."[46]

Cleaver confessed to Axelrod that his greatest fantasy was to open a bookstore. He wanted to call it Third World Books. "Have I told you about one of my secret dreams? A bookstore. I have long harbored the idea of owning a bookstore with a department that sells nothing but hardcore Jazz and another section that sells objects of art from Africa and Afro-America, the Caribbean, etc., and another department that sells a selection of clothing styles of the same genre, i.e. Black."[47] But most of all, Cleaver fantasized about being a writer. Now that his piece on Baldwin was coming out, he was growing surer of his abilities. "What I need is a studio somewhere away from everybody, with books lining the walls, my typewriter and reams of paper. Solitude. Then I will dredge the cracks and crevices of my being for a few well-chosen words. I told you before that just as soon as my essay appeared in *Ramparts* I would consider myself a writer. So I'm a writer and I intend to write forever more."[48]

While Cleaver worked away on *Soul on Ice*, Axelrod was the unsung hero of the book. She edited the full book before David Welsh of *Ramparts* took over. She cut up over fifty pages of their letters into pieces and then pasted them back together into a publishable form. Axelrod also started researching big magazines like *Esquire*, *Playboy*, and the *Saturday Evening Post* as potential places to publish individual essays. She was in constant correspondence with him about the editing. "And what do I do with all the bits and pieces on such a variety of topics?" she asked at one point. "And what about biographical things—shouldn't they be saved for a different kind of work? I'm really a baby, with no idea of how to go about this task, which didn't strike me as too much of a problem when I accepted it. I'm beginning to feel more and more useless."[49] Despite her misgivings, Axelrod provided much of the editing and behind-the-scenes work that made *Soul on Ice* into a bestseller.

In June, Axelrod obtained an oral promise from McGraw-Hill to publish *Soul on Ice*. Cleaver was so overwhelmed by this that he felt as though "Joe Louis punched me in the snout."[50] In July, Axelrod secured Cyrilly Abels as his agent. Abels had been the former editor of *Mademoiselle* and the literary agent for such luminaries as Paule Marshall, Frank O'Connor, and Katherine Anne Porter. In August, Axelrod flew to New York to negotiate Cleaver's contract with McGraw-Hill in person. When she arrived at its offices, she was told that the editor in chief, Frank Taylor, was not in. She barged into his office anyway, and after a two-hour discussion, she had obtained an agreement for a contract before Cleaver's parole hearing in November. He would get $2,500 upon signing and $2,500 upon delivery.[51] Axelrod was so ecstatic that she drove three hundred miles to Max and Anne Geismar's farm afterward to tell them that that she and Cleaver were in love and going to get married. Axelrod also edited three letters Cleaver had written to her, calling them "Prelude to Love—Three Letters." She sold the work to *Mademoiselle*, and she also sold Cleaver's story "The Saint" to *Esquire* for $450. Chief editor Harold Hayes at *Esquire* told Abels, "I'd like more from this writer soon." Axelrod was thrilled that she was able to help Cleaver. She was deeply, passionately in love, and she would have done anything for him. As she admitted boldly later, "If I had to pose naked on the middle of Broadway, I would have done it."[52]

Axelrod was also on the front lines, protecting Cleaver's interests against unscrupulous publishers. The new president of *Ramparts*, Warren Hinkle, tried to pressure Axelrod to accept a 70 percent royalty rate for Cleaver, while splitting the remaining 30 percent among Abels, David Welsh, and *Ramparts*. Cleaver was so grateful at the opportunity to publish that he wanted to agree immediately to the terms. "I don't want to make them feel that we dealt too sharply with them," he wrote Axelrod.[53] However, Geismar advised Axelrod to reject the deal. For one, Welsh's demand for 10 percent royalties was a reach, as editors were usually compensated with a flat rate and a line of recognition. Second, Abels had not brokered the book, so she didn't deserve 10 percent. Geismar stated, "I think you have yielded to a kind of group pressure, blackmail, out of fear for Eldridge perhaps or some kind of undue sentimentality that *Ramparts* brought him out. . . . Get over this; he is a genius; they have made their fame out of him."[54]

There were other shady financial dealings around Cleaver's publications as well. When Abels received payment from *Esquire* for Cleaver's story "The Saint," she sent the money to Warren Hinkle at *Ramparts*. Axelrod was furious. "I don't know how you got the impression that Warren was the caretaker of Eldridge's money," Axelrod wrote to Abels, "or that any arrangement had been made for payments for Eldridge's writings go to Warren, or that there was any agreement for any portion to go to him, but none of these is the case."[55] Cleaver was more circumspect about the whole thing. He saw this as a valuable opportunity to learn about the motivations of everyone involved. "Now we have a chance to see what everyone is up to, just what everyone's intentions are. If we were pressed for the money, it would be a very different thing, but this way we can afford to find out what's happening. If anything sneaky is afoot then it will well be worth it to pay this price."[56] Cleaver eventually accepted 75 percent of the royalties, and he signed a contract with McGraw in December.

As the date of the parole hearing approached, Cleaver became nervous. His work in his classes had become very uneven. He earned an A in world history, and his teacher said he was a fine student with real ability.[57] He also earned an A in sociology and was praised for his good work.[58] However, he got an F in creative writing, and Salisby reported that "this man could have earned the highest grade in the class, but for some reason he chose not to work."[59] He also failed American government and American literature. All his teachers agreed that Cleaver had high potential but a negative attitude.[60]

In truth, he was buckling under the pressures of writing and his upcoming parole hearing. As he wrote to Paul Jacobs, "I have no soul for reading and writing; been spending all my time playing chess, to escape the thoughts that come crashing into my skull about so much that's happening in this world."[61] He was particularly distraught about the book, especially as it was nearing completion and would soon be public. "It dawned on me how permanent a thing a book is, and that once it rolls off the press that's it forever more. So that there are terrible responsibilities involved on all sides."[62]

Cleaver had never been this close to freedom before. The tension was driving him crazy. He and Axelrod half-joked that if he were not granted parole this time, they would find a way to break him out. At the hearing, Cleaver made his case to the board. The next day, a slip of paper was delivered to his cell; it was supposed to have the verdict on it, but it came back blank. There had been some mistake, but since the board convened only once a month, he would have to wait four more weeks to find out whether he got parole.

On November 28, 1966, Cleaver was finally granted his freedom, and his release was scheduled for two weeks later. He had been in the California prison system for eleven years, his entire adult life. In the final days before his release, he attended his last African history and culture class. Later, Cleaver went to the clothing room where he was "dressed out"—given the clothes he would wear on the outside. He packed up all his papers and took them to Receiving and Release to be sent home. They told him it was too late to send them out, so he would have to carry them out by hand. He salvaged all of his critical and creative writing, but he dumped the boxes of legal casework he had collected for years. He kept the recent letters from Axelrod, including the last one, which she had sent on December 8, 1966. In it, she assured him, "We will live happily ever after. Despite the odds."[63]

9

OAKLAND (1966–1968)

On December 12, 1966, Cleaver walked out of Soledad prison for the last time. Axelrod picked him up in her tiny black MG, which Cleaver was barely able to fold himself into. As they drove up Highway 101 to San Francisco, looking out at the green hills, Cleaver was suddenly overwhelmed by his newfound freedom. "I had left my world behind me and now was speeding into the unknown," he later wrote, "feeling like an unarmed cowboy riding shotgun on a stagecoach through wild country."[1] Cleaver was suddenly unmoored from the strict life of the prison routine. He asked Beverly to pull over and let him drive. He needed to regain some sense of equilibrium. She handed over the keys reluctantly, since it was a violation of his parole.

As Cleaver drove into the city, he was overwhelmed by all the sights and sounds. "By now it was all a spaghetti bowl full of cars, trucks, people, and buildings, lights and the sound track of a movie about the chaos of the city. I had sucked in every sight and sound, through the pores of my skin, and by the time we reached Beverly's pad, in the Haight-Ashbury District, I was completely stoned."[2]

The next few days were a blur. Cleaver moved into Beverly's house, a four-story art deco home on Carmel Street. It was tucked away in Ashbury Heights, perched on a hill overlooking the Haight-Ashbury District. Cleaver checked in with his parole officer R. L. Bilideau, and then he and Axelrod took a trip up the Pacific Coast. They packed the car with clothes, a typewriter, a bag of weed, and a stockpile of guns that they borrowed from Axelrod's brother—a .45 automatic, a 30.06 rifle, and a 12-gauge shotgun. They drove to Mendocino, where Axelrod had borrowed a cabin near the ocean from a friend. It was isolated, on a cliff overlooking the blue expanse of the Pacific Ocean—a perfect place to relax.

But it was difficult for Cleaver to adjust to being on the outside. He kept looking over his shoulder, unable to shake the feeling that he was being watched. He tried to get rid of his paranoia by firing the guns off the cliff, reloading and firing again and again. But it only triggered traumas he had experienced in prison. "I kept firing the guns in earnest, against this fear, trying to shoot this panic. I was hearing again the sound of the guns in San Quentin and Folsom when the guards fired down at the convicts during the riots and fights in the prison yard. It always sounded to me like deadly thunder from the high heavens."[3]

Cleaver finally calmed down and began to relax after a few days. He spent the week making love to Axelrod, listening to records, smoking weed, and writing. He wrote to Max Geismar, expressing his near disbelief at his freedom. "I'm sitting at a window looking out at the ocean breaking into the land; from a cool little guest house on the lip of a cliff; just Beverly is here with the music, and the rest of the world is somewhere miles behind."[4]

When Cleaver and Axelrod returned from the trip, they began to settle into their new home. Axelrod hired her decorator, Adam, to refurbish Doug's old room for Cleaver. Because Adam was gay, Cleaver was at first against him decorating the room. Axelrod assured him that Adam was an artist and that he should keep an open mind. Adam painted the room a soft white with blue trim, laid down a thick green shag carpet, bought an executive desk and painted it green to match the carpet, and mounted a massive swivel chair behind it. Finally, he hung African masks made of ebony on the walls, and he placed long spears and cowhide shields next to a wicker chair that was as big as a throne. A zebra rug tied the room together. Cleaver loved the room. It was indeed a work of art, and it gave him the first real sense of control over his environment that he had ever felt. "As I arranged my typewriter, books, and papers in the room, I was pleased with what Adam had done, and agreed that he was something special."[5] Cleaver now had a room of his own. A few weeks after he moved in, the advance for *Soul on Ice* arrived. Cleaver received about $2,000, the most money he had ever had his life.

Cleaver began to explore the city, sometimes wandering around all night. Walking had been one of the things he had missed most in prison. It was intoxicating to be outdoors again. His favorite area was the Haight-Ashbury District, located about a mile downhill from Axelrod's house. It was originally settled by upper- and middle-class San Franciscans because of its close proximity to Golden Gate Park, and was one of the few areas spared by the 1906 San Francisco earthquake. Following World War II, many middle-class white people fled the neighborhood for the suburbs, and San Francisco's various urban-renewal projects pushed African Americans and gay communities to seek housing there. By the time Cleaver was released from Soledad, it had turned into a gathering place for all sorts of countercultural figures—hippies, beatniks, actors, musicians, poets, and spiritual gurus. Head shops, gay bars, and bohemian clubs could be found throughout the neighborhood, while psychedelic "happenings," acid-laced rock shows, and street performances attracted the city's spectacular subcultures. Cleaver came to the Haight at the very height of these developments, and he was drawn to this countercultural community.

Cleaver had confidence in this generation of young white people, feeling that they were "descendent[s] of the Boston Tea Party," potential rebels who might join blacks in the struggle for equality. Growing up in the age of the civil rights movement and the Vietnam conflict, these young white people saw through the lie of American exceptionalism. They rejected segregation and American imperialism abroad and joined marches, sit-ins, and other forms of protest. Cleaver saw that an alliance was necessary. "This is the key center of the eye of the storm, because whether they know it or not, whether they like it or not, neither white radicals nor black radicals are going to get very far by themselves, one without the other."[6]

As the weeks passed, Cleaver noticed that his feelings toward Axelrod started shifting. The day before Christmas, he and Axelrod drove to Los Angeles to share the holiday with Thelma and Cleaver's siblings. "Why do you have to marry an old white woman?" Thelma asked Cleaver when they were alone. He was shaken by his mother's disapproval, and by the time he got back to San Francisco, he decided to move into his own place.[7] Beverly was disappointed, but she understood that he needed space. She helped him find a studio on the top floor of an apartment building on Castro Street. From the fire escape, it had a magnificent view of the city and the Bay Bridge. It was his first apartment—he was thirty years old.

Cleaver began his job as a reporter for *Ramparts*, and he was at first overwhelmed. *Ramparts* started as a liberal Catholic periodical; under Ed Keating's direction throughout the 1960s, it evolved into a radical leftist magazine. When Cleaver began working there, he was paid $400 a month. He was so grateful that he told them he would have worked for free. The staff was welcoming and warm. They all knew his writings, and many of them had worked on editing his works for publication. They gave him his own office, thinking that it would convey their respect for his work. However, the room was about the same size as his cell back at Soledad, making him feel claustrophobic. Cleaver tried reading at the office, but he found that he no longer liked reading now that he wasn't confined to a prison routine. He also didn't really know how to interact with people on the outside. "To say that I was bashful would be an extreme euphemism," Cleaver later admitted.

"I was terrified at the idea of approaching anyone. The thought of initiating a conversation petrified me. A palpable fear, a deep inner dread, held me back like a chain around the neck of a dog. I realized the problem was that I didn't know how to talk to people, what to say to them."[8]

Cleaver was therefore excited when he received permission to accompany SNCC leader Stokely Carmichael across the United States for a speaking tour in February 1967. Carmichael was one of Cleaver's heroes. He had been a Freedom Rider in the early 1960s, before emerging in June 1966 as the chairman of the Student Nonviolent Coordinating Committee. Carmichael had popularized the rallying cry "black power," a call for a more militant approach to the civil rights movement than the one promoted by Martin Luther King. Cleaver traveled with Carmichael from Chicago to Pennsylvania to Washington, DC, to Detroit, reporting on his activities for *Ramparts*. He attended picket demonstrations, speeches on college campuses, and gatherings at churches. Cleaver was impressed with Carmichael's passion and commitment but bewildered that he didn't follow the teachings of Malcolm X more directly. He told him, "We must make Malcolm X a reference point, a source of inspiration, and the founder of a new political tradition among Afro-American people. No better way could be found to do this, than by specifically organizing, in Malcolm's name, the Organization of Afro-American Unity which was baptized in his blood."[9] Carmichael was unconvinced. "We can't follow a dead man. That's worse than following a blind man."[10] In early February Cleaver requested permission to spend three weeks with him in Egypt, Tanzania, Guinea, Liberia, and Ethiopia. The Adult Authority denied his request.[11]

On the surface, Cleaver was a model parolee. As his parole officer noted, he didn't really drink much, he held down a good job at *Ramparts*, and he seemed to settle into a stable life with Axelrod. They were planning to get married. Cleaver was just waiting for the restoration of his civil rights. "The case is proceeding without negative connotations," Parole Officer Bilideau reported.[12] But Cleaver was unsatisfied with his contribution to black struggles for freedom. He tried to find outlets for his political beliefs. He attended a mosque located in the

Fillmore District, but everyone knew that he was a follower of Malcolm and made it clear he was not welcome. He tried to track down the publishers of *Black Dialogue* magazine, but he couldn't find them. Finally, he got the address of Marvin Jackmon, a poet and playwright who had visited the African history and culture class at Soledad. Jackmon was an influential member of the black arts movement, and he and playwright Ed Bullins had established the Black Arts West Theatre in the Fillmore District.

Together, Cleaver, Jackmon, Bullins, and singer Willie Dale established an arts cooperative known as Black House, located in a two-story Victorian at 1711 Broderick Street. Cleaver used money from his book to pay the rent and phone bill and often slept in a room on the top floor. The Black House was frequented by all types of artists, including writers Amiri Baraka (a.k.a. LeRoi Jones), Joan Didion, and Sonia Sanchez, graphic designer Emory Douglas, musician George Murray, and activist Jimmy Garrett. For a short time, the Black House was the center of the black arts movement in San Francisco, featuring weekly readings and theater performances like *How Do You Do* by Bullins, *Madheart* by Baraka, and *Papa's Daughter*, starring Danny Glover. Cleaver was happy to be part of the Black House, though he still wanted to resurrect Malcolm's Organization for Afro-American Unity. Ultimately, the Black House was not radical enough for Cleaver in the fight against white oppression. Although *Ramparts*, SNCC, and the Black House all provided Cleaver outlets for his radicalism, they all fell short of helping him achieve his ultimate goal: the armed overthrow of the system.

At this crucial transitional moment, Cleaver met Black Panther Party leaders Huey Newton and Bobby Seale. Jackmon first introduced Cleaver to Newton outside a radio station, where Cleaver had been giving an interview. Newton was eager to recruit Cleaver. He had been in prison and could relate to the "brothers off the block," Newton's name for the black lumpen proletariat he wanted to enlist. Because Cleaver was a talented writer, Newton knew that he would be indispensable for articulating the goals of the party through its newspaper, the *Black Panther*. At first, Eldridge didn't want to join the

Panthers. He was still on parole, and he wanted to play it safe. That changed in February 1967.

Cleaver and the Black House organized an event to celebrate Malcolm X on the second anniversary of his death. Malcolm's widow, Betty Shabazz, was to be the keynote speaker for the event. Jackmon hired Black Panthers as security. When Shabazz arrived at the airport, the Panthers escorted her, openly brandishing shotguns, to the offices of *Ramparts*. Shabazz was an admirer of Cleaver's writings on Malcolm, so she wanted to meet him. When Cleaver saw the Panthers arrive, it was a revelation. "I spun around in my seat and saw the most beautiful sight I had ever seen: four black men wearing black berets, powder blue shirts, black leather jackets, black trousers, shiny black shoes—and each with a gun!"[13] A reporter named Chuck Banks tried to push his way through the bodyguards to get near Shabazz. Newton shoved him out of the way. A police officer that was standing nearby reached for his gun and made a menacing gesture toward Newton. Newton jacked a round into his chamber of the shotgun and challenged the cop, saying, "OK, you big fat racist pig. Draw your gun!" After a few tense moments, the officer retreated with Newton standing there defiantly. Cleaver was absolutely floored by Newton's boldness. He wrote later, "I fell in love with the Black Panther Party immediately upon my first encounter with it; it was literally love at first sight."[14]

The Black Panther Party had emerged in Oakland as a militant response to the institutional racism black people faced there. African Americans had been coming to the East Bay in massive numbers since World War II, drawn by the promise of jobs in the shipbuilding and war industries. The federal government was the largest employer in the Bay Area then, and, because of Roosevelt's outlawing of discrimination in wartime industries, tens of thousands of black people found work. This boom was short-lived, however, as deindustrialization set in over the next few decades following the war and those jobs dried up. By the early 1960s, Oakland was characterized as "depressed" by the federal government, and African Americans—who had been moving into the city in ever larger numbers throughout the 1950s—were hit hardest by economic decline. East Bay African Americans also faced racism in every aspect of life: segregated schools, prejudiced social-service agencies, and the criminalization of black youth. Almost all African Americans were crowded in West Oakland in the decades after World War II, hemmed in by discriminatory lending practices by banks and racist realtors. Black people in Oakland faced rampant police discrimination, as they were physically assaulted and unjustly arrested. The Oakland police department was nearly all white, and they targeted migrants, whom they viewed as a threat to the stability of white society.[15]

The Black Panther Party, formed by Bobby Seale and Huey Newton in 1966, emerged to combat these forms of racism. Like Cleaver, Seale and Newton were influenced by Frantz Fanon, Malcolm X, Che Guevara, Mao Tse-tung, and Robert F. Williams, and they saw American ghettos as internal colonies to be liberated from an occupying police force. They were inspired by the third-world guerrilla insurgency against white colonialism and were determined to develop their own tactics to take on internal colonialism. Newton and Seale sought to build an organization that addressed the concerns of working-class black people by directly confronting police brutality. Newton, who had studied the law closely, realized that the Second Amendment protected the rights of citizens to carry loaded guns. In late summer 1966, he and the other Panthers started armed patrols. Listening to dispatches over police radio, they drove to scenes where black citizens were being arrested. They stood at a short distance, openly displaying firearms and reading sections of the penal code. With their armed patrols, Newton and Seale started recruiting members to the party. They wore leather jackets, black berets, and dark sunglasses, creating a revolutionary style that was immediately recognizable and attractive to young black people.

Cleaver was mesmerized by the Panthers. For him, Newton represented Malcolm X reincarnate. "Huey P. Newton is the ideological descendant, heir and successor of Malcolm X," Cleaver decided. "Malcolm X prophesized the coming of the gun to the black liberation struggle. Huey P. Newton picked up the gun and pulled the trigger, freeing the genie of black revolutionary violence in Babylon."[16]

In early March 1967, the SNCC invited Cleaver to speak at the National Black Students Conference at Fisk University, a historically black college in Nashville, Tennessee. It promised to be an exciting event, featuring speakers like Amiri Baraka, Margaret Walker, and Julius Lester. Cleaver looked forward to the occasion, but he was even more excited to meet the militant women who organized for SNCC, whom he had nicknamed "puss in boots."

On March 23, the same day his civil rights were restored, allowing him to marry Beverly Axelrod, he flew to Nashville. It was Easter weekend, and an unseasonable snowstorm blanketed the East Coast. Cleaver was the only speaker to arrive. Fred Brooks, the president of the Fisk chapter, picked him up from the airport and drove him to his apartment where volunteers were scrambling. Cleaver was a bit overwhelmed by the chaotic scene and hung back in the doorway. It was a habit left over from his days in prison when he had to wait for permission to enter a room. A young SNCC volunteer named Kathleen Neal saw him in the doorway and was immediately struck by his imposing presence. He was sharply dressed in black high-top boots, gray slacks, and a green velvet pullover, and his face was completely inscrutable. "He was as tall as the doorframe," Kathleen later remembered. "He just stood there because he was going through prison count. Standing at attention. He had a mask on. There was no expression on his face."[17]

Kathleen's background could not have been more different from Cleaver's. Her father Ernest Neal had been a sociology professor and director of the Rural Life Council at Tuskegee Institute, the historic black college started by Booker T. Washington. Her mother, Juette Neal, was a teacher and singer who held an advanced degree in mathematics. When Kathleen was seven, Ernest took a job with the Foreign Service, and the family moved to New Delhi, where he worked on community-development agricultural programs. They lived in an area once occupied by British administrators and next door to India's first prime minister, Jawaharlal Nehru. As a child, Kathleen visited holy sites such as the Taj Mahal, and she was exposed to nationalist ideologies of Indian independence and self-rule following the end of British colonialism.

After Ernest's post in India was over, the family moved to Manila, where Kathleen lived a serene life. "I attended the American School in Manila, a truly international mix, participated in swimming competitions, graduated from eighth grade as class valedictorian, and generally breezed through adolescence with lots of friends and lived the careless leisure of life in a tropical island country."[18] As a teenager, Kathleen moved all over Africa. She lived in Monrovia, Liberia, and Freetown, Sierra Leone, before she was an adult. By the time she was college age, Kathleen was a cosmopolitan thinker with a global perspective and a passion for politics. She yearned to join the struggle of black people during the civil rights movement, and, in 1966, she left Barnard College to join SNCC. Her parents were not pleased, but Kathleen made a deal with her father that she would go back to school in a year if he supported her activism. He agreed and sent her $125 dollars a month. She used the money to set up an apartment in Atlanta, where she and her fellow SNCC members organized.

Cleaver was immediately struck by Kathleen's beauty and intellect. He had rented a car for the weekend, and since much of the conference had been cancelled, he chauffeured her around town, running small errands. He was nervous in Kathleen's presence, so he was overly formal. Newly freed from prison, the world outside for Cleaver was still an exciting novelty. He stopped at a laundromat because he had never been inside one before. Kathleen also showed him how a credit card worked. Cleaver was so excited to be among the young activists that he took them all out for wine and dinner and paid for it with money from his royalties. On the way home, he invited Kathleen to his hotel. She said no, but told him she didn't want to go home either. They drove to a little hill just outside of town with a view of the city. They sat under a full moon and talked until Eldridge fell asleep. Kathleen sat for a few hours and watched the sunrise by herself. At dawn, she finally woke him so he could drive her home.

After the conference, Eldridge received an extension from his parole officer to stay in Tennessee for another week. Cleaver told him that he wanted to report on Carmichael's upcoming college speaking tour for *Ramparts*, but in reality, he just wanted to spend more time with Kathleen. He was also inspired by the young radicals who worked for SNCC. Kathleen remembered, "Eldridge had been exhilarated by our total devotion to the struggle, and stimulated by our youthful enthusiasm. He had told us he was ready to jump parole and hide out in the hills of Tennessee in a revolutionary camp with us if we set one up."[19] Cleaver spent all of his time with the SNCC workers, and he even volunteered to take them to Atlanta, where they needed to take care of organization business.

Just as they were about to leave, Axelrod showed up wanting know why Eldridge hadn't returned. When Cleaver introduced her to Kathleen and the other members of SNCC, he told them, "This is my lawyer, Beverly Axelrod." Axelrod was irritated by this, as she wanted to be introduced as his fiancé. After a brief but heated discussion with Axelrod, Cleaver left with Kathleen and the other volunteers.

On the way to Atlanta, Brooks drove, while Cleaver and Kathleen sat in the back. They joked and teased one another. Cleaver kept touching her playfully. She was surprised but not put off by his advances. When Cleaver asked Kathleen how old she was, she replied that she was nineteen. "That's my baby sister's age!" he exclaimed, with some embarrassment. When they arrived in Atlanta, Kathleen and Cleaver went to her apartment alone. Kathleen didn't own much, just a mattress on the floor and a coffee table with a chess board set up on it. After a decade in prison, Cleaver had become a skilled player, though he didn't tell Kathleen. She was just learning to play, and when he expressed noncommittal interest, she challenged him to a game. She won and was so happy with her victory that she didn't realize that he had let her win. They ended up in the bedroom, where Cleaver fumbled through sex. Besides his experiences with Axelrod, most of his sexual encounters had been violent.

The next day, as they were about to leave, Eldridge turned to Kathleen and ominously held his thumb and pointer finger up to his forehead about an inch apart and told her "I'm about this far away from being crazy."[20] Kathleen had no idea what this meant, but she figured it had something to do with prison. It was an omen of the volatile life they would share in the future.

They spent a few days in Atlanta together. Kathleen read a rough copy of *Soul on Ice* that he had brought with him. She felt that it was the most powerful piece of writing she had ever read. They carried on interminable conversations, and Cleaver realized that this was the first time he had met a black woman he felt he could talk to. By the time they returned to Nashville, they were totally in love. On April 6, Kathleen flew to Washington, DC; on the same day, a riot broke out in Nashville following the arrest of a disruptive student at a campus restaurant. Cleaver was ordered home under threat of parole revocation.

When Cleaver returned to San Francisco, he threw himself into the activities of the Black Panther Party. On April 15, 1967, he joined one of the largest antiwar protests in American history, marching with sixty-five thousand demonstrators from Market Street to Kezar Stadium. He joined Julian Bond and Coretta Scott King onstage and gave a stirring speech calling for the end of the Vietnam war.

Cleaver's speech gained the attention of his parole officer, Mr. Bilideau. The day after the rally, Cleaver was called into his office, and his rights were severely curtailed. The official report read, "These conditions restrict or forbid Mr. Cleaver from making speeches, writing certain governmental criticism, or traveling across the San Francisco Bay to the East Bay area." Cleaver was prohibited from visiting Oakland because, Bilideau claimed, it was "the center of black political turmoil." Bilideau also cautioned Cleaver against criticizing the prison system or state administration, because it would "surely anger other influential state officers, thereby accelerating the parole revocation."[21] Cleaver promised to comply, though he had no real intention of letting up. "Because I was violating neither any law of the land nor any rule of parole, upon being assured by my attorney [Axelrod] that [I] was strictly within my rights, I decided not to accept these warnings and continued exercising my right to free speech and to write what was on my mind."[22]

Cleaver quickly became an active member of the Black Panther Party. After a black construction worker named Denzil Dowell was killed by the police, he helped launch the *Black Panther: Black Community News Service* newspaper on April 25, 1967. The main headline on the first issue read, "Why Was Denzil Dowell Killed?" The Panthers threw a rally, where Cleaver, Seale, and Newton told a crowd of four hundred people that they could not trust the government or the police and that they had to arm themselves.[23] In early May, Cleaver joined a delegation of thirty Black Panthers who traveled to the state capitol to protest the Mulford Act, a gun-restriction bill that prohibited the practice of openly carrying loaded firearms on public streets. The bill repealed the right to "open carry," but only in urban areas, where the majority of black people lived. White people living in rural areas were not affected at all. The bill had been introduced as a response to the armed patrols organized by Huey Newton and the Panthers and was supported both by Governor Ronald Reagan and the NRA, both later staunch supporters of Second Amendment rights.

On the day of the so-called March on Sacramento, twenty-four men and six women from the BPP walked into the capitol armed with shotguns and M1 rifles. As per Newton's instructions, they pointed their guns in the air or at the ground so that they could not be accused of threatening anyone. They were followed by a mob of reporters, with Cleaver among the group as a member of the press, on assignment from *Ramparts*. He carried only a camera and a notepad because of his parole restrictions. Some of the Panthers entered the assembly chambers, where the legislature was in session, and Bobby Seale read Executive Mandate Number One, protesting the Mulford Act as an attempt to disarm and disempower black people.

The Panthers were eventually forced outside by the police, where Governor Ronald Reagan had been having a picnic with a group of elementary school children. He was annoyed by the protest and told reporters, "There is no reason why on the street today a citizen should be carrying loaded weapons." As Cleaver and the other Panthers departed for Oakland, they were stopped at a gas station and surrounded by police with guns drawn. Cleaver grabbed his camera and started snapping pictures. A cop singled him out. "A policeman told me to come along. I showed him my press card, identified myself as a newsman, but his response was that he was just following orders. I had no choice but to get into the paddy wagon because the police were getting both nervous and angry and I didn't want to get shot."[24] Cleaver denied that he was a Black Panther, but they arrested him anyway and charged him with "conspiracy to commit a crime." Other Panthers at the scene were arrested for obscure Fish and Wildlife violations prohibiting loaded guns in a car. Seale felt bad that Cleaver had been arrested, worried that he would lose his parole. But Cleaver wasn't bothered by it. He told Seale, "Fuck it. It was worth it, because we did it."[25]

At the Sacramento jail, Cleaver took charge. He was the only one who had been in prison before. When the cops beat up one of the Panthers, it was Cleaver who urged them to take him to the hospital. When the cops refused to feed them, he told the cops, "We're going to get some food in this motherfucker, or don't you motherfuckers never come up to this door no more because you come to this door, there's eighteen of us and maybe three, four, five, of you."[26] Two days after the arrest, Axelrod went before the court and made an impassioned plea for Cleaver's release, saying that he was not armed and had attended the event as a reporter. The charges against him by the DA were dropped.

Following the Sacramento protest, officials decided to "drastically restrict" Cleaver's privileges.[27] They limited his movements to the city limits of San Francisco, he was no longer allowed to give any speeches, and he was to keep his name and face out of the news.

A few days later, the Panthers turned their focus to expanding the *Black Panther* newspaper. Newton knew that the Mulford Act would pass, and he would have to shift tactics to organize the black community. He decided to use the newspaper as a mouthpiece for the organization. As editor, Cleaver was at first reluctant to do what he considered tedious work, but Newton convinced him that "a newspaper is the voice of a party."[28]

Cleaver and Barbara Arthur wrote the articles for the issue. The artwork was handled by Emory Douglas, another new party member who had created posters for the Betty Shabazz visit. Douglas had grown up in San Francisco, and, like Cleaver, he had been arrested for juvenile delinquency when he was young. In reform school, he was introduced to graphic design, and he mastered his craft as a commercial artist at City College of San Francisco. He brought these skills to bear on the production of the *Black Panther*, creating a unique proletarian style that would come to define the paper.

In the early days, Cleaver, Douglas, Seale, and Newton laid out the design of the paper at Axelrod's home. Cleaver bought multiple jugs of red wine, and they sometimes worked through the night to complete it. In the second issue of the newspaper—which was the first full-format issue—they published the party's Ten Point Program, as well as the now-famous photograph of Newton sitting stoically in the wicker chair with spear in one hand and gun in the other. It was the scene that Adam had created in Cleaver's room. It was also in this issue that the group starting using the symbol of the pig to represent the police. Douglas drew a woodblock picture of a pig with the caption "Support Your Local Police," and it became an instant sensation.[29]

Newton wrote a series of articles over the summer of 1967, criticizing the police as an occupying imperial force and anointing the Black Panther Party as the vanguard party of the black community. Through its bold imagery and insightful articles by Newton, Cleaver, and others, the paper brought forth issues important to the black community, including police violence and economic justice. As chapters of the Black Panther sprung up in cities all over the country in the late 1960s, sales of the paper exploded. Weekly circulation reached anywhere from 139,000 to 200,000 per week, and the paper became the main economic engine of the party.[30]

Cleaver's involvement with the Panthers, as well as his newfound feelings for Kathleen, accelerated his changing emotions toward Axelrod. He had not stopped loving her, but he felt differently toward her now that he was free. By early May 1967, Cleaver had to admit to himself that he was going to leave her. He recalled, "I felt a clean and pure emotion for Beverly, born under circumstances that tested its weight, and it was heavy. I know that it was love. It was a surpassing love. My secret was revealed to me at that moment. I wasn't going to marry Beverly Axelrod." Faced with this realization, Cleaver tried to find some middle ground with her. He suggested an open relationship, but she refused. They took LSD together in an attempt to find new solutions, but they had a bad trip. Finally, Cleaver had to face the fact that he was in love with Kathleen, and his role in the Black Panthers was incompatible with his relationship to Axelrod. He realized he had to leave her. "But it was clear to me that, given the state of opinion and the relationship between black people and white people, no black man with a white woman was going to organize many black people. For the first time, I faced the truth that I was easing out on Beverly."[31]

Axelrod was heartbroken. She had spent years of her life helping free Eldridge from prison, and now he was abandoning her. Her relationship with him represented the union of her most deeply felt personal and political aspirations. She recalled, "I felt like we were really going to have an impact on life in America—the kinds of things that we would be able to do. So it was as though everything I'd ever been or planned in my life was leading up to this, and then it all explodes. So it wasn't just the love affair, it was my whole political life, it was everything."[32]

Axelrod became deeply troubled when she realized Cleaver was not coming back to her. She threatened to commit suicide, and at one point she swallowed a handful of Benzedrine tablets.[33] Cleaver recalled, "She said she would come in front of my house and, you know, start the motor of her car and kill herself with the exhaust fumes on my doorstep, and leave a suicide note that would land me in prison for the rest of my life."[34] Axelrod on one occasion got ahold of Cleaver's gun and threatened to use it on herself in his apartment. Cleaver didn't know what to do, so he called a friend of hers named Reggie Major for help. "She's got my gun," he told Reggie over the phone. Reggie rushed right over to the apartment. As he told the story, "I get up there. Beverly is definitely depressed. And not only is she depressed, she's waving this goddamned .45 around." Reggie tried everything to get it away from her. He tried gently coaxing. He tried wrestling it away from her, but she was too strong. As they were sitting on the bed together, the gun suddenly went off in Axelrod's hands and made a massive hole in the wall. It stunned her, and she handed the gun to Reggie and left.[35] On May 7, 1967, she wrote to Cleaver, "There is not one single vestige left of the things that were the basis of our love.... The love I have is for a man that doesn't exist anymore—it is not for you as you are now."[36]

Throughout spring and early summer, Cleaver and Kathleen had been exchanging passionate love letters and phone calls. In early July, they decided she should come out for a visit. He picked her up from the airport, and Kathleen was impressed with his new look. Cleaver wore a tight-fitting black leather jacket that all the Panthers wore, and he sported a tiny gold post in his left ear. Even his walk seemed somehow different. He almost seemed to sway as he approached her. "He looked like a pirate," Kathleen thought.[37]

Cleaver took Kathleen back to his apartment on Castro Street. It was a modest setup. He had taken the green shag rug and matching green desk from Axelrod's apartment, and he kept a record player on a low table by the window. There was no bed, just a mattress on the floor. It did have a fireplace, however, and the fire escape looked out over Duboce Park to the city beyond. Kathleen was mesmerized by the neighborhood. She thought Castro Street was named after the Cuban president. *Castro Street,* she thought. *A revolutionary street.*

Summer 1967 was the "summer of love," when tens of thousands of people—college students, hippies, military personnel, artists, musicians, drug addicts, and political radicals—descended upon the Haight-Ashbury District in San Francisco. Cleaver and Kathleen immersed themselves in this world, walking through the neighborhood every day. Kathleen described the scene: "The sidewalks of Haight Street were clogged with throngs of people that summer of euphoric abandon when thousands of young people flocked into San Francisco to join the hippies. Barefoot young girls wearing loose fitting gowns, boys with long hair, baggy pants, and headbands, or cowboy hats, some people draped in blankets with feathers stuck in their hair."[38] Cleaver and Kathleen built a little home out of the small studio. Kathleen put up curtains and photos, and she decorated the bed with colorful pillows and a bedspread. Cleaver scrounged up an old oak table so that they had a place to eat. Neither he nor Kathleen really knew how to cook. He had spent his entire adult life in prison, and she had attended a boarding school. They ordered a lot of takeout from a little place down the street. They listened to jazz numbers like Donald Byrd's "Cristo Redentor" while they ate meals by candlelight.[39] They were revolutionaries in love.

Kathleen was just one of the many women who joined the Black Panther Party in summer 1967. A number of women—such as Barbara Arthur and Judy Hart—challenged the traditional gender roles in the male-dominated party by writing in the *Black Panther*. Others took part in armed demonstrations alongside male members. Kathleen herself emerged as a highly committed leader of the party, speaking at rallies, organizing demonstrations, and recruiting members. She was the first woman to serve on the Panthers' Central Committee, and she was a model for other Panthers dedicated to the cause.

Cleaver soon asked her to marry him. "I had no doubt that Eldridge was the man with whom I wanted to spend the rest of my life," Kathleen later reflected. "We thought alike, we were both committed to the black revolution, and we loved each other deeply."[40] On August 2, 1967, Cleaver requested retention of his civil rights to marry Kathleen. The parole board was surprisingly encouraging. "S's current fiancée, Ms. Neal, appears as a mature young lady eager to assist him in his career. It is felt marriage might exert a stabilizing influence on S. Approval is being recommended."[41]

Even as Cleaver attempted to start his new life with Kathleen, he was still maintaining contact with Axelrod. She sometimes parked in front of his apartment and sat in her car for long periods. She called the apartment repeatedly, and he would sometimes spend hours talking with her. One day, Kathleen discovered the stack of letters that he and Axelrod had written one another while he was in prison. When she read through them and realized the intensity of their connection, she was devastated. She also found the religious medal that Axelrod had had made for him with their initials engraved on it. She confronted Eldridge about the letters and the jewelry. As she remembered it, "I grabbed that tarnished pendant off the closet shelf, darted past Eldridge and flung it out the kitchen window. He stood there stunned for a second, and then leaped to stop me, but by the time he grabbed my hand the pendant was flying toward the sidewalk."[42]

This conflict led to the first time Cleaver physically assaulted Kathleen. One night, after he had been talking with Axelrod on the phone, Kathleen decided that she had had enough. "When he asked me to go downstairs to get the mail, I snapped back that he ought to ask Beverly Axelrod to go get it. He stared at me for a second, his eyes glinting in rage, and then slammed his fist into my face. I reeled back, stunned, and then ran out of the living room crying."[43] The bruise around her eye was so bad that she wore sunglasses for weeks to cover it. When she told him later that she would not tolerate him treating her that way, he replied, "If you don't like it, you'll have to get something to stop me."[44]

A few days later, when Cleaver threatened her again, she pulled his .45 from the desk drawer and pointed it at him. She wasn't going to shoot; she just didn't want him to hit her again. Realizing that Kathleen wasn't going to pull the trigger, he knocked the gun out of her hand and slapped her across the face. These were the first of many such abuses that Kathleen would endure throughout their marriage.

In mid-October, James Baldwin passed through the Bay Area as a part of a lecture tour for the Congress of Racial Equality (CORE). Reggie Major was friends with Baldwin and talked him into meeting Cleaver. Baldwin was reluctant to meet, as Cleaver had viciously attacked him for his homosexuality in "Notes on a Native Son." In that essay Cleaver had written, "Homosexuality is a sickness, just as are baby-rape or wanting to become the head of General Motors."[45] Major insisted Cleaver would be cool, and Baldwin agreed to meet.

On a Friday evening, they met up and walked over to a party at Connie's West-Indian Restaurant. Cleaver had been feeling anxious about meeting Baldwin, so he brought along Huey Newton. Baldwin and Newton became fast friends, feeding off of one another's manic, intellectual energy. As they all walked down Haight Street, people rushed up to Baldwin to get his autograph. Meanwhile, Cleaver quietly stayed off to the side, too embarrassed to talk to Baldwin. As Major put it, "Eldridge was sorta shit kicking. First time I'd seen it. He had talked all that shit, and he just couldn't face Baldwin."[46]

Cleaver was ashamed, not only for what he had written, but also for what was probably his attraction to Baldwin. As Newton remembered it, "When we arrived, Cleaver and Baldwin walked into each other, and the giant, six-foot-three-inch Cleaver bent down and engaged in a long, passionate French kiss with the tiny (barely five feet) Baldwin. I was astounded at Cleaver's behavior because it so graphically contradicted his scathing written attack on Baldwin's homosexuality in his article 'Notes on a Native Son.' I later expressed my surprise to Cleaver, who pleaded that I not relay this incident to anyone."[47] Despite the outspoken homophobia present in his writings, Cleaver had a complicated relationship with same-sex desire. For Cleaver, homoerotic desire and queer panic were competing parts of his personality. His virulent homophobia toward Baldwin was not simply an expression of disgust; it was also an attempt to mask his erotic feelings for him and for men more generally.

Two weeks later, on October 28, 1967, Newton was pulled over by the Oakland police. The cops carried lists of license-plate numbers of cars owned by the Panthers, and they constantly harassed them. What happened at the scene is a matter of dispute, but after a gun battle, Officer John Frey was dead and Newton was shot in the stomach. Newton made it to Kaiser Hospital, where he was handcuffed to the bed and tortured by officers. For the murder of Frey, Newton faced the death penalty.

Cleaver committed himself to freeing Newton. Even though it endangered his parole, he felt Newton was the key to the liberation of black people. He decided that "staying out of jail [was] not as important as Huey Newton staying out of the gas chamber." On November 23, 1967, he wrote an editorial for the *Black Panther* entitled, "Huey Newton Must Be Set Free." In it, he called for armed self-defense against the police. "Every week, from every corner of America, we hear the reports of how some cop has shot and killed some black man, woman or child. We are sick and tired of hearing such news and we don't want to hear any more. The only way that it can be from now on is that there will be no more reports of black people being massacred or we want to hear more reports about more dead cops shot down by black men."[48] Cleaver cultivated relationships with white radical groups, using his connections with *Ramparts* to form alliances with anti-war demonstrators as well as the leftist Peace and Freedom Party. They agreed to agitate for Huey Newton's freedom in exchange for black votes for the Peace and Freedom candidates. Cleaver coined the slogan "Free Huey or the Sky's the Limit," which became the rallying cry of the new coalition.

In late 1967, the FBI had started taking notice of the Black Panthers, which it characterized as the "greatest internal threat to the security of the country." In late August, FBI director J. Edgar Hoover sent a memo to his field offices across the country announcing the creation of a new counterintelligence program. "The purpose of this new counterintelligence endeavor," he wrote, "is to expose, disrupt, misdirect, discredit, or otherwise neutralize the activities of black nationalist, hate-type organizations and groupings, their leadership, spokesmen, membership, and supporters and to counter their propensity for violence and civil disorder."[49] He encouraged his agents to be "enthusiastic and imaginative" in this endeavor and promised monetary incentives to reward innovative approaches to neutralizing the Panthers.[50]

FBI agents took various actions against the Black Panthers. They kept tabs on all Panther events, compiling lists of who attended, what was said, and what was planned. In their reports, agents summarized activities, located specific targets, proposed counterintelligence actions, and even created a "Rabble Rouser index." They passed along their reports to local police and intelligence agencies, as well as the army, navy, air force, and United States attorney general, and they coordinated with local police departments to raid Panther events. Agents also created a "ghetto informant program," which trained black men and women to spy on the Panthers and other radical groups. The FBI also created internal conflicts within the party through anonymous letters and set off deadly violence between the Panthers and rival groups, like US (United Slaves) Organization.[51]

By November 16, 1967, the FBI had compiled a sixty-page report about the BPP, containing detailed information about officers and membership, the location of headquarters, the content of speeches, and connections to other militant organizations. Agents tracked their purchases of guns, alarm clocks, electric fencing, and anything else that might be used to create a weapon.[52] The FBI also began to follow Cleaver. It placed him on the Security Index and tracked his movements. When Cleaver flew to Manhattan in the fall to talk with McGraw-Hill about the publication of *Soul on Ice*, the FBI field office in San Francisco wrote to the New York office to warn of his arrival. "Subject has close contacts with Negro militant organizations in this area. He may possibly contact black nationalist leaders while in New York."[53]

In December, Eldridge and Kathleen moved to an apartment at 850 Oak Street, near the Haight-Ashbury District. It was a much larger apartment than Cleaver's last one. They were so busy with the campaign to free Newton that they hardly had time to fix up the apartment at all. They hung up prints of Emory Douglas's revolutionary drawings as well as a poster of SNCC Chairman H. Rap Brown, built bookshelves from concrete blocks and some lumber, and made a makeshift couch out of a mattress and a few pillows.

On Christmas, Cleaver and Kathleen drove to Los Angeles to spend the day with Thelma and the Cleaver family. When Cleaver announced to his mother over dinner that he was getting married, Thelma joked with Kathleen, "Watch out. Eldridge likes big money." A few days later, Cleaver took Kathleen down to Central Avenue—a few miles down the boulevard from where he had grown up—to locate a wedding chapel. He found a small stucco building with a blue sign that read WEDDING CHAPEL. Kathleen was disappointed. Cleaver had sprung it on her at the last minute, and they were dressed in casual clothes. The only witnesses were Bunchy Carter, Cleaver's comrade from Soledad, and his brother Arthur Glen Morris. Worst of all, Cleaver had not even bought a ring. He asked Kathleen to borrow the gold ring her father had given her years earlier.[54]

Kathleen had her reasons for marrying Cleaver, despite his insensitivity and physical abuse. She was a true revolutionary, and she wanted to be with someone who was as committed to the cause as she was. As she explained, "I was afraid marriage would have completely inhibited my participation in the Movement. That fear dissolved completely when I fell in love with Eldridge, for he wanted a wife who would be as committed to the black revolution as he was. Our interests, desires, and political beliefs coincided perfectly—and we had enjoyed almost immediately an exhilarating communication we knew was rare."[55] Kathleen was young, idealistic, and deeply committed to the struggle for black freedom. She was even willing to bear Cleaver's violence for the sake of the movement. Her love for Cleaver and her love for the cause were one and the same. At Christmas, she composed a poem that expressed her feelings:

> My love for you
> runs endless like a stream.
> Into the deeper currents
> of the broad rivers of my love.[56]

With Newton now in jail, Cleaver was emerging as a leader of the party. He was appointed the minister of information, a title that he downplayed as a "courtesy title" when interrogated by his parole officer.[57] Cleaver was older than most of the Panthers by ten years. Through his time in prison, he had taught himself history, literature, and politics. He was equally comfortable discussing the finer points of guerrilla warfare as he was talking about the theoretical intricacies of Marx. He was widely respected by the young people of the party, including a young lieutenant named David Hilliard, who admired

Cleaver for using education to save himself from prison. He said, "There's no one more self-taught than Eldridge. He was left to destroy himself in prison. Instead he has mastered language and made the entire society listen to him."[58] The Panthers also respected him because of his criminal background, which he had not entirely disavowed. At one Panther meeting, Cleaver said to Panther members that they "should feel justified to rob, steal, and, if necessary, to kill in order to get what they need to the support of their organization."[59] Many Panthers called him "Papa Rage."

Cleaver advanced the party in a number of ways. He helped organize the first Panther chapter outside of Oakland, enlisting Bunchy Carter to start a Los Angeles branch. Carter recruited regular members and special cadets for an underground wing of the party. It was the starting point of Cleaver's involvement in organizing a secret force that could be used to fight white power structures. He also gave a number of speeches in support of Huey, criticizing white society and calling for a revolution. "Ours is a struggle against Community Imperialism," he told crowds. "Our black communities are colonized and controlled from outside, and it is this control that has to be smashed, broken, shattered, by whatever means necessary. The politics in our communities are controlled from outside, the economics of our communities are controlled from outside, and we ourselves are controlled by the racist police who come into our communities from outside and occupy them, patrolling, terrorizing, and brutalizing our people like a foreign army in a conquered land."[60] In mid-January, he gave a speech at the Alameda County Courthouse. The Panthers made huge posters that read COME SEE ABOUT HUEY, displayed while they played the Supremes hit "Come See About Me." They gave out hundreds of leaflets, covering Berkeley and Oakland with them.[61]

Cleaver continued his work publishing the *Black Panther*. In January 1968, he helped transform it from a monthly to a weekly and used it to protest Newton's incarceration. Cleaver, Kathleen, and Emory Douglas were a solid team. Cleaver wrote the articles, Douglas created the art, and Kathleen handled the administrative details. Douglas created bold images that represented black people carrying guns and pigs dressed up like police officers. They laid out the proofs at Kathleen and Eldridge's apartment, often working late into the night when against deadlines.

Cleaver's work with the party began attracting the attention of law enforcement. On January 15, 1968, at 3:30 in the morning, the Special Tactical Squad of the San Francisco Police Department banged on his door. "Police! Open up," they yelled. Cleaver knew that he didn't have to let them in without a warrant, so he stated, "I'm not letting you in." They threatened to kick in the door, to which Cleaver replied, "Well, you are going to have to kick the door in then."[62] The police knocked the door off its hinges. "Suddenly, at least five tall white men wearing heavy, navy blue uniforms and high, black leather boots stormed into our apartment, their long guns pointed at us," Kathleen recalled. "Two of them leaped past the front door they kicked down, and others climbed through the kitchen window in the back. They blitzed through the bedroom, the living room, and the dining room yanking drawers open, looking under the bed, under the sofa, in the closets."[63] These cops were part of the city's new tactical squad, and they wore shoulder holsters in addition to their regular sidearms. Some carried .357 magnums, which they pointed at the Cleaver and Douglas. They ransacked the apartment, looking for weapons and drugs. When Cleaver asked why they were there, they claimed there had been a burglary in the area committed by someone who matched Cleaver's description. Three days after the incident, Cleaver hired civil rights lawyer Charles Geary to sue the police and bring charges against the officers.[64] The FBI did an inquiry, but nothing ever came of it. In response, Huey Newton issued Executive Mandate Number Three, stating that all Panthers had to buy guns to defend against the police. He recommended that each Panther should own a shotgun, a .357 magnum, and a .38 pistol.

After this incident, the harassment only increased. Cleaver's phone rang at night, but when he answered it, no one was there. Cleaver was followed. On occasion, he spotted a car tailing him from three cars back. He recounted it later: "I was constantly followed about by persons whom I assumed were agents of the Federal Bureau of Investigation. I became afraid that they intended to kill me, and on many occasions, would not sleep at home, but rather seek out other residences where I felt they would be unable to locate me. Despite my best efforts, however, these people were constantly on my tail."[65] When he arrived at a location, someone would call him on the phone and say, "Thought you could shake us, didn't you, Eldridge?"

The day after the police kicked down his door, he gathered together seventeen Panthers to brainstorm ideas for how to retaliate against the police. As FBI informants recorded, "For publicity purposes, the BPPSD plans to get about two hundred Negro males, including several BPPSD members, to file into the Hall of Justice building in Oakland, California, and demand that Chief of Police Charles Gain give them applications for employment with the Oakland Police Department for police officer positions."[66] In late February, the FBI got ahold of all the phone numbers Cleaver had called from his apartment between December 12 and December 25. Agents followed him when he visited Newton in jail, opened his mail, and sent informants to monitor all meetings he attended. At Cleaver's apartment in February, informants made note of the people present, the weapons they carried, and the plans they made.[67] As the Black Panthers started to build a relationship with SNCC, the FBI called Stokely Carmichael's mother to warn her that the Panthers were going to kill her son.

As he emerged as a leader of the party, Cleaver enlarged his ambitious plan of building black and white political coalitions. On February 17, Cleaver and the Panthers held a rally for Newton's twenty-sixth birthday, where they announced a merger with SNCC. The mood was electric at the event, with over five thousand people in attendance. Many people dressed in African clothing, and the Duncan Company Dancers troupe danced to drums that echoed through the auditorium. The Panthers set up the wicker chair from the Newton photograph in the middle of the stage to represent his presence. A range of black and white radicals and politicians attended the rally, with speakers including city councilman Ron Dellums, Bobby Seale, Bunchy Carter, Ron Karanga of US Organization, and SNCC leaders H. Rap Brown, Stokely Carmichael, and James Forman. Cleaver, the master of ceremonies, captivated the crowd while reading Claude McKay's militant poem, "If We Must Die." He conferred the title of honorary prime minister on Stokely Carmichael, minister of foreign affairs on James Forman, and minister of justice on H. Rap Brown. It was a symbolic changing of the guards. As an organization, SNCC was starting to collapse. It had been created during the height of the civil rights movement, and because that era was on the wane, SNCC was left without a constituency or institutional framework. The ceremony marked the rise of Cleaver and the Panthers in national politics. The Black Panther Party was now the vanguard party of the black working class.[68]

Cleaver continued to build relationships with the Peace and Freedom Party, a left-wing socialist organization of white radicals newly founded by *Ramparts* editor Robert Scheer. It was organized around anti-war, free speech, and anti-racist issues. Although the Panthers did not allow white people to join their organization, through the Peace and Freedom Party they did encourage coalitions with them. As a Leninist-Marxist, Cleaver himself rejected separatist black politics and saw black-and-white alliances as necessary for the revolution against capitalism. Cleaver forged a relationship with the Peace and Freedom Party, talking them into donating a truck and $3,000 in exchange for black votes in the 1968 election.[69]

In late February 1968, *Soul on Ice* hit the bookstores. Just weeks before, Cleaver and Axelrod had come to an agreement about royalties. Because he felt guilty, and because he owed her a debt of gratitude, Cleaver offered her half the royalties. Axelrod refused his gesture, wanting him to keep the lion's share. On Valentine's Day, 1968, they signed a contract that would give her 25 percent of all royalties for *Soul on Ice,* which included book and serial form as well as motion-picture and television rights "of every nature and description, throughout the world."[70] *Soul on Ice* was an instant success. An additional three hundred thousand copies were printed by the end of first month. It sold two million copies in the first few years of publication and was named by the *New York Times* as one of the top-ten books of the year.

Soul on Ice stunned critics; many praised it as an important diagnosis of race relations. *Time* magazine wrote of Cleaver, "He is an authentically gifted prose stylist capable of evoking picturesque images and fiery moods. *Soul on Ice* is a collection of impassioned letters and heated essays lamenting the fact that American 'negritude' has been forced to cool it for too long: the book points prophetically and menacingly at the new world that had better be coming soon."[71] *Publishers Weekly* called it "grim, bitterly funny, tense, emotional, and intellectually arresting," while Shane Stevens of the *Progressive* compared it to Dante's *Inferno*.[72] Critics were drawn to the rawness and anger of Cleaver's writing. The *New York Times Book Review* called *Soul on Ice* "an enraged statement of Negro revolt," while Robert Hughes argued in the *Spectator*, "*Soul on Ice* . . . is worth a thousand white papers prepared on 'the problem' by Washington sociologists. It is a deeply invigorating, challenging book: what is more, it is, I believe, one of the rare books without which our history—let alone our future—cannot be understood."[73]

Not everyone, of course, loved Cleaver's book. Some white critics predictably bristled at Cleaver's confrontational politics. Robert Coles complained in the pages of the *Atlantic Monthly*, "I don't like the way he lumps all white men together, and I'm sick and tired of a rhetoric that takes three hundred years of complicated, tortured American history and throws it in the face of every single white man alive today."[74] More significant were the feminist critics who criticized the book's misogyny and seemingly prorape stance. Even though Cleaver unequivocally rejected rape as a revolutionary act in *Soul on Ice*, many believed that his book still endorsed it. In Susan Brownmiller's influential history of rape, *Against Our Will: Men, Women and Rape*, she challenged Cleaver's formulation of rape as a political gesture. And in Michele Wallace's acclaimed volume of black feminist criticism, *Black Macho and the Myth of the Superwoman*, she took issue with Cleaver's representation of black women more broadly. "The black woman, who is at the white women's knees, under the black man's heel, and gets the black man's hand, he described as an Amazon. What warrior would have put up with that kind of abuse?"[75]

Cleaver became a national celebrity. In New York, McGraw-Hill threw a book party for him at the Algonquin Hotel, where he and Kathleen rubbed elbows with Max Geismar, Norman Mailer, and other writers from the literary left. In late March, he went to Chicago to appear on *The Irv Kupcinet Show* on television. When he returned home to the West Coast, Marlon Brando arranged to meet Cleaver to discuss the screenplay for *Queimada* (a.k.a. *Burn!*), the story of a nineteenth-century black revolution. Brando wanted advice from someone he considered a real revolutionary. Cleaver was suddenly part of the zeitgeist of America. His most famous slogan, which had actually been created by Kathleen, was now everywhere. Max Geismar remembered, "In the town of Mamaroneck near Westchester, I saw—though I can hardly believe it still—a United States mail truck with another Cleaverism plastered on the outside: 'If you are not part of the solution you are part of the problem.'"[76]

10

REBELLION (1968)

In late March, Huey Newton ordered his lieutenants to break him out of the Oakland jail, an imposing twelve-story spire located on the edge of Chinatown, where he was held on the top floor. Axelrod was Newton's lawyer, and she brought word to Panther field marshall Donald Cox. He and other Panthers formulated a plan: on the day of the breakout, Axelrod would take the elevator to the top floor and distract the guards. Meanwhile, Cox and the Panthers would run up the twelve flights of stairs, and Axelrod would let them in through a side door. They would crawl past the guard station on the floor, enter the visitation room, and free Newton. Cox and the other Panthers started running stairs to get into shape. Charles Geary insisted that he could free Huey through the court system, but Cox and Axelrod continued with their plans. A few days before they were going to free Huey, everything changed.

Cleaver and Axelrod. *Courtesy of Lani Kask*

Cleaver in February 1967, just before he joined the Black Panther Party. *Courtesy of Lani Kask*

With Bunchy Carter in 1968.
Courtesy of the Bancroft Library

Eldridge Cleaver smokes a cigarette on a stage at American University, where he addressed crowds on October 18, 1968. *Bettman/Getty Images*

Cleaver for president poster

In Cuba in 1969.
Courtesy of the Bancroft Library

Eldridge and Kathleen Cleaver attend the Pan-African Festival in June 1969. *Photo by Bruno Barbey*

Giving a press conference in Algeria in June 1969, while Julia Herve translates. *Courtesy of the Bancroft Library*

Eldridge Cleaver and Stokley Carmichael discuss Marxism versus black nationalism at the Hotel St. George during the Pan-African Festival. *Photo by Guy Le Querrec*

Cleaver and members of the American People's Anti-Imperialist Delegation protest US imperialism at the border separating North Korea and South Korea. *Courtesy of the Bancroft Library*

Cleaver and the American People's Anti-Imperialist Delegation in Vietnam in 1970. *Courtesy of the Bancroft Library*

Cleaver gives the black power salute while visiting in Vietnam in 1970. *Courtesy of the Bancroft Library*

Eldridge Cleaver and Elaine Brown in China in 1970. *Courtesy of the Bancroft Library*

The former site of the International Section of the Black Panter Party in Algiers, Algeria. *Justin Gifford*

With unknown companions in Algeria. *Courtesy of the Bancroft Library*

Cleaver displays his new Cleavers pants in Paris. St. Eustache reflects in the window. *Photo by Rene Burri*

Eldridge Cleaver and Kathleen Cleaver in Paris, making arrangements to come back to the United States. *Courtesy of the Bancroft Library*

Eldridge Cleaver in jail after he returned to the United States in 1975. *Courtesy of the Bancroft Library.*

Cleaver shows off his controversial pants in his Los Angeles shop. *Courtesy of the Bancroft Library*

Cleaver and Reverend Vincent Thompson survey the land near Lake Lahontan in 1979. Cleaver planned to build a ministry and compound there. *Courtesy of the Bancroft Library*

Cleaver and the 4th of July organization in the early 1980s. *Courtesy of the Bancroft Library*

Eldridge Cleaver gets into an argument with a protester at one of his speeches in the early 1980s. *Courtesy of the Bancroft Library*

Fading from political activism and public view, Eldridge Cleaver starts an illegal recycling business in the late 1980s. *MediaNews Group/Oakland Tribune via Getty Images*

WANTED BY THE FBI

INTERSTATE FLIGHT - ASSAULT WITH INTENT TO COMMIT MURDER

LEROY ELDRIDGE CLEAVER

FBI No. 214,830 B

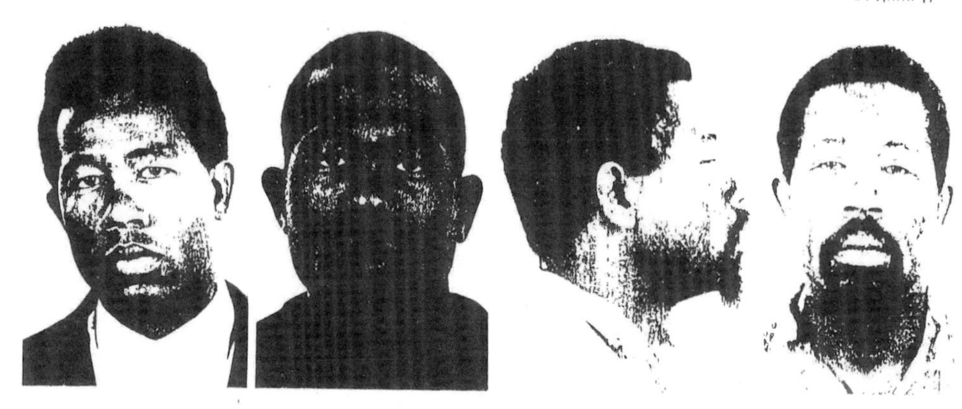

Photograph taken 1966 Photographs taken 1968

Aliases: Eldridge Cleaver, Leroy Eldridge Cleaver, J

May All Your Dreams Come True!

Eldridge Cleaver

DESCRIPTION

Age:	33, born August 31, 1935, Little Rock, Arkansas		
Height:	6' 2"	**Eyes:**	Brown
Weight:	185 to 195 pounds	**Complexion:**	Medium
Build:	Medium	**Race:**	Negro
Hair:	Black	**Nationality:**	American
Occupations:	Author, clerk, laborer, magazine editor, reporter, writer		
Scars and Marks:	Numerous pock scars on back		
Remarks:	Sometimes wears small gold earring in pierced left ear lobe		

Fingerprint Classification: 24 L 13 U OOM 19
1 2 U 001

CRIMINAL RECORD

Cleaver has been convicted of assault with intent to commit murder, assault with a deadly weapon and possession of narcotics.

CAUTION

CLEAVER ALLEGEDLY HAS ENGAGED POLICE OFFICERS IN GUN BATTLE IN THE PAST. CONSIDER ARMED AND EXTREMELY DANGEROUS.

A Federal warrant was issued on December 10, 1968, at San Francisco, California, charging Cleaver with unlawful interstate flight to avoid confinement after conviction for assault with intent to commit murder (Title 18, U. S. Code, Section 1073).

IF YOU HAVE ANY INFORMATION CONCERNING THIS PERSON, PLEASE NOTIFY ME OR CONTACT YOUR LOCAL FBI OFFICE. TELEPHONE NUMBERS AND ADDRESSES OF ALL FBI OFFICES LISTED ON BACK.

J. Edgar Hoover
DIRECTOR
FEDERAL BUREAU OF INVESTIGATION
UNITED STATES DEPARTMENT OF JUSTICE
WASHINGTON, D. C. 20535
TELEPHONE, NATIONAL 8-7117

Wanted Flyer 447
December 13, 1968

FBI Poster of Eldridge Cleaver. At the end of his life, Cleaver autographed copies for fans after his speeches with slogans like "May all your dreams come true" and "I faced the guns of the oppressor."

On April 4, 1968, Martin Luther King was assassinated in Memphis at the Lorraine Hotel. His murder triggered the largest uprising in American history since the Civil War, as riots broke out in over one hundred cities.[1] It was chaos at the Panther office. Cleaver recalled later, "And niggers was mad, niggers had come all [the way] from San Jose and all kinds of places down there and they came directly to the office of the Black Panther Party and they wanted guns. . . . All kind of jive motherfuckers came, motherfuckers came in the office with a box of dynamite, a motherfucker came in with some guns, but the majority of the people there wanted guns, they wanted some direction, and they wanted some blood, they wanted some pig blood because Dr. Martin Luther King had been murdered by racist Babylon."[2] Like Newton, Cleaver didn't believe rioting solved anything, so he didn't just hand out the guns. But Cleaver did believe in retaliation, and he believed that attacking the police could spark a revolution. "Then what we was going to do is go down there in the area where Huey Newton had had the shootout with the cops, and we would get out of the cars, get on foot, and then we'd find ourselves some cops, kill them, and just let it start. And then brothers in L.A. was going to start. People in San Francisco was going to start, and we were just going to make this the unleashing of attack[s] upon the cops."[3]

Cleaver recruited members for the assault and collected weapons. Tensions were high at Panther headquarters the day before the attack. At one point, an older African American man came to the headquarters on 4421 Grove Street and showed a badge, claiming he was a San Francisco police officer. He said was willing to be a double agent for the Panthers and a pipeline for information. He appeared to be drunk. An FBI informant on the scene recorded the interaction: "He told Eldridge Cleaver that the Oakland Police Department was planning to start genocide on the BPP. Cleaver immediately became aroused and said, 'We'll take care of that, we'll get them first.'"[4] The identity of this individual was never revealed. Whether he was another informant, a police officer, or an everyday citizen was never made clear. But this incident set the stage for the deadly confrontation to come.

Cleaver went around picking up weapons from stash houses in

anticipation of the ambush. He wrote in his unpublished book *Uptight in Babylon*, "I was to drive to a friend's house, pick up an AR15 rifle, and transport it across the Bay Bridge, to Oakland, where it was to be used, that very night, against whatever member of the Oakland Police Department happened to appear before its sights."[5] By the evening, the platoon of Panthers was well-armed and ready for combat.

On the night of April 6, a group of Panthers—Bobby Hutton, Warren Wells, Wendell Wade, John L. Scott, Charles Bursey, David Hilliard, Donnell Lankford, and Terry Cotton—loaded themselves into three cars and headed to a small neighborhood near the Oakland waterfront, a beat for the Oakland police. Cleaver, in the lead car, planned to ambush any cops coming down the street. As soon as they pulled up to the curb, police officers Nolan Darnell and Richard Jenson came around the corner in a cruiser. Like other Oakland police officers, they had been given a list of vehicles owned by the Black Panthers. The officers pulled up next to the second car and started checking the list. One of the Panthers from the trailing car panicked and ran up to Cleaver's window asking what he should do. Cleaver barked at him, "Man, don't you think we can see the pigs? That's what we came over here for. Looking for the pigs. Get back to your post."

Cleaver started the assault. "I said OK, man, let's do it. I had a machine gun. I got out of the car on this side and r-r-r-r-r- and started shooting at the two cops in the car. Then the other guys, naturally they going to go in action when they hear this shit."[6] Panthers fired shotguns and handguns at point blank range into the cop car. Forensics later revealed that forty-nine bullets had been fired into the car. Jensen was hit nine times but somehow survived. At that moment, police reinforcements showed up and began firing on the Panthers. Cleaver could hear the bullets whizzing by his head as the cops shot at him. He made a run for the alley with Bobby Hutton, and they broke into the basement of a house at 1218 Twenty-Eighth Street.[7] Hutton was only seventeen years old, the first member of the party recruited by Seale and Newton. Cleaver and Hutton stationed themselves at the window next to the basement door and began firing out the window. Cops took up positions in front of the house and from the windows of nearby houses. Over the next ninety minutes, they unloaded two thousand rounds into the house. The only thing that saved Cleaver and Hutton was an eighteen-inch foundation that served as a shield. The owner of the house survived by hiding in the bathtub.

As the firefight wore on, the situation became increasingly precarious for Cleaver and Hutton. The cops shot gas canisters into the basement. One hit Cleaver in the chest, and it hurt so bad, he thought he had been shot. They took off his shirt to check for bleeding, but there was only a bruise where he had been struck. Cleaver was shot in the foot and was bleeding badly. The house caught on fire from the barrage of gas canisters. As the fire moved closer, Cleaver called out to the cops, "We're going to burn up in here."[8] Cleaver and Hutton contemplated what to do next. Cleaver remembered, "[Hutton] said he could see that if we stayed in here like this we going to die and so we discussed whether we just make it like a suicide rush out there and just kill every cop we could and fuck it or just stay in here and shoot out like we were doing or surrender." They decided to surrender.

The cops told them to throw out their guns. Hutton came out first, then Cleaver, stripped naked. The police took them into custody and beat them as they dragged them to the front of the house. A police officer told Cleaver to run to the paddy wagon parked on the street. He refused, pointing at the bullet wound in his leg. "So he looks at my leg, and then he saw all the blood and shit, and, the son of a bitch, he kicked me—he kicked my leg—and then he stomped my foot. And then he hit me on the head with his gun, and then he knocked me down, and then while I was down they turned to Bobby. And they just shoved him, man, shoved him down the sidewalk, and they shot him twelve times and killed him."[9]

The neighbors who were standing on their lawns yelled out "Murderers!" when they saw the cops shoot Hutton. Although the police claimed that Hutton had tried to run, various witnesses, and even one of the cops, disputed this claim.[10] According to the County of Alameda's coroner's report, Hutton died of "gunshot wounds involving both thighs, back, left arm, right chest, neck, and head." The official cause of death was "shock and hemorrhage due to gunshot wounds."

After the cops killed Hutton, they dragged Cleaver to the paddy wagon. When they called in, he shouted his name to the dispatcher over and over again to make sure the dispatcher knew he was in custody. He was afraid the police were going to kill him in a dark alley somewhere.

The police took Cleaver to the California State Medical Facility at Vacaville, where they continued to beat him, even shoving him down a flight of stairs. The nurses eventually intervened and treated Cleaver's wounds. "We had so much tear gas on us, the people's eyes started burning when they brought us in. The sister did the best she could, she was washing all over my body, trying to get that gas out, which was in my hair, my beard, and my groin. All the skin was off my groin for three or four weeks."[11]

When Kathleen got to the hospital to visit him, she was shocked at what she saw. He was hardly recognizable. "Eldridge looked like a captured giant, cuts and scratches on his face, his hair burned off the top of his head, his foot covered by a huge white bandage. When the guard wheeled him into the room, I could see that Eldridge's eyes were swollen, his face puffy, and his beard was matted."[12]

When he was questioned by the police, Cleaver lied about everything. He told them that the police had fired on him and the other Panthers first after he stopped to urinate in front of his car. As a practice, the Panthers refused to take responsibility for any illegal actions taken against the police. Said Cleaver, "We always denied everything that we did. Even when they would come and catch us with guns blazing, we'd plead not guilty. Consequently, the cops got worse of a name than they deserved, because even when they were innocent we blamed them, because that was just a propaganda technique. You never admit fault."[13]

The next morning, Cleaver's parole was revoked for possession of a firearm, associating with individuals of bad reputation, failure to cooperate with a parole agent, and failure "to conduct himself as a good citizen."[14] The city council and mayor congratulated the policemen involved and decried the Panthers for causing anarchy. Despite the failure of the mission and the tragic death of Hutton, Cleaver felt that shooting it out with the police was one of the most significant moments of his life. He admitted years later, "I will tell anybody that that was the first experience of freedom I ever had."[15]

While Cleaver sat in Vacaville County Jail, the Panthers mourned Bobby Hutton by mobilizing. At the site of the shootout, people brought flowers. On April 11, 1968, Kathleen wrote Cleaver to tell him of various events they had planned in response to Hutton's death. She organized a press conference, funeral, courthouse march, and a rally at Vacaville, where Cleaver was being held. "Exhausted, dazed, wasted—we're all here in the pad finalizing and planning the day tomorrow, the Bobby Hutton–Eldridge Cleaver day."[16]

On the day of the funeral, 1,500 people, about half black people and half white people, gathered at the park beside Lake Merritt. Kathleen made a poster from a picture of Hutton wearing a newspaper boy's cap and smiling broadly at the camera. Marlon Brando attended the funeral and said that he would work to inform white people about the problem of police violence. "I'm here to try to dig it," he told the crowd. Other celebrities showed up, including James Baldwin, Ossie Davis, and Susan Sontag. After the rally, a caravan of buses and cars drove up to Vacaville to protest Eldridge's incarceration.

The police tried everything to pin the attempted murder of Darnell and Jenson on Cleaver. They threatened his accomplices, trying to get them to sign guilty confessions. Two days after the shooting, Sergeant Stevenson and his partner questioned Warren William Wells, who had been involved in the shooting. He demanded a lawyer, but they refused. As Wells stated in his affidavit, "They said they wanted a statement from me to prove that Cleaver's statement was not true. They told me that if I did not cooperate with them and give them the statement that they wanted, they had the power to see that Eldridge Cleaver and I would be convicted of the murder of Bobby Hutton and that we would both be sent to the gas chamber." They promised him a misdemeanor gun charge if he cooperated. After three hours of questioning, Wells finally caved and signed a document that he wasn't even allowed to read. "About fifteen minutes after the two officers left my room, I was told by the officers guarding me that they heard that I had been charged with assault to commit murder and that my bail had been set at $40,000."[17]

The other Panthers in custody reported similar treatment. Donnell Lankford stated that Stevenson intimidated him with threats. "I then made a statement because I was frightened, and to get rid of him and wanted him to stop bothering me, but the things I said in that statement were not true."[18] Another Panther, Charles Bursey, reported, "But he said if I didn't make a statement, he would personally see to it that I would be charged with an assault to commit murder."[19] Terry Cotton testified that the police sent in a cop posing as a lawyer to try to get him to make false statements against his friends.[20] Wendell Wade stated that a police officer pulled out a gun and pointed it at him: "And then he pulled out a snub nosed pistol and asked if the gun I had was loaded and would shoot and said 'my gun can shoot, too.' During all this he was pointing the gun right into my face. He then asked me more questions. I then signed the statement he had written without reading it because I was afraid he would shoot me if I didn't."[21]

On April 24, a grand jury indicted five Panthers on two counts of attempted murder and two counts of assault. Cleaver was indicted on three counts of each. There were no prints found on the guns matching the suspects. The AR-15 that Cleaver had used was so burnt from the fire that it also did not have prints. None of the officers could identify any of the men shooting at them, but based on the forced confessions of the Panthers, the grand jury felt there was enough evidence to indict. Cotton and Lankford were eventually acquitted on all charges. Wendell Wade was acquitted but was later sent to San Quentin for five years for robbery. Wells was given a fifteen-year sentence in the state prison for assault by an all-white jury, while Bursey was given a one-to-fifteen-year sentence. John Scott jumped bail.

The FBI worried that Cleaver's activities signaled a growing influence over radical elements in the black power movement. As early as February 29, 1968, the FBI urged agents to "prevent the rise of a leader who might unify and electrify these violence-prone elements, prevent these militants from gaining respectability and prevent the growth of these groups among America's youth." Following the shootout, the FBI moved Cleaver up on its list of priority targets. On April 18, 1968, it added him to the "Rabble Rouser/Agitator Index,"[22] and a month later, the FBI director gave the San Francisco branch permission to review all telephone calls from Cleaver's phone "to identify other black nationalists with whom Cleaver may be in contact."[23] Central headquarters scolded FBI informants for failing to uncover Cleaver's plan beforehand, and it even harassed news agencies like the *Sun Reporter* for not doing enough to cast the Panthers in a negative light. In early June, the FBI Central Office advised the special agent in charge in San Francisco: "You should continue to obtain details concerning the subject's arrests, it being noted that he had narcotic and burglary arrests in Los Angeles between 1950 and 1954 in view of the prominence of the subject in the Black Panther Party. Such data should be obtained for information and for possible future use."

At the same time he was under increased surveillance, there was an outpouring of public support for Cleaver. The confrontation with the police earned him notoriety as a real revolutionary and exposed him to the public in bigger ways. The International Committee to Defend Eldridge Cleaver was created to support his legal fees. It included writers Noam Chomsky, Arthur Miller, Paule Marshall, Adrienne Rich, Howard Zinn, and Kurt Vonnegut. Even James Baldwin was a contributing member. While Cleaver was being held at Vacaville, the Adult Authority received numerous letters from people protesting the revocation of his parole. They accused the Adult Authority of acting illegally, and some even stated that even if Cleaver had fired on the police, he had only done so out of protest of white racism. The letters came from diverse groups, including Health Professionals for Peace, the Medical Committee for Human Rights, and Students for a Democratic Society, as well as a range of individuals, such as university faculty, activists, artists, and everyday citizens. They were inspired by Cleaver's armed resistance, and they wrote messages like, "In the white power structure, we should be imprisoned and not Eldridge Cleaver, Huey Newton, or any other Black man fighting for freedom and self-determination," or "Release Cleaver. Stop harassing black leaders." Cleaver became so popular that he decided to run for president of the United States with the Peace and Freedom Party.

Cleaver's family was also supportive. In late May, Thelma wrote

Cleaver a letter, telling him that she was praying for him. "Keep your chin up and always remember that God is still in your life and that he loves you as well as anybody else. I never have stopped praying for you and will do anything I can to help you."[24]

Kathleen was the most encouraging of all. She brought him the things he needed to survive prison, including a typewriter, a dictionary, and a stack of books, including *The Confessions of Nat Turner*.[25] She visited him once a week and organized rallies and press conferences demanding his freedom. She kept him informed about Panther affairs, including the status of SNCC and the Peace and Freedom Party, the reception of *Soul on Ice*, and the everyday business of the Panthers. She wrote him passionate letters nearly every day, pledging her undying love, both to him and the cause. "Eldridge, I love you so totally," she wrote in her first letter to him. "As long as you are in jail, my soul, my heart, my spirit is in jail."[26] She offered her unconditional support and tried to boost morale by praising his writing. "Everywhere I go I hear talk about *Soul on Ice*. It's raging like wildfire over the Bay Area, and being reviewed and talked about everywhere. You are the Black Writer now. You have surpassed, in the minds of this generation, Wright and Baldwin and Malcolm, and have become the political writer of black America. I love you. I adore you, I worship you, and I want you to come home and deal with this shit so I can return to being your wife and not your advocate, agent, and lonely political mobilizer."[27] Eldridge was deeply touched by these letters and wrote back, "I am not the black writer of this age, you are. Your letters are bestsellers with me every time."[28]

Cleaver was harassed endlessly at Vacaville. Prison officials delayed his meeting with his lawyer Alexander Hoffman and would not allow him to use the tape recorder. Hoffman asked prison officials sarcastically, "May I expect that the next time I come to visit a long-standing rule will be discovered that attorneys may not bring in a pencil or paper?" Officials opened his mail, citing a potential breach of institutional security as their excuse. Cleaver and his lawyers filed a complaint, but they were told, "If security of a penal institution is to be preserved, the right of inspection can admit of no exception." They would not allow certain letters to go out because the prison deemed that "the contents are non-legal and do not pertain to any legal aspect of your case." Cleaver complained to Charles Geary that one guard in particular hounded him and invaded his privacy. "His name is Henshaw and he is always fucking with my mail. He is the one who reads my letters and goes around discussing their contents with other guards and even with inmates, making all kinds of snide, petty, racist remarks about me and the people to whom I write."[29] In response, Cleaver wrote a thirteen-page open letter to Governor Ronald Reagan on May 13, accusing the Oakland police, the criminal justice system, and even the governor himself of prejudicial treatment. "I am writing to you to call your attention that certain persons who are responsible to you have conspired to violate my rights and are now holding me as a political prisoner, at Vacaville Medical Facility."[30]

In late May, Cleaver and his lawyers protested the revocation of his parole, alleging that his confinement was illegal and he was being held without cause. On June 3, Cleaver appeared in court to testify concerning his writ of habeas corpus. He arrived at the courtroom in shackles, which his lawyer Geary asked to be removed. Cleaver testified that he and other Panthers had been transporting potatoes to David Hilliard's house to make into potato salad for a picnic the next day. He had stopped to urinate on the sidewalk when the police ambushed him and started firing. When the prosecutor Ed O'Brian asked who was with him on the night of the shootout, Cleaver replied: "A man who was murdered by local police." In his closing summary, Geary painted Cleaver as a model parolee who had paid his debt to society. "He's pulled himself by his own bootstraps, went in there as an ignorant young man and educated himself, went to the facilities and availed himself."[31]

On June 12, Cleaver arrived in court to hear the verdict concerning his parole. The Solano County Courthouse was packed. Members of SNCC, the Black Panthers, and the Peace and Freedom Party showed up, as did Stokely Carmichael and comic and actor Godfrey Cambridge. Policemen, FBI agents, and prison officials from the Adult Authority were on hand. After the Adult Authority failed to offer any testimony, the judge let Cleaver go on his writ of habeas corpus. Judge Raymond Sherwin wrote in his decision, "The uncontradicted evidence presented to this court indicated that the petitioner had been a model parolee. The peril to his parole status stemmed from no failure of personal rehabilitation, but from his undue eloquence in pursuing political goals. Not only was there absence of cause for the cancellation of parole, it was the product of a type of pressure unbecoming, to say the least, to the law enforcement paraphernalia of this state." Cleaver was freed on $50,000 bail. Friends and supporters contributed much of the money, and Ed Keating put up his house as collateral. After he was released, the FBI informed the Secret Service that Cleaver "should be considered armed and dangerous."[32]

When Cleaver got out of jail, he and Kathleen went back to their home at 850 Oak Street. However, they worried that they might be attacked by the police, so they soon moved to 2777 Pine Street, a large three-story house that served as home and makeshift Panther headquarters. Armed Panthers staked out every window and door, and they cut a hole in the floor to install a fireman's pole in case they needed to make a quick getaway.

Cleaver was now a political celebrity. In the post–civil rights era, his angry and defiant message filled the vacuum left by King's assassination. By surviving what many viewed as an ambush by the Oakland police, Cleaver became a hero both to white and black radicals. He was a symbol of dissent who openly criticized America's racism and its imperialist activities abroad. He had been in a gunfight with police and lived to tell about it. Cleaver was also a bohemian who loved the Haight scene. He smoked weed, practiced "free love," and hung out with countercultural figures like Jerry Rubin. In his speeches and writings, Cleaver turned profanity into poetry, and his ear for the American vernacular made him a popular cultural figure. He was followed by the press wherever he went and received boxes of letters—fan mail, donations, hate mail, and love letters. He tried to read it all, but there was too much. He was now making money from the royalties on *Soul on Ice*, so he bought a gold Pontiac and had a phone installed in it.[33]

The surveillance from the FBI and local police increased. Cleaver was followed everywhere. A repair truck had been parked outside the house since his release from Vacaville. Kathleen was so worried about a possible attack that she bought a shotgun and planned to buy a pistol for self-defense. Since this was a parole violation, Cleaver decided to move out rather than risk it. According to parole reports, "He stated that although he agreed with her in principle, he had no desire to languish in prison while she proved her point."[34] Cleaver moved into a small room in the home of white radicals Stew and Judy Albert.

Cleaver conducted Panther business out of the room but also used it as a crash pad to cheat on Kathleen with a parade of girlfriends. Ever since he had become a literary celebrity, he had started sleeping with more women. There was Tricia Baldock, a Berkeley librarian and supporter of the movement, and Karen Wald, a political activist. He told the Alberts, "I'll be bringing female guests by, and I want you to keep a loaded gun in one particular spot. I need protection if the pigs vamp. It doesn't matter where, just as long as it's always in the same place."[35] Cleaver called the place the Hippie Palace.

Throughout the summer, Cleaver intensified his Panther activities. He gave a number of provocative and inflammatory speeches. At a rally for Newton on July 14, 1968, Cleaver told the crowd, "From now on we niggers have got to stop killing other niggers and start killing police."[36] At a speech at the Barristers Club, he half joked that the Panthers would rob white people in the audience if they didn't make contributions to the cause. "We're very uptight for money, and I don't think we'll take up a collection here, but we'll accept any donations. Because we need that, and if someone don't give us that, we will rob you, kill you, burglarize your homes, catch you on dark streets and take your big fat wallet. Up against the wall, motherfucker!"[37] He also encouraged audience members to pick up guns and shoot up courtrooms full of lawyers and judges. "I hope that you will go out in your courtroom with your gun, you dig, and shoot some of these prosecuting attorneys, some of those lying policemen; throw them off the stand."[38] When a member of the audience asked Cleaver what white people could do to help the cause, he replied, "Kill some other white people."[39]

In July, Cleaver traveled with Bobby Seale and Emory Douglas to New York to appear at the United Nations. Since its creation after World War II, African American activists had viewed it as a place to protest the human-rights abuses experienced by black people in the United States. Among those was Malcolm X, who attempted to gain support among African nations to launch a UN investigation of the racist treatment of African Americans. At a news conference there, Cleaver told reporters that the Panthers would not allow Newton to be executed. "They will have to kill us first," he stated defiantly.[40] The Panthers filled out an application with the UN to become a recognized nongovernmental organization. They also met with Cuban officials to seek permission to set up a military training facility in Cuba. Cleaver had studied Che Guevara and Castro closely and was eager to learn guerrilla warfare from the Cubans. They promised both facilities and training if Cleaver came to the island.

Cleaver secured the nomination for president of the United States with the Peace and Freedom Party. He promised, if elected, to withdraw troops from Vietnam, disband the police, and promote self-determination for all racial groups. He claimed that the United States was the number-one successor to Nazi Germany and biggest obstacle to human progress. Cleaver was popular among voting white radicals. On August 3, 1968, he received the most votes by California delegates to win the nomination, beating out comedian Dick Gregory. He was only thirty-three years old and Constitutionally ineligible to win, but the party nominated him anyway.[41] Cleaver was incredibly idealistic about his candidacy. In a journal entry titled, "Why I Am Running for President," Cleaver made a list of all of the reasons he wanted America's highest office: "To inspire the outcast and downtrodden, the poor and disinherited, the hated and the scorned. To take hold of our own destiny, with our own hands, our own efforts, our own sweat, blood and tears. To harness our despair with machinery that will change our lives, give our lives back to us. To unleash and liberate and set in motion and focus America's New People."[42]

In September, Cleaver was invited to teach a course at Berkeley called "Social Analysis 139X: Dehumanization and Regeneration in the American Social Order." A sociology student by the name of Lawrence Magid came up with the idea of the class, and he enlisted the support of psychology professor Edward Sampson to organize it. It was an attempt to make up for the lack of black-studies courses on campus. One thousand students immediately signed up to take the class. Ronald Reagan was an ex officio member of the board of regents; when he heard about it, he pressured the university to bar Cleaver. "If Eldridge Cleaver is allowed to teach our children, they may come home one night and slit our throats," he famously said.[43] Max Rafferty, state superintendent of public instruction, sent letters to every county and district school superintendent in California threatening a loss of credentials and state aid if Cleaver were allowed to speak at their school.[44] The state senate voted to censure the university for allowing him to speak. The board of regents voted ten to eight to bar him, though fearing accusations of suppressing free speech, they decided to allow him to perform one lecture.[45] Students and faculty were outraged at this infringement of academic freedom. Students held massive protests. Two thousand showed up for a demonstration and voted unanimously to allow him to lecture. In response to the demonstrations, the academic senate voted 668 to 114 to defy the regents. The class was finally offered to one hundred students for no credit, and Cleaver was paid a $400 honorarium and travel expenses.[46]

When Cleaver arrived for the first class on October 9, 1968, he surprised everyone with his restraint. Although he had once considered calling the Berkeley course "Pigology," he spoke throughout without his usual barrage of obscenities.[47] "I'm not here to be a demagogue today, to stir up the rabble or anything of that type," he told the class. "This is supposed to be a little quiet dissertation on racism or what that's about." Cleaver covered an array of topics that he had studied in prison, ranging from American literature to the origins of the slave trade. In his hour-long lecture, he explored Melville Herskovits's foundational anthropological work on African culture, Thomas Jefferson's contradictory status as Founding Father and slave owner, and the landscape of contemporary racism. Cleaver spoke extemporaneously, drawing from the deep body of knowledge he had acquired through a decade of close study in prison. It was improvisational, but academic. As he quipped near the end of his lecture, "This is an experimental course, right? I'm just experimenting with this shit, don't quote me on that."[48]

The following week, Cleaver expanded on his literary and cultural analysis. He performed close readings of *Moby Dick*, analyzing America's social structures through the metaphor of the ship. He outlined the significance of the slave trade by explaining its economic underpinnings, and he recounted the history of the Fugitive Slave Law and the abolitionist movement. As a provocative in-class activity, he had students explain American slavery to a Martian who had traveled to earth, which challenged them to conceptualize America's racial history from an outsider's perspective. Over the course of next few weeks, he taught them about John Brown and the white radical element of racial struggle, the period of Reconstruction after the Civil War, the Great Migration, and the rise of the Ku Klux Klan and white nationalism. Cleaver believed in history and literature's capacity to resurrect the collective memory of black America. He saw literature, "like music, dance and technology," as necessary for the survival of the oppressed.

Cleaver was riding a wave of political fame and literary success. In October, he signed a $25,000 contract with McGraw-Hill for a forthcoming book on black power. Over the next two months, he crisscrossed the country, making incendiary speeches attacking Ronald Reagan and racist America. In early October, Cleaver gave a speech at Stanford University's Memorial Hall to a crowd of 1,700, with another 800 standing outside. "Ronald Reagan is a punk, a sissy and a coward," Cleaver declared, "and I challenge him to a duel to the death or until he says Uncle Eldridge. I give him a choice of weapons—a gun, a knife, a baseball bat or marshmallow."[49] The next day, he spoke at Sacramento State College, where he openly defied authorities. "I know that my parole officer has his comrades here today, his agents here, same thing for Ronald Reagan, same thing for the adult authority, the same thing for all the wardens of all the prisons, and the pigs, the hogs who patrol the prisons, fuck you."[50]

He repeated versions of this speech at other venues across the country. In mid-October he visited New York and gave speeches at the Algonquin Hotel and New York University.[51] Don Cox remembered, "Eldridge made a memorable swing through the country. I recall the song he composed and that he convinced every audience to rise and sing with him at the end of every speech. At New York University, I even saw two nuns in their habits stand with the rest of the audience and sing 'Fuck Ronald Reagan.'"[52] Cleaver saw profanity as a way to connect strategically with the masses. He peppered his speeches with the word "motherfucker" accordingly. On October 20, 1968, he gave a speech at American University, where he concluded, "I am not here seeking votes. I am the Presidential candidate of the Peace and Freedom Party, but it's only the visionaries in the party who think we are going to have a president in the White House this time around. As a matter of fact, if I was elected, I would not enter the White House. I would send a wrecking crew there to burn the motherfucker down."[53]

The FBI followed Cleaver everywhere and attempted to undermine him. They mailed anonymous phony letters to various branches of the BPP accusing him of stealing funds. They made one hundred copies of the speech in which he threated Ronald Reagan and sent them to school boards, clergy, and parent-teacher associations.[54] The FBI sent letters to Kathleen, telling her that Cleaver was having sexual relationships with underage girls. "I also cannot understand why he has a group of 13- and 14-year-old girls around him. He even takes some of them on trips with him. I cannot imagine anything that they do that you cannot do better. Your friends used to think that you loved your husband very much but now, I'm afraid, they are beginning to feel sorry for you because you are married to such a bum. Signed by your friend, Mr. X."[55] The FBI even sent Cleaver letters stating that his life was in danger. "Some of these Black Cats are planning to kill you because they think you are uptight with the Man. I don't dare sign this letter for fear of my own life." It was signed "Soul Brother."[56]

As November 27 approached—the day when Cleaver was

scheduled to return to prison—his lawyers tried to keep him free. On November 20, 1968, the Cleaver team filed a stay issuance of remittitur. The Supreme Court denied it.

Cleaver promised the parole officer that he would come quietly, saying that he "did not want to give the police any excuse to shoot him." However, in various speeches leading up to his return, he repeatedly said he would die before he would allow himself to be taken back to jail.[57] Cleaver considered a number of extreme options. "I was surrounded by escape plans. One group had me riding into the Rockies on horseback and then escaping into Canada. I was no Lewis and Clark Operator, but I expressed interest in the deal. A couple of white sympathizers offered to hijack a jet (with hand grenades) and whisk me off to the islands. That was vetoed by everybody."[58] Cleaver was drawn most to the idea of shooting it out with the police in public:

> I began to concentrate solely on my plan. I chose Merritt College because it was ideal from many points of view. In the first place, it was in the heart of the Black Community of Oakland. Secondly, it was a physically sound structure, more like a fortress than anything else. Merritt College had been constructed to serve as a High School, and like most High Schools in Babylon, it was solid stone. . . . Also, it commanded the immediate terrain. It had solid strong towers rising up from the roof of its second story that surveyed the area for hundreds of yards in either direction.[59]

Cleaver studied blueprints drawn up of the college, including underground tunnels, plumbing, and the electrical system. He began stockpiling guns, gas masks, and medical supplies in preparation for a final gun battle.

Newton vetoed Cleaver's plans for martyrdom and ordered him to make an escape to Cuba instead. On the day before his scheduled return to prison, things were tense. A group of one hundred protesters, mostly white, demonstrated outside of Cleaver's house with signs that read ON WATCH AGAINST MURDER BY THE POLICE and STOP POLICE

EXECUTIONS.[60] Armed Panthers were stationed on the porch, scanning the crowd for plainclothes policemen. Inside the house, windows were armored with sheet steel and three-quarter inch plywood. Panthers, armed to the teeth, were positioned strategically throughout the house in anticipation of an attack. Cleaver didn't show up for his last class at Berkeley. The next morning, he failed to arrive at the San Francisco State Building in downtown San Francisco, where he was supposed to be taken into custody. Charles Geary led a group of reporters to his house at 2777 Pine Street, but Cleaver was long gone. The authorities issued a warrant for his arrest by 11:00 AM. Kathleen claimed that she knew nothing about his whereabouts, though the police were suspicious, as she had recently withdrawn $33,000 from their bank account. When she was questioned by the media if she had withdrawn money and given it to Cleaver, she responded sarcastically, "No, it was 40 million and if he wanted to go to Cuba, he could buy his own plane."

In truth, Cleaver hadn't told Kathleen or anyone about his real plan. He was worried about FBI infiltrators. He only told Ralph Smith, who doubled for him at his house to fool police. An acting troupe helped Cleaver escape. They covered his face in makeup to age him forty years. He dressed up like an old man to fool security at the San Francisco Airport. He flew to New York and then traveled to Montreal, where he hid out for two weeks at safe houses provided by professors, students, and other radicals. He had to wait for the St. Lawrence Waterway to unfreeze enough to steer the freighter out to the Atlantic Ocean.[61] Some American members of the Students for a Democratic Society were traveling to Cuba to establish the Venceremos Brigade, a coalition of Americans who worked with young Cubans to show solidarity with the Cuban Revolution. Among them was Karen Wald, a Berkeley activist with whom Cleaver had been carrying on an affair for the past few months. Cleaver despised Wald, but he didn't pass up any opportunity for sex. Cleaver passed the time on the voyage by reigniting the affair with her, which he described in his journals with his usual explicitness. "I fucked her all the way to Havana. When the freighter pulled into Havana Harbor on Christmas morning, she was sucking my dick. I came when they lowered the gang plank."[62]

11

CUBA (1968–1969)

Christopher Columbus arrived in Cuba in 1492, looking for gold. Following his first reconnaissance, the Spanish king sent conquistadors to colonize the island. Over the next two centuries, Cuba emerged as Spain's staging ground for its conquest of the Americas. Spaniards founded the port city of Havana as headquarters and established a slave system known as *encomienda*, working natives to death in the gold mines. Those who resisted were killed, and many others died from diseases like measles and smallpox. By the time Cuba's gold deposits had been exhausted in the mid-sixteenth century, nearly all of the original indigenous inhabitants of Cuba had been wiped out.

Following the genocide of the native population, Spain began importing African slaves to Cuba to work on coffee, tobacco, and sugarcane plantations. Following the Haitian Revolution and collapse of the sugar industry in Haiti, Cuba emerged as the largest sugar producer in the world. Cuba's slave system grew quickly and massively. Hundreds of thousands of slaves were brought to Cuba from West Africa aboard slave ships in just a few decades in the early nineteenth century. The ships were so crowded and unsanitary that anywhere from one-quarter to one-half of the slaves died en route.[1] By the 1840s, slaves made up more than half the Cuban population.

Conditions on the plantations were extremely harsh. Slaves cleared land, planted cane, and harvested by hand. It was backbreaking work in the hot sun. Slaves worked up to twenty hours per day during harvesttime, and they were often locked in *barracones* at night. They were whipped for the smallest offenses, and many died from overwork. Slave insurrections broke out regularly throughout Cuba's history until slavery was finally outlawed by royal decree in 1886. Many of these insurrections were well-organized campaigns for collective freedom. In the Aponte Rebellion of 1812, for instance, hundreds of enslaved and free black people joined together in a loose gathering of uprisings in an attempt to overthrow slavery. One of the leaders, José Aponte, was beheaded, and his head was displayed in an iron box at Havana's entrance as a warning to other would-be rebels.[2]

When Cleaver pulled into Havana Harbor on Christmas morning 1968, he felt a mix of excitement and caution. He romanticized Cuba's insurrectionary past against colonial powers and fantasized that the Panthers would continue that legacy. He once wrote, "Cuba had a glorious tradition of fighting, of uprisings drowned in blood, and yet continuing, writing a history of black rebellion that has been one of the brightest flames in the fires of our struggle."[3] Cleaver was less sure about the Castro administration's commitment to the Panthers and black people more broadly. Following the end of the Cuban Revolution in 1959, Castro had pledged to end racial discrimination on the island. He outlawed all forms of racism, and he increased opportunities for Cuban black people in education, housing, and the economy. However, just a few years after the revolution, Castro declared racism eradicated, even though the fundamental structures of prejudice had not been addressed. Black struggles for equality became taboo in Cuba, and so Cleaver wondered if he could really count on Castro's support.

Cleaver was relieved that they had made it to Havana. Over the course of the fifteen-day journey, he worried that the navy might intercept the boat and take him back to the United States. Or worse, it might torpedo the freighter. But Cleaver had survived and felt he had won a small victory in his escape from the police. "I was happy because no matter what happened now, no matter how it turned out in the end, we had beaten the pigs. There was a nation-wide manhunt going on back in the United States for me but I had gotten away."[4]

A small delegation of Cubans in full military regalia greeted Cleaver at the dock and gave him an olive-colored uniform and a Luger. He was glad to get his hands on a gun, as he hadn't been allowed to carry one aboard. Now that he was being hunted by the US government, he wanted to have a sidearm with him at all times.

Cuba treated Cleaver as an honored guest and gave him an apartment located on Calle L, just two blocks away from the Hotel Habana Libre. It had once been a dentist's office, but, following the revolution, it had been confiscated by the Ministry for the Recovery of Misappropriated Assets. It had four bedrooms, a dining room, four baths, a kitchen, a greenhouse, and two terraces. A dentist's chair was bolted to the middle of the floor in one of the rooms. One terrace faced the sea and the other faced the street. The latter was covered with clinging vines and foliage, which Cleaver liked because it allowed him to watch the street without being seen.[5] The apartment was well stocked with food, rum, and cigars, and the government even provided a maid. "I felt more than a little puffed up with all the royal treatment," Cleaver later recalled.[6]

For the next few weeks, Cleaver was given grand tours of the island to view the transformations that had occurred since the revolution. He was taken to every province and given detailed descriptions of the lives of the people there.[7] He was shown farming cooperatives and was taken to desegregated beaches, parks, schools, and housing complexes. Cleaver took classes on Cuba's history, and he learned about the antidiscrimination and literacy campaign that Castro had launched in 1959 to end prejudice in Cuba. He even got to shake Castro's hand. At least initially, Cleaver saw a country that under communism had addressed social inequality through socialist programs and antidiscrimination laws.

Cleaver was therefore optimistic that the Blank Panthers might get logistical support from the Cuban government for their own rebellion. There was certainly precedent for a relationship between Cuba and American black people. In 1960, Fidel Castro had stayed at the Hotel Theresa in Harlem during a visit to the UN, where he met with Malcolm X. The summer before Cleaver arrived, Castro had welcomed Stokely Carmichael as a guest of the island for three weeks.

Castro had also backed Robert F. Williams, author of *Negroes with Guns* and a hero to Cleaver. Williams had grown up in Monroe, North Carolina, and, following a tour as a marine during World War II, he had returned home to take over leadership of the local branch of the NAACP. He started the Black Armed Guard, a gun club created to protect civil rights activists in the South. He provided weapons for members and trained them on how to defend themselves. After he was falsely accused of kidnapping, he fled to Cuba with his wife, Mabel, and two children, where he was given asylum by Castro. Williams operated the radio program *Radio Free Dixie*, on which he encouraged black GIs to rebel against the United States government. He and Mabel also published an underground newspaper, the *Crusader*, in which they critiqued US racism. In 1962, Williams published his memoir, *Negroes with Guns*, which recounted his efforts to organize a gun club in the racist South. It was a major inspiration to Cleaver as well as to the rest of the Black Panthers. Cleaver hoped that Castro might also grant him asylum and provide him the resources for his own radio program and newspaper.

Now a fugitive and an outlaw, Cleaver turned more of his attention to supporting the underground militant wing of the Black Panther Party. He was eager to be trained by the Cuban military in combat. He had read Che Guevara's *Guerrilla Warfare* while in prison and felt ready to experience the real thing. When Cleaver had met with Cuban officials at the UN in July 1967, they had assured him he would be given a training facility. Now that he was in Cuba, he planned to bring Bunchy Carter and a few others over for training and then sneak them back into the United States, where they could run insurgent operations against the police from the Appalachian Mountains. "I wanted to get started on the revolutionary training center for American Black Panthers. There were people in the States ready to join me as soon as I gave the word, so I was anxious to get started. It was a matter of urgency with me."[8]

But for months, the Cuban government did not answer any of Cleaver's requests to create the training center. Officials continued to take him on tours of the island and provide education classes. To keep his presence on the island a secret, they didn't allow him to visit restaurants or hotels. He tried to get permission to bring Kathleen to the island, but he was prevented. Because of the US blockade, he couldn't send letters or make phone calls. "The Cubans reneged on certain promises they had made before I had even arrived, such as a permanent, well organized facility, and the right to make broadcasts," Cleaver commented later. "They had no intention of ever allowing the things that they promised."[9]

While Cleaver waited on the Cuban government, he passed much of his time drinking and smoking weed and writing. Cleaver worked away at a memoir (unpublished) of his time in prison called "Book of Lives," which he later changed into a novel called "Ahmen's Jacket." He bought a pound of marijuana from a local connection he had found. He drank from the stores of rum left in his apartment. He got ahold of a recording machine and taped himself in the aftermath of these binges. "I just woke up, all fucked up in the mind," he said at the beginning of one tape. "God, I feel like I been drinking a lot of rum or smoking dope or something. I ain't get no sleep. It's gonna fuck me up today." Cleaver also slept with prostitutes, whom he called "haints." As Cleaver recalled it, some of these interactions were violent, as when one prostitute bit his penis during oral sex. "They got haints running around here. They got star haints. And I just thought of a haint that's fucked up my dick. And went around bragging about it. My dick ain't ever going to be right again."[10]

After months of waiting, Cleaver demanded to see Castro directly. The Cuban leader had told Cleaver upon their meeting to contact him if there were any problems. He quickly found himself on the defensive. "As a result of my demands, the situation changed dramatically. I was taken to a dinner meeting where I was verbally attacked by a number of people. They said the Black Panther Party was infiltrated by the CIA and they couldn't trust us. Then they accused me of attending secret black power meetings in Havana. I was stunned because I hadn't done anything like that. In fact, I didn't even know there was a black power movement in the so-called people's paradise where they said everyone had equal economic opportunity."[11] Cleaver was invited to stay in Cuba as long as he wanted as a private citizen, but all other requests were denied.

In his enthusiasm for Cuba as a socialist state, Cleaver had misread the contentious racial dynamics there. Although Castro had declared racism eradicated in 1961—just two years after the implementation of the antidiscrimination policies—the truth was that racial discrimination had not been addressed. Following the classic Marxist analysis, Cuban officials believed that racism was a mere effect of economic forces, and therefore a properly socialist system would end prejudice. Because they were so invested in this ideology, they believed that the mere mention of racism was counterrevolutionary, and they outlawed black social, political, and religious groups.[12] They began to see Cleaver as a threat because his sympathy for black liberation movements challenged the socialist vision for Cuba's raceless society.

At this time, Cleaver met a number of black American hijackers fleeing to Cuba. Between 1968 and 1972, Cuba was the single most popular destination in the world for skyjacking exiles, criminals on the lam, and would-be political revolutionaries.[13] Dozens upon dozens of hijackers—including a number of Black Panthers—commandeered commercial airliners in the late 1960s and headed to Cuba, which they believed would offer them political asylum and a new life. What hijackers found was often different than the fantasy. The Cuban government regarded many of them as petty criminals, mentally ill individuals, or potential spies. They were arrested and placed in "immigration jails" until sentencing for illegally entering the country. The Cuban government often sent hijackers to agricultural work camps in the Camagüey Province five hundred miles from Havana. They performed hard labor cutting sugar cane, and some were later freed to live in Havana.

Through Karen Wald, Cleaver met Moziah Kenyatta in March 1969. He was a hijacker who had worked in the labor camp and now lived at the Hotel Habana Libre. Through Moziah, Cleaver passed the word on to other imprisoned hijackers at the camp, encouraging them to make their escape to his apartment. In this fashion, Cleaver recruited half a dozen new Panthers. He explained, "And whenever anyone got to my pad, I would baptize him in the name of the Father, Son, and the Holy Ghost, and make him a Black Panther. I told the Cubans that I was authorized by the Black Panther Party to induct Afro-Americans into the Black Panther Party anywhere, anytime as I saw fit, and I took these people in."[14] Cleaver offered shelter to a number of people. There was James "Akili" Patterson; his wife, Gwen; and their daughter, Tanya. Patterson was a member of the New York Black Panther Party, as was another hijacker named Omar Talib. Byron Booth and Clinton Smith joined Cleaver in Havana after escaping from the work camp. Cleaver had been friends with Booth in the African culture and history class in Soledad. In January 1969, Booth and Smith had escaped from Soledad, hijacked a plane at LAX, and made their way to Cuba. Cleaver's apartment quickly became known as *la casa de las Panteras* because of all the hijackers he was harboring.

Cleaver and his small group of Black Panthers began stockpiling guns. The tensions between the Panthers and the Cuban government grew until one day the police tried to force their way into Cleaver's apartment to arrest Raymond Johnson, a young student organizer who had hijacked a plane to Cuba from Louisiana. "We were in that siege frame of mind, that Afro-American, 'Custerism—LAST STAND' frame of mind," Cleaver remembered later in an interview. "So we were all in this together. We would go down together. We took that position. We told them that we were not going to let them take the dude and that we were going to resist. We made our last will and testament on tapes, sent them to the States."[15] Cleaver made it known to the police that they were willing die to protect their comrade, and the police finally backed down.

Cleaver soon realized that he could not carry on the struggle for black liberation in Cuba. As he wrote in his journal, "I came to the conclusion that an island is automatically a prison. And that every government in existence and every government that has ever existed is or was oppressive and corrupt. It was inevitable that I began to compare Cuba with Alcatraz."[16]

Cleaver was removed from the island by the government after reporter James Pringle published a story in May 1969 that he was in Havana. Cleaver had been sleeping with Bunny Hearn, a pro-Cuban American who knew Castro and the governmental elite. After Cleaver reportedly hit her, she told Pringle about his presence. Not wanting to get into conflict with the United States, Cuba apparently rushed Cleaver out of the country. He explained, "When the news hit the wire, the Cubans started jumping. They started taking me to clinics to get shots and check-ups, getting me fitted for a couple of suits, taking my photograph, etc. I felt exactly the way I felt each time I had gotten out of prison."[17] According to Cleaver, he was forced out of Cuba because his view of racial struggle was incompatible with Cuba's socialist vision of a raceless society. He wrote later, "I had observed Cuba from top to bottom, and decided that if this was communism, it wasn't the kind I was looking for. I had a very disappointing opinion of what was supposed to be a utopian society, an ideal society of the future. Cuba posed the first serious challenge to my communist beliefs, but it did not turn me against the communist doctrine. I just thought that the Cubans were doing it wrong."[18]

The FBI reported that Cleaver was removed from Cuba for more nefarious reasons. One surveillance document read, "We have received information that Cleaver is unable to return to Cuba because of a rape charge against him there." Another claimed, "Eldridge Cleaver was persona non grata in Cuba because he had raped a young Cuban girl while he was enjoying the hospitality of the Cuban Government. Cleaver has stated since that time that he left Cuba for other reasons."[19] Because of Cleaver's history of rape, it is certainly possible he committed this crime. However, given the FBI's notorious history of using sexual innuendo and rumor to smear various black leaders—including Dr. Martin Luther King and Huey Newton—this charge cannot be seen as credible. No other specific evidence exists to indict him beyond the FBI reports, and the fact that the FBI did not choose to make this accusation public suggests that it was most likely not legitimate. Whatever the case, Cleaver's dream to receive guerilla training from the Cubans and expand the underground section of the Black Panther was shattered. The Cuban political leadership, looking to suppress black nationalist activity in its own country, regarded Cleaver's Panther activities as a threat. And once he had been outed by the press, he was seen as a liability. In June 1969 the Cubans loaded Cleaver onto a plane heading for Algiers, Algeria.

12

ALGERIA (1969–1970)

When Cleaver arrived in Algiers in early June 1969, his future looked uncertain. The Cubans had hustled him onto the plane so fast that they failed to provide him with any contacts. They didn't even inform the Algerian government of his arrival. At the airport in Algiers, Cleaver was disguised as a Cuban national and shuttled downtown. He was driven through the French quarter, where white colonial buildings stood shoulder to shoulder along the downtown boulevards. They were holdovers from French colonial rule, which began in 1832 and had lasted 130 years. During their occupation, the French had seized Algerian lands, created feudal patrimonies, and turned many Algerian peasants into sharecroppers. They demolished the old central city in Algiers and redesigned the streets in Parisian style. Just adjacent to Cleaver's hotel was the Casbah, an ancient labyrinth of narrow walkways and whitewashed homes winding up away from the sea into the hills. Here, the Algerians fought and won the insurgency against the French during the Algerian War of Independence. The Algerians had only been free of French colonial rule for seven years when Cleaver arrived.

Cleaver was taken to the Hotel Victoria in the heart of downtown, which had served as a stopover for tourists from Europe and America half a century earlier. Kathleen was waiting for Cleaver when he arrived. A few weeks earlier, she had prepared to depart for Cuba. She kept a suitcase at the *Ramparts* office so she could leave at a moment's notice, and she filled a copper box with as much cash as she could carry. Being eight months pregnant, Kathleen was nervous about flying, but she hoped Cuba would be a romantic place to reunite with Cleaver. "Havana is where I imagined Eldridge and I would have our revolutionary honeymoon."[1] The FBI followed her constantly during this time. "Most of the telephones I used were tapped; most of the people I knew and worked among were considered subversives. FBI agents tailed me everywhere."[2]

On May 21, 1969, Ed Bullins drove Kathleen and bodyguard Emory Douglas to San Francisco Airport to catch a flight to Paris in order to get to Cuba. In Paris, they met Ellen Wright, a literary agent and widow of novelist Richard Wright. They also met her daughter Julia Herve, who showed Kathleen around Paris and helped her shop for baby clothes. The day before she was going to depart to Cuba, a journalist named Lee Lockwood tracked her down and told her that Cleaver was about to be taken to Algiers. Emory and Kathleen took a flight on May 30 that landed in Algiers in the middle of the night just a few days before Cleaver arrived.

Cleaver had not seen his wife in eight months, so when she opened the door of the hotel room, he was shocked by her changed appearance. As he joked later, "I went to the room and knocked on the door, and when it opened there was a fat lady standing there. She had my wife's hair."[3] Kathleen filled Cleaver in on the details of the struggle since he had been away. With a shrinking central committee and ongoing FBI harassment, she had taken on more of a leadership role in the movement. She explained later, "I had become involved in gun running, hiding fugitives, and bitter interparty political struggles. I had learned to drive. I had traveled across the country to speak at rallies, organized mass demonstrations, and established my own network of friends, supporters, and allies in the Bay Area radical community. I had learned to cope with betrayals, manipulations, shoot outs, and assassinations. My new sense of independence unnerved him as well as my new appearance."[4]

Cleaver, Kathleen, and Douglas stayed at the Victoria while they waited to see how the government would handle their case. It was shabby and run-down. Twin beds sat side-by-side in the Cleavers' tiny room, and cheap curtains hung over the windows. A shower crowded the already cramped space. The once-elegant balcony, which looked out over the Mediterranean Sea, was now weather-beaten. A communal toilet was at the end of the narrow hallway, so there was very little privacy. Since there were no dining facilities, Cleaver and Emory ate at local restaurants, and they brought back a stew called chorba for Kathleen. She was exhausted from the trip.

Once Kathleen was rested, they all ventured out into the streets to explore the city. Downtown Algiers was a world completely alien to them. The call to prayer echoed through the cavernous boulevards five times a day. It was a haunting and beautiful sound that made Algiers seem all the more mysterious. Kathleen described the city: "In the narrow alleys and passageways of the quarter, dusky Arabs and Berbers, cloaked in dark colored woolen burnooses, shuffled alongside young Mediterranean-looking men wearing short sleeved shirts and tight pants. A few women, their attractive faces half concealed by diaphanous veils worn like surgical masks, their clothing wrapped up in dingy white cloths draped from their heads to their feet, clutched underneath the chin by one hand, mingled in the sidewalk crowds."[5] The Algerians mostly looked back at them with benign interest, but every once in a while, they were confronted by someone. One night, as they were coming home from a restaurant, a drunk man approached them and said to Cleaver in French, "Well, you got yourself a white woman." Kathleen knew enough French to translate. Cleaver was enraged and had to resist the urge to knock the man out. He realized that Algeria had some of the same sexual taboos concerning black men and light-skinned women as America. After this incident, he made sure he carried his gun wherever he went.[6]

Cleaver was becoming frantic. He had no contacts, no diplomatic relations, and no official permission to be in the country. The Cuban officials suggested sending him to an Al Fatah training camp in the Middle East. With Kathleen eight months pregnant, this idea seemed ludicrous. Cleaver also had no access to his finances. Soon after he arrived in Algiers, he reached out to his agent, Cyrilly Abels, to find out the status of his royalties. "I want to know what's happening to all of that money, and I want to know how much is there and I want to know everything that has transpired since the last check you sent to me. It is disgusting and disappointing that things have been allowed to degenerate to this stage and I want to see this situation rectified immediately."[7] A week later she wrote him back with the bad news: the Treasury Department had frozen his bank account. The official notice stated, "Eldridge Cleaver is a designated national of Cuba under the Cuban Assets Control Regulations of the Treasury Department, a copy of which is enclosed. Property in which Eldridge Cleaver has any interest of any nature whatsoever, direct or indirect, is blocked property under these regulations."[8] For his travel to Cuba, Cleaver was characterized as a foreign national. This designation was eventually lifted in late September 1969, but for the first months in Algeria, Cleaver had no access to money.

Elaine Mokhtefi (née Klein), an American employee at the Algerian Ministry of Information, came to Cleaver's rescue. She had served as press secretary for Algeria's first president, Ahmed Ben Bella, and she was as an ally of liberation groups. Mokhtefi got a call late one night from Charles Chikerema, a representative of the Zimbabwe African People's Union, telling her that Cleaver needed help. The next morning, she went to the Victoria to find him. He told her what had happened in Cuba and how the Cubans now planned to ship him off to a training camp. "Can you help me?" Cleaver pleaded.[9] Mokhtefi discussed the matter with Slimane Hoffman, who was in charge of the office that handled liberation movements. She asked that Cleaver be allowed to give a press conference and permission to stay in the country. She got both.

On July 15, Cleaver publicly surfaced, giving a press conference at the University of Algiers to a room packed with university students, foreign journalists, and freedom fighters. Cleaver was nervous. This was his first public appearance since he had fled the United States eight months before. Cleaver told the crowd he was thrilled to be in Africa and believed an alliance could be built between black American struggles and African anticolonial movements. "Our struggle is revolutionary," he told them.[10]

Mokhtefi secured invitations for the Cleavers to attend the Pan-African Festival. In the late 1960s, as many African nations had achieved independence from European colonial powers, Algeria decided to host a celebration of these liberated nations. The country put together a massive festival, featuring arts and culture from African nations and African diasporic groups. The official invitation promised, "This gathering, the first of its kind and certainly the most unique in history, will bring together some 5000 artists and intellectuals of Africa and the African American community. Every category of artistic expression will be represented—ballet, sculpture, painting, folklore, modern instrumental and vocal groups, cinema, and theater." Cleaver himself was invited to participate in a political symposium on "African culture, its realities, its role in the liberation struggle, in the consolidation of African unity and in the economic and social development of Africa."[11] Cleaver was excited about the opportunity. The festival was sponsored by the Organization of African Unity, a group founded by various African countries in the early 1960s to promote human rights for Africans. The group influenced Malcolm X on his trip to Africa so much that he established the American version, the Organization of Afro-American Unity, which Cleaver had tried to revitalize at Soledad and Black House. Cleaver had finally made a pilgrimage to Africa like his hero Malcolm X, and he was determined to finish the work that his mentor had started. He was so grateful for the opportunity that he told Mokhtefi, "You saved my life."[12]

Cleaver knew little about Algeria when he arrived in summer 1969. He had studied psychiatrist and philosopher Frantz Fanon and his manifesto of decolonization, *The Wretched of the Earth*, in San

Quentin, but that was the extent of his knowledge. Cleaver was influenced by one of Fanon's central ideas that "decolonization is always a violent phenomenon." Drawing from Fanon, Cleaver adopted the idea that African Americans were colonial subjects under police occupation. He therefore saw violent overthrow as the ultimate answer to police repression and colonial domination.

Algeria's significance was therefore for Cleaver primarily symbolic. As a nation that had expelled an occupying colonial force, it was an emblem of anticolonial radicalism and Arab nationalism. Algeria's victory put it at the forefront of decolonization efforts and inspired freedom fighters from around the world to seek aid there. President Houari Boumediene—who had been a military commander of the Algerian National Liberation Front during the resistance—nationalized the country's oil and gas industry and used the money to fund liberation armies across the globe. Boumediene sought to create anticolonial unity with groups still fighting European powers. Now that Cuba no longer offered support, Cleaver believed that Algeria represented the best hope for the Panthers to receive the international recognition, funding, and training they needed to create an American revolt. At the time he stated, "I believe that by 1972 we will have a military *coup* in the United States and a military dictatorship, because by that time there will be a full-scale war going on in the United States, and an election for the presidency will be out of the question."[13]

The Pan-African Festival began on July 21, 1969, the same day as the Apollo moon landing. "I don't see what benefit mankind will have from two astronauts landing on the moon," Cleaver told the *New York Times*, "while people are being murdered in Vietnam and suffering from hunger even in the United States."[14] The festival was unlike anything that anyone had seen before. The French boulevards that had once been symbols of colonial domination were now stages for the expression of African identity. On the first day, four thousand participants flooded the streets. Delegations from thirty-one African countries and six liberation movements paraded down the boulevard in brightly colored attire. Uniformed freedom fighters marched in formation, with dance troupes, swordsmen, jugglers, and belly dancers all entertaining the crowd. Tuareg Horsemen galloped through the streets, firing their rifles in the air. Museums throughout Europe and Africa lent art collections, while acting troupes put on plays. Drums could be heard echoing up and down the boulevard day and night.[15]

The Black Panthers were at the center of it all. Algeria's minister of information, Mohammed Benyahia, gave them use of an empty storefront on the Rue Didouche Mourad, the main artery running through downtown. The storefront was sleek and stylish, with plate glass windows, stretching twenty feet tall, framing the entrance and a balcony overlooking the gallery-like space. The Panthers hung Emory Douglas's brightly colored artwork on the walls and plastered the windows with posters of Cleaver, Seale, and Newton. On July 22, the Panthers gathered in front of a crowd of young Algerians to open the center. Cleaver wore a vibrant orange dashiki that Kathleen had given him. Julia Herve gave a short speech praising the Panthers as heirs to Malcolm X. Even with the sweltering heat, Algerians packed the store, as they were attracted to the bold style and provocative artwork of these black American freedom fighters. The Panthers gave out posters and fliers, which the Algerians took with gratitude. For days during the festival, the Panther information center was the focal point of downtown. Algerians gathered out front, chanting "Power to the People!"[16]

Cleaver and the Panthers were put up by the Algerian government at the Hotel Aletti, an art deco hotel that had been inaugurated by Charlie Chaplin in 1930. It was now owned by the government, which used it to house various revolutionary groups and other guests of Algeria. A broad white building ten stories high with massive columns and a circular driveway, it sat on a French boulevard surrounded by palm trees and bright orange flowers, just down the street from the famous Grande Poste. The sidewalks around it were crowded with cafés, and during the festival they were packed with delegations, journalists, filmmakers, freedom fighters, and representatives from all over the African continent. The inside of the hotel was magnificent: the lobby was decorated with velvet drapes and hand-carved furniture, and chandeliers hung from the ceiling. Cleaver and Kathleen were given a lavish room on the third floor with gold satin chairs, large beds with matching bedspreads, French Provincial furniture, and a large window that looked out onto the port.[17]

Every night of the festival, delegates gathered in the Aletti's grand ballroom. Chandeliers lit the high-ceilinged dining room, where dozens of tables were covered in gleaming white tablecloths. The mood at these gatherings was warm and exuberant. Cleaver was happy to be surrounded by his old Panther friends, and he also found a joyous comradeship among this group of African radicals. As Kathleen remembered it, "Being among Africans and knowing that we had widespread understanding and support for our struggle, instead of being persecuted, harassed and constantly criticized as we were in America, was a pleasant change for us all. This persecution drew us closer together, for in our movement we knew life may be preciously short, and this increased the beauty of the time we could all share together."[18]

The festival also attracted black artists and political figures. The guest list included playwright Ed Bullins, sociologist Dr. Nathan Hare, jazz great Archie Shepp, singer Nina Simone, and Stokely Carmichael. They stayed at the famous Hotel St. George, a palatial compound perched high up on the hillside overlooking the sea. It had been built on the site of an Ottoman palace at the end of the nineteenth century and featured Moorish architecture and sprawling botanical gardens. Persian rugs covered the floors of the lobby, and the walls were ornamented with Byzantine mosaics. A pair of colorful peacocks made of tile watched over a fountain in the central lobby. Dwight Eisenhower and Winston Churchill had used the hotel as a base during World War II; more recently, literary celebrities like Jean-Paul Sartre and Simone de Beauvoir had been guests.

Cleaver had his final falling out with Carmichael at the Hotel St. George. Carmichael had publicly resigned from the Black Panthers months earlier and had openly criticized the Panthers' alliance with white political groups. Carmichael's Afrocentric vision of revolutionary struggle had always been at odds with Cleaver's Marxism, but it finally came to a head in Algiers. Cleaver was a dialectical materialist, which meant that he didn't subscribe to Marxist dogma but rather to a method of critical thought that adjusted to material conditions. For

Cleaver, anticolonial Marxism was alive to the struggles of peoples of color throughout the globe and helped forge connections with other groups fighting against capitalism and colonialism. Carmichael's black nationalist approach, on the other hand, endorsed the idea of a collective black identity around which the oppressed could rally. Cleaver and Carmichael had a number of heated exchanges at St. George's restaurant over these conflicting views. As Dr. Nathan Hare remembered it, "I saw him and Stokely sitting in a very private and serious huddle. They appeared as old friends—or better yet, as estranged spouses—in a deliberately subdued huddle."[19] Their relationship was broken after this. A month later, Cleaver published an open letter to Carmichael in the pages of the *Black Panther* criticizing his views as racist. He repeated the words his mother had once told him, "An undying love for black people that denies the humanity of other people is doomed. It was an undying love of white people for each other which led them to deny the humanity of colored people and which has stripped white people of humanity itself."[20]

During the conference, Cleaver met representatives of a number of third-world countries. Elaine Mokhtefi first put him in contact with North Vietnam. Cleaver believed that the occupation of Vietnam by the US military was analogous to the police occupation of American ghettos, and he was eager to discuss this with the Vietnamese. They greeted Cleaver as an ambassador, presenting him with a ring made from the metal of a downed American fighter jet.[21] Through Mokhtefi, Cleaver met with the ambassador of North Korea, who invited him to attend the upcoming journalist conference in Pyongyang. Cleaver visited the Chinese embassy, and he participated in a panel with representatives from Haiti, Angola, Mozambique, and Zimbabwe to discuss techniques to overthrow colonial powers. He even struck up a friendship with Yasser Arafat, who occupied the Al Fatah office just down the street.[22] Through his conversations with Arafat, Cleaver came to believe that the struggle of Palestinians was akin to other global struggles against Western hegemony. Cleaver took a hard line against Israel, claiming it was a "tool of international imperialism" and supported the armed resistance by Palestinian freedom fighters against the Zionists.[23]

As the festival came to a close, Kathleen returned to Algiers from the small town of Tiaret, where she had she given birth to her first child at a Cuban hospital in Algeria. Cleaver and Kathleen named their firstborn son Maceo after the famous Cuban revolutionary Antonio Maceo. They hoped that he too would become a radical and leader of his people someday. The blissful moment of his birth was short-lived, however, when Kathleen came home to find Cleaver carrying on an affair with Tricia Baldock. Cleaver had been sleeping with Baldock in Berkeley, and when he landed in Algiers, he sent for her to come to the Aletti. Kathleen was devastated. Cleaver tried to defend their relationship, saying she could be useful acting as courier and messenger. Kathleen didn't buy it. A few days later, after Cleaver had not come home by 2:00 AM, she went down to Baldock's room with a butcher knife, and she planned to stab them both if Baldock didn't leave the country. When she couldn't find them, she went back to her own room, where Cleaver was waiting for her. He started choking her. As Kathleen described it in a letter to him later, "I was down on the floor beside Maceo's bed and you were choking me, calling me insane, and it wasn't until I gasped that you were the one who was insane for choking me over a white woman that you stopped. You told me that you felt like killing me. I didn't feel like killing you, but I sure did want to kill that bitch you were fucking. And there's nothing insane about that. Check Fanon."[24]

Over the next few months, Kathleen wrote a series of letters to Cleaver demanding that he send Baldock back to the States and that he stop brutalizing her. These letters were angry, defiant, and sometimes darkly funny, as Kathleen fought to retain her dignity and sanity in the face of Cleaver's behavior. She wrote in one, "If you cannot manage to have your relationship with Tricia, your darling little devil who loves the very air you breathe and the shit in your underpants like niggers love port, cool enough now so as not to violently attack me physically and emotionally when I cut the bitch up because I don't relate to white women whose relationship to the people's war is based on their relationship to a black dick, then we will just have to make other arrangements."[25] Kathleen's letters pointed out the hypocrisy of

Cleaver's actions as a revolutionary race leader who abused his black wife in order to protect his white mistress. He had not destroyed the image of the ogre. In Kathleen's assessment, he was more entangled with her than ever. She challenged him, "If you want to off me for her, please go ahead—and let the whole world know that even the great Eldridge Cleaver is still talking revolution and sleeping counter-revolution. Anything you want is yours for the taking, and take her if that's what you want—but don't expect me to sit around and catch blows and lose blood and sleep and weight and sanity over something as insignificant as a little Miss Muffet."[26]

At the end of the festival, the Cleavers were unsure what to do next. They had made important contacts with third-world countries that shared their passion for the fight against imperialism. However, they were still without resources or a home base. Cleaver had hoped that the Organization for African Unity would grant the Panthers official status as a liberation group. This would institutionalize the Panthers as an sanctioned organization on the international scene. They were denied, however, and Cleaver was left without a plan. Furthermore, hijackers Rahim Smith, Byron Booth, Akili Patterson, and Gwen Patterson had arrived from Cuba and needed a place to stay. With nowhere else to go, they threw in their lot with the Cleavers.

Ellen Wright lent Cleaver some money, and they all found a house near Pointe Pescade, a dilapidated fishing village a few miles outside town. The house had been abandoned because it had once belonged to an Algerian loyal to the French, who had been killed by the National Liberation Front (FLN). The community was isolated. The Cleavers had no car, and none of the neighbors spoke English. The house had no appliances, hot water, closets, toilet, or telephone. The smell of gasoline flooded the house from the garage below. The house was constantly damp, and only an old kerosene heater warmed the place.[27] Kathleen's mother arrived just in time. She bought a refrigerator and stove for them, and she helped with the baby. Even with her mother's presence there, Kathleen thought that the stone building was like "a tomb."[28]

Money was becoming an ongoing concern. Cleaver wrote to Abels, "This is urgent and not debatable. Obtaining operational cash is a serious difficulty, and those funds do us no good lying up in a NY bank, earning money for the stockholders while we must have food, clothing, shelter, transportation, and other basic tools for survival."[29] Cleaver wondered if he might make money by writing a quick book. Perhaps he could publish something like his recent *Post-Prison Writings and Speeches*, a loose collection of essays he threw together in early 1969. Abels urged him to work on a more substantial project. "I feel that *Post-Prison Writings* was fine, for what it was, but I feel your next book, as I've said, should be more solid—ether a sustained political work or a sustained autobiography or a sustained novel."[30] Cleaver thought of combining and developing his two best autobiographical short stories about his childhood, "The Black Moochie" and "The Flashlight," into a novel, but Abels shot that idea down as well. She told him that "Moochie" was more immediate, while "Flashlight" was a recollection, and they didn't belong together.[31] She wanted him to produce something entirely new. Cleaver wasn't sure that he could do it. He wrote to his old friend Max Geismar, "According to my desires, I should be doing a lot of writing at this time, but according to my needs, I write seldom if at all."[32]

In 1945, the newly formed United Nations divided Korea along the thirty-eighth parallel. It was understood that this was a temporary arrangement, and that in 1948, a countrywide election would be held to reunify the country. The United States took control of the southern portion, arguing that doing so would expedite the transition from four decades of Japanese colonial rule. It installed the dictator President Syngman Rhee. Rhee was virtually unknown to Koreans. He had been brought over on Douglas MacArthur's personal airplane from the United States, where he had been living off and on since 1904. Rhee was anticommunist and pro-American, and as president, he cracked down on dissidents and communists. He retained the colonial-era police force that had been maintained by the Americans after 1945, using them to protect the property rights of landowners and industrialists. He kept tens of thousands of communists in prison, and when an uprising broke out on Jeju Island, Rhee's police and military massacred over fourteen thousand people.

The North was controlled by a communist worker's party and ruled by Kim Il-sung as president. President Kim was an effective guerrilla leader who had fought against the Japanese colonizers. He was highly respected by Koreans on both sides of the thirty-eighth parallel. Between 1945 and 1948, as a principal administrator, he nationalized heavy industry that had been owned by the Japanese, implemented an eight-hour workday, established a health-care system, and redistributed vast tracts of land to peasant farmers. In 1950, President Kim decided to reunify the two Koreas by invading the South. This was after Rhee had held an election and declared himself president of the entire Korean peninsula. A war ensued. The United States came to the aid of South Korea, attempting to "stop the spread of communism." Americans dropped over thirty thousand tons of napalm and six hundred thousand tons of bombs on North Korea. American forces burned entire villages they suspected might be harboring guerrillas. They dehumanized Koreans, calling them "gooks."[33] Despite the heavy losses to its infrastructure and population, North Korea emerged as a symbol of anticolonial might, warding off the world's biggest superpower. Cleaver wrote later, "The defeat of the United States' war of aggression against the Korean people was an important turning point in the history of the world struggle against imperialism. The great example of the Korean People's struggle against the United States is a beacon light of hope to all of the peoples of the world who are struggling for liberation and national salvation."[34]

In early August, Cleaver received the official invitation to attend the internationalist journalist conference in Pyongyang. The North Koreans promised to pay his expenses, and they invited him on tours of Mt. Kumgang and the seaside city of Wonsan. The letter informed Cleaver, "The visit of your delegation to our country and its participation in the Conference will contribute to the strengthening of the solidarity of the journalists of the world in their joint struggle against U.S. imperialism and to the consolidation and development of friendship and solidarity between journalists of our two countries."[35] Cleaver was eager for this once-in-a-lifetime opportunity, and he felt that it would strengthen the Panthers' standing on the global stage. He wrote to David Hilliard on the eve of the trip, "We are laying the groundwork for continuing and improving relations with our comrades from North Korea. We should be able to generate some very strong support in Korea and throughout Asia. Look forward to messages from us."[36]

On September 11, Cleaver and Byron Booth took a plane from Algiers to Moscow, then another to Pyongyang. During their first few days in North Korea, they were given a tour of the city and surrounding countryside. They were taken to museums, where they were taught the history of North Korea's resistance to Japanese and American imperial rule. Cleaver was impressed with the capitol city. "Pyongyang was an incredible site. From the blackened ruins of the war, these people have built a beautiful modern city with wide tree lined boulevards interspersed with gardens and parks. The buildings in the heart of the city are mostly 6 or 7 stories high and white or pastel colored. The predominant impression of the whole city is of light and space and greenery."[37]

On September 22, Cleaver delivered an address to Kim Il-Sung and the Korean people, titled "Solidarity of the Peoples Until Victory or Death!" Cleaver was in true revolutionary form. He attacked American imperialists, calling them "bloodsucking capitalist vultures and the bloodletting warmongers." He urged people all over the world to pick up arms and drive the imperialists out of Vietnam, South Korea, Guantanamo Bay, Africa, Asia, and South America. He implored freedom fighters to kidnap ambassadors, blow up buildings and pipelines, and shoot anyone who stood in their way. He urged people to create revolutionary literature so as to inspire soldiers to form firing squads and execute "President Nixon, ex-President Johnson, all the generals of the U.S. Armed Forces, all warmongers and exploiters."[38] This speech was not heard outside of Korea, though Cleaver later included this anti-American rhetoric in his introduction to a collection of speeches by Kim, published in 1972.

During his few weeks in Korea, Cleaver was an earnest student of North Korean political and military philosophy. He took eighty pages of handwritten notes, carefully documenting his experiences, which he titled "Revolutionary Spirit of Comrade Kim Il Sung."[39] He tried to record every aspect of what he learned, integrating Kim Il-sung's teachings into his larger Marxist framework. Cleaver was particularly interested in Juche, a philosophy that combined Marxism-Leninism, Maoism, and nationalism.[40] It emphasized self-reliant struggle against imperialism and cautioned against applying Marxism without first understanding the specific national situation. For Cleaver, Juche offered a compelling synthesis of materialist and anticolonial thinking that could be applied to the American context.

Cleaver also mapped out how Korean military tactics might be adopted by black freedom fighters. He studied strategies for guerrilla warfare, including training of troops and propaganda. His made exhaustive lists of his objectives. Under the column labeled "Military Training," he wrote: "Killing. Expert on Weapons. Shooting, geography and map reading. Map making; strategy; attack, ambushed. (Idea: put sand in socks to make body strong). Avoid all obstacles; know how to survive land mines, chemicals. Wet handkerchiefs make good gas masks. Self-defense with hands and feet."[41]

In North Korea, Cleaver was lonely for Kathleen. He knew that he treated her badly, but that didn't stop him from abusing her. Although he would never acknowledge it, he resented her privilege and her light skin, and he punished her for the way that made him feel. Only when he was away from her did Cleaver express his affection for her through his letters. He wrote on the first night apart, "But love, it is only out of a sense of duty that I was able to tear myself away to take this trip. Secretly I kept hoping that something would happen to block it. When I return, let us both be a little nicer and more considerate of each other. Because I can think of nothing as precious to me as you and your love. I will always love you."[42] A few days later, he wrote to Kathleen again. He was even more vulnerable in this letter, almost apologetic for his abuse: "I am anxious to get back so that I can be with you and Maceo. I miss you both in the strongest way. I am very sorry about the insanity that crept into our relationship. . . . I was getting very depressed because I was convinced you were losing interest in me and becoming interested in others. It seemed to me that this was showing in many little ways. I want you to know that I love you and only you and there is not the slightest chance of my ever loving anyone else."[43]

The week after Cleaver left for Pyongyang, Kathleen intercepted a packet of love letters intended for him from Tricia Baldock. This was the breaking point for Kathleen, and she decided to sleep with Clinton "Rahim" Smith as revenge. She told Cleaver in a letter, "I finally realized that the only thing to do was to try and experience what you had experienced, to see how I felt about fucking somebody else, because words weren't bringing me any nearer to an understanding, and all my efforts to discuss it with you were futile."[44] Kathleen started spending more time with Smith. He took her to a fortune-teller and to a seaside restaurant named Cercle du Baron. They went to a dance club, where friends saw them kissing. One night, the Cleavers' cleaning lady tipped over a bucket and spilled water all over Kathleen's mattress, which was on the floor of the bedroom. Smith offered to let her share his bed. Kathleen remembered those events much later: "I was so tired and disoriented that I didn't realize the position he was putting me in—because he intended to sleep there as well. His promise to leave me alone was empty. Unceremoniously, soon after I settled into the bed, he approached me sexually, and I did not turn him away. It was not my idea, but I took a certain perverse pleasure in sleeping with another man after being humiliated by Eldridge's relationship with Tricia Baldock."[45]

When Cleaver returned from North Korea, she told him about the affair. He became insanely jealous. Even though Cleaver cheated on Kathleen all the time, he was maddened by her infidelity. A few days after the incident, Smith disappeared from the house. Cleaver had kindapped him and shot him with an AK-47 given to him by Kim Il-sung. Then, unable to carry the body on his own, Cleaver enlisted Byron Booth to help bury it. Booth was so afraid for his own life that he left Algiers the next day and did not return. Within a week, Smith's body was found half-concealed in the hillside behind Pointe Pescade. Cleaver told Mokhtefi he had killed Smith because he was stealing their money and planning to leave with it. But that was a lie. He had killed Smith out of rage and jealousy, and because, in Algeria, he had the power to get away with it. As Cleaver admitted to fellow Panther Don Cox, "I killed the motherfucker. The minute he fucked Kathleen, he was a dead man."[46] Mokhtefi and Cox were both disturbed, but they knew the government would do nothing about it, so they kept silent.

Cleaver became more abusive toward Kathleen after Smith's murder. One night, he invited Mokhtefi for dinner. Kathleen was too tired to cook, but he forced her to make dinner anyway. As Mokhtefi remembered, "He went to tell Kathleen that I would stay for dinner. Kathleen said 'I won't make dinner.' He gave her a black eye. And she made dinner. And I had to eat it. It was terrible. I could never forget that. Later I asked him why he treated her so badly. He said, 'Some people demand to be treated that way.'"[47]

Cleaver also took revenge on Kathleen by starting up numerous affairs with Algerian women. He sometimes went out two or three times a day to meet them. In spring 1970, he started a relationship with a fifteen-year-old girl named Malika Ziri. She was intelligent and beautiful, and Cleaver fell in love with her. They used Mokhtefi's apartment as a meeting place and eventually became very public about their relationship. They could be seen together around town all the time. Kathleen was pregnant with the couple's second child, and Cleaver ignored her to spend time with Malika. The affair was scandalous, especially considering that the country was Muslim. Cox remembered, "I would go with him to pick her up from school. And we'd be sitting out the car waiting for her at lunch time and I'd see all these men in their cars, but they're coming to get their daughters or sisters or something. But Eldridge is there to pick up his girl, you know. Oh, it was terrible."[48] Cox inwardly condemned Cleaver for dating an underage girl, but because of his loyalty to him and the cause, he said nothing. Kathleen was traumatized by Cleaver's behavior. She was racked with guilt over his murder of Smith, and she was outraged by his infidelity and abuse. But she was alone and isolated in a country where women had little voice. She wrote in her journal, "These days are very trying, although the components of the strain are not particularly new, they are of a sort that repetition makes practically unbearable.

I am now five months pregnant, Maceo is eight and a half months old, and Eldridge—Eldridge is busy with his work and his women. How many affairs can one wife stand? How many sleepless nights and torturing empty silences and withheld complaints and tears can be tolerated?"[49]

The Americans had no official embassy of their own in Algiers. Algeria had broken off diplomatic relations after the Six-Day War between Israel and Egypt, Syria, and Jordan in 1967. The Americans did run a consulate out of the Swiss embassy, however, as the United States still had significant oil interests in the country. Soon after Cleaver's arrival, the American consulate started keeping tabs on him. It wasn't difficult, as he visited the consulate regularly. In the fall, American diplomats gave a Thanksgiving party for oil executives from the United States. Cleaver and the Panthers crashed the party. William Eagleton, head of the American consulate, described it: "They entered in a phalanx, early in the reception, creating a bit of a stir. Black leather coats, light blue turtle-neck shirts, black trousers, Afro hair-do's, four of them counting Cleaver, and accompanied by an American negro girl in the same outfit. Quite a few Texans and Oklahomans working for SONATRACH were present, and you could have heard a pin drop." As it turned out, the Panthers were eager to get help with their passport applications. Everyone drank and started to relax, and officials helped them fill out the forms. Eagleton speculated that Cleaver made such a big show of coming to the party because he and the other Panthers were homesick. "I think more germane is that they feel 'dépaysé' in Algiers, out of touch with the States, bored, and eager for some contact with Americans."[50]

Throughout 1969 and 1970, FBI and law enforcement in the United States stepped up its attacks on the Panthers. The bureau created conflict between the Panthers and Ron Karenga's US Organization. It created propagandistic cartoons that were made to appear as though each organization were ridiculing the other in an attempt to spark violence. On January 17, 1969, the conflict turned deadly, when

Panther members John Huggins and Bunchy Carter were killed by US Organization members on the UCLA campus. The shooters were suspected of being agent provocateurs for the FBI.

The death of Carter was a tremendous blow to Cleaver. Carter had established the L.A. chapter and built that organization from the ground up. In the process, he had created the first underground component of the Black Panther Party, which Cleaver saw as necessary in the struggle against the police. Carter was also a close friend, and as a street-gang-leader-turned-revolutionary, he was a symbol of everything the Panthers could achieve.

In December 1969, Chicago police murdered Panther leaders Fred Hampton and Mark Clark while they slept in their beds. The FBI had used informants to help them map out Hampton's apartment and then passed along the information to law enforcement. Just a few days later, the Los Angeles Police Department's new special weapons and tactics (SWAT) unit attacked L.A. Panther headquarters. Geronimo Pratt, who was a decorated military veteran and appointed head of the Los Angeles Panthers after Carter's death, had fortified the offices by piling sandbags against the walls and digging tunnels in the basement. Policemen fired five thousand rounds of ammunition into the headquarters, but the Panthers inside survived the five-hour onslaught. However, many Panthers elsewhere did not survive other attacks. According to civil rights lawyer Charles Geary, "In a period of two years—December, 1967–December, 1969 . . . twenty-eight Panthers were killed [by police]. And we have documented all of these cases. Since then other Panthers have been murdered."[51]

In the spring of 1970, the FBI began a campaign to drive a wedge between Cleaver's International Section and the Central Committee of the Black Panther Party. The FBI hoped to create mutual suspicion between Cleaver and David Hilliard, and they wanted Cleaver to feel isolated abroad. As they reported, "It is expected that at least some doubts will be created in Cleaver's mind and a serious breach may result between him, Hilliard, Hewitt, and Howard. More severe consequences could occur resulting in the possible expulsion of Matthews and/or Hewitt. If sufficiently angered it could even cause Cleaver to return to the United States."[52]

The FBI first sent a forged letter to David Hilliard ostensibly from fellow Panther Connie Matthews stating that Cleaver was becoming erratic. "I think that something is really wrong with him [Cleaver] and that his thinking is so clouded at this time that he could be a danger to you and the party." The letter went on to claim, "He really has been gone so long that he seems out of touch with reality and you should know this."[53] The FBI also sent a letter to Cleaver, again ostensibly from Matthews, stating that David Hilliard had been stealing funds. It also warned Cleaver that he was becoming less relevant in the party. The letter concluded, "I may be mistaken in this, but from what I have heard, it looks like you fall in the category 'out of sight, out of mind' and except for your name and reputation, you have become a drag to the party." Cleaver responded just as the FBI had hoped. He expelled Louise Wibecam, James Patterson, and Gwen Patterson from the International Section, fearing that they might be informants. James Patterson left for Liberia, while Gwen Patterson stayed behind to act as caretaker for the children of the International Section members. Wibecam fled the country. J. Edgar Hoover was so pleased that he gave out incentive awards to the agents who created the letters.[54]

During summer 1970, a number of new Panthers showed up in Algeria, including Sekou Odinga, Larry Mack of the New York chapter, and Pete O'Neal, head of the Kansas City branch of the Panthers. Even as Cleaver expelled members, the International Section kept growing in size, as Panthers from all over abandoned the United States for Cleaver's organization.

Cleaver's money woes eased somewhat in early 1970, when the federal government lifted its lien against him after it determined he was not a Cuban national. He once again had access to his royalties. At this point, Abels, Mokhtefi, and others advised him to get out of his agreement with Axelrod, which still gave her 25 percent of the royalties. Abels wrote him multiple letters, pushing him to change the agreement. "As you know, I do think Beverly should have come to some other arrangement with you. I have for some time. But it was a personal arrangement from the beginning (between you and Beverly) and I can see it's being changed only by you."[55] Abels reasoned that no one could have known how much *Soul* was going to make or how much Cleaver's revolutionary activities were going to cost. Besides, Abels stated, "Beverly has already received a considerable amount of money under the assignment Eldridge made."[56] Cleaver adamantly refused. He owed her his life for getting him out of prison, and she had helped him publish *Soul on Ice*. Despite his betrayals of many others in his life, Cleaver still felt a deep loyalty to Axelrod. She had helped secure his freedom, and for that he would be eternally grateful.

In May 1970, Kathleen flew to Pyongyang to give birth to her second child, a daughter named Joju. Cleaver insisted on sending her there, as he wanted to spend more time with Malika alone. Kathleen and Maceo were installed in a large guest house on the shores of a lake near Pyongyang. They were provided with a cook, driver, maid, and interpreter. From here, Kathleen wrote Cleaver a series of letters, making an impassioned demand that he change his behavior. She was tortured by his cheating, writing him, "I have been tormented with the results of your relationships with various white women ever since I first came to San Francisco up to the present, and this situation MUST be resolved."[57] The next day, she wrote again, with even more force. "I am tired of being given a back seat to white women, tired of being denied any social existence, any consideration, and any respect. It's gotten to the explosive point now where our relationship holds no emotional satisfaction, no mental satisfaction, no physical satisfaction, and no genuine companionship for me—and for you either, from what you say. It's all misery, suffering, frustration, and sickening."[58]

Over the next month, Kathleen wrote a series of letters to Cleaver. She deliberated over the state of their marriage, the future of their children, and their plans for the revolution. For Kathleen, her marriage to Cleaver and the black revolution were connected, and she believed both could be saved if they could find some reconciliation. Despite all of Cleaver's abuses, she was willing to forgive him for the sake of the marriage, the family, and, most of all, for the revolution. "To rise above the level of petty personal concerns, either material, emotional, or physical, and surmount the pinnacle of a liberated existence in the genuine revolutionary spirit—this is the key to solving many small problems and complex difficulties we face now."[59]

Her letters fell on deaf ears. When Kathleen returned to Algeria with her two small children in summer 1970, Cleaver ignored her pleas for reconciliation. He was distant and cold. He was also paranoid, knowing that he was being watched by the FBI. He was drinking or smoking marijuana too much now. With his grasp on things slipping away, he turned his attention toward trying to strengthen the International Section of the Black Panther Party.

In July 1970, Cleaver led a group of writers and activists on a tour of North Korea, North Vietnam, and China. The group, known as the American People's Anti-Imperialist Delegation, traveled to Asia to show support for struggles against imperialism across the globe. The members included Bob Scheer and Jan Austin of *Ramparts*; Ann Froines, John Froines, and Andy Truskier of the Peace Movement; Elaine Brown of the Black Panther Party; Pat Sumi of the Movement for a Democratic Military; Alex Hing of the Chinese Radical Organization; Randy Rappaport and Janet Kransberg of New York Newsreel; and Gina Blumenfeld of the Peace and Freedom Party. The trip represented the height of Cleaver's efforts to build an international and domestic coalition of radicals from diverse backgrounds to protest white supremacy and empire.

Cleaver was paranoid after receiving the letters from the FBI, so he took extreme measures to control the dynamics of the trip. He acted almost like a warden as soon as the delegation met in Moscow. Delegate Randy Rappaport remembered, "He made it clear that we were henceforth his prisoners. He took our passports from us. I think he was high or drunk. He was high or drunk most of the time. He basically laid out the dynamic we were going to be in where he was essentially going to be in total control of our lives."[60]

Cleaver's drug and alcohol use lately had gotten a bit out of control. During the stopover in Moscow, he invited Alex Hing and Bob Scheer to his room to smoke some marijuana. He had filled a cassette player with it, which he carried on the trip. He was afraid that the KGB agents patrolling the hallways would smell it, so he poured some perfume from a bottle that Scheer had picked up for Kathleen in Paris into a dish and set it next to the door. He then lit it on fire, hoping to cover the marijuana smell. But the door caught fire, and Cleaver was barely able to put it out before it got out of control.

The day after the delegation met in Moscow, the group flew to North Korea, where group members visited museums, schools, and factories. They traveled to the demilitarized zone at Panmunjom, where American soldiers still guarded the border between North and South Korea. They protested with signs that read, GO HOME USA! They went to the Museum of Anti-Japanese Revolutionary Struggle as well as the Sinchon Museum of American War Atrocities. Sinchon was where thirty-five thousand Koreans were allegedly killed by American forces in just fifty-two days. The delegation members were invited to write in a guest book. After everyone signed it, Cleaver read through the entries. Rappaport remembered, "I wrote something somewhat emotional. I am a person with a very high level of empathy, and I get very emotional in a lot of situations. Everybody had written something. Eldridge was looking at what everyone had written, and he said 'Who wrote this?' I actually didn't identify myself. I was terrified. He was referring to what I had written. And he tore it apart."[61]

During the trip to North Korea, the delegation was unexpectedly invited to Hanoi, North Vietnam. With the war raging, Cleaver saw the side trip as an opportunity to protest the war from inside the site of struggle. He did not give anyone an option. He wanted to be recognized as the revolutionary anti-war hero and decided they were all going to Hanoi. The decision sprang from a combination of ego and political calculation. He saw himself as a great historical figure and believed that with the help of the third world, he could bring about revolutionary military action in the United States.

When they arrived in Vietnam, they were treated as official delegates. They met with Norodom Sihanouk from Cambodia, Vietnamese premier Pham Van Dong, and General Vo Nguyen Giap. Cleaver later wrote that the greatest moment of his life was when Pham Van Dong toasted him. Officials gave the delegation gifts of books and a vase made of aircraft parts from a downed American jet. They also held an International Day of Solidarity with Afro-American People.[62] Cleaver and Elaine Brown gave a speech on Vietnam Radio, encouraging American GIs to turn their weapons against their commanding officers. Some US troops wrote Cleaver later to tell him that they deserted after listening to his message. The Vietnamese government gave them hundreds of letters from American POWs to their families back home.[63] At the end of their stay in Vietnam they visited China for a week, where they met with officials and toured Peking.

From one perspective, the trip had been a grand success. Cleaver and the Panthers had deepened ties with socialist countries in Asia and promoted the Black Panther Party as a global political group. However, Cleaver had also ruined alliances with domestic political groups. He did not allow the female delegates to make decisions, he forbade everyone from talking to others outside the delegation, and he violently policed everyone's movements. Alex Hing even overheard Cleaver joking with Bob Scheer at one point that "the masses are asses," which undermined everything he believed as a Marxist and as a third-world delegate.[64] Elaine Brown, a member of the Black Panther Party, wrote a forty-page report about Cleaver's behavior on the trip, called "Hidden Traitor." According to Brown, Cleaver drank excessively, vulgarly hit on both delegates and hosts, and made disparaging remarks about the countries they were visiting. "By this time, E. C. could no longer be viewed by me as a respected leader of the BPP, and he had developed in my mind as an adversary who was maniacal in his thoughts, and who would often attempt to carry out maniacal thoughts through the use of other people's various own personality problems."[65]

Even when the trip was over, Cleaver exercised extreme control over the delegation. He transported them to the apartment out at Pointe Pescade. He gathered them together and announced that he had read their journals. He demanded that they destroy any part that made reference to him. Rappaport explained, "It was possible that we would be arrested when we came back, that our journals would be confiscated, and then there would be too much information available to the FBI or CIA or whoever about him. So he tells us we should go through our journals and pull out and destroy any pages that had any of that kind of content in them." Rappaport believed that they had little choice. "He basically said you will be killed if in any way, shape, or form betray or show any negativity toward me or the Black Panther Party. He basically threatened our lives, and he had our passports."[66]

In little more than a year since his arrival in Algeria, Cleaver had created a viable international section of the Black Panther Party with significant connections to third-world communist countries. But Cleaver also used seized power for himself, which he used to murder a rival lover and member of his own party with impunity. Fueled by alcohol and marijuana, Cleaver as autocrat succumbed to his most violent impulses, particularly in his relationship with Kathleen. In response to the sabotage perpetrated by the FBI, Cleaver grew paranoid, expelling members and taking hostages. He was becoming a dictator who used intimidation and humiliation to control everyone in his orbit. Cleaver was no less committed to the cause of black freedom than before. Indeed, his primary motivation was to create meaningful relationships between black Americans and the third world. But because Cleaver believed he was an important actor in the history of black liberation, he felt that he could act above the law.

13

THE INTERNATIONAL SECTION OF THE BLACK PANTHER PARTY (1970–1972)

Over the summer of 1970, Algeria's Revolutionary Council granted the Panthers status as a liberation movement. Cleaver had approached Mokhtefi about the matter before he left on the trip to Asia, and she had worked behind the scenes to make it happen. On September 13, 1970, the Algerian government inaugurated the embassy for the International Section of the Black Panther Party. It was monumental for the party and for Cleaver personally. Recognized as an official international organization by the Algerian government, the Panthers now had a centralized home base through which to run their operations. By this point, the community of Panthers was growing substantially. Don Cox and his wife Barbara Easley, Pete and Charlotte O'Neal, Sekou Odinga, and Larry Mack had all fled the

United States to join Cleaver, and there were more Panthers showing up all of the time.

The Panther embassy was housed in a white stucco villa located at 4 Rue Vivani in the suburban neighborhood of El Biar. The modest two-story complex had once been occupied by the National Liberation Front of South Vietnam. It had a library and high-ceilinged meeting rooms as well as a large balcony in the front. The Panthers transformed one room into an office for creating newsletters and recordings and another into a nursery for the growing number of children. They were given quasi-diplomatic status, a $500-a-month stipend, a mailbox, a telex, and identification cards. In just a few short years, Cleaver had gone from being an inmate to the leader of an international liberation movement backed by an African nation. He started to think of himself as the black Che Guevara. Now that they were housed in the villa and had access to media and financial resources, the possibilities seemed endless.

A month after the opening, countercultural guru Timothy Leary and his wife, Rosemary, arrived on Cleaver's doorstep. With the help of the radical Weathermen organization, Leary had escaped a minimum-security prison in California. Stew Albert and his wife, Judy, brought him to Algeria to meet Cleaver. Leary was a hero to the white left, and in the interests of solidarity, Cleaver agreed to house him and his wife.

Leary proved a difficult guest. One of his fans had smuggled one thousand hits of LSD into Algeria, and Leary and Rosemary were very public about using it. They repeatedly went to the Bou Saada region, an oasis in the desert, where they tripped naked on acid. One day the police picked them up and dropped them off to Cleaver. He responded by placing the Learys under house arrest. Leary had a sense of humor about the whole thing. "We saw ourselves as historic figures, as the first white Americans to seek the protection of the first black American government in exile. And now we have become the first whites to be busted by that black government. It's far out."[1] The Algerians, on the other hand did not like Cleaver's response, believing that he had overstepped his authority. As the State Department reported, the "Algerian government was very angry with the local colony of Black Panthers as a result of the Panther 'arrest' of Timothy and Rosemary Leary. The Panthers had taken the law into their own hands."[2]

A few days later, Cleaver put out a videotape condemning Leary's use of drugs as counterrevolutionary. It was a total about-face from his position in 1968, when he felt drug use was a way to organize people politically. Cleaver stated, "Leary seems content to continue advising people to 'Turn on, tune in and drop out', and that he really means it when he says that freedom means getting high. While this is in direct conflict with the needs of the American revolution, because we feel that we need people with clear heads, sober people who [have] their wits about them, because we're confronted with murderous fascist pigs who will stop at nothing." Cleaver made exceptions for booze and marijuana, but he believed psychedelics had no place in the revolution to come. He proclaimed to Leary's followers, "Your god is dead because his mind has been blown by acid."[3]

In August 1970, Huey Newton was released on a $50,000 bail bond. His manslaughter conviction for the murder of Officer Frey had been thrown out by an appellate court. He had survived three years in prison and was ready to retake control of the party. Cleaver was thrilled to have Newton visit Algeria to see the operation. However, now that Newton was free from prison, an ideological struggle between the two men started to emerge, one that would tear the party in half in just a few short months. Cleaver was a staunch supporter of anticolonial violence and international cooperation among third-world nations. He believed in proletariat solidarity and the overthrow of the capitalist system through guerrilla warfare. At first, Newton supported these radical ideas. Just after his release, he asserted that armed struggle was the only path to black liberation, which earned the support of George Jackson, the infamous revolutionary who founded the San Quentin branch of the Black Panther Party. However, Newton quickly shifted his focus to local community survival programs, such as free breakfast for children.

Although Cleaver and Newton are now usually seen as diametrically opposed in their views, they were not so rigid in their ideologies as people think. Newton kept the Panthers militarized by employing bodyguards to control members of the party, while Cleaver himself had initially supported the breakfast program when it was first started out of a church basement in 1968. The Panthers had gathered there many mornings to cook food, and the kids smelled it while walking to school. One day they asked if they could come in, and the Panthers invited them to eat. The program grew from there. Cleaver remembered, "They'd show up every morning for breakfast and more and more kids but we had so much food we had all them ranges, we had all them ranges and we had all these seats, big auditorium sized dining room, cafeteria, so we just cooked more food, man, and pretty soon it was more kids coming to breakfast than the Panthers, man. You used to have to really get there early and get in line to get in there because we gave priority to these kids cause they had to get to school. We could eat later on." The program emerged somewhat spontaneously to meet the direct needs of the community. Continued Cleaver, "We didn't set out and say, look, let's start a breakfast-for-children program. We never had that idea. It was just discovered that through our own practice, and that became a very powerful counter to the attempts by the government to isolate us."[4]

Following Cleaver's departure from the United States, the breakfast program became the cornerstone of the Panthers' community-organizing effort. The organization fed twenty thousand children in 1968, and the popularity of this program led to the creation of others, such as free health clinics, clothing giveaways, and sickle-cell-anemia testing.[5] The new approach was incredibly successful in recruiting new members and earning the community's respect.

The FBI recognized that the Panthers' new strategy was effective, so it tried to destroy the breakfast program. Agents intimidated church and school officials in an attempt to deny the Panthers venues to serve food. They spread rumors about food being poisoned and even considered lacing it with laxatives to make everyone sick. This final measure was considered too dangerous and was vetoed, but the FBI made every effort to sabotage feeding hungry children. Hoover justified this to his agents by reminding them that the Panthers were their true targets. "In neutralizing the 'Breakfast for Children Program' we do not desire to prevent needy children from these breakfasts, but are attempting to prevent the poisoning of the children's minds by hard core BPP members."[6]

As soon as Newton was free from prison, the FBI acted quickly to intensify the conflict between him and Cleaver. Hoover sent out a notice the day after Newton's release: "All offices consider counterintelligence proposals to initiate and/or exploit existing dissension within BPP including conflicts between Newton and other leaders such as Hilliard and Cleaver over BPP policy, ideology, day-to-day operation, finances, and personal matters." After Newton wrote an article in the August issue of the *Black Panther* calling for oppressed groups, including gays, to unite with the Panthers, the FBI sent forged letters to David Hilliard denouncing Newton's support of homosexuals and accusing him of being gay. When Cleaver took in Timothy Leary, the FBI sent letters to Newton accusing Cleaver of "playing footsie" with him.

In October, Newton started exhibiting strange behavior. He carried a swagger stick and started calling himself "supreme commander." He snorted cocaine and took over a nightclub called the Lamp Post. In its reports, the FBI noted, "Huey Newton is apparently unstable and suffering some sort of complex." Agents felt they could exploit this erratic behavior to create further dissension within the party. They sent him a letter, playing on his paranoia. "Here abroad Eldridge and his close advisors in consort with David and June and others in Babylon are conspiring to set you up, take away your leadership and make you our 'Impotent Commander'."[7] In another letter to Newton, the FBI wrote, "Eldridge is rapping with [redacted] to cut you out. Watch out for [redacted] and the others that keep oinking to Eldridge about you. You are the man Huey and all of us are for you but you have got to watch out. Maybe you can tell everybody that all letters to or from Eldridge have to clear through you."[8]

The FBI also sent fake letters to Cleaver, ostensibly from other Panthers, complaining about Newton's leadership style. "Dear Eldridge, It's about time somebody told the Supreme Commander to get himself together and maybe you're the only one that can do it. Huey lacks the aggressiveness to deal with the present situation at the correct level."[9] By December, it was clear that these efforts to sabotage the interaction between Huey and Cleaver were working. Communications from central headquarters to Cleaver came in sporadic letters or phone calls. At Christmas, Cleaver wrote a frustrated letter to Newton, "As a whole, we are being blocked, by you, because of your refusal or failure to communicate with us, to inform us, and to keep us up to date on developments, particularly on the ideological plane."[10]

In the new year, the FBI stepped up its efforts. They sent letters to both Kathleen and Huey Newton's brother threatening them with assassination. They also sent letters to Newton, criticizing him for his "inept" handling of the recent gathering of Revolutionary People's Constitutional Convention (RPCC) and implying that Cleaver was going to stage a coup.[11] One letter read, "You as supreme commander must be held responsible for this fiasco and it is due to your total incompetence for selecting stupid lazy niggers to do the job and you and your whole party have set the revolution back five years."[12] Newton became increasingly paranoid. He believed an informant had infiltrated the organization, and he was afraid Cleaver was plotting something.

In late January, the FBI sent a letter to Cleaver, blaming Newton for the decline of the party. "The Black Panther Party has failed miserably. No longer can the Party be looked upon as the 'Vanguard of the Revolution'."[13] Another FBI-authored letter urged Cleaver to start a coup. "Things around headquarters are dreadfully disorganized with the comrade commander not making proper decisions," the letter stated. "We must get rid of the Supreme Commander or get rid of disloyal members."[14] The FBI exploited the vanities and insecurities of both Panther leaders, which drove them both to act in desperate and volatile ways, and set the stage for the destruction of the party. The FBI wrote in the days before the split, "BPP are at a low ebb. Expulsions and defections during the last quarter have removed many of the prominent members and a good portion of the New York Chapter. Newton is positive there is an informant in Headquarters. Cleaver feels isolated in Algeria and out of contact with Newton and the Supreme Commander's secretary has disappeared."[15]

The party began to fall apart in January 1971, as the ideological contradiction between Cleaver and Newton was fully exposed. Newton first expelled Geronimo Pratt from the Panthers. Pratt was a Vietnam veteran who had fortified the Los Angeles Panther office and heroically survived a five-hour gun battle with police. Under the instructions of the Central Committee, Pratt went underground and set up a secret camp in Texas to train guerrillas. Pratt was later arrested, and because Newton was trying to make the Panthers into a reformist organization through community programs, he purged Pratt from it for his underground activities.[16] Later Pratt was imprisoned for a murder he didn't commit and served twenty-seven years in prison, until it was revealed that the chief witness against him, Julius Butler, was an informant for the FBI. Pratt's guilty verdict was finally reversed in 1997.

Newton also expelled the Panther 21, a group of Panthers who had been framed for plotting terrorist activities. They had been indicted on conspiracy to commit murder charges for supposedly planning to dynamite five midtown department stores, the Bronx police station, and the New York Central Railroad tracks at 148th Street. In January 1971, the Panther 21 published "Open Letter to the Weathermen," in the *East Village Other*, criticizing the Black Panther Party for not freeing them from prison. The Panther 21 argued that the Panthers were no longer the true vanguard of the party because they weren't willing to engage in guerrilla warfare. Newton expelled them for their criticisms. It was the end of the Central Committee's support of clandestine guerrilla activity.

Cleaver was baffled by Newton's decisions. As one FBI report put it, "he was totally confused over the current affairs of the BPP."[17] For Cleaver, the underground militant element of the party was a necessary instrument of the struggle against imperialism. As a Marxist-Leninist, he believed that the vanguard party must at some point lead the working class in a violent overthrow of capitalism. Pratt and the Panther 21 were important figures in this campaign. Cleaver called Huey on January 27 to talk him out of the expulsions. Newton launched into a tirade about the Panther 21, complaining about their lack of loyalty. Cleaver tried to protest, but Newton cut him off, saying, "All the twenty-one down." Cleaver also broached the topic of Pratt. Newton called him a "snake" and accused him of betraying the Panthers.[18] Cleaver attempted on multiple occasions to convince Newton to bring Pratt and the Panther 21 back into the organization, but Newton wouldn't hear of it.

FBI officials who were spying on these conversations felt they should continue to exploit Newton's mistrust ever further. A report stated, "[Newton's] extreme sensitivity to any criticism and jealousness of other top Panthers have recently led to his capricious expulsion of dedicated Panthers. Based on the above we have intensified our counterintelligence activity in selected office[s] to further disrupt and aggravate this situation and our efforts are undoubtedly responsible for some of the Panthers' current problems."[19] A few days later, Hoover himself sent out a call to all agents to focus on manipulating Newton's erratic personality. "Primary cause of these internal problems appears to [be] dictatorial, irrational and capricious conduct of Huey P. Newton. His extreme sensitivity to any criticism, jealousness of other leaders and belief he is some form of deity are causing severe problems within the group."[20]

Throughout February, the FBI intensified the campaign against Cleaver and Newton. It sent letters signed by the Panther 21 to Cleaver complaining about Newton's leadership, and continued to urge Cleaver to take over leadership of the party: "As the leading theoretician of the party's philosophy and as a brother among brothers, we urge you to make your influence felt. We think that The Rage is the only person strong enough to pull this factionalized party back together."[21] Prompted by these letters and by his interactions with Newton, Cleaver sent a telegram to the New York Panthers on February 15. "We now have clear picture of what happened to Geronimo and Panther 21. We disagree with action taken by Hilliard controlled right-wingers. We are going to move soon and hard against this madness. All power to the people. Eldridge."[22]

The FBI sent more letters to the Central Committee. It continued to barrage Newton with bogus letters from delegates complaining about his handling of the RPCC, and it sent one to Newton's brother saying that Cleaver was going to have Newton killed. In mid-February, the FBI mailed the following: "Please warn Huey. He doesn't know the danger he is in. Huey has handed out suspensions and discipline wholesale with no idea who is loyal and who is not. Where does he think all of our trouble started? Why doesn't he look to Algiers and figure it out? First he lost the support of a good part of the white radicals and now the New York chapter."[23]

The final split occurred on February 26, 1971. After lengthy discussions with other members of the International Section, Cleaver and his cohort voted unanimously to demand the resignation of David Hilliard and ask for the reinstatement of both Geronimo Pratt and the Panther 21. They felt that they had no choice but to publicly call out the leadership for their anti-revolutionary actions. Jim Dunbar hosted a television program in San Francisco on which Newton appeared as a guest. Cleaver called in to join the conversation from Algiers. They were promoting the Intercommunal Day of Solidarity to be held in March. At the end of the interview, Dunbar asked Cleaver if he had anything else that he wanted to say. Unexpectedly, Cleaver made the call for the reinstatement of the expelled Panthers:

> I just want to comment on the present situation that exists, antiblack sensibility, specifically in reference to the purge of Brother Geronimo, the expulsion of the Panther 21. Our position over here, and we have three members of the Central Committee of the Black Panther Party over here, is that this action is regrettable, it should not have taken place. It took place without proper consultation with the other members of the Central Committee and we lay the responsibility at the feet of David Hilliard and we demand that David Hilliard be dismissed or resign from the position of chief of staff of the Black Panther Party, so that we can go about the work of putting the party back together again. Because it looks to us as though, as a result of the actions taken by David Hilliard over long periods of time, the party is falling apart at the seams.[24]

This statement spelled the end of the International Section of the Black Panther Party. Elaine Mokhtefi remembered, "I don't think he realized that it was the end of the organization. And neither did anyone else, including DC. They voted. They were all in favor to go on that show and say those things. It was not a decision made off the top of his head. It was a decision made by the International Section. They got together and had a meeting, and they decided to have a showdown."[25]

A few hours later, Cleaver got on the phone with Newton. Cleaver hoped they could resolve things swiftly and peacefully. Instead, the conversation spiraled out of control. Newton expelled the entire International Section, and he threatened to write the Algerian government to have them kicked out of the country. "I like a battle, brother, we'll battle it out," Newton goaded. Cleaver was calm, but pleading: "That's not the best way to deal with that." Newton threatened, "But I think I have the gun." Cleaver responded, "I've got some guns too, brother." Finally, Newton called Cleaver a coward and a punk and hung up the phone.

The conflict escalated quickly following the split. Newton expelled everyone in the International Section. Cleaver in turn expelled Newton and David Hilliard. The New York faction took Cleaver's side and called for a people's trial of Huey Newton. On March 5, Elaine Brown published the article "Free Kathleen Cleaver and All Political Prisoners," accusing Cleaver of murdering Rahim Smith and holding Kathleen Cleaver hostage. This was followed by a number of articles in the *Black Panther* attacking Cleaver's manhood and commitment to the party. Newton published a public expulsion, stating, "Eldridge Leroy Cleaver is a murderer and a punk without genitals." He even commissioned Emory Douglas to create a poster of a naked Cleaver missing a penis.

The fallout of the split was deadly. On March 8, Robert Webb, a Panther loyal to Cleaver and the Panther 21, was murdered on 125th Street in Harlem in broad daylight by three men. The New York faction blamed Huey Newton's henchmen for the crime. A month later, the *Black Panther* manager Sam Napier was murdered in retaliation by members of the New York Panthers. Panthers across the country took sides in the conflict, and the stakes were lethal. The Panthers at San Quentin wrote to Cleaver: "We felt like in all fairness to let you know just how we stand, not only as Party members, but Convicts to Convict. You know our language, and we know yours. We know you're going to be sent here [Quentin] or Folsom. And you know it too, nigger. If so, then you'd better give your last respects to your wife and children, because you're never going to leave here again."[26] The whole situation was a nightmare. According to Kathleen, "We each had to adjust to the sickening reality of being threatened and attacked by our comrades, people we thought of as friends, people we thought we loved."[27]

The Oakland Panthers began to demilitarize their image after this, showing fewer weapons in the *Black Panther* and promoting the free breakfast and free clothing program more than ever.[28] The Central Committee renounced the spirit of insurrection promoted by Cleaver and abandoned philosophies of armed self-defense in support of survival programs. Cleaver and the International Section suddenly found themselves isolated.

The FBI congratulated itself on the "chaotic state" of the BPP. "It should also be noted that the split which has developed in the high level leadership of the BPP with the falling out of Newton and Cleaver, together with the purging of the 'Panther 21' from the BPP, may be utilized as evidence that the counterintelligence efforts of the NYO have born some fruit."[29] So confident was the FBI that it decided to cease the sabotage campaign against Cleaver and Newton. "Since the differences between Newton and Cleaver now appear to be irreconcilable, no further counterintelligence activity in this regard will be undertaken at this time, and new targets must be established."[30]

The International Section floundered following the split. There were now sixteen adults and eight children living at the villa and in various apartments around the city. Even with the $500 stipend from the government, money was tight. After his trip across Asia, Cleaver had been designated a national of North Korea, North Vietnam, and China under the Trading with the Enemy Act. His royalties were frozen once again. In a letter to Abels, he estimated that he needed at least $5,000 a month to keep the operation running.[31] In late February 1971, Kathleen wrote to Abels to ask for a loan of several thousand dollars. "You probably cannot imagine our financial situation over here, but it is extremely desperate at this point. As money gets shorter and tighter, our financial responsibilities have become greater and greater."[32]

The United States consulate was watching Cleaver closely, looking for an opportunity to get him expelled from the country. Eagleton wrote to the State Department, "We are keeping our eyes open for something in the Panther picture here on which we can hang an effort to neutralize or remove them from Algeria. We are prepared to use all our channels. Perhaps the Newton 'expulsion' of the New York faction and Cleaver can be exploited in this respect. Please keep your eyes open for this kind of ammunition."[33]

Cleaver tried to find creative ways to make money. He charged journalists anywhere from $500 to $1,500 for interviews.[34] He tried to sell his Berkeley lectures to a publisher, but there was no interest. Cleaver worked away on what he was billing a sequel to *Soul on Ice* called *Uptight in Babylon* about his shootout with the police.[35] It featured some interesting biographical sections with the Panthers, but it was also weighed down by lengthy discussions of Malcolm X, Martin Luther King, and John Kennedy. Kathleen sent a manuscript of her own to Simon and Schuster that focused on women's liberation. She wanted $15,000 for it. The publisher decided to reject it, writing, "There was great enthusiasm here about the idea of the project but the actual material submitted did not, unfortunately, meet our expectations. We felt that the manuscript did not offer enough new ideas or concepts about the subject."[36]

To keep their revolutionary hopes alive, Cleaver and Kathleen created the Revolutionary People's Communication Network, an international organization designed to bring together freedom fighters from all over the world. The RPCN had few resources and little outside support, but it retained connections with a loose collective of radicals, including the Panthers in New York, ex-GIs stationed in Germany, and the People's Progressive Party in Guyana, among others. Kathleen traveled extensively to maintain connections with other groups, and she and Cleaver stayed connected by making propaganda tapes with a Sony Portapak, one of the first portable video cameras in existence. Cleaver felt that this new audio-visual technology would transform the efforts to organize revolutionaries. He called it "Voodoo." The International Section published the newspapers *Right On!*, *Babylon*, and *Voice of the Lumpen*, offering alternatives to the *Black Panther* newspaper and providing institutional legitimacy to the Cleaver faction.[37] In these papers, Cleaver continued to push an agenda of international solidarity and guerrilla warfare in the service of overthrowing the United States and all imperialist powers. In the article "Towards a People's Army," he wrote, "To cope with this situation, we have one and only one path open to us: to arm and organize ourselves into a powerful, deadly, invincible bloc inside the United States so that the United States cannot do anything of which we do not approve."[38] Under the threat of neocolonialism, Cleaver saw guerrilla violence as a necessary response to white supremacist power.

Under the banner of the RPCN, the International Section identified with a number of guerrilla organizations across the globe. Cleaver applauded the efforts of the Palestinian Black September group, which staged hijackings and kidnappings and which famously kidnapped athletes at the 1972 Munich Olympics. He inspired members of the Red Faction Army, a left-wing German organization that carried out a series of shootings and bombings in an attempt to bring about revolution in West Germany. He also tried to forge ties with the Black Liberation Army (BLA), a contingent of Black Panthers mostly from New York that rejected the community-based programs of Newton. Cleaver planned to employ this group to wage guerrilla warfare within the United States. The BLA organized assassinations of police officers and other guerrilla actions before it was forced underground.[39]

For Cleaver, these groups were proponents of anticolonial violence and the true vanguard of the revolution. However, lacking mainstream political power, they were ultimately unable to organize people or inspire revolutionary change through violence. By the early 1970s, they had been neutralized, leaving Cleaver with little institutional support for his revolutionary ideas. With the death of George Jackson after a failed prison escape in August 1971, the last of the Panthers who publicly supporting anticolonial violence were gone.[40]

The International Section survived during these difficult months in large part because of Kathleen's hard work and administrative genius. According to her logs, her days were jammed full of party tasks. She read mail, ran errands, typed memos, and took phone calls. She dealt with plumbers and landlords, typed up Cleaver's statements and lectures, translated Panther material into French, ordered books, and drove people to doctor's appointments. She was the one who initially organized the nursery at the international headquarters. She ordered cookbooks and taught herself to decently cook Chinese food. She did interviews for the *New York Times* and *Le Monde*, and she met with ambassadors from China and Korea and dissidents from Haiti.

In April 1971, Cleaver had new hopes for international legitimacy when he was invited to the People's Republic of Congo by the first secretary of the Congolese Workers Party, Claude-Ernest Ndalla. He was asked to participate in a conference focused on the struggle of Africa's Portuguese colonies. Hosted by a Congolese youth organization, it was attended by dozens of representatives from liberation movements and socialist nations. The Panther delegation was made up of Cleaver, Kathleen, Denise Oliver-Velez, and Michael Tabor. They hired Bill Stephens of the Paris-based company Video Out to film the whole thing. Tabor had been a member of the New York Panthers and escaped with Connie Matthews after Newton had held them hostage in New York. Cleaver liked the tough and intelligent Oliver-Velez, a member of New York's Young Lords, and decided to mentor her. He brought her books on African politics by Nkrumah, Léopold Senghor, and Fanon. He assigned her readings and then quizzed her. Oliver-Velez remembered, "He was one of the first people that forced me [to] sit down and read a lot of things that I had not bothered to read. I will always be grateful to Eldridge for him to have forced [me] to be a lot more aware of the politics of Africa."[41]

Cleaver and the delegation arrived in Brazzaville in the People's Republic of Congo in late April. Brazzaville had once been the capital of French-controlled Congo, a colony since 1880. The free and independent People's Republic of Congo had only been formed recently in 1969. It implemented a Marxist-Leninist form of government and kept close ties with North Vietnam, North Korea, and the USSR. Cleaver was particularly excited about the trip because it gave him an opportunity to witness the union between Marxism and sub-Saharan African culture. In the article "After Malcolm," Cleaver wrote, "We now have an African model, the People's Republic of the Congo, which is a black nation with a Marxist-Leninist state. All arguments over the synthesis of our history, our culture, and Marxism-Leninism can now be dealt with objectively, because we have an example of where this has already been done successfully."[42]

Cleaver and the other delegates attended panels, rallies, and speeches. They went to receptions and visited with other delegations. Cleaver was invited to speak at a presentation to delegates from all over the world. He gave his customary speech condemning imperialism and racism, but he also attacked socialist countries for their own racism. Kathleen was listening to the French translation, and realized the translator was intentionally mistranslating Cleaver's speech. The translator changed Cleaver's phrase "so-called Communist brothers in the USSR. . ." to "our beloved Comrades in the USSR." Kathleen sprang into action. Denise Oliver-Velez remembered, "She jumps up out of her chair and runs up to the stage and snatches the microphone away from the person who was doing the translating in French." Kathleen did the translation for Eldridge into French herself, and at the end there were mumbles of disapproval. It was taboo to talk about race in socialist Africa, and it was even more dangerous to openly criticize the USSR.

In the middle of the night, Congolese soldiers woke Cleaver and the delegation and moved them out of the location. The KGB was staying in their hotel, and there were reports that they might assassinate Cleaver. Oliver-Velez recalled, "That night there was banging on the doors. I opened the door and all these guys with guns in military uniforms came into the room. They said, 'We are taking you to a place that is safe, because the Soviets are going to kill you.'"[43]

After the conference, the delegation explored Brazzaville and the Congo. They walked through the streets during the May Day parade, where people listened to radios and danced. There was a vibrancy that reminded Cleaver of Harlem, which he had visited back in 1968. They visited Brazzaville's cultural center, whose entrance had a two-story mural with scenes from African history. It included slaves being marched at gunpoint to sea and the Berlin Conference of 1884–85, where European powers carved up the African continent among themselves. They visited the workshop of the famous sculptor Grégoire Massengo and took video of themselves walking next to the Congo River. They flew to Pointe-Noire and Diosso, the former slave port, where millions of slaves had been trafficked as part of the Atlantic slave trade. Kathleen remembered the visit as a powerful experience for them all: "There we were, five black people born in the United States, standing facing the Atlantic, on the exact shore where millions upon millions of bound African captives had been loaded onto slave ships. Awe, anger, sadness, and amazement mingled together as I listened to the waves rolling gently over the sand and back into the ocean, again and again." As they stood at the shore, Cleaver turned to the group and said, "We are the descendants of those people taken away. . . . We have come back."[44]

From Pointe-Noire, they flew by helicopter to Cabinda, an Angolan enclave where guerrilla fighters of MPLA (Popular Movement for the Liberation of Angola) were waging war against the Portuguese. The delegation was taken to the base camp in the mountains. It was a dream come true for them all to meet true guerrilla freedom fighters. Kathleen said, "Now, we were together at one of MPLA's early camps in the hills of Cabinda—where the dreams of revolution had turned into concrete practice, where flesh and blood freedom fighters seized their peoples' land and reclaimed their own future. We felt an exquisite thrill being among guerillas at their base in Angola."[45] Cleaver and Kathleen were impressed by the Congo's socialist governance and its aggressive anticolonial stance. They felt at home there. When they returned from the camp, they met with President Marien Ngouabi and officially requested to set up a Panther office there. The Cleavers wished to move to Brazzaville. The president said he would consider their request.

At home in Algiers, they never heard any word. Finally, they received reports that politician Ange Diawara had led a failed coup against President Ngouabi. The country was in chaos, and it was impossible at this time for the Cleavers to return.

Cleaver came back to Algeria to face a number of revelations. The break-in of an FBI office in Media, Pennsylvania, in April 1971 led to the discovery of COINTELPRO activities. Although Cleaver had always suspected the Panthers had been spied on and sabotaged, he had never been totally sure until now. It was a relief to know that he had not been paranoid. Cleaver also found out that McGraw-Hill had canceled his book contract for *Uptight in Babylon*. He had received a $50,000 advance for *Babylon*, and he was supposed to turn in a manuscript in June 1970. After multiple delays, McGraw-Hill decided to cancel the book and recover money from royalties for *Soul on Ice*. After the contract was cancelled, Cleaver started shopping around a manuscript of his speeches. He was so desperate that he tried to sell it behind his agent's back. Abels wrote to him, a bit irritated, "You know Eldridge, that's not good tactics: since I am your agent, you should let me handle it. I have worked very hard for you and still do. I don't believe anyone else could have done as well. Not only isn't it good ethics, it gums up the works and is not to your advantage. Publishers get sore when they hear several people are offered the same thing."[46]

The International Section of the Black Panther Party limped along for the next year. Cleaver was able to communicate with other groups through their newspapers and video tapes, but without support from the well-connected Central Committee, the section was alone. Worse yet, they were always short on money. That looked like it might change when Roger Holder and his girlfriend, Cathy Kerkow, hijacked a plane and headed for Algiers with $500,000. Holder was a veteran of the Vietnam War, a tank and helicopter gunner who had deserted after witnessing so much violence. Kerkow was a twenty-one-year-old who worked at a massage parlor. Together, Holder and Kerkow pulled off the longest hijacking in history. When they landed in Algiers, a dozen military vehicles surrounded them. The military seized the money and took Holder and Kerkow into custody. They held them at the Aletti for two weeks and finally released them to Cleaver with asylum.

Cleaver thought that the Algerians would let the International Section keep the money. He believed in hijacking as a revolutionary tactic in the fight against capitalism. He said in a RPCN newsletter, "In this early age of armed struggle in the U.S. the liberation fighters are in constant and desperate need for many things to survive and advance. It is a just and correct tactic to expropriate all we can from the big capitalist countries and corporations who exploit billions from the people."[47] However, the Algerians gave the money and plane back to Western Airlines. They were in the midst of striking lucrative oil-industry deals with the United States, and they didn't want to upset them. A week after the incident, Kathleen wrote her friend Fredrika Teer: "Things are getting increasingly negative and uptight for us in Algeria, they have been declining for the past year very steadily as the importance and influence of American business interests intensifies . . . neo-colonialism on the horizon. The hijacking—which we thought was a beautiful thing, a gift from heaven of ½ million $$$$$$$—has turned to be a provocation for all the enemies of Algeria to jump on the bandwagon to put pressure of all sorts upon the government behind the hijackers." She wondered if this was a sign of the beginning of the end. "You can imagine then how we feel—just what kind of pressure will it take for them to be forced to turn us in?"[48]

On August 1, another hijacked airliner arrived in Algiers. It carried an army deserter named Melvin McNair, his wife Jean and their two kids, a political radical named Joyce Tillerson Burgess, as well as George Wright (aka Larry Burgess) and George Brown, who had both broken out of Leesburg State Prison in New Jersey in 1970. They had with them $1 million in ransom money. At the airport, the Algerians confiscated the money and placed everyone under arrest. They began driving the group downtown, when Cleaver and the Panthers pulled up next to the police escort. Cleaver yelled, "Don't give up the bread!"

The escort stopped, and men armed with submachine guns commanded him to turn around.[49]

Cleaver was desperate for the money. He tried contacting government officials repeatedly with no response. As a group, the International Section considered many options to retrieve the money, including public protests. They finally decided to write a letter to the president, demanding the ransom back.

On August 2, 1972, the day after the hijacking, Cleaver sent an open letter to Houari Boumediene, asking for the $1 million taken from the hijackers. He gave a press conference to make sure the message was heard. Cleaver was glib in his tone, recklessly criticizing the government for their lack of response to his inquiries. "My main reason for making this an 'open letter' is that at least I can be assured that it will come to your attention, which is something I cannot say with the same confidence about my other attempts to communicate with you recently." Cleaver argued that the hijacking was "an internal problem between the American people themselves." He concluded, "To carry out our struggle for the liberation of our people, as any and every revolutionary and freedom fighter understands, we must have money."[50] Cleaver also told the hijackers to write a letter of their own to the president on August 8. In the letter they thanked the president for the hospitality he had shown them and then concluded rather forcefully, "We request that if the Algerian government will not give us back our one million dollars and allow us to remain in Algeria, then give us back our one million dollars and we will go somewhere else."[51]

Calling out the president directly was foolish as well as dangerous, and Cleaver suddenly found himself a target of the Algerian government. On August 10, the Panthers held an International Day of Solidarity event at the villa and had invited communist diplomats, journalists, and political exiles. Two busloads of policemen pulled up to the gates and surrounded the villa. They turned away everyone who wanted to attend the event. As they were entering the compound, Roger Holder fired off his gun from the balcony, which only alarmed the police more. The police corralled everyone in the living room while they searched for weapons. They confiscated all their guns, including a gun the Congolese government had given Cleaver as a gift. They turned off their telephone and telex. The chief of police told them that no one could leave the building. They were kept there for two days under house arrest.

On August 15, 1972, military police brought a summons for Cleaver. He and Kathleen went to the police headquarters to see Salah Hidjeb, the head of state security. Hidjeb told Cleaver the hijacking was exclusively an Algerian issue, and they could not keep the money without angering powerful people in the United States. Throughout the early 1970s, Algeria had been working out a deal with the United States for a twenty-five-year contract, whereby El Paso Gas of Texas would receive ten thousand billion cubic meters of natural gas per year. It represented billions of dollars of revenue. For the sake of business, Algeria did not want to disrupt the delicate relationship with the United States. When Cleaver pointed out that it put national interests above those of oppressed people, Hidjeb told him, "This is Algeria's gas, and we can sell it to whoever we like, capitalist, communist, it doesn't make any difference."[52] Cleaver was obstinate. He argued Panthers could not operate a liberation force without money. He also demanded his favorite gun back. Hidjeb told them that they could not act as a state within a state, and he dismissed the Panthers as "Palace Revolutionaries."[53]

Following this, the Panthers were quarantined. Support from China had already begun to evaporate after President Nixon made his highly publicized visit there. But now the Panthers were no longer even invited to gatherings by the North Korean and North Vietnamese embassies, as they feared reprisal by the Algerian president. Not long after Cleaver's meeting with Hidjeb, the Algerian government demanded that Cleaver step aside to allow Panther member Pete O'Neal to take over as head of the International Section. Cleaver was happy to do so, as he was starting to plan his escape from the country. One of the first things O'Neal did was to request passports for himself, his wife, and several other Panthers who wanted to leave Algeria. On September 16, O'Neal and Charlotte left for Tanzania without telling Cleaver. A week later, Larry Mack and Sekou Odinga left for Egypt. Other Panthers left soon after. Roger Holder was left in charge of the

International Section. What had once been a community of almost thirty was reduced to just a handful. Police agents began to follow Cleaver everywhere he went. One day, two men in suits approached Cleaver on the street and told him, "You are welcome to stay until diplomatic relations are reestablished with the United States."

In December, Cleaver was feeling hopeless about the possibilities for any further revolutionary activity in Algeria. He wrote to Reggie Major, "As you can well imagine, our future in Algiers is pretty limited—any possibility of effectiveness has been destroyed by the combined forces of afro-american jackanapes, Algerian pro-capitalists, and American oil interests."[54] The plainclothes policemen who followed him grew more aggressive. On December 13, 1972, eight policemen ambushed the Cleavers as they were coming out the front door of the villa. As Kathleen described it, "Eldridge walked back in to one group of the pigs, with his hand on his piece just like they were moving at him—they all backed off, fumbled, didn't shoot, and melted off."[55] It was a close call. They needed to get out of Algeria immediately. They decided to sneak into France for the time being. They got fake passports through Elaine Mokhtefi and prepared for the move.

By late December, they were stressed to the point of collapse. State Department officials reported on the situation: "The Cleavers were described as crestfallen, pessimistic, and restless. Kathleen was said to look particularly sour. Always a very slim person, she is now described as excessively thin and pale."[56]

The Cleavers created their last will and testament on December 13, just in case anything went wrong. Kathleen took the children to her mother's house in the United States, and then she traveled across Europe to try to find a place that would give them official asylum. Cleaver said his goodbye to Malika, with whom he was no longer sexually involved. Over the years, Cleaver became involved with other women, though he still felt he had a connection with Malika. She now worked as an organizer and militant for a workers' rights organization, and Cleaver saw himself as her mentor.[57]

On New Year's Day, a friend drove Cleaver to Tunisia. He flew from Tunis to Geneva, and then he was driven to a safe house in the south of France. The Black Panther Party as he had known it had all but been destroyed, and his plans to raise a guerrilla army had failed. His alliance with socialist countries was finished. Cleaver was faced with the difficult decision of what to do next. One thing was sure: his life as a revolutionary was over.

14

PARIS (1973–1975)

When Cleaver reached France, he wrote to Kathleen to let her know he was safe. To avoid detection, he used the pseudonyms "Richard" and "Mercedes." "Just to let you hear a word from me," he wrote. "Everything went as planned, without a hitch. Everybody did their part very well. The people with whom I'm staying are nice as they can be, so I anticipate no problems. There are very good prospects of working out a situation very soon so that we can be together. I hope that on your end you will be prudent and careful so as not to leave a trail."[1] Kathleen planned to meet Cleaver in Paris with the children when things stabilized.

Cleaver spent a month at a safe house in Gordes and then surreptitiously moved to Paris. Elaine Mokhtefi helped arrange a modest apartment for him in the Latin Quarter. He had just a few allies in Paris, such as Paul and Carole Roussopoulos, filmmakers and activists who had originally introduced him to video recording in Algiers. Otherwise, he was alone.

Cleaver had few options. The International Section of the Black Panther Party was in shambles, and he did not have the resources to continue the RPCN in Paris. He was cut off from the liberation groups and was disillusioned with socialist dictatorships. With few other avenues available, Cleaver decided to seek political asylum in France and pursue writing. He hoped finally to become a great author. He hadn't had the time or mental energy to write a true follow-up to *Soul on Ice*, and Paris potentially offered him an opportunity to do so.

In the spring, Cleaver started the asylum-seeking process. Through Paul and Carole, he met Jean Genet. Genet, in turn, introduced Cleaver to famed lawyer Roland Dumas, who had once been legal counsel to Pablo Picasso. Dumas agreed to help Cleaver. He started a public campaign on his behalf, giving interviews to the French and English press. He enlisted intellectuals Jean-Paul Sartre, Simone de Beauvoir, and others to write letters on Cleaver's behalf. He applied to Prime Minister Pierre Messmer directly for Cleaver's asylum, citing the French Constitution as support for his request. "Any man persecuted because of his action in favor of liberty has the right to asylum in the Republic."[2]

In his request, Cleaver claimed that he was a political leader victimized by the United States government. "I am sought and persecuted precisely for the struggle I have carried out until this day. It is because I have fought for black Americans and demand the recognition of their rights that I find myself today, in fact as in law, in an apartheid situation." Cleaver promised to cease all radical political activity and devote himself to his art. "I would commit to respect the laws of the country granting asylum and I would not, during my stay in France, undertake any political activity. I would devote myself to my literary career."[3]

The French government rejected his request. Interior Minister Raymond Marcellin explained, "It does not seem, in addition, that the person in question runs any particular risk in his present country of residence because of his political convictions or his ethnic origin. In the absence of these elements and given the past activities of the person making this request, it was not judged apt to authorize him to come to France."[4] In the face of this rejection, Cleaver decided to remain in Paris illegally.

Cleaver spent the next few months exploring Paris and writing. As always, he was short on money, but he got some help from the Roussopouloses. He became a regular patron at Shakespeare and Company, the famous bookstore on the Left Bank near Notre Dame Cathedral. Cleaver fashioned himself as an expat American writer, like Hemingway, Wright, or Baldwin. He told a friend, "I've been reading Hemingway's little book about Paris, *A Moveable Feast*, going to all the places he mentions, and ordering the same drinks in the cafes he talks about. I absolve myself by writing it all off as research, telling myself that I will write a book about Paris someday. I gave up on trying to follow Henry Miller's path through this city, because it leads into too many dark prostitute infested alleys."[5] People sometimes recognized Cleaver out in parks or cafes, and he urged them to keep quiet. "I'm underground," he told them.

In early 1974, Cleaver was able to secure visas for himself and the family. Throughout his time in Paris, he had been carrying on a number of affairs. There was the filmmaker Carole Roussopoulos as well as Marie-Laure de Decker, a photographer and journalist. Decker was romantically involved with Finance Minister Valéry Giscard d'Estaing. Cleaver persuaded her to arrange a meeting between them so that he could make his case for asylum. They met in d'Estaing's apartment inside the Louvre, and he offered to help. After President Georges Pompidou died in office in April and Giscard replaced him, he was true to his word and gave residence permits to the whole family. The Cleavers could finally relax and make Paris their home.

Kathleen retrieved the children from the United States and met Cleaver in Paris. They moved into a house at 9 Rue Bruant, situated between the Chevaleret metro station and the Pitié-Salpêtrière Hospital. The house had once been the location of a moving company, so there were large gates and a courtyard. It was an ancient two-story house with three bedrooms. Cleaver used one for his office, which looked out over the hospital. As he later remembered, this was one of the truly happy times he spent with his family. "The largest room, with a wonderful, huge fireplace, contained our TV and was where we really lived as a family. It was here, in this room, that I got to know my children again after having been separated from them for [a] year."[6] Kathleen liked to shop at a store down the street, and the children enjoyed riding bikes around the courtyard. The walls surrounding the house were large enough that Cleaver could plant marijuana in the front yard. He dried large bushels in the attic, which made the whole house stink.[7]

It was difficult for the Cleavers to adjust to Paris. Kathleen wrote to Abels, "Things are moving along here, always a slow process of regroupment after changing countries, re-establishing a home, when two small children are involved. It's the slowness of it that is so exasperating to me, plus the confusion that's unavoidable—but it wreaks havoc with my desire and need for efficient and well programed activities."[8] The children were especially affected. They did not initially go to school, and the parks in Paris didn't have playgrounds or many trees to climb. It was a difficult life for them.

As always, they were hard up for money. In spring 1974, they only had a few hundred dollars in their back account, and Kathleen again wrote Abels for a loan. "Therefore, it would be a big help to receive that some-odd 200 dollars so we can prevent ourselves from becoming three months behind in the rent, and just stay at two."[9]

Cleaver continued to struggle with his writing. In Algeria, he had started an autobiographical prison novel, "Promises." He tried to work on it when he moved to France, but he had not made much progress. As he wrote Kathleen, "I was optimistic about being able to complete the book within a couple of months, but I stopped writing do [*sic*] to the pressure of events and so have not been able to finish."[10] In February 1974, Peter Hyun of Doubleday visited Cleaver to help with the book. Hyun was one of the few people who still believed Cleaver was a gifted writer. He rented him an apartment so that he could write in solitude. He took Cleaver and Kathleen to the Eiffel Tower for dinner, where they toasted the future book. At the end of the trip, Hyun took sections home to read.

A few weeks later, Hyun wrote Cleaver with his specific criticisms. They were not positive. He told Cleaver that the book suffered from an inconsistent literary style and tone. There were too many incidents strung together, and the book had little sense of direction. Hyun accused Cleaver of providing too few descriptions of his own dreams, ideas, and philosophy. Worse yet, Huyn remarked that Cleaver's ideas about race and gender were firmly out of step with the times. "American black and white politics have changed. There is a wariness about rhetoric and a sensitivity to the oppression of women and homosexuals."[11] In Hyun's assessment, Cleaver's writing didn't have the focus or political relevance that it once did. He told Cleaver to make drastic changes if he wanted to publish. "Eldridge, don't let your publishers, friends and fans down this time—please," he warned. "You can't afford it."[12]

Cleaver bristled at these criticisms. He responded, "I feel that my publishers are some chickenshit, petty, calculating profiteers, capable of disregarding my fate, able to relate to me only from the perspective of a Balance Sheet."[13] He told Hyun if he really wanted to help, he should send money for rent.

As the realities of Cleaver's new existence in Paris set in during 1974, his worldview began to shift dramatically. He started to move away from the radical left, the Black Panther ideology no longer holding any attraction for him after the falling out. As he said to Kathleen in a letter, "I am glad to put an end to that whole Panther Cowboy image, which, regardless as to what value it might have had in the past, is definitely useless at the moment."[14] Cleaver also rejected Marxism. Having witnessed deeply flawed socialist dictatorships in his five years abroad, Cleaver decided that Marxism in practice was doomed. As he later recalled, "I began to have more anti-Communist feelings. I began to rethink my basic beliefs. I went back and re-read the *Communist Manifesto* and the other books in light of what I had seen, realizing I had to temper my philosophy with reality. I had to face the hard truth that the beautiful philosophies of Marx and Lenin were nothing more than philosophies. They did not tie into reality because they simply did not work, not anywhere where people had attempted to apply them."[15]

Stripped of the belief systems that had once defined him, Cleaver grew more depressed throughout 1974 and early 1975. He was restless, and he spent much of his time with his mistresses or walking around Paris. Kathleen told him that he was more belligerent than usual: "First, of course, is your nasty attitude. Nasty remarks, hostile comments, sullen non-communicativeness. Secondly, to be constantly uncertain about when or where you may be or may be going. That is, your blatantly maintaining a highly exclusive social existence, while simultaneously demanding to know ever[y] o[u]nce of detail about where who when I am going."[16] Cleaver grew increasingly unhappy living in France. The children started speaking better French than English, and Maceo expressed a preference for soccer over American football. That broke Cleaver's heart, as he had always dreamed of him growing up to play American football professionally.

Cleaver finally grew so depressed that he decided to kill himself. His dreams to build an international coalition of freedom fighters were dashed, and without the support of the Panthers, he felt alone. In the spring of 1975, he traveled to Rocheville, a small city near the sea where he rented an apartment. As he told it later, "I was sitting on the balcony, the thirteenth floor of the building. I had a pistol in my hand. I just felt the spirit would come over me at any time and I would raise the gun to my head and pull the trigger. It would all be over."[17] Just when he was at his most hopeless, Cleaver claimed that he saw the face of Jesus Christ in the moon, which convinced him to give up life in exile and face trial in the United States. He later reported that this was the turning point in his life. Many detractors claimed that Cleaver made this story up, suggesting that his conversion was only a ruse to convince the public that he was a political and religious convert. It is true that Cleaver later used this story as the basis of the ministry he established, a ministry he created to make a living after he returned to the United States. However, Cleaver, who had spent over ten years of his life in prison, ultimately volunteered to come home and go back to prison in order to face the charges against him. Something moved him, and his decision to come home was an act of faith, rather than calculation. As Cleaver wrote in his unpublished autobiography, "I had received a spiritual message that I must surrender to the authorities, go into that prison cell, and I would come out the other side. There was no fear. I just knew I would come out the other side."[18]

Kathleen didn't really care what the reason was that Cleaver wanted to go home. She was sick of Paris and ecstatic to return to the United States. She told Cleaver, "Everything in this city is a triple hassle, and they've got a right to think their culture is superior to all others, fuck, it costs 80 francs to fix a leaking pipe." She concluded the letter, "I cannot take too much more of Paris, Rue Bruant, and all these francs and francais shit."[19]

Cleaver started to figure out how he was going to return to the United States. He reached out to Congressman Ron Dellums to get help with safe passage. Dellums, a black representative from California, was known for his leftist views and his support of the Black Panthers. Dellums told Cleaver that he should learn French, because nobody on the left wanted him to come back. With Bobby Seale's and Elaine Brown's recent near-successful bids for office, the Panthers were moving into the political mainstream. With his fringe ideas about black insurrection, Cleaver was seen by Dellums and many Panthers as a dangerous liability. One of Cleaver's friends told him, "Should you come back, your situation would be different. There is no one out here you can count on, for anything. On the contrary, you can count on them to do you in."[20]

Cleaver felt tortured by the loss of the Panthers. "I began to experience a severe depression," he remembered later. "Perhaps I have been crazy all my life, but I never went around brooding or tormented or anything like that."[21] Cleaver's pain turned to anger, and he swore that he would have his revenge on Dellums and all those who had shunned him.

In April, Cleaver walked into the law office of Samuel Pisar to seek help. He told Carl Salans, an attorney with the firm, about his life since the shootout with the Oakland cops. Cleaver was willing to stand trial for the gun battle with police, but he didn't want to sit in jail pending trial if possible. He wanted to know if Salans could help him make a deal.

On May 5, Salans wrote to Brent Scowcroft, the deputy assistant to the president for national security affairs. "Mr. Cleaver says, in effect, that he has been all around the radical world and has become disenchanted with it. He has rejected the Marxist-Leninist world view which he formerly advocated. He no longer wants to tear down the American system; he wants to come home and live with it." Salans suggested that it might be a good move politically for President Ford to bring Cleaver home as a gesture of reconciliation. "The idea I had was that it might not be bad for the United States, particularly in the current rather depressed state of affairs, for Cleaver to 'come back into the fold' saying that he has been everywhere else and has concluded that the United States is still the land of opportunity. This might be particularly fitting in the bicentennial year. It also coincides with President Ford's effort to turn the American people away from recriminations and despair about the past to hope and opportunities which America offers for the future."[22]

Scowcroft put the matter to the Justice Department, which said it was an issue for the state of California to resolve. The feds couldn't make a deal to keep Cleaver out of jail, but they would arrange for an escort to American soil where the arrest would be made. He would have to face jail time while he was on trial. Cleaver, desperate now to come home, agreed.

At first, Cleaver was unsure that he had made the right decision. It seemed crazy that he had deliberately chosen to go back to prison. "I was climbing the walls, having dreams at night about being in jail, waking up asking myself what I was doing, remembering how much I hated prison."[23] In April 1975, he traveled back to Rocheville for some peace and quiet. He hoped to get some writing done, and he wanted to improve things with Kathleen. It always helped when he was away for a time. On his way out the door, he wrote her a note. It was the kind of love letter that he always gave her when he was going out of town. "In a few minutes I will be going," he wrote. "You, Joju, and Maceo are still sleeping. I want you to know that you three are the most important thing in my life. I love you all very much. I know that I am hard to get along with. But I hope that you never doubt that I love you from the bottom of my heart."[24]

Cleaver was productive in Rocheville, and things improved with Kathleen. As she wrote to him, "I'm really glad to hear that you're getting into your thing. It must be a relief. For concentrating on writing, solitude has no substitute, no superior, and . . . seems like nothing can come out right without it."[25] Over the next few months, they exchanged loving letters. Kathleen told him about taking the kids to parks where they picked flowers, played in the sandbox, and watched fish in the pond. She also talked about her concerns about the kids. Maceo was often sick, and both of the kids were losing their grasp of the English language. Joju had begun asking for her to stop speaking English because it hurt her ears. Kathleen suggested that they rent a beach house for the family over the summer. "When you come, why not bring some information on near-by beach houses for rent, so we could split from Paris soon. In June there should be enough money for tickets, so just have to find a place to stay near a beach, or even a heated swimming pool. . . . I'd go for a hotel with big gardens myself."[26]

Over the summer, Cleaver brainstormed new ideas for making money. Since his confrontation with Hyun, he had all but given up on writing. With no prospects for publishing a bestseller, Cleaver reimagined himself as, of all things, a fashion designer of men's pants. The pants Cleaver wanted to create were no ordinary pants. They had an exterior codpiece affixed to the front, called an "appurtenance." Cleaver considered many names for the pants, such as the Satyr, the Incubus, the Stag, or the Stud, but he settled on the Cleavers.

The idea partly came out of his experience making clothes in prison. "When I was in prison they made me work in the clothing factory and I learned how to operate every sewing machine. I learned how to make patterns and design clothing and everything. I considered it to be a bad experience because I learned it in prison. I never thought of it as a skill until I went to France. I realized that the ability to make patterns—that people go to school to learn this—that the ability to operate all these sewing machines and the cutting machine—that these were highly praised skills, one could make money doing that."

Cleaver's pants were also an expression of his ambiguously homophobic reaction to the world of men's fashion in Paris. As he told it, he attended a seminar where Yves Saint Laurent and Pierre Cardin were discussing how to design pants to make a man's behind "a hot fashion item."[27] "One night, I heard one of the Kings—or Queens—of High Fashion discussing a new pair of pants. To my dismay, I learned that he was deliberately cutting his clothes to enhance the rear end of a man, to turn him into a sexual object."[28] Cleaver feared that regular pants promoted "penis binding" and that gay designers were "pushing a homosexual ideology" through clothing. He believed that homosexuality was a medical or psychological problem and that gay men were the rivals of women who were killing the life of the male sperm. He felt his unique pants would restore men to their proper heterosexual gender role. With the focus on the "appurtenance," the Cleavers were supposed to be a symbol of heterosexual male potency. However, with the style designed to attract attention to the codpiece, the pants more accurately reflected Cleaver's own conflicted attitudes concerning homosexuality, as they were both heteronormative and deeply homoerotic at the same time.

Cleaver pursued the pants idea with a manic single-mindedness. He made some sketches of the pants, and he wrote Kathleen an excited letter from Rocheville. "I see immediately that these are the pants the world is waiting for. They are revolutionary in design because are revolutionary in concept."[29] Cleaver was so taken with the idea of the pants that he worried it might be stolen before he could get them on the market. The next day he wrote Kathleen again. He believed that his idea would solve all of their money woes, and his conviction bordered on madness. "If you would get on top of this and forget about all those bullshit translations bullshit you are doing, we could solve our financial situation overnight and for many nights to come."[30]

Cleaver also wrote to an up-and-coming graduate student by the name of Henry Louis Gates about his big plans for the pants. "It's fantastic, you will love it, and I am worried about the repercussions. These pants will be banned in Boston, but they are going to explode on the world like blue jeans—in fact, I predict, blue jeans and everything else will have to incorporate this new principle." Cleaver felt that they were so radical that they would be denounced by the pope and made illegal in Muslim and communist countries. On occasion, "people will be busted for wearing these pants, possibly killed."[31] He asked Gates to come up with an investor who would contribute a million dollars. Gates responded that he looked around, but didn't find anyone. In the face of extreme financial hardship and his disintegrating relationship to the left, Cleaver was becoming increasingly disconnected from reality. The Cleaver pants were representative of his desire to regain his cultural relevancy in a moment when the black radicalism he had helped usher in was fading into obscurity.

Throughout the summer, Cleaver worked earnestly on the design for shirts, pants, and vests. He put out an ad in the *International Herald Tribune* calling for investors. "Eldridge Cleaver is seeking legitimate business associates to finance and organize marketing of his revolutionary design in male pants." He promised that the Cleavers were "destined to revolutionize men's fashion and corner [the] world market." In interviews, Cleaver sounded insane promoting the pants. He claimed to be an "unwashed sexologist" who was freeing men from what he called "the fig leaf mentality." "Clothing is an extension of the fig leaf, it put sex inside our bodies. My pants should put sex back where it should be."[32] He also claimed that his pants would eventually make blue jeans look like "girl pants" and that the Cleavers would be as popular as the "brassiere phenomenon for women."[33] In honor of the bicentennial, he wanted to create a pair with an eagle, red and white stripes, and thirteen stars on the appurtenance. In October 1975, he put out an ad for the Cleavers in *Rolling Stone*. It featured pictures of Cleaver wearing a pair of his pants. They were black and white with a black codpiece. The ad read, "Walking Softly But Carrying it Big . . . You'll be Cock of the Walk with the New Fall Collection from Eldridge de Paris." The Cleavers were a flop.

By late fall, Cleaver was ready to give himself up. He and Kathleen sent the children ahead to Cleaver's mother's house in Pasadena. On November 17, 1975, Cleaver announced at a news conference that he would give himself up to American authorities the next day. It was the end of the era. Abels had died only a week earlier, and it looked like Cleaver's writing career might be over. He assured the public that he was getting no kind of deal from the American government. He told reporters that he was weary of exile, and he was tired of "living under dictatorships." He believed America had changed, as symbolized by the recent revelations of Nixon's wrongdoing, and that he would get a fair trial. He also believed that the conditions for black Americans were better than they had ever been. In a statement to reporters, he said, "A new situation now exists in the United States. The war in Vietnam is over. The status and condition of black people has undergone a fundamental change for the better. The American people have been shocked into objectivity and vigilance by the exposure of the massive, systematic and conspiratorial subversion of their democratic rights."[34] In an op-ed in the *New York Times* titled "Why I Left the U.S. and Why I Am Returning," Cleaver wrote, in a statement that infamously signaled the death of his radical principles, "With all of its faults, the American political system is the freest and most democratic in the world. The system needs to be improved, with democracy spread to all areas of life, particularly the economic. All of these changes must be conducted through our established institutions, and people with grievances must find political methods for obtaining redress."[35]

On November 18, Cleaver went to Paris's Charles de Gaulle Airport. He wore a white turtleneck and a dark jacket. He had wanted to wear his Cleaver pants with the specially designed codpiece made of a black velvet sheath and a ruby red tip.[36] Kathleen and his lawyer convinced him that it would set the wrong tone. He would be arrested in the United States, so he was met by two FBI agents in Paris who escorted him on the plane but didn't place him in custody. "I was relaxed and feeling great, but they were looking around, their hands close to their guns, on the lookout, perhaps thinking there were terrorists hiding somewhere to hijack the plane or something. I was just happy to finally be going home."[37]

The party arrived on TWA Flight 803 just after 5:00 PM at John F. Kennedy International Airport. As soon as the plane landed, an agent read a warrant for his arrest, and Cleaver was placed in handcuffs. He was also served a subpoena to appear before the Internal Security Subcommittee of the Senate Judiciary Committee. After clearing customs, he met three more FBI agents. In the main terminal, roughly seventy-five to one hundred reporters rushed toward him. He was a bit startled as the crowd jostled him. US customs agents had to form a barrier. Reporters fired questions at him, and he responded, "I think it's ridiculous to question me under these circumstances." No friends or family came, nor did any supporters.

Cleaver was arraigned at Federal District Court in Brooklyn and placed under $100,000 bail. The next morning, he was flown to San Diego under federal prison guard.[38] The FBI questioned him constantly about his involvement with foreign governments. Even though he was back in jail, Cleaver was excited to be home, where he could fight the charges against him. It would be a difficult battle, and he would have to carefully calculate his every move. As Cleaver wrote to Carole Roussopoulos (who he called Cher Revy to shield her real identity from the authorities), "The FBI has been vamping on me with all kinds of questions, and as I am now a big Patriotic Shit I have to deal with it in a very delicate matter."[39]

15

BORN AGAIN (1975–1981)

In early December 1975, Cleaver found himself behind bars after seven years on the run. He was held at the Metropolitan Correctional Center, San Diego, a federal detention facility that housed Timothy Leary after he was captured in Afghanistan in 1973. From the inside of a cell, Cleaver at first regretted his decision to return home. He missed the French cafés and strolls through the city. "It is not so bad right now, but at first I felt like to cry," he wrote to Carole Roussopoulos in Paris. "I couldn't believe it. It was impossible to sleep. I lay awake in my bed at night and wonder if I have gone crazy. I thought maybe I was crazy. I wanted to go back in time and wake up from a bad dream."[1]

Over the first month, Cleaver settled back into the rhythms of prison. He worked on a number of creative projects to pass the time. He wrote screenplays, outlined essays on African economic development, and developed a marketing plan for his pants. Prison had always suited Cleaver the creative artist. The constricted solitude and the routine made him disciplined and focused. He admitted to Roussopoulos in late December, "For work this place is good because I have all my energy for my brain. No fuck, no dope, no café. Just nice clean living and much time to think."[2] Behind bars, Cleaver felt calm and productive for the first time in a long time.

Cleaver's defense strategy started to come together in the first few weeks of his return. Georgia State Senator Julian Bond visited him and promised to canvas for him. Kathleen busily assembled a defense committee. Cleaver himself crafted a public relations plan to beat the attempted murder charges against him for the 1968 shootout with the Oakland police. He intended to subpoena the FBI records of the Panther surveillance to prove that the shooting was the result of harassment and sabotage by law enforcement. Hoover and the FBI were clearly guilty of sabotaging the Panthers. Cleaver felt that he just had to show how their harassment had catalyzed the shootout with the police.

Cleaver also wrote a series of articles and propagandistic press releases announcing his new pro-nationalist stance. It was his hope to convince the court of public opinion that he was a political convert who rejected radical Marxism and now embraced American exceptionalism. He figured that if he could present himself as Panther-turned-patriot, he might have a chance to win his freedom. It was a play that Cleaver had been using since he started going up in front of the parole board when he was in prison, and he hoped that his narrative of reform would work here.

Cleaver's new identity was partly created out of an honest rejection of the third-world socialism in places like Cuba and the Congo. He came away from his time abroad convinced that Marxism-Leninism failed in practice, as it was too easily corrupted by dictators and opportunists. Cleaver rejected his radical identity, because he was tired of what he viewed as the failure of communism abroad.

But Cleaver also honestly believed that his unique experiences qualified him to be an important national spokesman. Imagining himself to be the political focal point of the moment, he thought that he could bring together America's various factions. In his narcissism and delusion, he didn't see how his conservative stance was alienating his old friends. He believed he was on the cusp of breaking back into national politics. He wrote to Roussopoulos, "I am very happy with the new political line I was running, am running, because it is badly needed here. Here everybody is completely fucked up, confused, and a little shaky from so much heavy shit coming down: the end of the war in Vietnam, Watergate, Shaky Ford, Patty Hearst, Squeeky Fromme, nothing but violence, many people killed each day, lots of unemployment. It really looks like the country is falling apart. I am the only one who has some ideas of how to deal with this shit."[3] There was a crisis in America, and Cleaver thought that only he could solve it.

Cleaver's transformation was regarded by many on the left as suspicious. Nikki Giovanni insinuated that Cleaver had colluded with law enforcement, while *Newsweek* hinted that he had made bargains with the federal government. In mid-December, Elaine Brown put out a statement of behalf of the Black Panthers: "The Party cautions the black community to be on guard against giving support to [him] until it can be clearly established that he is not playing the Judas role . . . in return for his own personal freedom."[4] Cleaver, of course, had made a request to federal government to allow him to stay out of jail pending trial, but the government had denied it. Cleaver had made no other deals. Like most aging exiles, he just wanted to come home, though he saw why people doubted him. "To tell you the truth, I can see how everybody could be suspicious," he conceded to Roussopoulos. "I changed my political line, then I surrendered. It does look suspicious."[5]

Cleaver tried to reach out to the Panthers. He called headquarters collect, but they refused to accept the charges. He was devastated. He later wrote in a private journal that losing that final connection with the Panthers was the worst moment of his life.[6] "I began to realize that all my old friends didn't want me to get out of prison; the communists, the Black Panther Party members. They laughed at me. They wouldn't visit me. My wife would go around to ask them to help me. They would tell her to go away. I realized I didn't have any friends any more. Except for my family, I was isolated. In that jail, the days and nights got very long."[7] Cleaver began to blame the left and the Panthers for his predicament: "They are completely crazy, just drunk from the fucked up, stupid Left ideology that Babylon is a fascist police state. Yet they are living a very good life, doing no revolutionary work, but talking, talking, talking. If those motherfuckers would support me, I could be free on bail right now, je te jure [I swear]!!!! The new Governor Brown would move on my case if motherfuckers like Tom Hayden and his Jane Fonda, and all those bullshit people, would support me."[8]

On January 2, Cleaver was transferred to Alameda County Jail in Oakland over his protests. He was afraid that he might be killed in a county facility, where there were pro-Newton Panthers and other potential enemies. It was a tough situation. Cleaver had no typewriter. A radio system with no volume control blasted music at 6:00 AM every morning, waking him up. Cleaver was jailed in the middle of Oakland, and yet no one visited him. He felt abandoned by his comrades and the organization he had helped build. He was deeply depressed and lonely.

A week later, Cleaver went before the judge for his bail hearing. His publicly appointed defender asked that bail be reduced from $100,000 to $50,000, as he had come home voluntarily. Judge Lionel Wilson, who would become the first black mayor of Oakland, denied his request, saying the original $50,000 bail had not been enough to keep him in the country in the first place. The judge also continued the case for thirty days so Cleaver could secure a lawyer. His money was still tied up with suits and liens, and he had not been able to find counsel.

Cleaver was at a crossroads. Without support from the left, he had difficulty raising money for bail. He was isolated and longed for a sense of community. In February 1976, Cleaver for the second time in prison turned to religion for support, this time converting to Christianity. A religious outreach program group known as the God Squad visited the prison to hold prayer meetings. The volunteers were ridiculed by the inmates. As Cleaver remembered, "When the missionaries would close their eyes and hold hands with the prisoners who had joined them, to pray, the other prisoners would throw wet bars of soap, salt shakers, and wet toilet paper at them."[9] Despite the mockery he faced, Cleaver himself joined the prayer circle, as he was searching for any sense of belonging. A prison chaplain named Morrison encouraged Cleaver and gave him a bible. Later, alone in his cell, according to Cleaver, "I confessed the name of Jesus Christ. I asked him into my life. I asked him to be my personal Savior. I laid all my sins at the foot of his cross, and he set me free."[10] Anxious to belong to a group again and feeling bereft of spirituality, Cleaver invested his remaining personal and political fortunes in the Christian faith. It was in many ways his final disavowal of his old life.

Cleaver's religious transformation was to some degree an act, designed to gain support from conservatives and the religious right. The late 1970s witnessed the emergence of evangelicalism, and born-again celebrities were all the rage.[11] Both *Newsweek* and *Christianity Today* declared 1976 the year of the evangelical, while one-third of Americans in a Gallup poll identified as born again. Even Jimmy Carter claimed that he had a close personal relationship with Jesus. Cleaver hoped to capitalize on America's obsession with born-again Christianity by publicly repenting for his political sins and then being accepted back into American life.

Cleaver cultivated his own born-again persona by studying Charles Colson's bestselling book *Born Again*, which came out in February of that year. Colson had served as a special counsel and "hatchet man" to President Nixon, and he had been indicted for obstruction of justice. He served seven months in federal prison. *Born Again*, an account of his time in prison and his conversion to Christianity, sold forty thousand copies before the official release date and half a million copies before fall. It was later made into a film. At the height of Colson's popularity, he got forty to fifty letters a day from fans. He eventually established the largest prison ministry in the world, and *Born Again* became the most celebrated spiritual memoir of the 1970s and the definitive book of the emerging evangelical movement.[12]

Born Again gave Cleaver an idea. If Colson could write a bestseller about his religious conversion, then so could he. Cleaver wanted to take advantage of the public's fascination with religious conversion narratives and solidify his pro-America identity in the minds of the public. He developed a narrative of his own, which he called the "moonshot" speech. He adapted it from Colson's narrative, in which he looks out at sea until he accepts Jesus as his savior. Cleaver based his own narrative on his experience in Rocheville, where he saw Jesus's face in the moon. As he described it, "As I stared at this image, it changed, and I saw my former heroes paraded before my eyes. Here were Fidel Castro, Mao Tse-tung, Karl Marx, Frederick Engels, passing in review—each one appearing for a moment of time, and then dropping out if sight, like fallen heroes. Finally, at the end of the procession, in dazzling, shimmering light, the image of Jesus Christ appeared."[13] Cleaver's moonshot speech—which recounted his own path from Marxist to international freedom fighter to Christian—became the cornerstone of his ministry as well as of the conversion narrative he would publish in 1978, titled *Soul on Fire*. Over the next twenty years, he told versions of this story many times in churches, schools, and even police stations. It formed the basis of his income for the rest of life, and it was the final remnant of his days as a fiery orator.

Cleaver knew that his conversion would be greeted with extreme skepticism, so he tried to keep it secret. But news leaked after the pastor did an interview about his mission work with the *Los Angeles Times*. Cleaver was suddenly inundated with letters. Some were from the Christian community, who welcomed him. One read, "There was a time when I believed in your vision 100%. And then I hated you. And then I didn't care. And then—the courage it takes a person to stand up and simply say 'I've changed'. And now I'm proud."[14] Many more of the letters were racist and hateful. "Animals belong in cages, or let loose in the African jungles where he can rape snakes," read one. "Jig-a-boo nigger shit-colored ass-eater," read another. One letter that was signed by "A real gentleman of a Christian Faith" read, "A miserable dirty filthy minded nigger to commit so many rapes on women and girls. Just suppose someone jumped out behind a bush and grabbed your 6 year old daughter, God forbid." Some letters were very threatening: "Cleaver, you nigger asshole—our contribution to you—will be a bullet in your fucken brain—SOON!"[15]

Cleaver's conversion narrative achieved the desired effect. People started to take interest in the reformed Panther. By February, Kathleen had put together the Cleaver Defense Fund, which featured many prominent members. In addition to Julian Bond, it included Bayard Rustin, president of the A. Philip Randolph Institute; Dorothy Height, head of the National Council of Negro Women; and Frederick O'Neal, president of Actors Equity Association. A lawyer named George Higgins read about Cleaver's religious turn in the paper and volunteered his services. By the summer, there was some progress on Cleaver's case. More public figures joined the Cleaver Defense Fund, including State Assemblyman Willie Brown, Minister Cecil Williams from the Glide Church, and even cult leader Jim Jones. George McGovern, Walter Mondale, and John D. Rockefeller III all wrote letters of support for Cleaver. He received contributions from various Christian and Jewish groups, as well as some labor unions. Daniel Patrick Moynihan and Pat Boone both raised money for the fund. Boone stated to him in a letter, "Jesus says that He will be with you until the end of the world—and since we're one in Him, it looks like we're stuck with each other."[16]

In June, there was a snag when Higgins left the case after "substantial differences" with Cleaver over how it should be handled. Cleaver refused to take any plea deal. Senate hearings had recently exposed the extent to which the FBI used illegal tactics to monitor and sabotage the Panthers. Cleaver planned to fight the case all the way, because he wanted to use it as a vehicle to expose the illegal actions of the FBI. Cleaver wanted to secure his freedom, but he also wanted to politicize the trial.

In July, Cleaver received good news. Superior Court Judge Spurgeon Avakian ruled that the Adult Authority could not hold him for his parole violation. California had recently gotten rid of indeterminate sentencing, and the judge felt that under the new law, Cleaver should be free from the parole hold. But he still had to raise a $100,000 bail. In August, the owner of the National Liberty Corporation, Arthur DeMoss, posted almost half of the money for Cleaver's bail. DeMoss, a devout Christian, had read about Cleaver in the *Los Angeles Times*. After having written to him in prison, he visited Cleaver a number of times and was so impressed with his story that he put up his own money. The rest was raised by friends, his legal-fund team, and the born-again community. On August 13, Cleaver was let go from jail on parole. He still faced the assault charges for shooting at the Oakland police, but he was a free man until the trial got underway.

After Cleaver was released from prison, the Panthers attacked him more vehemently. In mid-April, the Panthers published an article in the *Black Panther*, stating, "Today the Black Panther Party formally condemns and denounces Eldridge Cleaver as an active and willing agent in the FBI's COINTELPRO plan to destroy Black organizations by creating internal dissension." They accused him of pushing Bobby Hutton into the gunfire of the Oakland police and claimed that he had Sam Napier killed. What was printed by the Panthers was patently false. Cleaver had always been one of the main targets of COINTELRO and never one of its agents. As for him pushing Hutton, it simply wasn't true. The police had pushed him and gunned him down, as multiple witnesses attested. And though it had been Cleaver-affiliated Panthers who had killed Napier, there was nothing specifically tying him to the shooting. Cleaver was guilty of many crimes. He had expelled Panthers for small infractions and had killed one of his comrades. He had beaten Kathleen and openly defied the Central Committee. But in this case, the Panthers printed lies and exaggerations designed to destroy any remaining credibility that Cleaver might have had.

Cleaver was devastated by these accusations. He felt betrayed by the Panthers, who had gone out of their way to ruin his reputation. He wrote to Ellen Wright in Paris, "I have had to get me some brand new friends. All of the bastards who called themselves Black Panthers, Communists, etc., have tried to crucify me with lies that I've become an F.B.I.-C.I.A. agent and/or informer. They really did a good job smearing me. And the fact that I returned voluntarily to the U.S.A. made everybody a little suspicious. On top of that, I have been running down political positions which clash violently with the traditional positions of the Left. But I insist that I am right and the outmoded positions of the Left are exactly that—outmoded."[17]

Now out of prison, and with few other options to make a living, Cleaver decided to become a preacher, a revolutionary-turned-evangelist. In part, his decision simply came down to a matter of money. The born-again community was the only form of financial and emotional support he was getting at the time, and he depended entirely upon it. But there was also something more to becoming a preacher for Cleaver. His grandfathers had both been preachers, and his mother had always dreamed he would step in their shoes someday. There was something sacred about this work, and he believed he was uniquely suited to do it. For Cleaver, his decision to become a preacher was not only financial, but also spiritual. As he wrote to Roussopoulos just before he was released from prison, "I think you have the wrong idea about me becoming a Pasteur [*sic*]. It doesn't mean that I will become a Catholic Priest to wear strange clothes or anything like that. It is a very important thing because to really become a serious, stable power in the classical tradition of the Afro-American people, it is very important to have the support of God and the religious leaders. In fact the religious leaders are giving me support at this time. Without them, I would be completely cooked—but completely."[18]

When Cleaver was released from prison, he went on an interview tour to promote his new political and religious line to the public. He appeared on *Good Morning America, Meet the Press*, and *Firing Line* and talked with numerous newspaper reporters. He was under a gag order, so he couldn't talk specifically about the shooting case, but he could discuss his new ideological positions. Cleaver talked up the police and the United States military, criticized the oppressiveness of communist dictatorships, and even praised the CIA and FBI as superior to other secret police around the world. He reversed his views on the Palestine-Israel conflict, claiming that Arabs were the "world's worst racists," and said that with Watergate and the end of Vietnam, America was a freer place for African Americans. He also criticized the Panthers for being too aggressive, saying, "I think that we were a little naïve in our approach that we were excessive in our language that we scared a lot of people."[19] When reporters asked if he had made a deal with the federal government, he retorted, "I made a deal with Jesus."[20]

Cleaver quickly became an important figure in the born-again world. He met both Billy Graham and Charles Colson following his release; they encouraged him to join the religious industry. A month after Cleaver was released from prison, be announced that he was going on the circuit as an evangelist. He signed a contract with Word Books to publish his own Colson-inspired conversion narrative, *Soul on Fire*, for $20,000. Cleaver and Kathleen were baptized in the pool of the Arrowhead Hotel in Burbank in October by Colson, and then he left on tour. Throughout the fall of 1976 and spring of 1977, Cleaver traveled all over the United States. He made multiple television appearances, including on Jerry Falwell's *Old Time Gospel Hour*, Jim Bakker's *The PTL Club*, Pat Robertson's *The 700 Club*, and Robert Schuller's *Hour of Power*. Cleaver's story was billed as the "Conversion Story of the Century," and it was eventually seen by thousands of college students, inmates, and congregants across the country. He sold out massive venues, getting standing ovations. When he and Colson gave a rally at the San Diego Sports Arena in February 1977, it was packed with nine thousand people.

In his moonshot speech, Cleaver recounted stories of his upbringing and his early life with his two grandfathers, who had inspired him to become a preacher. He told them about his mother's religious teachings, as well as her warning him against harboring racism toward white people. "It makes you a dead man," she had told him. He talked about his years as a troubled teenager and his incarceration, where he studied Marxism and black history. He recounted his time as a Black Panther and his life abroad in Cuba and Algeria. Following the birth of his children in France, Cleaver began to put his faith in a Creator. After he witnessed the appearance of Jesus's face in the moon, he converted to Christianity. He told audiences that all of this had resulted in a shift in his belief that all of the world's problems were not economic and political ones, but were spiritual ones. He concluded, "We need a spiritual revolution in the world." Cleaver's role as a preacher restored to him a sense of community and the adoration of crowds that he so desperately sought. Although he was now on the opposite side of the political spectrum from his days as a Panther, Cleaver found in evangelicalism the redemption he was looking for.

Emboldened by his success, in spring 1977, Cleaver decided to start his own organization, the Eldridge Cleaver Crusades. He modeled his ministry on evangelists such as Jim Bakker and told people that he wanted to be the "black Billy Graham." Cleaver hired a booking agent and signed with a national speaking bureau. Christian periodicals such as *Eternity* magazine, *Christian Life Magazine*, and *Christian Reader* featured Cleaver and reported on his new ministry. The evangelical leadership strongly supported Cleaver. DeMoss advised him on everything from managing salaries to following tax codes for his new organization.[21] Charles Colson told Cleaver he should hire a sharp administrative assistant. "You need someone hard-headed who is running this for you. Delegate the responsibility to them and then let them do it. You shouldn't be making hiring decisions or office policy questions. Your time is too valuable and people will take advantage of you."[22]

In the fall 1977, Cleaver started putting the team together for the organization. One day, he ran into Marvin Jackmon from the Black House while crossing Market Street in San Francisco. They met for lunch, where Cleaver asked him to become an administrative assistant for the Cleaver Crusades. Jackmon agreed, but only on the condition he be well compensated. "One of the most important things Eldridge and I insisted upon when I began conducting his affairs with white Christians was that we must be treated first class, especially in terms of travel and lodging."[23] They then had to hire a staff. Cleaver wanted to hire black Christians to give some much needed credibility to his ministry, but they were wary of his organization. "He couldn't get the black Christians," Jackmon recalled. "He tried. They were afraid. They were mortally afraid that the white folks were going to kill him and kill them in the process. They felt he was playing a game with the white man. They suspected that he was lying about the moon." They turned to the only people still loyal to Cleaver. Jackmon explained, "So the only people I could get were the fearless black Muslims. So that's who his whole staff became: black Muslims—the graphic man, the office help, you know. If they were[n't] black Muslims, they might as well have been, because most of them were antiwhite."[24]

Cleaver created a highly organized and tightly controlled operation. He wrote up a set of rules that had to be followed by the congregations he visited. No literature, copies of his text, or recordings could be sold without his consent. Cleaver was obsessive about monitoring the collections as well. One guideline in the contract stated, "Any offering taken for Eldridge Cleaver shall be counted in the presence of an Eldridge Cleaver staff member. The disbursement should occur immediately after his lecture and or testimony." He also put restrictions on his interactions with the audience. "At the conclusion of his lecture, Eldridge must be allowed to mingle with the congregation until HE decides it is time for him to depart."[25]

On the surface, the Cleaver Crusades was a successful operation. Cleaver looked the part of born-again preacher, with his gray blue suit, white shirt, striped tie, and casual loafers. He gave speeches to massive crowds all over the country. He started publishing his newsletter on July 1, and he received hundreds of small checks and dollar bills every month. In 1977, Cleaver earned $21,000 for speaking engagements and another $20,000 from public donations. Billy Graham even donated $5,000 in support of Cleaver's ministry. Cleaver branched out into a number of projects with his ministry. He made a deal with Gospel Films to create a movie about his life called *The Eldridge Cleaver Story* for $35,000, and he even signed on to do an Eldridge Cleaver comic book.[26]

But behind the scenes, Cleaver was barely holding the ministry together. For one, he often appeared as though he were just going through the motions onstage during his speech. He lacked the fervor or conviction that had defined his oratory when he was a Panther. Denise Oliver-Velez saw him at a prayer breakfast in Washington, DC, in spring 1977 and noticed how out of place he was there. She remembered, "He had this bible that Billy Graham's wife had given him. Me and my roommate looked at him and laughed. I said, 'Yo, Rage, you need to open that bible up . . . the edges are still stuck together. Make it look like you reading this shit."[27]

Cleaver made a mockery of the organization in other ways. It was rumored that he was sleeping with the wives of some of church leaders, and he and Jackmon snorted a lot of cocaine on their tours. Jackmon later remembered, "Before we left to get on the plane, we had to do some lines from here to L.A. . . . Then we get on the plane and we take turns going to the bathroom. Yeah, then get on back and sit down. Flying high in the friendly sky. Trying to get to Jesus."

The churches themselves were engaged in shady dealings. According to Jackmon, all of the preachers were stealing from the "love offerings" from the congregation. "When we did gigs in the churches, I had to go in the room and count the money with the preachers because they would skim off the top."[28] After seven months of this hectic schedule of working seven days a week, Jackmon quit in summer 1978 and moved to Reno to be with his father and brother. Cleaver stayed on tour for another year, but the long days and the pressure were wearing on him, and he began looking for a way out.

Protests erupted at many of Cleaver's speaking events. At Irvine, the Black Student Council boycotted his lecture. At Amherst, he was booed and interrupted with cries of "sell out!" When he spoke at Wisconsin State Prison, inmates interrupted him with catcalls and verbal attacks. When he yelled out to the crowd, "Jesus Christ is the only path," a prisoner shouted back, "He was a warden of the mind."[29] He told them that he related to their struggle as a fellow inmate, but they were so disruptive he had to relinquish the mic. At a theater in Seattle, a representative from the Anarchist Party of Canada threw a pie in Cleaver's face. The group issued a press release, in which it said the following: "The Anarchist Party of Canada (Groucho Marxist) have pushed this Oreo Cookie Cream Pie in the face of Eldridge Cleaver because he is a turncoat fink and front man for what is alleged to be a CIA-fronted religious group."[30] In 1977, the American Atheists association named Eldridge Cleaver the Religious Hypocrite of the Year.

The Cleaver family moved constantly because of financial strain. By April 1977, Cleaver had only collected about $20,000 in donations for his legal defense, and he had personal and legal bills, as well as back taxes, totaling about $100,000. The Cleavers owed money to lawyers and employees, in addition to IBM, Sears, the Hertz car-rental agency, and a camera shop. In just a few short years, the family moved to Cupertino, Menlo Park, Redwood City, Palo Alto, Los Altos, San Francisco, and different parts of Los Angeles. The Cleavers were continually running away from their debts.

Despite his breakneck schedule, Cleaver recommitted himself to studying and expanding his mind. He started maintaining a library again. He was ravenous for information, and he read widely. He read periodicals on both sides of the political spectrum, including *Freedomways* and *Dissent* on the left, and the *Moral Majority Report*, the *Messianic Vision Newsletter*, and the *Evangelical Women's Caucus* on the right. Cleaver also saved newspaper articles about a range of topics, including the Symbionese Liberation Army, black women in art, James Baldwin, black Muslims, the Organization of African Unity, Jews for Jesus, among many other topics. He was a fastidious note taker, and he created an elaborate system for learning and storing information. His son Ahmad remembered, "He definitely had a library and a store of books in every one of the seven or eight houses we lived in—in the Bay Area especially—and always he would have these notepads with markings of where he put things and stored things. He was in the process of studying this information and writing. And he would have different folders and box files that he stored different things he was writing." Whenever the family moved, Cleaver carefully packed his papers and folders for transport.

Cleaver enjoyed a good relationship with his children during this tumultuous period. He was still cheating on and physically abusing Kathleen, but he was not abusive toward his kids. Perhaps because of his difficult relationship with his own father growing up, Cleaver tried to show his kids the affection that he never had. Ahmad remembered, "His relationship with the children was warm. My sister and I, we had a warm relationship. Even throughout his difficulty and struggles with our mother and abuse issues and hardship with economic difficulties and various sundry attempts to overcome them, the relationship with my sister and I was always warm." As a parent, Cleaver emphasized respect and discipline. When Cleaver came home for the day, the children were to remain silent. The kids played sports, and Ahmad learned karate. Spankings were rare but were doled out to teach important lessons. "I can remember the worst beatings I ever got," Ahmad once recalled. "Spare the rod, spoil the child—we had this kind of philosophy. The worst one was for sleeping in church. It was a church down the street. I did not know what the man was talking about at the time I went to sleep, but obviously it wasn't catching my attention. So he [Cleaver] pulled me ahead of my mother and sister until we got to the house, and I got a beating. He said, 'Don't sleep in church. That's the house of God.'"[31]

Education was very important in the household. Like his mother before him, Cleaver also gave the children books as gifts. According to Ahmad, "My sister and I . . . would always get specific types of books, not just any type of Winnie the Pooh and Donald Duck and Popeye books. We got Malcolm X coloring books, George Washington Carver books, black photography books, and storybooks about Africa, and coloring books, but children's books that were very focused about know who you are, know your background. These are your heroes from your past and your ancestors." Cleaver even revived his discussion about opening a bookstore someday. But this was a dream that he could not make come true given circumstances. He was deep in debt and still faced the attempted murder charges of those Oakland police officers. Staying afloat was the best he could do. Ahmad said, "His leaning toward opening a bookstore . . . was right in line with his personal skills. But for him to be able to do the next steps as far as getting a building and getting a license for a business and getting loans or whatever financial support is needed, this is where his attempts to take these enterprises to the next step ran into a brick wall."[32]

By 1978, Cleaver was frantically looking for a way out of the Cleaver Crusades. He wasn't making enough money, and he had witnessed firsthand how corrupt the preaching circuit was. Evangelical culture was wearing him down. Cleaver turned to his pants design as a potential way out. Colson and others were alarmed with Cleaver's pants project, so he figured if he could launch a successful clothing business, it could help him break from the religious circuit. He studied a range of books to increase his knowledge of fashion, including *Designing Apparel Through the Flat Pattern*, *Introducing Pattern*

Cutting, *Inside Fashion Design*, and *Textiles, Fabrics, and the Theory of Fashion Design*.

Cleaver borrowed $42,000 from unknown donors and incorporated Eldridge Cleaver Unlimited on January 18, 1978. After hiring two full-time seamstresses, two designers, and an aid, he held his first staff meeting in February 1978, where they discussed potential designs for underwear, swimwear, and leisurewear. During market week, he rented a small showroom to show off his collection. In late summer, he opened a tiny boutique on La Cienega Boulevard in West Los Angeles with a small sign out front that read ELDRIDGE CLEAVER UNLIMITED.

Business was slow throughout 1978. Despite publicity in the pages of *Newsweek* and *Jet,* Cleaver hardly made any sales. At twenty to thirty dollars a pair, the Cleavers were mostly popular among men in discos. Ironically, even though Cleaver had designed the pants as a heterosexual fashion icon, they seemed to be more popular with gay men. Cleaver then tried to turn the shop into a community outreach center for young men. Seeing himself as an educator and mentor, he wanted to transform his shop into a finishing school for boys. Its purpose was to teach them how to interact with girls "without having to resort to rape," as he put it.[33] He also wanted to establish a rape hotline for men who were tempted to sexually assault women. He thought of himself as providing a public service.

Cleaver's efforts to alienate the Christian community with the pants worked. When he tried to advertise them at the Convention of National Religious Broadcasters, they shut him down. The world-premiere of *The Eldridge Cleaver Story* was also cancelled.[34] Cleaver admitted to the press, "A lot of people stopped talking to me, especially some of my Christian friends."[35] Even though sales were sluggish, Cleaver was optimistic that the president would be wearing his pants during inauguration. The company folded after a year.

In 1978 and 1979, Cleaver suffered a number of additional financial setbacks. In 1978, his conversion narrative, *Soul on Fire*, was published. Despite the title's allusion to Cleaver's first bestselling book, *Soul on Ice*, his follow-up failed to garner much public attention. Even with the Christian community's interest in the book, sales were low.

Critics were unimpressed. Richard Gilman in *The New Republic* wrote, "A slipshod, ill-written, spiritless piece of work from any point of view."[36]

In February 1979, Cleaver suffered another financial blow when Beverly Axelrod won a royalties case against him. Back in 1972, with mounting financial difficulties, Cleaver had finally reneged on his agreement with Axelrod at the request of Cyrilly Abels. He wrote Axelrod a letter in September 1972, telling her the deal was off. "Furthermore, the agreement signed in February of 1968 was signed under duress, and in my relationship to Atty. Axelrod as her client. This relationship no longer exists, and Atty. Axelrod is acting in bad faith by attempting to continue to use this agreement against my wishes and in violation of the understanding under which it was signed."[37] Axelrod sued after she received this notice. The judge ruled that the original agreement "is now and always has been valid and binding" and that Cleaver's attempt to revoke the original agreement "is now and has always been of no force and effect." The court decided that Cleaver owed her $53,486 plus 7 percent interest.[38]

Cleaver continued giving his moonshot speeches regularly throughout spring and early summer 1979 in order to bring in an income, making between $1,000 and $3,000 per speech. He was still looking for a way out of the church circuit, even though his stump speeches paid the bills and debts. Then in the summer, it looked like he might have an opportunity. Marvin Jackmon invited Cleaver to come to Reno, where he had been teaching at the University of Nevada's English department and working at the Community Services Agency. Through the Nevada Humanities Committee, Jackmon was awarded two planning grants from the National Endowment for the Humanities. The goal was to produce conferences for Reno's small black community. He put together an Excellence in Education conference, and he asked Cleaver to be a speaker.

When Cleaver arrived, Jackmon introduced him to Reverend Vincent Thompson of the African Methodist Episcopal church. He was married to a rich white woman who owned land on Lake Lahontan in Silver Springs, Nevada. The couple decided to donate forty acres to Cleaver to establish a ministry and compound. Cleaver wrote out an excited letter to his followers. He claimed that the ministry would give him an opportunity to create a new kind of outreach organization: "We shall use this land to develop the programs which the Holy Spirit has made clear to us: publications (magazines, newspapers, books, brochures); a prison ministry; Finishing School for problem boys and girls from urban areas; a retreat for students, workers, artists, writers, ministers, and all peace-loving Children of God. We want to develop a new approach to the prevention of rape, violence, child and spouse abuse, family counseling; a marriage chapel; facilities for seminars, workshops, and conferences."[39] Cleaver's compound sounded like a utopia.

In June, Cleaver brought the press out to the site in the high desert for a photo op. He showed them where he was going to build a massive spiritual center, which would have space for retreats, seminars, and Christian education.[40] Cleaver now preached a spiritual approach to social problems: "The deterioration in our cities and national life, the breakdowns in our system that are social, political, and economic have to be grappled with in a correct manner—the spiritual aspect solves a lot of problems."[41] There were whispers of disproval from the planning commission. Cleaver received threats of violence, and he started traveling with a trunk full of guns. He was finally run out of town when Jackmon heard of plans to lynch him. Jackmon said, "One day my boss at the CSA (Community Services Agency) called me in to tell me he had just left a meeting with state officials who told him to inform me that if Eldridge Cleaver did not leave the State of Nevada they were going to kill him. I gave Eldridge the message and he soon packed up and returned to California."[42]

Cleaver tried ever-crazier schemes to distance himself from the born-again circuit. In late summer 1979, he joined the Unification Church. The organization had originally been founded as an anticommunist political tool by Kim Jong-pil, the former head of the Korean CIA and prime minister of South Korea. It was run by Sun Myung Moon, who claimed to have met Jesus and been chosen as his successor. A mix of Christianity, Confucianism, and anti-Communism, the

Unification Church was widely known as a cult, which used a practice known as "love bombing" to recruit members. Lonely people were targeted with physical affection so that they would turn away from their own communities and give their possessions to the church. Many people considered the so-called Moonies to be practitioners of brainwashing. Cleaver became interested in the Moonies after he met a woman at a luncheon who had been arrested for kidnapping her own daughter back from the Moonies. He felt that what had happened to this woman was unjust and decided to infiltrate the Moonies to rescue young people from the camps.

In August 1979 he went to the Unification Church's Camp K in Sonora for a six-week retreat. Later, he related, "I put myself in their hands, and I allowed them to do whatever they would with me. They subjected me to the same program that they subjected other people to. And I watched these other people become Moonies. And I said before that I feel that the reason that it didn't work on me is because I'm older; I've been through more experience, plus my prison experience where I've been in the hands of expert brainwashers."[43] On October 20, 1979, he pledged loyalty to the Unification Church. He attended Moonie gatherings in Oakland and worked with the group Project Volunteer. In public, Cleaver said, "I'd rather be the littlest Moonie than with Billy Graham."

While in public, Cleaver used his conversion to the Unification Church to distance himself from born-again Christianity; behind the scenes, he kidnapped and deprogramed victims of the Moonie group. Cleaver practiced his own "love bomb" on girls he encountered at the camp. In part, he did this to rescue them from the Moonie cult. Jackmon said, "When the Moonie girls gave him the love bomb, Cleaver applied it back to them, essentially turning them out and rescuing them from Moon's cult. He actually saved several lost and turned out white youth, reconnecting them with their parents. Sometimes the parents paid Eldridge for kidnapping their children and returning them." But Cleaver's aims were far from altruistic. Again, according to Jackmon, "He'd try to seduce the girls, or did seduce them, and then try to deprogram them."[44] As with many of Cleaver's social justice crusades, his motivations to liberate girls from the Moonie camp were anything but pure. Although his initial interest in the Moonies stemmed from fascination with the organization, he remained in the camp to exploit vulnerable girls.

In fall 1979, Cleaver's shooting case with the Oakland police was finally decided. Throughout the pretrial preparation, he had tried everything to have it dismissed. In one instance, he had requested that it be dropped for insufficient evidence, and in another, because none of the officers could identify him as the shooter. He had tried to implicate the FBI in an illegal campaign of surveillance and harassment that began months before the shooting occurred. All of these attempts failed. Each time, the court sided with the prosecution, and it determined that the FBI surveillance had not been directly connected to the shooting. In November 1979, Cleaver finally made a plea deal for his freedom. He pled guilty to three charges of assault and told the court that he was willing to work with the unemployed and children doing community service. The charges of attempted murder were dropped. He was given parole and two thousand hours of community service. By this point, he had accumulated $350,000 in legal fees. Judge Winton McKibben of Alameda County Superior Court declared him free, stating, "I believe people should have a chance to rehabilitate themselves. I feel you have changed for the better, and I feel it would be highly vindictive to send you to jail."[45]

With the court case behind him, Cleaver now looked to create a conservative social justice movement to combat the radical left. He was bitter that the Panthers had treated him so harshly, and he decided to build an organization to attack them. In January 1981, he established the 4th of July Movement, an organization established to promote anti-left propaganda. In a letter to Art DeMoss's wife, he explained, "I am working with a San Jose–based group to organize a movement and organization to carry a positive, American message to the college campuses, to refute the communists and other alien ideologies that now dominate our nation's college campuses."[46] The organization was blatantly ideological and nationalistic. According to the articles of incorporation, the aim of the institute was: "a) the defense and restoration of the Constitution of the United States of America in the tradition of the founding fathers and b) the research and commemoration of the 4th of July and the patriotism deriving therefrom, which is the glue holding our society together."[47] The organization created a newspaper called the *Eagle*, made T-shirts, and wrote patriotic songs. One of their immediate goals was to bring back the Pledge of Allegiance to all major public events.

Ironically, Cleaver borrowed much of the organizational structure of the Black Panther Party in organizing the 4th of July Movement. He adopted the "What We Believe" and "What We Want" configuration from the Panthers' Ten Point Program for the organization's manifesto, and he stated that the goals of the organization were to end all violence and crime.[48] Although the Black Panther Party and the 4th of July Movement were located on opposite sides of the political spectrum, the same idealistic impulse that drove Cleaver to support the Panthers also informed his political views in the early 1980s. As he stated in the "Launching Plan," the 4th of July Movement was "Revolutionary and Utopian, because when we look at the world we do not like the way it is organized and run—not in the natural world which God has made, but in that manmade world of society, commerce, law making and breaking, in that world of finance and banking and affairs, of inflation and high prices,—and the impulse to change this world, to make it better, is the beginning of the revolutionary motion."[49] Throughout his life, Cleaver had searched for utopian solutions for real world problems. His interest in the 4th of July Movement, even as it was informed by conservative ideologies, was yet another attempt to realize his dream of an equitable and just society.

It was also in early 1981 that Cleaver shocked the world by dabbling in Mormonism. He had always looked to religion as a source of communal support and power, from his time behind bars as a Muslim to his tenure as a born-again minister. Even so, for much of the public, it was a surprising turn, as the Mormon Church had only been allowing black men to be priests since 1978. Cleaver responded to these criticisms by pointing out that the Mormons, unlike Christians, had never owned any slaves. Although there might have been some of his characteristic contrarianism in his conversion of Mormonism, he also seemed drawn to it because it offered him a sense of spirituality. Cleaver initially became interested in Mormonism through the figure of Melchizedek, an old testament priest after whom Mormon founder Joseph Smith named the church's high priesthood. Reading about Melchizedek, Cleaver was so struck by the figure that he wrote in his private journal, "There was a spiritual quality about this experience, the same spiritual feeling I had experienced in that apartment in southern France."[50]

Throughout the early 1980s, Cleaver expanded his involvement in the Mormon church. He ran into Carl Loeber, a 1960s ex-radical who had once helped him on his campaign for president. Loeber had since become a Mormon. "I didn't recognize him because he was so clean shaven," Cleaver remembered. "He had a short, neat haircut, and was wearing a suit. The last time I saw him he was so greasy, you'd needed ice prongs to grab a hold of him. He used to wear a beard, never combed his hair. He was an anarchist. I had been a communist believing in a dictatorship, but he wanted all government thrown down."[51] Loeber brought Cleaver to the Mormon church in Menlo Park, and he began attending services. At first, he felt out of place. He was the only black person in a church of white people. "Sometimes I felt very strange, looking around seeing nothing but white people. Still, I felt good being there, that there was a purpose for me being there. I had the faith that I should just hang in there and keep going."[52] Cleaver followed the church until his parole was lifted. He was finally baptized on December 11, 1983, in the Oakland LDS Tri-Stake Center (now more commonly known as the Interstake Center). It gave Cleaver great pleasure to know that after his baptism, he was the best-known African American Mormon in the United States.[53]

Cleaver's involvement in the church gave him an opportunity to expand his work as a conservative organizer. Through Loeber, Cleaver met W. Cleon Skousen, a former FBI agent who had become a professor of religion at Brigham Young University. In February 1981, Cleaver gave a talk to the nine hundred members of the Century Club there. He gave his moonshot speech and ended his talk with "I believe that our Salt Lake City is becoming a political and spiritual message that can rescue this country from the stagnation that it's now in, and help us to go into a brave new world." Skousen thanked Cleaver for his testimony and added, "J. Edgar Hoover would be proud of you."[54]

The Century Club was so impressed that it hired Cleaver as a lecturer for the Freeman Institute, a conservative political education organization. The organization believed in returning to the gold standard, abolishing the Environmental Protection Agency, and ending other so-called abuses of the federal government. Cleaver explained on radio on the *Ray Briem Show* that the Freeman Institute had similar goals to the 4th of July Movement: "The Freeman Institute is dedicated to teaching American people the formula of the Founding Fathers of this country for government and for regulating the economy and the lives of people. They have a formula that they have searched out and studied and it was the formula upon which they based this country when it was first founded."[55] Cleaver toured campuses giving a speech called "International Terrorism and Communism vs. Capitalism." He insisted that communist governments were corrupt and evil, claiming they tortured dissidents: "If you disagree with the government, they'll take you into a hospital and surgically alter your brain; they'll cut part of your brain out; they'll give you chemical injections, they'll give you shock treatments and change your brain through forceful means like that."[56]

Cleaver ramped up his antisocialist rhetoric during these speeches for the Freeman Institute, becoming more alarmist in his views. In addition to telling audiences that the communists performed illegal brain surgeries, he also insisted, "The Soviet Union and Warsaw Pact countries fully intend to take control of the whole world and turn it in into a Communist empire." If Cleaver started to sound more unhinged from reality, it is because he began borrowing many of his ideas from the *Christian Anti-Communist Crusade Newsletter*, a right-wing nationalist publication that peddled conspiracy theories. It featured such anti-left articles as "The Communist Master Plan for the Conquest of the USA," "Marxist Teachers Promote University Riots," and "Communism Means Mass Murder." The company that published the newsletter sold bumper stickers that read, COMMUNISM IS A CAUSE, NOT A CURE, OF POVERTY, DISCRIMINATION AND OPPRESSION. The newsletter scapegoated immigrants, university professors, refugees, and communists, and it stoked fears of foreign invasions. At a time when Cleaver was trying to strengthen his credentials as a left-bashing neo-conservative, he adopted these conspiracy theories to provide credibility for his own controversial persona.

In the fifteen years that Cleaver and Kathleen had been together, he had never stopped cheating on her. He was a profoundly selfish person who had never respected his vows or remained faithful, even in the first months of their relationship. At home, and when he went on the road for speeches, he carried on affairs with multiple women. Some of these affairs ended badly, as Cleaver often used women for sex and discarded them. One letter signed by "A Colored Girl" read, "Why have you broken down the bindings of our wonderful friendship? Is it another woman? And probably 'WHITE' too. I don't give a damn about another bitch. I am still me and you are still you."[57] Cleaver often pursued these affairs until they bored him, and then he quietly pulled away.

Cleaver continued to abuse Kathleen physically as well. He even bragged about it in *Jet* magazine: "I don't mind being known as a wife beater; I've done it throughout my marriage. When I no longer have a right to that, my marriage will be terminated. There are all kinds of institutions to service and defend the so-called battered wives. What nobody is saying is that most of the time the bitch needed her ass kicked."[58]

Kathleen was finally fed up of the cheating, abuse, and financial worries. She was also sick of Cleaver's increasingly crazy behavior: "Eighty-five percent of what he says, I don't like. I don't like any of it, the codpiece pants, the Mormons."[59] After the court case was over, Kathleen felt she no longer had a reason to stay. Cleaver was finally free of the police, and she had done her part as his loyal wife to help him win his freedom. In August 1981, Kathleen left. She had applied to Yale as an undergraduate a few months earlier, and once she had been accepted, she took the kids and moved to the East Coast.

Cleaver's family life was destroyed. He loved his wife and children fiercely, even as he was a deeply imperfect family man. Ahmad remembered, the separation represented the end Cleaver's life as he knew it. "His debts and economic difficulties played definitely a role in the decision by my mother to move out of California and go to New Haven, Connecticut, to go back to finish her BA and then go directly to law school. So all those decisions, which were in a sense breaking up the family, came because of those economic difficulties and barriers and debts on the one side. And on the other side some of the unfortunate consequences of abuse in the relationship. So those two together sent the father to one side of the country and the mother to the other."[60]

With no place to go and little money, Cleaver started working as a tree trimmer for Loeber, who owned Blue Ox Tree Company. He lived in a house with nine other employees. With Kathleen and the kids now gone, Cleaver would have to start his life over one last time.

16

AMERICA (1981–1998)

Cleaver was lost after Kathleen and the kids left. With their departure, gone was his last source of stability in his life. Desperate for a sense of community, he reached out to Huey Newton and the Panthers again to make amends. Given the revelations that the FBI had turned them against one another and sabotaged their party, Cleaver believed they could rebuild their relationship. He wrote an open letter to Newton, "We have been slaughtered and traumatized by the onslaught of COINTELPRO and by our own mistakes and shortcomings."[1] Newton felt it was too late. Even though he too wanted reconciliation, the blood of Panther members had been spilled. To honor their sacrifice, there could be no reunion.

Cleaver also reached out to Bobby Seale in a letter. He swore that he was not an informant and explained that his turn to the right had been tactical response to the waning political influence of the left. "When I began to move in a different ideological direction, it was because I recognized that what we were into in the BPP and 'movement' was exhausted, had run its course; and I was looking ahead—way down the line, and I was positioning myself for the future—which is now." Cleaver proposed that they build a memorial for Bobby Hutton and that they try to free the Panthers who still remained in jail. In certain portions of the letter, it sounded like the Cleaver of old: "The capitalist system is in a state of general crisis and black people are being sacrificed on the altar of national recovery. The police departments are preying upon the people and are poised to crush them." At the end of the letter, he announced to Seale that he was going to run for mayor, and he wanted his help: "I am asking you to join me and we can win. Then we can bring a whole new political climate to the entire nation. We hold the keys to victory in our hands."[2] Seale responded by publicly denounced Cleaver, saying, "He's not a true representative of the Black Panther Party. Eldridge was always trying to start a shoot-out while I was trying to organize breakfasts for children."

With few options to make an income, Cleaver returned to a rigorous speaking tour in early 1982. He was desperate, and so he turned again to right-wing organizations, as they were the only ones who would financially support him. He signed up to speak at sixty college campuses with the Collegiate Association for the Research of Principles (CARP), the campus ministry arm of Sun Myung Moon's Unification Church. According to its brochure, CARP was created to inspire a spiritual renaissance, reinstitute conservative moral practices concerning sex and drugs, provide an alternative to Marxism, and reinvigorate American patriotism.[3] In fact, it was part of a network of institutions designed to attack communism. CARP was funded by CAUSA International, a Unification Church–sponsored entity that funneled millions of dollars into anticommunist efforts throughout Central and South America. Cleaver had an ambiguous relationship with these organizations. Even while he worked for CARP, he tried to distance himself from the Unification Church, repeating in interviews that he wasn't officially a part of it. However, when he was asked about the brainwashing at Moonie camps, he defended the organization. "It's not brainwashing. It is simply their conversion process, like boot camp."[4] Without the support of the Panthers or his family, Cleaver searched desperately for a sense of belonging in the early 1980s and found instead only uncomfortable political alliances that he could never fully embrace.

Cleaver toured colleges all over the United States, preaching his hardcore anticommunist line. His speech was called "America's Role in the World Revolution." In it, he warned that America was on the brink of a political and economic crisis and therefore voiced support for Ronald Reagan's foreign and domestic policies. He believed in making cuts to the national budget and social programs, because, he claimed, "no one is starving in America."[5] He felt that a class war in America would lead to a takeover by the Soviet Union, so he proposed that the proletariat and the bourgeoisie work together. Cleaver's rhetoric was often extreme. "Let's roll out the heavy guns, draw a line and not let them come over that line. And if they do, let's blow them off the face of the earth."[6]

Cleaver toured widely, speaking at several prestigious schools, such as Harvard, Yale, Cornell, the University of Chicago, and Columbia, as well as major state colleges in Kansas, Wisconsin, Washington, Alabama, and California. He was like a carnival sideshow, a black radical turned conservative, who drew large crowds of supporters and detractors. Working for the Unification Church was not his first choice, though at least he could again enjoy some of the adoration and political controversy that had made him such a fixture of the black power moment. Cleaver was enough of a narcissist that he was willing to peddle conservative ideologies for the chance to electrify and scandalize crowds. And as long as groups like CARP were paying his bills, Cleaver was toeing the right's party line.

Students protested Cleaver wherever he went. He was booed at Yale's Afro-American Cultural Center. Communist groups at Florida State University and the University of Georgia opposed him. Students from the Progressive Labor Party (PLP) and the International Committee Against Racism (a front group of the PLP) shouted him off stage. Eight demonstrators were arrested at the University of Wisconsin for protesting, and Cleaver was chased away from the microphone. Some stormed the stage, tearing down the American flags placed behind him. Others threw eggs. At Berkeley, a protester threw a cup of water on him, and Cleaver punched him with a left jab.[7] The crowd called him a traitor, fascist pig, and bootlicker, and they carried signs that read, EC WORLD RECORD-BREAKING BELLY CRAWLER and NO FREE SPEECH FOR RACIST SLIME; SMASH THE MOONIES AND THEIR KIND. In South Carolina, a man shouted out, "This is the real Eldridge Cleaver" and then played a tape of him giving a speech during his Black Panther days.

Cleaver reacted with characteristic bravado to these confrontations. To one protestor who challenged him, he commanded, "Shut up, loudmouth punk," and he threatened to dance on the chest of another student who called him an Uncle Tom. He called one student a slave and told another group, "To those blacks here today who say they're slaves, with the powers vested in me, I set you free." The conflicts between Cleaver and the audiences kept escalating, and CARP had to beef up security and create new guidelines to protect him. "Don't allow anyone to jump up on the stage and if they do, deal with them strongly. Have a clear plan for arrival and departure points," the new rules read. CARP readied a car at the end of Cleaver's talk for a quick exit. As the organization warned, "The assassination attempt on Reagan happened as he exited the hotel."[8]

By early 1984, Cleaver had become disillusioned with the Moonies. He had never been entirely comfortable with its cultish status, and the protests were starting to wear on him. They were also cheating him out of money, which outraged Cleaver. He wrote to a friend, Odd Inge, "I am very sorry that I ever trusted the family, that I ever worked with CARP, that I stuck my neck out and suffered much persecution and rejection. And now, overnight, they stab me in the back. It is EVIL to act this way."[9]

With no income and no place to go, Cleaver moved back to Berkeley. He was directionless and lonely. For a time, he squatted in the abandoned house where he and Bobby Hutton had had their gunfight with the Oakland police.[10]

Cleaver carefully considered his next move. He wanted to write a memoir, which would be a sequel to *Soul on Ice*, but without the discipline of prison life, he was unmotivated to work on it. He was sick of speaking circuits, which was problematic as his only marketable assets were his public speaking abilities and his infamy as a black conservative. Cleaver was still bitter about Ron Dellums and the black political establishment's rejection of him when he came home from France. It was an old wound, but one that Cleaver still obsessed over. In January 1984, he decided suddenly to run against Dellums in California's Eighth Congressional District as an independent candidate. At first, he fared well getting donations. In the first few months of his campaign, Cleaver raised nearly $30,000 dollars, and he got support from the National Conservative Political Action Committee. He hired Decision Making Information Company and Prince and Associates for $13,000 to help his campaign. It looked like Cleaver might break into politics as one of the few black conservatives with a national reputation.

Cleaver ran on a conventional conservative platform. He proposed eliminating school busing, getting rid of social programs, and giving aid to the Nicaraguans to fight communism abroad. He summarized his ideology in his campaign materials: "I want you to take interest in my campaign, as I feel my strong support for a 'second to none' defense establishment, my support of the Free Enterprise system, of replacing welfare with work, of steadfastly and vigorously supporting free institutions and the democratic process, while vigorously opposing Communism and all forms of oppression, exploitation, and totalitarianism, will be supported by you."[11] Cleaver also proposed some more provocative and controversial ideas designed to appeal to racist and jingoistic voters. He suggested the United States should close borders entirely and create identification cards to control illegal immigration. He claimed that thousands of communist agents were operating within the United States, trying to overthrow the government. He even defended the use of police chokeholds. He hoped to gain support through shock and awe, and he felt he could win as a political novelty.

In truth, Cleaver cared little for politicians on either side of the spectrum. He was a political dilettante who stirred up controversy in order to remain in the public eye. "You can have Tweedledee or Tweedledum," he told the media. "The Democrats postpone problems, and the Republicans aggravate problems."[12] Cleaver's main purpose in running was to seek revenge against Dellums and the black democratic establishment, against whom he had a personal vendetta. In meetings with the press, Cleaver accused Dellums of being associated with "fringe elements of Communists and left-wingers."[13] His campaign literature stated, "He is a pliable tool in the hands of the Marxist-Leninist puppet masters of Berkeley, which has become an ideological cesspool of anti-American intrigue, where even the city council refuses to pledge allegiance to the American flag. The masters pull Dellums' strings with strings around their own necks stretching to Havana, Moscow, Peking, Tehran, Damascus, Tripoli, and beyond."[14] In a bizarre turn, Cleaver accused Dellums of precisely what he himself had done, which is to work with communist countries all over the world to overthrow American imperialism. Hoping to exorcise the last vestiges of his revolutionary identity, Cleaver projected onto Dellums all of the ideological characteristics that he once possessed, and then tried to beat him in a political election.

Cleaver also tried to elevate the campaign to the national level. He wrote an open letter to Jessie Jackson, attacking him for negotiating for the freedom of an American fighter pilot shot down in Syria. He claimed that Jackson was playing politics, and he advised the presidential candidate to purge his ranks of "unreconstructed Sixties radicals, U.S. haters, ex-SNCC racists, and outright pro-Communists, like my congressman, Ron Dellums."[15] To boost his conservative credentials at the local level, Cleaver attacked flag burners and communists. He showed up to city council meetings, where he insisted that members recite the Pledge of Allegiance before the start of the proceedings. Berkeley mayor Gus Newport, who attended these meetings, used to shout, "Shut up, or we'll have you removed." Desperate for any kind of attention, Cleaver spouted reactionary right-wing ideologies and pulled off a variety of publicity stunts in order to maintain a public presence.

In August 1984, Cleaver withdrew from the race, claiming that his contribution funds had been stolen by a man named Howard Ruff from the Ruff Political Action Committee. He then tried to run for a seat on the Berkeley City Council, but only finished eleventh out of the fourteen candidates.

Cleaver tried to remain active in city politics in Berkeley throughout the mid-1980s, banking on his profile as a Panther-turned-conservative. Because he could not get attention at the national or even state level as a politician, he turned to local issues to maintain his presence in the political sphere. He became an advocate for Claire Morrison, a woman who had had a nervous breakdown in 1980 after her father and brother died. She left her house to her sister-in-law and checked into a retirement home. The sister-in-law rented it to tenants, and when Morrison tried to reoccupy the house in 1982, the rent-control laws prohibited her from evicting the occupants. She was arrested twice for trespassing on the property. She moved in with a neighbor named Karen Koelker, who helped organize protests on Morrison's behalf. Cleaver joined the conflict in 1984. He publicly criticized the local rent-control board, claiming that they were using rent control as an "ideological weapon to get rid of all free enterprise in Berkeley."

Cleaver saw himself as a hero in this struggle. He threatened vigilante action against the renters and issued a call for "fearless, courageous, ready-for-action volunteers, preferably some Vietnam veterans" to throw them out.[16] He and other demonstrators picketed the home, and the renters filed a restraining order against him. He was arrested when he showed up at the house repeatedly.[17] As Morrison's protector, Cleaver saw himself as defending the rights of the downtrodden. He represented himself this way in an unpublished screenplay called *The Rose Garden*. "E.C., a black writer who used to be part of the ruling political party, but is now passionately opposed to them, having split with them over the issue of Rent Control, has adopted the tactic of showing up at public meetings to critique the policies and practices of the City Government."[18]

It was through this controversy that Cleaver was given a second chance at family life. Through Morrison, Cleaver met Karen Koelker, and they started a relationship. In 1986, Koelker gave birth to their son, whom they named Riley. He was born with Down syndrome, and Cleaver loved him fiercely. He remembered, "The people at the hospital urged her to have an abortion, and I began to realize that this was a serious problem. But we wanted the child, and when our son was born, I didn't see anything bad about him. I just saw that he was little."[19] Though Cleaver did not marry Koelker, they shared an intimate relationship through their coparenting of Riley. No matter his other problems, Cleaver had always had a soft spot for children, and Riley provided a much-needed source of affection throughout the rest of his life.

In late January 1986, Cleaver announced that he was running for office one last time, as a Republican for the United States Senate. He was desperate to stay in the spotlight and believed that this Senate race was his final chance for a career in politics. Cleaver stuck to his conservative playbook. He blasted Democratic incumbent Alan Cranston for his communist sympathies. His political platform included opposing abortions, stopping the flow of immigrants from Mexico, and reducing the scope of the welfare program. At the California Republican Assembly Convention, Cleaver got the biggest laugh when he told the delegates that he was a Ronald Reagan Black Panther. He also got a standing ovation from the hundreds of Republicans delegates present. But Cleaver was at a disadvantage as he struggled to get donations. By February, he had reportedly only raised fifty dollars.[20] However, he remained typically overconfident about his chances. "I'm the candidate with the smallest bankroll but I predict I'm going to win this nomination," he told reporters.[21] Faced with irrefutable defeat, Cleaver nevertheless maintained his brash and even narcissistic self-confidence. It was this kind of blind faith in his ability to overcome all odds that made him so tragic.

Cleaver campaigned intensely for the Senate seat and attended a host of meet and greets, including for the California Federation of Republican Women, the League of Women's Voters, the Long Beach Republican Party Fundraiser, the California Republican League, and many more. His competition was unfazed. Cranston remarked that he would like to face Cleaver because he said "terrorists aren't popular now." Politician Ed Davis also dismissed Cleaver, remarking, "I don't think Cleaver is a very good Republican. Not many Republicans ever try to kill cops."[22] Cleaver got about twenty-two thousand votes in the primary or about 1 percent of the total vote, placing tenth out of thirteen candidates. The result marked the end of his attempt at a political career.

With the collapse of his political aspirations and the end of his work with religious organizations, Cleaver was left without direction. With no revolutionary cause to defend, he spiraled. In his desperation, he turned to using crack cocaine, which was flooding Oakland and other inner-city neighborhoods across the United States in the mid-1980s. Cleaver was just one of many former Panthers who became addicted to crack. David Hilliard and Huey Newton could be seen hanging out at crack houses in Oakland reminiscing about the old Panther days. Cleaver bought his crack from a dealer named Cadillac Brown in the Acorn housing projects. He spent most days smoking with his old friend Marvin Jackmon.

Crack consumed Cleaver. When he ran out of money, he sold all of his bookcases and furniture. Then he sold all of his prized books to the stores lining Telegraph Avenue. Cleaver also threw little crack parties, where he traded drugs for sex. Jackmon recalled, "Cleaver needed a woman with his Crack, similar to many other brothers who didn't think of getting loaded without a Crack ho. So when I met with Cleaver and he had the funds to make a Crack run, he would tell me to bring back a Crack ho or two. I got the shock of my life one night when Cleaver told me to make a run and bring him back some boys. Shocked, I told him naw, I was not going to do that, even though he seemed disappointed."[23]

Cleaver's relationship to his homosexuality had always been contradictory, and it remained ambiguous during this period. While he was seeking young men for sex at his parties, he was also publicly condemning homosexuality. He wrote an open letter to Harvey Milk's assassin, Dan White, offering him a place to stay in his home. He defended White's actions and claimed that the homosexual community was viewed as "leprotic and unclean by the majority of the people."[24] It was this ambivalent stance toward homosexuality that defined Cleaver, who concealed his own attraction to men with vehement disavowals of homosexuality.

Cleaver turned to increasingly zanier schemes to stay in the public eye. As a race leader, a religious zealot, and a politician, he was washed up. But he could still pull off a publicity stunt. He founded the Treasure Island Liberation Front and claimed that he had discovered a map to buried treasure located under the military installation on Treasure Island, which rests between San Francisco and Oakland. Calling himself Captain Cleaver, he requested that San Francisco remove the naval presence on the island so that he could dig up the $1 million in jewels. He maintained that it had been buried there fifty years earlier but had been forgotten because of the war. He hoped to dig up the loot and then have the city transform the island into a baseball park for the Giants. He sent letters to Mayor Dianne Feinstein and Assembly Speaker Willie Brown, demanding something be done. Nothing ever came of it.[25] Cleaver was now a cartoonish parody of his former self. Disconnected from political life and a larger community, he turned to increasingly desperate exploits to maintain his relevancy. But by this time, few people cared about Eldridge Cleaver, and he again found himself alone.

A week after the Treasure Island stunt, Cleaver was arrested for possession of crack. It was the first of a series of arrests that would plague him for the last decade of his life. He blew through a stop sign at Fifty-Ninth Street in Oakland, drove the wrong way down the street, and then nearly crashed headfirst into a cop car. When he saw the cops, he tossed his stash out the window. But the cops found two pieces of crack on the car floor and charged Cleaver with possession. His bond, set initially set at $11,000, was lowered to $2,500. Cleaver insisted that he had been "ambushed" by the police, who only arrested him because he was a famous writer.[26] Following this charge, Cleaver held a yard sale in Berkeley to raise money for his defense. He sold old Panther signs and framed pictures, as well as signed copies of *Soul on Ice*. It was the last stockpile of materials from his days as a radical, and although he was reluctant to give up his memorabilia, he didn't have any other options to make money. He only managed to raise $250, which hardly seemed like adequate compensation, given all that he had sacrificed.[27] Cleaver eventually received probation for possession and had to attend a rehabilitation program. He had every intention of kicking his habit.

Cleaver's trouble with the law continued into the next year. Without a reliable source of income, and with all of his books and valuable possessions now gone, Cleaver turned to theft to support his drug habit. In February 1988, he and Jackmon were arrested for stealing a desk and table from an abandoned two-story Victorian home. They had just gotten it on the roof of the car when the neighbors spotted them and called the cops. The police pulled them over on Martin Luther King Jr. Way. In addition to the stolen desk and a table, the police confiscated a fourteen-inch sword, which was part of Cleaver's Treasure Island costume. He was charged with burglary, possession of a dangerous weapon, and having an unsafe load on the car. In court, Cleaver sold out Jackmon in order to save his own skin. He claimed that the furniture had been abandoned by the previous owners, and that he was going to sell it to help his homeless friend Jackmon. Cleaver was released on $13,050 bail.[28] Jackmon did not have the $5,000 bail and remained stuck in prison. He was angry with Cleaver for leaving him to languish behind bars, and they hardly spoke again. Once again, the court was merciful toward Cleaver. On June 29, 1988, he was placed on three years' probation and received a 180-day suspended jail sentence for burglarizing a house. He got two hundred hours of volunteer work, and he pled no contest to misdemeanor second degree burglary.[29]

For the next few years, Cleaver managed to scrape by. He had been off the national stage since he dropped out of the Senate race and was now practically forgotten. Hard up for money, he formed an organization called the Greater Taker Recycling Service. He collected recycling after people put it out on the curb but before the city-contracted recycler picked it up. He claimed it was legal because of the nonprofit status of the 4th of July Movement, even though the organization had been suspended since May 1983. Cleaver called it a "*Sanford and Son* inspired useful enterprise," and he estimated that he made about $150 on a good day. Cleaver's outgoing message on his answering machine was campy and bizarre, reflecting his drop into obscurity in the late 1980s: "Hello, you have reached the Church of the Divine Greater Taker. Well, folks, we can't do much about your soul, but we can do something about your recyclables. City of Berkeley, was it the masked bandit? Or could it be . . . Satan?"[30]

Even while Cleaver used this recycling hustle to make ends meet, he was still ambitious to make a return to the national spotlight as a writer. Hoping to repeat the success of *Soul on Ice*, Cleaver worked on a wide range of artistic projects throughout his last years. He wrote screenplays, including one called "The Dog Catcher" about his teenage years with the Pachuco gang in Rose Hills. He wrote another about his time at Nelles School for Boys. He worked on an Eldridge Cleaver anthology and an autobiography. He also outlined a history of the United States, which he described as "an interpretation of some salient American history from the end of the Civil War, down to our own times, with a peep into the future."[31] He wrote songs, including a dark, pro-life tune called "The Altars of Satan—A Pro Children Song": "We sacrifice our children on the altars of Satan / When we slay them inside the womb. It should be a spirit's safe haven / It's God's little waiting room."[32] Cleaver also wrote the dialogue for a music video called "Scenario," which was inspired by the cultural phenomenon "We Are the World."

Cleaver hoped to sell these works and take a trip abroad. He really wanted to see Paris one last time. In December 1990, Carole Roussopoulos reached out to him after a decade of silence. He was ecstatic to hear from her after all these years apart, and he wanted to come back to France to rekindle their romance. As he wrote her, "But it is true that you have been on my mind and in my heart at all times. I have come to understand that I really love you with a love that has not diminished with time. I miss you totally. I need you totally. No one has or can take your place. What we shared together is still alive and waiting. I want to see you and be with you just as soon as possible."[33] Cleaver swore that he was on the verge of selling some of his screenplays so he could use the money to visit her. But Cleaver would never see Roussopolous again, because he would never sell any of his writing again. All of his outlines were broad and unfinished, and his mind was too warped from the crack to create anything with discipline and polish. Cleaver would write poetry, music, and screenplays and create other projects for the rest of his life. There were flashes of Cleaver brilliance in many of those pieces. However, he could never quite capture the zeitgeist again in his writing the way he had with *Soul on Ice*. Without the daily structure of prison to organize his life or the creative energy of someone like Beverly Axelrod to assist him, Cleaver struggled to find the discipline or the distinctive voice that had made him indispensable to the black power moment. Sadly, lacking the intellectual community to help give shape to his work, Cleaver meandered from one project to the next, and in the end, there were only a few boxes of partly finished manuscripts to show from the last years of his life.

No matter how hard he tried to quit, Cleaver could not resist the allure of crack cocaine. In June 1992, he was again arrested for possession. He was outside a crack house on Adeline Street when he was approached by the police, who searched his truck. He was arrested for carrying .12 grams of cocaine and was held on $8,000 bail.[34] At first, he said that it was not cocaine. "The officers did claim what I had was cocaine, but that is subject to analysis. I don't think it was. It was just something I got from someone."[35] The charges were eventually dismissed when a judge determined that the officers made an illegal search of his truck and an improper arrest.

In early 1994, Cleaver was nearly killed over a crack deal gone bad. On March 1, he was robbed and hit hard on the head with a blunt object. He was found by the police wandering near a woman's home at four o'clock in the morning and knocking on her window. He had no wallet or keys on him. He was arrested for public intoxication and possession of crack and a pipe. After twelve hours in jail, Cleaver was rushed to the hospital after he was found vomiting in his cell. He underwent five hours of surgery for bleeding between the brain and skull, and doctors removed some of his skull to relieve the pressure.[36]

He didn't speak or eat for three days after surgery. On March 24, he was transferred to San Leandro rehabilitation hospital. He barely survived.

When Cleaver recovered from surgery a few months later, he was a changed man. He had mild brain damage, and he was physically weaker. He would now have to walk with a cane for the rest of his life. Cleaver's brush with death had convinced him to abandon the conservative identity he had once so carefully cultivated. At the end of his life, he moved to the left one last time, attacking the republican establishment with fervor. He was searching for redemption, and he hoped to find it by returning to some of the political leanings that had once defined him.

Even though he was not completely recovered from his brain injury, Cleaver started giving his moonshot speech again at churches, high schools, and museums to make ends meet. It had many of the same elements that characterized his early speech. It was still basically a religious conversion story, but he slyly adapted it into an attack on right-wing politics. He started by hurling a copy of the Republican manifesto, *Contract with America*, across the room in disgust. He called Newt Gingrich a "gargoyle" and Rush Limbaugh a "precursor to fascism." After Gingrich called Hillary Clinton a "bitch," Cleaver began campaigning to elect her president, using the slogan, "Let's put a bitch in the White House."[37] After his near-fatal injury, Cleaver's feelings toward women had softened, and he came to believe that only a female president could unite a divided nation. In his journals, he wrote, "What is missing from our politics right now, is the heart of a mother, and this is exactly what we need. We must demand that both parties nominate a woman. The one that refuses to will most certainly be defeated."[38]

Cleaver also reached out to the Panthers one last time, asking Bobby Seale to give a series of lectures on college campuses about the legacy of the Panthers. Even though Seale had been disappointed by Cleaver's rightward turn in politics, he reluctantly agreed. When the Black Panther Party had started as an organization, Cleaver was the one who had supported it with his royalty money from *Soul on Ice*. Seale never forgot that act of generosity. So they toured together, reminiscing about fighting the "pigs" to auditoriums full of college students and professors. "We believe in ambushes," he told audiences. "People tell me that I shot some white police," he said. "I shot some black ones too. I am an equal opportunity shooter." Cleaver was thrilled to stand in front of a university audience again. He loved the attention, of course, but he also felt at home back in his role as a Panther. He had come full circle. He told audiences, "I am a revolutionary. I do not accept injustice. I do not accept inequality. I do not accept oppression. I do not accept exploitation."

Even though Cleaver suffered from severe health problems, including brain damage, heart trouble, and diabetes, he continued to tour widely to give speeches and informally campaign for Hillary Clinton. He had no other source of income, so he was forced to keep up a rigorous schedule. He delivered talks at coffeehouses, houses of worship, medical centers, and university commencements. With his typical flair for the dramatic, he brought photocopies of his FBI poster and signed autographs on them with messages like "Power to the People" and "May All Your Dreams Come True." He spoke at Santa Rosa Christian Church to protest the wave of church burnings across the country.[39] He delivered a speech at the Confederated Salish Kootenai Reservation in Pablo, Montana, where he asked the Native Americans there to forgive what the United States had done to them. He spoke at an Earth Day celebration in Portland, Oregon, where he told the excited crowd there that he had hugged his first tree that very day.[40]

Cleaver even spoke to police departments, which he felt was important work to bridge the divide between progressives and conservatives. As he wrote to Berkeley student Lani Kask, "Yesterday I made a speech to the Pasadena Police Department. My goal is to speak to police departments all over the country. I have something to say, and they are listening."[41] Cleaver was proud of his new role as a religious radical. Late in life, he tried to merge his contradictory personalities as a religious leader and seeker of radical justice. As he wrote to a friend, "I am getting very good at preaching. In fact, all of my talks are becoming excellent. I believe that God has his hand upon my life and is using me in a very special way."[42]

In July 1996, Cleaver caught a momentary break when he was hired as a consultant to a multicultural diversity task force at the University of La Verne in California. It was his first steady paycheck in a while, and it gave him a forum to articulate some of his most radical ideas of his late years. He wrote the "La Verne Manifesto" for the program, which argued that multiculturalism was an important tactical response to white supremacy and colonial power. Echoing his views from his time living in exile in Algeria, he wrote: "Viewed from the perspective of Multicultural Diversity, we must comprehend facets of the chaos, destruction, and dislocation in the lives and social structures of the peoples and lands plundered and ravaged by the Colonial, Imperialist powers of Europe. Because of their military, political and economic domination of the world, Europeans were able to impose cultural supremacy upon the world, relegating all other cultures to inferior status." Cleaver argued that multiculturalism and diversity offered marginalized people some protection in the face of imperial exploitation. "It is the result of the assertion of independence by the once subjugated peoples. It is part of their attempt to affirm their humanity and to validate themselves."[43]

Cleaver became a rogue social crusader who pitched a range of outlandish ideas to maintain his public presence. He wrote a proposal demanding Vatican to return all stolen artifacts to the colonized countries from which they had been taken: "UN Resolution calling upon the Vatican to turn over to the people of the Western Hemisphere all the artifacts and relics plundered and confiscated by the missionaries and conquistadors and shipped to the Vatican."[44] In speeches, he floated the idea of a moon prison that would house rapists, batterers, and environmental criminals. "Toxic polluters must be exiled to the moon. Environmental felonies and crimes against the person. Restore pain and deterrence. Child molesters should be exiled to the Lunar Penal Colony for life." He also suggested that men who abuse women should have more severe punishments than just jail time. "Beater gets locked in a room with two men chosen by the woman."[45] Some of

Cleaver's ideas were totally bizarre. On *The Savage Nation* radio talk show with Michael Savage, he claimed that an organization called the Franchise, masterminded by Robert Kardashian, sold cocaine to pro athletes. "This organization is the one that provides cocaine by the kilo—they do not sell anything less than a kilo—to the athletes of the United States of America," he said.

By spring 1998, Cleaver was truly destitute. The job at the University of La Verne had only been temporary, and he suffered more than ever with money troubles. For a while, he was sleeping on the couches of different friends. He then moved to the Pomona Arts Colony, where he eked out a living making flower pots. He had two vinyl couches that he used for a makeshift bed, and his phone had been cut off for nonpayment. He e-mailed Bobby Seale in March, desperate for help: "I earn pretty good next month, April, but right now I am up against the wall. My landlord told me that they have some people who have money who want my apartment. So I have until April 30 to get out. Right now I can't even afford to get out. How about making a direct deposit into my account?"[46]

Cleaver also suffered badly from failing health. He had developed prostate cancer, and he didn't have medical insurance to treat it fully. He feared for his life, and he became so desperate that he explored nontraditional forms of care. He wrote in his journal, "I am going to devote much more effort to alternative treatment. In addition to the medicine which I got from San Bernardino County, I am taking some herbal capsules that I purchased from a Chinese acupuncture specialist. The herbs have me glowing with vibrant good feeling, but I really don't know what's happening with my cancer, because I was supposed to have a check-up in April to see if the treatment is working, but they refused to schedule me an appointment because of my change of address. I am furious. I feel like going to the clinic and shooting the clerks who schedule appointments. Of course I wouldn't do that."[47]

To make matters worse, Cleaver had never been able to overcome his addiction to crack. Even after he was almost killed, he continued to use drugs to deal with his pain and loneliness. His son Ahmad reached out to him a number of times, begging him to stop. "You need to consider your health and your family or at least your son Riley and stop using Crack cocaine. I work now with many a drug fiend here at Project Renewal Inc. My job is a Job Developer. I help recovering addicts most of who were formerly homeless seek employment. After your near death head injury you are only setting yourself up for the grave by smoking crack. What will you tell the CREATOR if your soul left your body while you were in a drug stupor?"[48] Tragically, Cleaver never heeded this warning. He had been an addict too long. Besides, crack offered him a temporary escape from a life full of despair and failed hopes.

There was one bright spot in his life: his children. He was close to his son Riley, and he kept in contact with Karen Koelker to make sure everything was going well with him in school.[49] Cleaver often penned Riley letters. In one birthday card, he wrote, "Dear Riley: I love you. I was very happy to see you and spend a few days with you and mom. I hope you still like your new school. I look forward to seeing you again. Love, Dad."[50] One of Cleaver's favorite pastimes was to write short stories for Riley. In a series of fantastical tales, he turned his son into a "fierce pirate leader" who goes on many adventures, combatting mermaids who sing siren songs to lure sailors to their death. Even in the midst of his desperate personal struggles, Cleaver was a tender and loving father who tried to supply his son with a sense of stability.

In the spring of 1998, a few weeks before his death, Cleaver was deeply depressed about his poor health. His daughter, Joju, urged him to reconnect with some of his old Panther friends to lift his spirits. In 1997, Geronimo Pratt had been released from prison when it was revealed that the star witness against him in the case had been an informant for the FBI. Cleaver had been at the courtroom that day to embrace his old comrade, but since then had been isolating himself. Joju met Geronimo and Stokely Carmichael in April 1998, and she wrote to her father: "Everyone asks about you all the time. They tell me great stories about meeting you, hearing you speak, hanging out with you. They all love you and miss you too. But you're not easy to keep up with. Geronimo says he's got friends who live down your way and if he asks them they can find you for him. But he says he didn't know where you were. Everyone says you'll always be their hero. Geronimo calls you Papasan. I like that."[51]

Joju also met Don Cox's son, who suggested that they all go visit him in France, where he now lived. Joju wrote to her father excitedly, "He says we should all go to France together, since I speak French, and visit his Dad. He hasn't seen him in a few years. That would be fun. Maybe we could [go] all together if we plan it right. Would you like to go back to France?"[52] Cleaver felt a rising sense of hope. He had been dreaming of going back to the cafes and bookstores of Paris for twenty years. He could reminisce with his old friend Cox about all of their underground activities when they were with the Panthers. Roussopoulos would be there too, and who knows? Perhaps there was still time to reignite their romance. Yes, Cleaver decided. He would find a way to raise the money to go to Paris.

A few days later, Cleaver gave his last talk at the Firelight Church of Religious Science. He was in good spirits and entertained the crowd with his moonshot speech. At the end of his sermon, he said something strange. Speaking of his mother at the end of the sermon, he told the crowd prophetically, "We will all be together again at another time and another place."[53] Within the week, he suffered a heart attack and was taken to Pomona Hospital. Because he was also struggling from diabetes and the prostate cancer, Cleaver was very weak. He was in and out of consciousness, and at one point when he saw some police lights flashing outside his window, he told his family, "Those people—they ruined my life."[54] Cleaver died on May 2, 1998, and his official cause of death was probable acute myocardial infarction due to atherosclerotic cardiovascular disease (a heart attack).[55] After he died, the Los Angeles Police stole Cleaver's body and kept it for three days. What they did with it is anybody's guess, but when Joju went to pick it up from the coroner, he said that the police had just dropped it off. Not even in death, as Cleaver would put it, did the "pigs stop fucking with him."

Cleaver's funeral was held at the Wesley United Methodist Church on May 9, 1998. Even though Cleaver had lived as a loner for the last twenty years of his life, a crowd of over two hundred people packed the church. It was a diverse crowd, with a mix of white and black mourners.

Kathleen and the kids were in attendance, as were former Panthers, ex-cons from Soledad, radical Muslims, former *Ramparts* staff, and born-again Christians. Among the mourners were artist Emory Douglas, Tarika Lewis (the first woman to join the Black Panther Party), old friend Reggie Major, sociologist Nathan Hare, Muslim leader Yusuf Bey, and Jamal Al-Amin (formerly chairman of SNCC and formerly known as H. Rap Brown). Marvin Jackmon coordinated the service, even though he and Cleaver had had a falling out during the 1980s. Even Beverly Axelrod came, sitting toward the back of the church, silently paying her respects. Cleaver was dressed in a burial robe of brilliant yellow and red in an open casket. He was surrounded by Christian and Black Panther banners, as well as an American flag. The church was filled with the music of African drums and the Crenshaw High School Choir.

One by one, mourners got up and spoke about Cleaver's life. A number of speakers praised his work as a Christian minister. At one point, Ted Prasatek, a white man in his sixties, forced his way to the pulpit unscheduled. He had been suicidal in 1976 when he saw Cleaver on television giving his moonshot speech and talking about his conversion to Christianity. "I was one of those rednecks," he told the crowd. "Used to be full of hate. But I came all the way from Baltimore, 2,400 miles, to pay tribute to my brother. . . ."[56] The crowd cheered.

Many others remembered Cleaver as a revolutionary, comparing him to Nat Turner, W. E. B. Du Bois, and even the prophet Mohammed. Emory Douglas celebrated him as a radical leader, who inspired thousands of people to join the cause of freedom for black people during the black power movement. Bobby Seale struck a conciliatory tone, remembering Cleaver as someone who rediscovered his radical roots in the last years of his life. He told the crowd, "In all the mistakes and in all the positive progressive efforts he contributed we must take time to remember and know his contribution. He must live in history as one of the many who struggled for all human liberation."[57] But it was eulogist Geronimo Pratt who was probably Cleaver's most loyal and ardent supporter. When Pratt had been ousted from the Black Panther Party by Huey Newton for going underground, it had been Cleaver who had stood up for him. Cleaver himself was expelled from the Party defending Pratt, and Pratt never forgot that. In his eulogy, Pratt joked that Cleaver had made him promise to curse and smoke weed at his funeral. Even at his own memorial, Cleaver wanted to inject a little irreverence. Pratt gave a thunderous speech praising him as the epitome of a revolutionary. "We wanted our bodies flung out into the street so young people could see. . . .that's what revolution means."[58] A number of people in the crowd threw up black power salutes and yelled "Power to the people!" At the end of the service, Cleaver's body was accompanied to Mountain View Cemetery in Altadena by an LAPD motorcycle escort.

When Eldridge Cleaver was about twelve years old, his mother encouraged him to study hard so that he could grow up to be a leader of his race. She introduced him to the accomplishments of NAACP lawyer Thurgood Marshall and race leaders like Booker T. Washington and W. E. B. Du Bois. Cleaver remembered that she told him, "You have to be like Thurgood Marshall. He's a freedom fighter. You have to make a contribution, so that on the day that you die, you will have advanced the cause of freedom and made a contribution to the freedom of our people."[59] Soon after this, Cleaver's father Leroy abandoned the family and Cleaver started his precipitous slide into a life of crime. Thelma's dreams of her son becoming the next Thurgood Marshall were crushed when he was sent to reform school and then prison.

Although Cleaver did not become a race leader in the conventional sense, it was during his incarceration that he emerged as a radical activist, willing to endure torture and imprisonment for black people. He became a self-made scholar of Marxism and African American history, and he transformed himself into an intellectual while behind bars. Following Malcolm X, he converted to the Nation of Islam and fought for civil rights on behalf of incarcerated black Muslims. He read widely—Nkrumah, Fanon, and Mao—and became a dynamic thinker, never locked into any one philosophy. As a leader of the Black Panther Party, Cleaver called for the violent overthrow of the American government, going so far as to orchestrate an ill-fated shootout with the police. On the run from the law, he took shelter in countries around the world that had recently won struggles over colonial occupation, including Cuba and Algeria, and he sought to build alliances with the communist governments of North Korea, Vietnam, and China.

Cleaver also performed acts of monstrous violence. He raped women early in his late teens and abused his wife Kathleen repeatedly over the course of his life. He threatened and intimidated people, bending them to his will, and he killed a man for sleeping with Kathleen. When he returned to the United States, he betrayed the radical spirit of the Panthers by becoming a born-again Christian and an apologist for right-wing politics. Toward the end of his life, which was plagued by loneliness and drug addiction, Cleaver scrambled for a sense of belonging and found limited comradeship with the Moonies, the Mormons, and the Republican Party.

Cleaver's life was a contradiction, shot through with heroic acts of defiance against white oppression *and* emotional and physical violence against the innocent. He was a profoundly selfish and narcissistic person, who manipulated and controlled people in order to boost his own fragile ego. He also believed profoundly in the fight for race and class equality and was willing to put everything on the line for it. At his most relevant, Cleaver preached a message of revolution or death, and he meant it. At his worst, he denounced black radicalism and supported some of the most regressive policies of the Reagan-era Republican Party. Following his brush with death in 1994, Cleaver returned to a more radical political stance, but years of crack abuse and untreated mental illness kept him from recapturing the national spotlight he had once held. He died an obscure and somewhat forgotten figure.

It therefore may be tempting to discard Cleaver, to throw him into the dustbin of history. His abuse of women alone could be seen as grounds enough to push him to the margins of our collective memory. His story, however, with all its contradictions, remains important because it helps us understand America's own tragic history. Cleaver's life brings into focus America's racist institutions—from slavery and Jim Crow to mass incarceration—while also highlighting its people's aspirations for freedom, from the rise of black education to the Great Migration to black liberation politics. Over the course of his life, Cleaver was many things: a prison philosopher, a freedom fighter, a religious charlatan, a fashion designer, and a neo-conservative. Cleaver was above all a man who masterfully adapted to ever-changing historical circumstances. His singular life provides us a unique and unified view of black cultural politics in the twentieth century.

Even though he has been pushed to the edges of history, Cleaver's impact on American life has been profound, if mostly hidden from view. He helped establish early prison activism at places like San Quentin Prison, and he was one of the main architects of the Black Panther Party. His book, *Soul on Ice*, sold millions of copies upon its publication, and it emerged as one of the critical texts of the black power movement. Even with the waning influence of the radical left in the 1970s, it was Cleaver who kept the insurrectionary spirit of the Panthers alive by supporting guerrilla activism on a global scale. Donning a black beret, leather jacket, and dark glasses, Cleaver helped influence the style of black activism and the cultural politics of cool, and groups like Black Lives Matter can be traced back directly to Cleaver and the Panthers.

Cleaver was no Martin Luther King; he was no Malcolm X. But the same forces of history that created those men also created Eldridge Cleaver. The debatable choices that he made to battle oppression and capitalist exploitation, as well his later turn to the religious right, themselves offer new perspectives on the pernicious effects of racism and trauma under global imperialism. Cleaver was profoundly imperfect because the world that made him was imperfect, and rather than rise above that world, he reveled in its contradictions. Cleaver challenges us because he refuses easy classification. He in fact delighted in contrariness and iconoclasm. Ultimately, Cleaver's life offers us an opportunity to perform the difficult task of understanding the perspective of someone whose horrific actions severely complicated, if not undermined, his fight for freedom. However unlikely, Eldridge Cleaver happened, and we must face him if we want to come to terms with our past and perhaps even imagine a better future.

NOTES

PROLOGUE: ESCAPE

1 Donna Jean Murch, *Living for the City: Migration, Education, and the Rise of the Black Panther Party in Oakland, California* (Chapel Hill: University of North Carolina Press, 2010), 8.
2 Eldridge Cleaver, "Slow Boat to Cuba," carton 2, folder 27, Eldridge Cleaver Papers, Bancroft Library, University of California, Berkeley, 28.
3 Eldridge Cleaver, "Cuba Journal," December 15, 1968, box 1, folder 15, Eldridge Cleaver Collection, Cushing Archive, Texas A&M.
4 Eldridge Cleaver, "Barrister Club Speech," 1967, carton 2, folder 74, Eldridge Cleaver Papers, Bancroft Library, University of California, Berkeley.
5 Memorandum by G. C. Moore to W. C. Sullivan, February 23, 1968, carton 21, folder 27, Eldridge Cleaver Papers, Bancroft Library, University of California, Berkeley.
6 Memorandum, "Agitator Index," SAC (special agent in charge) San Francisco to FBI Director, April 18, 1968, carton 21, folder 27, Eldridge Cleaver Papers, Bancroft Library, University of California, Berkeley.
7 Cleaver, "Slow Boat to Cuba," 3.
8 Cleaver, "Cuba Journal," 3.
9 Cleaver, "Slow Boat to Cuba," 18.

CHAPTER 1: SLAVERY AND THE AMERICAN SOUTH

1 National Archives and Records Administration—Southeast Region, Morrow, GA, "U.S. Southeast Coastwise Inward and Outward Slave Manifests, 1790–1860," Coastwise Slave Manifests, 1801–1860, RG 36, Records of the U.S. Customs Service, ARC identifier: 1151775, https://www.ancestry.com.
2 Walter Johnson, *Soul by Soul: Life Inside the Antebellum Slave Market* (Cambridge, MA: Harvard University Press, 1999), 5.
3 William Warren Rogers et al., *Alabama: The History of a Deep South State* (Tuscaloosa: University of Alabama Press, 1994), 97–99.
4 William A. Owens, *A Fair and Happy Land: A Chronicle of Frontier America* (New York: Charles Scribner's Sons, 1975), 232.
5 Arkansas State Archives, Little Rock, AR, "Ouachita County Records: Tax Books 1846–1857," microfilm county roll 003741-003742.

6 Hannah Rosen, *Terror in the Heart of Freedom: Citizenship, Sexual Violence, and the Meaning of Race in the Postemancipation South* (Chapel Hill: University of North Carolina Press, 2009), 95.
7 Arkansas Compiled Census and Census Substitutes Index, 1819–1870, "1860 U.S. Federal Census—Slave Schedules," Provo, UT, https://www.ancestry.com.
8 Owens, *A Fair and Happy Land*, 261.
9 Grif Stockley, *Ruled by Race: Black/White Relations in Arkansas from Slavery to the Present* (Fayetteville: University of Arkansas Press, 2008).
10 "United States, Freedmen's Bureau Labor Contracts, Indenture and Apprenticeship Records, 1865–1872," FamilySearch website, https://www.familysearch.org/search/collection/2475025. The source cites National Archives and Records Administration, Washington, DC, Records of the Assistant Commissioner for the State of Arkansas, Bureau of Refugees, Freedmen and Abandoned Lands, 1865–1869, Employment, Arkansas, NARA microfilm publication M979, n.d., roll 41, FHL microfilm 1498738.
11 Stockley, *Ruled by Race*, 81–82.
12 Stockley, 60.
13 *Encyclopedia of Arkansas*, s.v. "Freedmen's schools," last modified May 24, 2016, http://www.encyclopediaofarkansas.net/encyclopedia/entry-detail.aspx?entryID=2170.
14 Eric Foner, *Reconstruction: America's Unfinished Revolution: 1863–1877* (New York: Harper and Row, 1988), 96.
15 Berna J. Love, *End of the Line: A History of Little Rock's West Ninth Street* (Little Rock: Center for Arkansas Studies, 2003), 31–33.
16 Gene Vinzant, "Mirage and Reality: Economic Conditions in Black Little Rock in the 1920s," *Arkansas Quarterly* 63, no. 3 (Autumn 2004): 262.
17 *Report of the Little Rock Vice Commission, May 20, 1913, and the Order of Mayor Chas. E. Taylor to Close All Resorts in Little Rock by August 25, 1913* (Little Rock, AR: Little Rock Vice Commission), 25, https://archive.org/details/reportoflittlero00litt.
18 Henry Louis Gates, "The Chitlin Circuit," in *African American Performance and Theater History: A Critical Reader*, ed. Harry J. Elam (New York: Oxford University Press, 2001), 139–140.
19 U.S. City Directories, 1822–1995, "Little Rock, Arkansas, City Directory, 1925," Provo, UT, https://www.ancestry.com.
20 U.S. City Directories, 1822–1995, "Little Rock, Arkansas, City Directory, 1930," Provo, UT, https://www.ancestry.com.
21 James D. Anderson, *The Education of Blacks in the South, 1860–1935*, (Chapel Hill: University of North Carolina Press, 1988), 209.
22 U.S. City Directories, 1822–1995, "Little Rock, Arkansas, City Directory, 1907," s.v., "Henry Robinson," https://www.ancestry.com.
23 "United States Census, 1930," FamilySearch website, accessed October 23, 2017, s.v., "Henry Robinson," https://familysearch.org/ark:/61903/1:1:MKV5-B94.
24 Johnny E. Williams, *African American Religion and the Civil Rights Movement in Arkansas* (Jackson: University Press of Mississippi, 2008), 33.
25 Eldridge Cleaver, *Soul on Fire* (Waco, TX: Word Books, 1978), 37.
26 Cleaver, 36.
27 Cleaver, 40.
28 Story L. Matkin-Rawn, "We Fight for the Right of Our Race: Black Arkansans in the Era of Jim Crow" (PhD diss., University of Wisconsin-Madison, 2009), 171.
29 Matkin-Rawn, 174.
30 Eldridge Cleaver, "Confessions of a Rapist," carton 1, folder 1, Eldridge Cleaver Papers, Bancroft Library, University of California, Berkeley, 4.
31 Cleaver, *Soul on Fire*, 38.
32 Cleaver, 40–41.
33 Cleaver, 41.

34 Eldridge Cleaver, "Memoir," carton 1, folder 1, Eldridge Cleaver Papers, Bancroft Library, University of California, Berkeley.
35 California Institution for Men (Chino), "Medical Evaluation of Eldridge Cleaver, July 28, 1954," carton 32, folder 9, Eldridge Cleaver Papers, Bancroft Library, University of California, Berkeley.
36 "1940 Federal Census," Little Rock, Pulaski, Arkansas, roll T627_166, enumeration district 60-10, 11A, https://www.ancestry.com.
37 Eldridge Cleaver, interview by Lani Kask, 1997, private collection.
38 Love, *End of the Line*, 11.
39 Cleaver, interview by Lani Kask.
40 Cleaver, *Soul on Fire*, 42.

CHAPTER 2: PHOENIX AND THE WEST

1 Bradford Luckingham, *Minorities in Phoenix: A Profile of Mexican American, Chinese American, and African American Communities, 1860–1992* (Tucson: University of Arizona Press, 1994), 145.
2 Cleaver, "Confessions of a Rapist," 8.
3 Cleaver, 9.
4 Eldridge Cleaver, "The Black Moochie, Part II," *Ramparts*, November 1969, 14.
5 Cleaver, 14.
6 Warren M. Banner and Theodora M. Dyer, *Economic and Cultural Progress of the Negro in Phoenix, Arizona* (New York: National Urban League, 1965), 148.
7 Banner and Dyer, 67.
8 Emmett McLoughlin, *People's Padre: An Autobiography* (Boston: Beacon Press, 1954), 41– 42.
9 Cleaver, *Soul on Fire*, 43.
10 Cleaver, 44.
11 Cleaver, "Confessions of a Rapist," 2.
12 Eldridge Cleaver, "My Autobiography" (unpublished manuscript, n.d.), Kathleen Cleaver Archive, private collection, 7.
13 Cleaver, *Soul on Fire*, 44.
14 Cleaver, 47.
15 Don Schanche, "Burn the Mother Down," *Saturday Evening Post*, November 16, 1968, 65.
16 Cleaver, *Soul on Fire*, 47.
17 Cleaver, 47.
18 Cleaver, 45.
19 Cleaver, 45–46.
20 Cleaver, 47.

CHAPTER 3: LOS ANGELES AND THE GREAT MIGRATION

1 Josh Sides, *L.A. City Limits: African American Los Angeles from the Great Depression to the Present* (Berkeley: University of California Press, 2003), 43.
2 Mike Davis, *City of Quartz: Excavating the Future of Los Angeles* (New York: Verso, 1990), 161.
3 Cleaver, "Black Moochie, Part II," 14.
4 Cleaver, 15.
5 Clora Bryant, ed., *Central Avenue Sounds: Jazz in Los Angeles* (Berkeley: University of California Press, 1998), 9.
6 Cleaver, "Black Moochie, Part II," 14.
7 Eldridge Cleaver, "The Flashlight," *Playboy*, December 1969, 124.
8 Eldridge Cleaver, "Black Moochie, Part I," *Ramparts*, October 1969, 26.
9 Cleaver, *Soul on Fire*, 55.
10 Eldridge Cleaver, "Sketches of John," carton 1, folder 2, Eldridge Cleaver Papers, Bancroft Library, University of California, Berkeley.

11 California Department of Corrections, "Reception-Guidance Center form for Cleaver, July 2, 1954," box 6, folder 1, Eldridge Cleaver Papers, Bancroft Library, University of California, Berkeley.
12 Eldridge Cleaver, reminiscences, Los Angeles (unpublished manuscript, n.d.), carton 1, folder 59, Eldridge Cleaver Papers, Bancroft Library, University of California, Berkeley.
13 Cleaver, *Soul on Fire*, 63.
14 Eldridge Cleaver, "The Tree," carton 1 folder 1, Eldridge Cleaver Papers, Bancroft Library, University of California, Berkeley.
15 Cleaver, *Soul on Fire*, 64.
16 "From Panther to Patriot," *Latter-Day Sentinel*, June, 19, 1981. The article can be found in oversize box 2, folder 2, Eldridge Cleaver Papers, Bancroft Library, University of California, Berkeley.
17 Cleaver, *Soul on Fire*, 62.
18 Cleaver, 48.
19 Cleaver, "Black Moochie, Part I," 21.
20 Cleaver, "My Autobiography," 3.
21 California Institution for Men (Chino), "Social Evaluation of Eldridge Cleaver, July 28, 1954," carton 32, folder 9, Eldridge Cleaver Papers, Bancroft Library, University of California, Berkeley.
22 Cleaver, "Black Moochie, Part I," 21.
23 Cleaver, 22.
24 Cleaver, 26–7.
25 Eldridge Cleaver, "Cleaver Testimony at the Valley Christian Center in Dublin, CA, January 23, 1977," carton 2, folder 83, Eldridge Cleaver Papers, Bancroft Library, University of California, Berkeley.
26 Cleaver, reminiscences.
27 Cleaver, "Cleaver Testimony."
28 Cleaver, "Cleaver Testimony."

CHAPTER 4: REFORM SCHOOL

1 Miroslava Chavez-Garcia, *States of Delinquency: Race and Science in the Making of California's Juvenile Justice System* (Berkeley: University of California Press, 2012), 52–56.
2 Chavez-Garcia, 47–48.
3 Eldridge Cleaver, "The Rose Garden," November 2, 1987, Kathleen Cleaver Archive, private collection.
4 California Institution for Men (Chino), "Social Evaluation."
5 Harvey Swados, "Old Con, Black Panther, Brilliant Writer, and Quintessential American," *New York Times Magazine*, September 7, 1969, 38–39, 139–154.
6 California Institution for Men (Chino), "Social Evaluation."
7 Cleaver, interview by Lani Kask.
8 Cleaver, reminiscences.
9 Cleaver, reminiscences.
10 California Institution for Men (Chino), "Social Evaluation."
11 Swados, "Old Con," 179–180.
12 Preston School, "A Day in the Life of a Ward," Preston Foundation.
13 "Instruction Book and Rules and Regulations for Preston School of Industry," 1938, 9.
14 California Institution for Men (Chino), "Medical Evaluation."
15 Selden Menefee, "Subjective Impact of an Industrial Training Program: A Panel Study," California Department of Youth Authority, June 8, 1964, 66–67.
16 Menefee, 96.
17 California Department of Corrections, "Cumulative Case Summary for Eldridge Cleaver, July 20, 1954," carton 32, folder 10, Eldridge Cleaver Papers, Bancroft Library, University of California, Berkeley.

18 California Institution for Men (Chino), "Medical Evaluation."
19 Superior Court of California, "Probation Officer's Report for Eldridge Cleaver, May 25, 1954," carton 32, folder 5, Eldridge Cleaver Papers, Bancroft Library, University of California, Berkeley.
20 Superior Court of California, "Probation Officer's Report."
21 California Department of Corrections, "Cumulative Case Summary."
22 California Department of Corrections, "Reception-Guidance Survey for Wilhelmina Cleaver," n.d., box 1, folder 1, Eldridge Cleaver Papers, Bancroft Library, University of California, Berkeley.
23 California Department of Corrections, "Reception-Guidance Survey for Mother Cleaver," n.d., box 6, folder 1, Eldridge Cleaver Papers, Bancroft Library, University of California, Berkeley.
24 Superior Court of California, "Probation Officer's Report."
25 Superior Court of California.
26 Lee Lockwood, *Conversation with Eldridge Cleaver: Algiers* (New York: McGraw Hill, 1970), 78.

CHAPTER 5: SOLEDAD PRISON

1 Min S. Yee, *The Melancholy History of Soledad Prison: In Which a Utopian Scheme Turns Bedlam* (New York: Harper's Magazine Press, 1973), 4.
2 California Department of Corrections, "Social Evaluation."
3 California Department of Corrections, "Vocational Summary of Eldridge Cleaver, July 28, 1954," carton 32, folder 9, Eldridge Cleaver Papers, Bancroft Library, University of California, Berkeley.
4 California Department of Corrections, Soledad, "Test for Shop Behavior," n.d., box 6, folder 1, Eldridge Cleaver Papers, Bancroft Library, University of California, Berkeley.
5 Cleaver, *Soul on Ice*, 22.
6 California Department of Corrections, "Report of Violation of Institution Rules, February 4, 1955," box 4, folder 2, Eldridge Cleaver Papers, Bancroft Library, University of California, Berkeley.
7 California Department of Corrections, "Inter-departmental Communication, February 3, 1955," Kathleen Cleaver Archive, private collection.
8 Yee, *Melancholy History,* 11.
9 Lockwood, *Conversation with Eldridge Cleaver,* 81.
10 Lockwood, 80.
11 Eldridge Cleaver to B. F. Russell, July 14, 1955, Lani Kask Archive, private collection.
12 Cleaver "My Autobiography," 6.
13 Cleaver, *Soul on Ice*, 21.
14 D. D. Evans, "Custody and General," July 25, 1955, box 6, folder 4, Eldridge Cleaver Papers, Bancroft Library, University of California, Berkeley.
15 Cleaver, *Soul on Fire*, 72.
16 Cleaver, *Soul on Ice*, 30
17 California Department of Corrections, Soledad, "Notice of Adult Authority Hearing, August 1955," Kathleen Cleaver Archive, private collection.
18 California Department of Corrections, Soledad, "Report Compiled by Classification & Parole Representative, August 1955," box 6, folder 5, Eldridge Cleaver Papers, Bancroft Library, University of California, Berkeley.
19 Cleaver, *Soul on Ice*, 30.
20 Cleaver, *Soul on Ice*, 29.
21 Irving Howe, "Black Boys and Native Sons" *Dissent* (August 1963): 353–368.
22 Eldridge Cleaver, "Malik as Hero," carton 1, folder 1, Eldridge Cleaver Papers, Bancroft Library, University of California, Berkeley.
23 Cleaver, *Soul on Ice*, 31.

24 California Department of Corrections, Soledad, "Adult Authority Report for Eldridge Cleaver," n.d., box 6, folder 4, Eldridge Cleaver Papers, Bancroft Library, University of California, Berkeley.
25 California Department of Corrections, Soledad, "Progress Report for Eldridge Cleaver, March 13, 1956," carton 32, folder 7, Eldridge Cleaver Papers, Bancroft Library, University of California, Berkeley; California State of Corrections, Soledad, "Education Progress Report, November 16, 1956," carton 32, folder 7, Eldridge Cleaver Papers, Bancroft Library, University of California, Berkeley; California State of Corrections, Soledad, "Education Progress Report, June 29, 1956," carton 32, folder 7, Eldridge Cleaver Papers, Bancroft Library, University of California, Berkeley.
26 California Department of Corrections, Soledad, "Report of Violation of Institution Rules," n.d., box 6, folder 2, Eldridge Cleaver Papers, Bancroft Library, University of California, Berkeley.
27 California Department of Corrections, Soledad, "Notice of Adult Authority Hearing, 1956," carton 32, folder 9, Eldridge Cleaver Papers, Bancroft Library, University of California, Berkeley.
28 California Department of Corrections, Soledad, "Evaluation of Parole for Eldridge Cleaver," carton 32, folder 11, Eldridge Cleaver Papers, Bancroft Library, University of California, Berkeley.
29 California Department of Corrections, Soledad, "Parole Progress for Eldridge Cleaver, May 31, 1957," carton 32, folder 10, Eldridge Cleaver Papers, Bancroft Library, University of California, Berkeley.
30 California Department of Corrections, Soledad, "Summarization of Activities for Eldridge Cleaver, May 29, 1957 to October 17, 1957," carton 32, folder 10, Eldridge Cleaver Papers, Bancroft Library, University of California, Berkeley.
31 Eldridge Cleaver to Beverly Axelrod, September 17, 1965, box 2, folder 2, Eldridge Cleaver Papers, Bancroft Library, University of California, Berkeley.
32 Cleaver, *Soul on Ice*, 33.
33 Eldridge Cleaver, "Book of a Rapist," carton 1, folder 1, Eldridge Cleaver Papers, Bancroft Library, University of California, Berkeley, 1.
34 Cleaver, 12.
35 Cleaver, 15.
36 Cleaver, 19.
37 Cleaver, 24.
38 California Superior Court, "Probation Officer's Report, March 11, 1958," box 6, folder 2, Eldridge Cleaver Papers, Bancroft Library, University of California, Berkeley.
39 California Department of Corrections, San Quentin, "Circumstances of Offense, May 14, 1958," carton 30, folder 11, Eldridge Cleaver Papers, Bancroft Library, University of California, Berkeley.
40 California Superior Court, "Petition for the Writ of Error Coram Noblis, December 14, 1964," carton 30, folder 13, Eldridge Cleaver Papers, Bancroft Library, University of California, Berkeley.
41 California Department of Corrections, San Quentin, "Circumstances of Offense."
42 California Superior Court, "Petition for the Writ."

CHAPTER 6: SAN QUENTIN PRISON

1 Eric Cummins, *The Rise and Fall of California's Radical Prison Movement* (Palo Alto, CA: Stanford University Press, 1994), 6–7.
2 Kenneth Church Lamott, *Chronicles of San Quentin: The Biography of a Prison* (New York: D. McKay, 1961), 233.
3 Clinton T. Duffy and Dean Jennings, *The San Quentin Story* (Garden City, NY: Doubleday, 1950), 250.
4 Cummins, *Rise and Fall*, 8.

5 Duffy and Jennings, *San Quentin*, 217–218.
6 Eldridge Cleaver, "Ahmen's Jacket" (unpublished manuscript, n.d.), carton 2, folder 47, Eldridge Cleaver Papers, Bancroft Library, University of California, Berkeley, 17–18.
7 California Department of Corrections, San Quentin, "Psychiatric Examination for Eldridge Cleaver, July 10, 1958," carton 32, folder 10, Eldridge Cleaver Papers, Bancroft Library, University of California, Berkeley.
8 California Department of Corrections, San Quentin, "Readmission Clinical Report of Eldridge Cleaver, May 14, 1958," carton 32, folder 11, Eldridge Cleaver Papers, Bancroft Library, University of California, Berkeley.
9 California Department of Corrections, San Quentin, "Psychological Evaluation of Eldridge Cleaver, May 14, 1958," carton 32, folder 11, Eldridge Cleaver Papers, Bancroft Library, University of California, Berkeley.
10 California Department of Corrections, San Quentin, "Progress Report in Accounting, September 1958," box 6, folder 4, Eldridge Cleaver Papers, Bancroft Library, University of California, Berkeley.
11 California Department of Corrections, San Quentin, "Progress Report in World History, September 1958," box 6, folder 4, Eldridge Cleaver Papers, Bancroft Library, University of California, Berkeley.
12 California Department of Corrections (San Quentin), "Report of Violation of Institution Rules, May 20, 1958," Kathleen Cleaver Archive, private collection.
13 California Department of Corrections, San Quentin, "Medical-Psychiatric-Dental, September 5, 1958," box 6, folder 4, Eldridge Cleaver Papers, Bancroft Library, University of California, Berkeley.
14 Cleaver, *Soul on Ice,* 34.
15 Eldridge Cleaver, "Promises" (unpublished manuscript, n.d.), carton 1, folder 51, Eldridge Cleaver Papers, Bancroft Library, University of California, Berkeley, 17.
16 Cummins, *Rise and Fall*, 17.
17 Rudolf Englebarts, *Books in Stir: A Bibliographic Essay About Prison Libraries and About Books Written by Prisoners and Prison Employees* (Metuchen, NJ: Scarecrow Press, 1972), 59.
18 Cummins, *Rise and Fall*, 28.
19 Eldridge Cleaver to C. Johnson (San Quentin), October 6, 1958, Lani Kask Archive, private collection.
20 Eldridge Cleaver to R. Butler, (San Quentin), March 29, 1959, Lani Kask Archive, private collection.
21 Eldridge Cleaver to Harold Ackerman, September 1, 1959, box 1, folder 1, Eldridge Cleaver Collection, Cushing Archive, Texas A&M, 12.
22 Harold Ackerman to Eldridge Cleaver, October 20, 1959, box 1, folder 1, Eldridge Cleaver Collection, Cushing Archive, Texas A&M.
23 Eldridge Cleaver to San Quentin Classification Committee, July 5, 1959, Kathleen Cleaver Archive, private collection.
24 Eldridge Cleaver to San Quentin Classification Committee, July 17, 1959, Kathleen Cleaver Archive, private collection.
25 Wilhelmina M. Robinson to Warden Fred Dickson, Letter, July 24, 1959, Kathleen Cleaver Archive, private collection.
26 Eldridge Cleaver to the San Quentin Classification Committee, n.d., Kathleen Cleaver Archive, private collection.
27 Eldridge Cleaver to San Quentin Classification Committee, November 4, 1959, carton 32, folder 9, Eldridge Cleaver Papers, Bancroft Library, University of California, Berkeley.
28 Cleaver to San Quentin Classification Committee.
29 California Department of Corrections, San Quentin, "Classification of Eldridge Cleaver, December 7, 1959," box 6, folder 4, Eldridge Cleaver Papers, Bancroft Library, University of California, Berkeley.

30 California Department of Corrections, San Quentin, "Adult Authority and Parole Referral Report, January 29, 1960," carton 32, folder 10, Eldridge Cleaver Papers, Bancroft Library, University of California, Berkeley.
31 California Department of Corrections, San Quentin, "Psychiatric Summary for Eldridge Cleaver, February 4, 1960," carton 32, folder 10, Eldridge Cleaver Papers, Bancroft Library, University of California, Berkeley.
32 Eldridge Cleaver to the Lieutenant Bartlett, March 25, 1960, Kathleen Cleaver Archive, private collection.
33 Cleaver, "Promises," 8.
34 Eldridge Cleaver, "Dirty Bosco" in "Ahman's Jacket," carton 2, folder 47, Eldridge Cleaver Papers, Bancroft Library, University of California, Berkeley, 14.
35 Eldridge Cleaver to Beverly Axelrod, April 1, 1966, box 2, folder 6, Eldridge Cleaver Papers, Bancroft Library, University of California, Berkeley.
36 Eldridge Cleaver to Beverly Axelrod, September 10, 1965, box 2, folder 2, Eldridge Cleaver Papers, Bancroft Library, University of California, Berkeley.
37 Cleaver, "Ahmen's Jacket," 3.
38 Cleaver, 13.
39 Cleaver, 15.
40 Cleaver, 20.
41 California Department of Corrections, San Quentin, "San Quentin Work Supervisor's Report for Eldridge Cleaver, February 11, 1961," box 6, folder 4, Eldridge Cleaver Papers, Bancroft Library, University of California, Berkeley.
42 California Department of Corrections, San Quentin, "Adult Authority and Parole Release Referral Report for Eldridge Cleaver," February 24, 1961, carton 32, folder 10, Eldridge Cleaver Papers, Bancroft Library, University of California, Berkeley.
43 California Department of Corrections, San Quentin, "Psychiatric Summary for Eldridge Cleaver, February 9, 1961," Kathleen Cleaver Archive, private collection.
44 California Department of Corrections, San Quentin, "Progress Report, September 15, 1960," Kathleen Cleaver Archive, private collection.
45 California Department of Corrections, San Quentin, "Inter-Departmental Communication, May 8, 1960," Kathleen Cleaver Archive, private collection.
46 California Department of Corrections, San Quentin, "Inter-Departmental Communication, May 16, 1960," Kathleen Cleaver Archive, private collection.
47 California Department of Corrections, San Quentin, "Psychiatric Summary for Eldridge Cleaver, February 9, 1961," Kathleen Cleaver Archive, private collection.
48 California Department of Corrections, San Quentin, "Psychiatric Summary, February 9, 1961," carton 30, folder 10, Eldridge Cleaver Papers, Bancroft Library, University of California, Berkeley.
49 Zoe Colley, "'All America Is a Prison': The Nation of Islam and the Politicization of African American Prisoners, 1955–1965." *Journal of American Studies* 48, no. 2 (2014): 393–415.
50 California Department of Corrections, San Quentin, "Report of Violation of Institution Rules for Eldridge Cleaver, April 11, 1961," Kathleen Cleaver Archive, private collection.
51 Cleaver, *Soul on Ice*, 63.
52 California Department of Corrections, San Quentin, "Inter-Departmental Communication, April 12, 1961," Kathleen Cleaver Archive, private collection.
53 California Department of Corrections, San Quentin, "Inter-Departmental Communication, August 17, 1961," Kathleen Cleaver Archive, private collection.
54 California Department of Corrections, San Quentin, "Report of Violation of Institution Rules for Eldridge Cleaver, September 6, 1961," Kathleen Cleaver Archive, private collection.
55 Eldridge Cleaver to Officer C. Thompson, September 17, 1961, Kathleen Cleaver Archive, private collection.

56 Eldridge Cleaver to Thelma Cleaver, December 19, 1961, carton 30, folder 22, Eldridge Cleaver Papers, Bancroft Library, University of California, Berkeley.
57 Eldridge Cleaver to Associate Warden L. S. Nelson, January 4, 1962, Kathleen Cleaver Archive, private collection.
58 Eldridge Cleaver to Associate Warden L. S. Nelson, January 11, 1962, Kathleen Cleaver Archive, private collection.
59 California Department of Corrections, San Quentin, "Transfer Request for Eldridge Cleaver, March 12, 1962," Kathleen Cleaver Archive, private collection.
60 California Department of Corrections, San Quentin, "Psychiatric Evaluation for Adult Authority for Eldridge Cleaver, January 24, 1962," Kathleen Cleaver Archive, private collection.
61 California Department of Corrections, San Quentin, "Adult Authority and Parole Release Referral Report, February 1, 1962," Kathleen Cleaver Archive, private collection.
62 California Department of Corrections, San Quentin, "Psychiatric Evaluation, January 24, 1962."
63 California Department of Corrections, San Quintin, "Evaluation at Time of Adult Authority Hearing for Eldridge Cleaver, March 6, 1962," box 6, folder 5, Eldridge Cleaver Papers, Bancroft Library, University of California, Berkeley.
64 Eldridge Cleaver to Walter Dunbar, May 17, 1962, Kathleen Cleaver Archive, private collection.
65 Eldridge Cleaver to Charles Geary, May 20, 1962, Kathleen Cleaver Archive, private collection.
66 Eldridge Cleaver to Governor Edmund Brown, May 20, 1962, Kathleen Cleaver Archive, private collection.
67 California Department of Corrections, San Quentin, "Inter-Departmental Communication, California State Prison at San Quentin, August 3, 1962," Kathleen Cleaver Archive, private collection.
68 California Department of Corrections, San Quentin.
69 California Department of Corrections, San Quentin, "Inter-Departmental Communication, California State Prison at San Quentin, August 5, 1962," Kathleen Cleaver Archive, private collection.
70 California Department of Corrections, San Quentin, "Inter-Departmental Communication, August 3, 1962."
71 California Department of Corrections, San Quentin, "Inter-Departmental Communication, August 5, 1962."
72 Eldridge Cleaver to Thelma Cleaver, August 6, 1962, Kathleen Cleaver Archive, private collection.
73 Eldridge Cleaver to Director of Corrections Walter Dunbar, August 1962, Kathleen Cleaver Archive, private collection.
74 California Department of Corrections, San Quentin, "Inter-Departmental Communication, California State Prison at San Quentin, December 28, 1962," Kathleen Cleaver Archive, private collection.
75 Eldridge Cleaver to Director of Corrections Walter Dunbar.
76 Eldridge Cleaver to Walter Dunbar, October 21, 1962, Kathleen Cleaver Archive, private collection.
77 Eldridge Cleaver to Mr. L. Marks, October 1, 1962, Lani Kask Archive, private collection.
78 Memorandum by D. B., "Note for Cleaver File," n.d., Lani Kask Archive, private collection.
79 Eldridge Cleaver to Warden Fred R. Dickson, October 19, 1962, Lani Kask Archive, private collection.
80 California Department of Corrections, San Quentin, "Disciplinary Report for Eldridge Cleaver, March 15, 1963," carton 32, folder 10, Eldridge Cleaver Papers, Bancroft Library, University of California, Berkeley.

81 Eldridge Cleaver to L. S. Nelson, January 10, 1963, Kathleen Cleaver Archive, private collection.
82 Cummins, *Rise and Fall*, 97–98.
83 California Department of Corrections, San Quentin, "Inter-Departmental Communication, December 28, 1962."
84 California Department of Corrections, San Quentin, "Disciplinary, October 23, 1962," Kathleen Cleaver Archive, private collection.
85 California Department of Corrections, San Quentin, "Report of Violation of Institution Rules for Eldridge Cleaver, November 8, 1962," Kathleen Cleaver Archive, private collection.
86 California Department of Corrections, San Quentin, "Inter-Departmental Communication, California State Prison at San Quentin, December 28, 1962," Kathleen Cleaver Archive, private collection.
87 California Department of Corrections, San Quentin.
88 Cleaver, "Promises," 8.
89 California Department of Corrections, San Quentin, "Adult Authority and Parole Release Referral Report for Eldridge Cleaver, April 10, 1963," carton 32, folder 10, Eldridge Cleaver Papers, Bancroft Library, University of California, Berkeley
90 Cummins, *Rise and Fall*, 73.
91 California Department of Corrections, San Quentin, "Chrono Items—General, June 18, 1963," box 6, folder 4, Eldridge Cleaver Papers, Bancroft Library, University of California, Berkeley.
92 Eldridge Cleaver to Adult Authority, March 9, 1963, Kathleen Cleaver Archive, private collection.
93 Cleaver to Adult Authority.
94 California Department of Corrections, San Quentin, "Inter-Departmental Communications, January 13, 1963," Kathleen Cleaver Archive, private collection.
95 Memorandum by W. D. Auchuff, March 18, 1963, California Department of Corrections, San Quentin, Kathleen Cleaver Archive, private collection.
96 Eldridge Cleaver to W. D. Achuff, March 26, 1963, Kathleen Cleaver Archive, private collection.
97 California Department of Corrections, San Quentin, "Adult Authority and Parole Release Referral Report for Eldridge Cleaver, April 10, 1963," carton 32, folder 10, Eldridge Cleaver Papers, Bancroft Library, University of California, Berkeley
98 California Department of Corrections, San Quentin, "Psychiatric Evaluation for Adult Authority, May 17, 1963," Kathleen Cleaver Archive, private collection.
99 Cleaver, "Promises," 3.
100 Cleaver, 4.
101 Memorandum, June 18, 1963, California Department of Corrections, San Quentin, Kathleen Cleaver Archive, private collection.
102 Cleaver, "Promises," 5.

CHAPTER 7: FOLSOM PRISON

1 Jim Brown, *Folsom Prison* (Charleston, SC: Arcadia Publishing, 2008).
2 California Department of Corrections, Folsom, "Initial Classification for Eldridge Cleaver, July 1, 1963," Kathleen Cleaver Archive, private collection.
3 California Department of Corrections, Folsom, "Adjustment Center Review, July 26, 1963," Kathleen Cleaver Archive, private collection.
4 Eldridge Cleaver to Beverly Axelrod, September 17, 1965, box 2, folder 2, Eldridge Cleaver Papers, Bancroft Library, University of California, Berkley.
5 California Department of Corrections, Folsom, "Psychiatric Evaluation for Adult Authority, November 1963," Kathleen Cleaver Archive, private collection.
6 California Department of Corrections, Folsom, "Adult Authority and Parole Release Referral Report, November 1963," Kathleen Cleaver Archive, private collection.

7 Cleaver, "Promises," 6–7.
8 Eldridge Cleaver to William Sharp, January 8, 1964, box 3, folder 18, Eldridge Cleaver Papers, Bancroft Library, University of California, Berkeley.
9 Eldridge Cleaver to Howard University Law School, January 27, 1964, box 3, folder 18, Eldridge Cleaver Papers, Bancroft Library, University of California, Berkeley.
10 Eldridge Cleaver to *DePaul Law Review,* January 31, 1964, box 3, folder 18, Eldridge Cleaver Papers, Bancroft Library, University of California, Berkeley.
11 Eldridge Cleaver to Legal Bookstore, February 2, 1964, box 3, folder 18, Eldridge Cleaver Papers, Bancroft Library, University of California, Berkeley.
12 Eldridge Cleaver to Office of the Clerk of the Supreme Court, February 10, 1964, box 3, folder 18, Eldridge Cleaver Papers, Bancroft Library, University of California, Berkeley.
13 Eldridge Cleaver to Carmen Leigh, July 1964, box 3, folder 18, Eldridge Cleaver Papers, Bancroft Library, University of California, Berkeley.
14 Eldridge Cleaver to Howard University, July 7, 1964, box 3, folder 18, Eldridge Cleaver Papers, Bancroft Library, University of California, Berkeley.
15 Eldridge Cleaver to Berkeley Law School, November 15, 1964, box 3, folder 18, Eldridge Cleaver Papers, Bancroft Library, University of California, Berkeley; Eldridge Cleaver to UCLA Law School, November 15, 1964, box 3, folder 18, Eldridge Cleaver Papers, Bancroft Library, University of California, Berkeley.
16 Cleaver, "Promises," 12.
17 California Department of Corrections, Folsom, "Adult Authority and Parole Release Referral Report, August 21, 1964," Kathleen Cleaver Archive, private collection.
18 California Department of Corrections, Folsom, "Psychiatric Evaluation for Adult Authority, August 25, 1964," Kathleen Cleaver Archive, private collection.
19 California Department of Corrections, Folsom, "Evaluation at the Time of Adult Authority Hearing," November 9, 1964," Kathleen Cleaver Archive, private collection.
20 California Department of Corrections, Folsom, "Adult Authority and Parole Release Referral Report, August 21, 1964," Kathleen Cleaver Archive, private collection.
21 Eldridge Cleaver, *Soul on Ice* (1968) (New York: Delta, 1991), 220.
22 Cleaver, "Promises," 19.
23 California Department of Corrections, Folsom, "Report of Violation of Institution Rules, March 18, 1965," Kathleen Cleaver Archive, private collection.
24 Eldridge Cleaver to S. P. Faustman, March 21, 1965, Kathleen Cleaver Archive, private collection.
25 Cleaver, "Promises," 14.
26 Cleaver, 19.
27 Cleaver, 30.
28 Lani Kask, "Soul Mates: The Prison Letters of Eldridge Cleaver and Beverly Axelrod," (PhD diss., University of California, Berkeley, 2003), 27.
29 Beverly Axelrod, interview with Lani Kask, May 1, 1993, Lani Kask Archive, private collection.
30 Kask, "Soul Mates," 158.
31 Cleaver, "Promises," 41.
32 Axelrod, interview.
33 Axelrod.
34 Beverly Axelrod to Eldridge Cleaver, June 4, 1965, box 2, folder 1, Eldridge Cleaver Papers, Bancroft Library, University of California, Berkeley.
35 Eldridge Cleaver to Beverly Axelrod, June 15, 1965, box 2, folder 1, Eldridge Cleaver Papers, Bancroft Library, University of California, Berkeley.
36 Eldridge Cleaver to Beverly Axelrod, August 16, 1965, box 2, folder 1, Eldridge Cleaver Papers, Bancroft Library, University of California, Berkeley.
37 Eldridge Cleaver to Warden Robert Heinze, August 22, 1965, box 2, folder 2, Eldridge Cleaver Papers, Bancroft Library, University of California, Berkeley.
38 Ed Keating to Arthur Barron, October 24, 1966, Lani Kask Archive, private collection.

39 Ed Keating to Max Geismar, August 26, 1965, Lani Kask Archive, private collection.
40 Eldridge Cleaver to Edward Keating, September 16, 1965, box 3, folder 19, Eldridge Cleaver Papers, Bancroft Library, University of California, Berkeley.
41 Eldridge Cleaver to Beverly Axelrod, September 19, 1965, box 2, folder 2, Eldridge Cleaver Papers, Bancroft Library, University of California, Berkeley.
42 Cecil Brown, "The Minister of Information Raps: An Interview with Eldridge Cleaver," *Evergreen*, October 1985, 85.
43 Cleaver, *Soul on Ice*, 172.
44 Cleaver, 173.
45 Cleaver, 173.
46 Eldridge Cleaver to Beverly Axelrod, September 10, 1965, box 2, folder 2, Eldridge Cleaver Papers, Bancroft Library, University of California, Berkeley.
47 Eldridge Cleaver to Beverly Axelrod, September 12, 1965, box 2, folder 2, Eldridge Cleaver Papers, Bancroft Library, University of California, Berkeley.
48 Eldridge Cleaver to Beverly Axelrod, September 19, 1965, box 2, folder 2, Eldridge Cleaver Papers, Bancroft Library, University of California, Berkeley.
49 Beverly Axelrod to Eldridge Cleaver, September 15, 1965, box 2, folder 2, Eldridge Cleaver Papers, Bancroft Library, University of California, Berkeley.
50 Beverly Axelrod to Eldridge Cleaver, September 16, 1965, box 2, folder 2, Eldridge Cleaver Papers, Bancroft Library, University of California, Berkeley.
51 California Department of Corrections, "Report of Violation of Institution Rules, September 21, 1965," carton 32, folder 7, Eldridge Cleaver Papers, Bancroft Library, University of California, Berkeley.
52 Eldridge Cleaver to Beverly Axelrod, September 24, 1965, box 2, folder 2, Eldridge Cleaver Papers, Bancroft Library, University of California, Berkeley.
53 Kask, "Soul Mates," 391.
54 Eldridge Cleaver to Beverly Axelrod, November 12, 1965, box 2, folder 3, Eldridge Cleaver Papers, Bancroft Library, University of California, Berkeley.
55 Memorandum by Robert A. Heinze to Walter Dunbar, November 24, 1965, Kathleen Cleaver Archive, private collection.
56 Axelrod, interview.
57 Edward Keating to Warden Robert Heinze, October 18, 1965, Kathleen Cleaver Archive, private collection.
58 Norman Mailer to Joseph Spangler, October 27, 1965, Kathleen Cleaver Archive, private collection.
59 John Howard Griffin to Joseph Spangler, October 13, 1965, carton 3, folder 1, Eldridge Cleaver Papers, Bancroft Library, University of California, Berkeley.
60 Eldridge Cleaver, "Dear Typewriter," November 10, 1965, carton 1, folder 70, Eldridge Cleaver Papers, Bancroft Library, University of California, Berkeley.
61 Eldridge Cleaver, "Secret Thoughts," November 7, 1965, carton 1, folder 4, Eldridge Cleaver Papers, Bancroft Library, University of California, Berkeley.
62 Eldridge Cleaver to Beverly Axelrod, October 28, 1965, box 2, folder 2, Eldridge Cleaver Papers, Bancroft Library, University of California, Berkeley.
63 Eldridge Cleaver to Thelma Cleaver, November 3, 1965, Kathleen Cleaver Archive, private collection.
64 Cleaver, "Dear Typewriter."
65 California Department of Corrections, "Adult Authority and Parole Release Referral Report, November 1965," Kathleen Cleaver Archive, private collection.
66 Eldridge Cleaver to Theophilus Cleaver, December 6, 1965, box 3, folder 19, Eldridge Cleaver Papers, Bancroft Library, University of California, Berkeley.

CHAPTER 8: CALIFORNIA MEN'S COLONY AND SOLEDAD PRISON

1 Cleaver, "Promises," 63.
2 Cleaver, 66–67.

3 Cleaver, 64.
4 Eldridge Cleaver to Edward Keating, December 17, 1965, Kathleen Cleaver Archive, private collection.
5 California Department of Corrections, CMC East, "Report of Violation of Institution Rules, December 27, 1965," Kathleen Cleaver Archive, private collection.
6 Eldridge Cleaver to Edward Keating, January 5, 1965, box 3, folder 20, Eldridge Cleaver Papers, Bancroft Library, University of California, Berkeley.
7 Eldridge Cleaver, "To My Love on New Year's Day," box 1, folder 1, Eldridge Cleaver Papers, Bancroft Library, University of California, Berkeley.
8 California Department of Corrections, CMC East, "Report on Attorney Visit, January 2, 1966," Kathleen Cleaver Archive, private collection.
9 California Department of Corrections, Soledad, "Classification Initial, January 18, 1966," Kathleen Cleaver Archive, private collection.
10 Cleaver, "Promises," 71.
11 Kask, "Soul Mates," 686.
12 Cleaver, *Soul on Ice*, 121.
13 Eldridge Cleaver to Beverly Axelrod, January 26, 1966, box 2, folder 4, Eldridge Cleaver Papers, Bancroft Library, University of California, Berkeley.
14 Cleaver, "Promises," 94.
15 Eldridge Cleaver to Beverly Axelrod, February 6, 1966, box 2, folder 4, Eldridge Cleaver Papers, Bancroft Library, University of California, Berkeley.
16 Eldridge Cleaver to Beverly Axelrod, February 3, 1966," box 2, folder 4, Eldridge Cleaver Papers, Bancroft Library, University of California, Berkeley.
17 Cleaver, "Promises," 18.
18 Eldridge Cleaver, "Bunchy," carton 2, folder 51, Eldridge Cleaver Papers, Bancroft Library, University of California, Berkeley, 38.
19 Eldridge Cleaver to Bernard Garrett, May 3, 1965, box 3, folder 19, Eldridge Cleaver Papers, Bancroft Library, University of California, Berkeley.
20 Eldridge Cleaver to Beverly Axelrod, March 17, 1966, box 2, folder 5, Eldridge Cleaver Papers, Bancroft Library, University of California, Berkeley.
21 Eldridge Cleaver, "Notes on Literary Craftsmanship," carton 1, folder 4, Eldridge Cleaver Papers, Bancroft Library, University of California, Berkeley.
22 Eldridge Cleaver, "Library Critical Essay, March 21, 1966," carton 1, folder 3, Eldridge Cleaver Papers, Bancroft Library, University of California, Berkeley.
23 Eldridge Cleaver, "Roots of Identity," carton 1, folder 2, Eldridge Cleaver Papers, Bancroft Library, University of California, Berkeley.
24 Eldridge Cleaver, "All capitalists will be dead," carton 1, folder 3, Eldridge Cleaver Papers, Bancroft Library, University of California, Berkeley.
25 Eldridge Cleaver, "Kwame," carton 1, folder 3, Eldridge Cleaver Papers, Bancroft Library, University of California, Berkeley.
26 Eldridge Cleaver to Beverly Axelrod, April 25, 1966, box 2, folder 6, Eldridge Cleaver Papers, Bancroft Library, University of California, Berkeley.
27 Cleaver, "Sketches of John."
28 Eldridge Cleaver, "Blood Money," carton 1, folder 3, Eldridge Cleaver Papers, Bancroft Library, University of California, Berkeley.
29 Eldridge Cleaver, "Stacy," carton 1, folder 1, Eldridge Cleaver Papers, Bancroft Library, University of California, Berkeley.
30 Eldridge Cleaver to Beverly Axelrod, February 12, 1966, carton 2, folder 4, Eldridge Cleaver Papers, Bancroft Library, University of California, Berkeley.
31 Eldridge Cleaver to Beverly Axelrod, letter, June 16, 1966. Quoted from Lani Kask, "Soul Mates: The Prison Letters of Eldridge Cleaver and Beverly Axelrod," (PhD diss., University of California, Berkeley, 2003): 1483–1484.
32 Eldridge Cleaver to Norman Mailer, February 27, 1966, box 3, folder 20, Eldridge Cleaver Papers, Bancroft Library, University of California, Berkeley.

33 Eldridge Cleaver to John Griffin, March 11, 1966, box 3, folder 20, Eldridge Cleaver Papers, Bancroft Library, University of California, Berkeley.
34 Kask, "Soul Mates," 80.
35 Eldridge Cleaver to Beverly Axelrod, February 16, 1966, box 2, folder 4, Eldridge Cleaver Papers, Bancroft Library, University of California, Berkeley.
36 Kask, "Soul Mates," 873.
37 Eldridge Cleaver to Beverly Axelrod, March 1, 1966, box 2, folder 5, Eldridge Cleaver Papers, Bancroft Library, University of California, Berkeley.
38 Axelrod, interview.
39 Beverly Axelrod to Eldridge Cleaver, April 21, 1966, box 2, folder 6, Eldridge Cleaver Papers, Bancroft Library, University of California, Berkeley.
40 California Department of Corrections, Soledad, "Custody and General Report, June 10, 1966," Kathleen Cleaver Archive, private collection.
41 California Department of Corrections, Soledad, "Report of Violation of Institutional Rules, May 18, 1966," Kathleen Cleaver Archive, private collection.
42 Eldridge Cleaver to Beverly Axelrod, April 23, 1966, box 2, folder 6, Eldridge Cleaver Papers, Bancroft Library, University of California, Berkeley.
43 Kask, "Soul Mates," 1306.
44 Cleaver, "Promises," 181.
45 Eldridge Cleaver, "Prison Memoir Father," carton 1, folder 1, Eldridge Cleaver Papers, Bancroft Library, University of California, Berkeley.
46 Eldridge Cleaver to David Welsh, August 7, 1966, box 3, folder 20, Eldridge Cleaver Papers, Bancroft Library, University of California, Berkeley.
47 Kask, "Soul Mates," 1400.
48 Kask, 1410.
49 Beverly Axelrod to Eldridge Cleaver, March 20, 1966, box 2, folder 5, Eldridge Cleaver Papers, Bancroft Library, University of California, Berkeley.
50 Kask, "Soul Mates," 1554.
51 Kask, 100.
52 Axelrod, interview.
53 Kask, "Soul Mates," 1967.
54 Max Geismar to Beverly Axelrod, October 25, 1966, Lani Kask Archive, private collection.
55 Beverly Axelrod to Cyrilly Abels, November 16, 1966, Lani Kask Archive, private collection.
56 Kask, "Soul Mates," 2002–3.
57 California Department of Corrections, Soledad, "Education Progress Report for History, August 19, 1966," carton 32, folder 7, Eldridge Cleaver Papers, Bancroft Library, University of California, Berkeley.
58 California Department of Corrections, Soledad, "Education Progress Report for Sociology, August 19, 1966," carton 32, folder 7, Eldridge Cleaver Papers, Bancroft Library, University of California, Berkeley.
59 California State of Corrections, Soledad, "Education Progress Report, June 10, 1966," carton 32, folder 7, Eldridge Cleaver Papers, Bancroft Library, University of California, Berkeley.
60 California State of Corrections, Soledad, "Education Progress Report for American Literature, June 10, 1966," carton 32, folder 7, Eldridge Cleaver Papers, Bancroft Library, University of California, Berkeley; California State of Corrections, Soledad, "Education Progress Report for American Government, June 10, 1966," carton 32, folder 7, Eldridge Cleaver Papers, Bancroft Library, University of California, Berkeley.
61 Eldridge Cleaver to David Welsh, August 24, 1966, box 3, folder 20, Eldridge Cleaver Papers, Bancroft Library, University of California, Berkeley.
62 Eldridge Cleaver to David Welsh, September 16, 1966, box 3, folder 20, Eldridge Cleaver Papers, Bancroft Library, University of California, Berkeley.
63 Kask, "Soul Mates," 2003, 2099.

CHAPTER 9: OAKLAND

1 Cleaver, "Promises," 122.
2 Cleaver, 120.
3 Cleaver, 128.
4 Eldridge Cleaver to Max Geismar, December 14, 1966, Lani Kask Archive, private collection.
5 Cleaver, "Promises," 134–135.
6 Eldridge Cleaver, "The New National Black Leadership," n.d., Kathleen Cleaver Archive, private collection.
7 Cleaver, "Promises," 139.
8 Cleaver, 135.
9 Cleaver, 195.
10 Cleaver, 196.
11 Report to Adult Authority, "Letter from *Ramparts* Magazine, February 23, 1967," Kathleen Cleaver Archive, private collection.
12 Report to the Adult Authority, "Case Conference, March 15, 2018," Kathleen Cleaver Archive, private collection.
13 Eldridge Cleaver, *Post-Prison Writings and Speeches*, ed. Robert Scheer (New York: Random House, 1969), 29.
14 Cleaver, 23.
15 Donna Jean Murch, *Living for the City: Migration, Education, and the Rise of the Black Panther Party in Oakland, California* (Chapel Hill: University of North Carolina Press, 2010), 3- 10.
16 Cleaver, *Post-Prison Writings and Speeches*, 38.
17 Kathleen Cleaver, in discussion with the author, April 17, 2018.
18 Kathleen Cleaver, "Outline for 'Memories of Love and War,'" Kathleen Cleaver Archive, private collection, 4.
19 Kathleen Cleaver, "Memories of Love and War" (unpublished manuscript, n.d.), Kathleen Cleaver Archive, private collection, 97.
20 Kathleen Cleaver, in discussion with author, April 19, 2018.
21 Donald Rothenberg, "Affidavit, June 3, 1967," carton 16, folder 1, Eldridge Cleaver Papers, Bancroft Library, University of California, Berkeley.
22 Cleaver, *Post-Prison Writings*, 6.
23 Joshua Bloom and Waldo E. Martin Jr., *Black Against Empire: The History and Politics of the Black Panther Party* (Oakland: University of California Press, 2013), 56.
24 California Corrections, "Emergency Report for San Francisco, May 3, 1967," Kathleen-Cleaver Archive, private collection.
25 Bobby Seale, *Seize the Time: The Story of the Black Panther Party and Huey P. Newton* (New York: Random House, 1970; Baltimore: Black Classic Press, 1991), 166. Citations refer to the Black Classic Press edition.
26 Seale, 167.
27 California Department of Corrections, "Report to Adult Authority, May 9, 1967," Kathleen Cleaver Archive, private collection.
28 Eldridge Cleaver, introduction to *The Genius of Huey P. Newton,* by Huey P. Newton (San-Francisco: Black Panther Party, 1970), 5.
29 Bloom and Martin, *Black Against Empire,* 79–80.
30 Sean L. Malloy, *Out of Oakland: Black Panther Party Internationalism During the Cold War* (Ithaca, NY: Cornell University Press, 2017), 81–82.
31 Cleaver, "Promises," 148.
32 Axelrod, interview.
33 Memorandum, California Department of Corrections, April 19, 1967, Kathleen Cleaver Archive, private collection.

34 *Beverly Axelrod v. McGraw-Hill Book Company, et al.*, "Deposition of Eldridge Cleaver, January 3, 1978," carton 28, folder 10, Eldridge Cleaver Papers, Bancroft Library, University of California, Berkeley.
35 Reggie Major, interview by Lani Kask, n.d., Lani Kask Archive, private collection.
36 Beverly Axelrod to Eldridge Cleaver, May 7, 1967, Lani Kask Archive, private collection.
37 Kathleen Cleaver, in discussion with the author, April 17, 2018.
38 Kathleen Cleaver, "Memories of Love and War," 230.
39 Kathleen Cleaver, 242.
40 Kathleen Cleaver, 233.
41 California Department of Corrections, "Report to Adult Authority, May 9, 1967," Kathleen Cleaver Archive, private collection.
42 Kathleen Cleaver, "Memories of Love and War," 250.
43 Kathleen Cleaver, 267.
44 Kathleen Cleaver, 268.
45 Cleaver, *Soul on Ice*, 136.
46 Reggie Major, interview.
47 Huey Newton, "On Eldridge Cleaver: He Is No James Baldwin," in *The Huey Newton Reader*, ed. David Hilliard and Donald Weise (New York: Seven Stories Press, 2002), 285–289.
48 Eldridge Cleaver, "Huey Newton Must Be Set Free," carton 26, folder 17, Eldridge Cleaver Papers, Bancroft Library, University of California, Berkeley.
49 Memorandum by J. Edgar Hoover, "Personal Attention to All Offices," August 25, 1967, carton 24, folder 1, Eldridge Cleaver Papers, Bancroft Library, University of California, Berkeley.
50 J. Edgar Hoover to SAC Albany, "Counterintelligence Program," August 27, 1967, carton 23, folder 18, Eldridge Cleaver Papers, Bancroft Library, University of California, Berkeley.
51 Select Committee to Study Governmental Operations with Respect to Intelligence Activities, Sen. Rep. No. (April 26, 1976), book 3, https://www.senate.gov/artandhistory/history/common/investigations/ChurchCommittee.htm.
52 Federal Bureau of Investigation, "Black Panther Party for Self Defense," November 16, 1967, carton 27, folder 11, Eldridge Cleaver Papers, Bancroft Library, University of California, Berkeley.
53 SAC San Francisco to SAC New York, "Leroy Eldridge Cleaver," October 4, 1967, carton 26, folder 17, Eldridge Cleaver Papers, Bancroft Library, University of California, Berkeley.
54 Kathleen Cleaver, "Memories of Love and War," 274.
55 Kathleen Cleaver, 47.
56 Kathleen Cleaver, "For Eldridge," December 12, 1967, Kathleen Cleaver Archive, private collection.
57 R. L. Bilideau to Issac Rivers, "Progress Report for Cleaver," February 21, 1968, Kathleen Cleaver Archive, private collection.
58 David Hilliard and Lewis Cole, *This Side of Glory: The Autobiography of David Hilliard and the Story of the Black Panther Party* (Chicago: Lawrence Hill Books, 1993), 141.
59 FBI SAC San Francisco, "BPPSD Meeting, St Philips Lutheran Church, January 21, 1968," carton 26, folder 17, Eldridge Cleaver Papers, Bancroft Library, University of California, Berkeley.
60 Eldridge Cleaver, "Black Information," carton 4, folder 6, Eldridge Cleaver Papers, Bancroft Library, University of California, Berkeley.
61 Kathleen Cleaver, "Memories of Love and War," 4.
62 Kathleen Cleaver, in discussion with the author, April 19, 2018.
63 Kathleen Cleaver, "Memories of Love and War," 6.
64 Charles Geary to San Francisco Police Commission, "Letter, January 18, 1968," Eldridge Cleaver Papers, Carton 26, Folder 16, Bancroft Library, University of California, Berkeley.

65 Eldridge Cleaver, interview by Lani Kask, March 1998 , Lani Kask Collection, private collection, Berkeley, California.
66 Memorandum, Federal Bureau of Investigation, "Black Panther Party," January 16, 1968, carton 24, folder 10, Eldridge Cleaver Papers, Bancroft Library, University of California, Berkeley.
67 Memorandum, SA to SAC San Francisco, "BPPSD," February 16, 1968, carton 26, folder 20, Eldridge Cleaver Papers, Bancroft Library, University of California, Berkeley.
68 Bloom and Martin, *Black Against Empire*, 112–113.
69 Kathleen Rout, *Eldridge Cleaver* (Boston: Twayne Publishers, 1991), 61.
70 Eldridge Cleaver and Beverly Axelrod, agreement on interest in literary work, February 14, 1968, carton 3, folder 6, Eldridge Cleaver Papers, Bancroft Library, University of California, Berkeley.
71 *Time*, "Books: The Funky Facts of Life," April 5, 1968, http://content.time.com/time/magazine/article/0,9171,900104,00.html.
72 Shane Stevens, "Quest for Dignity," *Progressive*, May 1969, 44.
73 Robert Hughes, "Black Cream," *Spectator*, February 7, 1969.
74 Robert Coles, "Black Anger," *Atlantic Monthly*, June 1968, 106.
75 Michele Wallace, *Black Macho and the Myth of the Superwoman* (London: Verso, 1978), 117– 118
76 Max Geismar, "Autobiography" (unpublished manuscript, n.d.), Lani Kask Archive, private collection, 291.

CHAPTER 10: REBELLION

1 Peter Levy, *The Great Uprising: Race Riots in Urban America During the 1960s* (Cambridge: Cambridge University Press, 2018), 153.
2 Eldridge Cleaver, "Political Education," March 21, 1971," carton 5, folder 12, Eldridge Cleaver Papers, Bancroft Library, University of California, Berkeley.
3 Eldridge Cleaver, interview by Charles Jones, March 24, 1995, Kathleen Cleaver Archive, private collection.
4 Memorandum, Federal Bureau of Investigation, April 10, 1968, carton 23, folder 18, Eldridge Cleaver Papers, Bancroft Library, University of California, Berkeley.
5 Eldridge Cleaver, "Uptight in Babylon" (unpublished manuscript), carton 1, folder 56, Eldridge Cleaver Papers, Bancroft Library, University of California, Berkeley.
6 Eldridge Cleaver, interview by Lani Kask, n.d., Lani Kask Collection, private collection, Berkeley, CA.
7 Department of Corrections, "Parole Violation Report for Eldridge Cleaver, June 14, 1968," Kathleen Cleaver Archive, private collection.
8 Sergeant E. Hilliard, "Addenda 4b," April 6, 1968, Kathleen Cleaver Archive, private collection.
9 Eldridge Cleaver, interview by Charles Jones.
10 "Ex-Officer Disputes Police Account of Panther's Slaying," *Los Angeles Times*, April 18, 1971, B.
11 Brown, "Minister of Information Raps," 80.
12 Kathleen Cleaver, "Memories of Love and War," 13.
13 Cleaver, interview by Lani Kask, n.d.
14 California Department of Corrections, "Report to Adult Authority from Parole & Community Services Division, June 14, 1968," carton 14, folder 4, Eldridge Cleaver Papers, Bancroft Library, University of California, Berkeley.
15 *Frontline*, season 16, episode 3, "The Two Nations of Black America," directed by Henry Louis Gates, with Eldridge Cleaver interview, aired February 10, 1998 on PBS.
16 Kathleen Cleaver to Eldridge Cleaver, n.d., Kathleen Cleaver Archive, private collection.
17 California Department of Justice, "Affidavit of William Wells," carton 19, folder 16, Eldridge Cleaver Papers, Bancroft Library, University of California, Berkeley.

18 California Department of Justice, "Affidavit of Donnell Lankford," carton 19, folder 16, Eldridge Cleaver Papers, Bancroft Library, University of California, Berkeley.
19 California Department of Justice, "Affidavit of Charles Bursey," carton 19, folder 16, Eldridge Cleaver Papers, Bancroft Library, University of California, Berkeley.
20 California Department of Justice, "Affidavit of Terry Cotton," carton 19, folder 16, Eldridge Cleaver Papers, Bancroft Library, University of California, Berkeley.
21 California Department of Justice, "Affidavit of Wendell E. Wade," carton 19, folder 16, Eldridge Cleaver Papers, Bancroft Library, University of California, Berkeley.
22 Memorandum, SAC San Francisco to FBI Director, "Leroy Eldridge Cleaver," April 18, 1968, carton 21, folder 27, Eldridge Cleaver Papers, Bancroft Library, University of California, Berkeley.
23 Memorandum, FBI Director to SAC San Francisco, "Leroy Eldridge Cleaver," May 16, 1968," carton 21, folder 27, Eldridge Cleaver Papers, Bancroft Library, University of California, Berkeley.
24 Thelma Cleaver to Eldridge Cleaver, May 21, 1968, box 3, folder 1, Eldridge Cleaver Papers, Bancroft Library, University of California, Berkeley.
25 Memorandum, Robert G. Thompson to Captain E. C. Brawley, "Cleaver," April 26, 1968, Kathleen Cleaver Archive, private collection.
26 Kathleen Cleaver to Eldridge Cleaver, April 25, 1968, Kathleen Cleaver Archive, private collection.
27 Kathleen Cleaver to Eldridge Cleaver, May 4, 1968, Kathleen Cleaver Archive, private collection.
28 Eldridge Cleaver to Kathleen Cleaver, May 7, 1968, carton 22, folder 2, Eldridge Cleaver Papers, Bancroft Library, University of California, Berkeley.
29 Eldridge Cleaver to Charles Geary, May 30, 1968, carton 16, folder 1, Eldridge Cleaver Papers, Bancroft Library, University of California, Berkeley.
30 Eldridge Cleaver to Ronald Reagan, May 13, 1968, carton 2, folder 19, Eldridge Cleaver Papers, Bancroft Library, University of California, Berkeley.
31 California Department of Justice, "Redirect Examination," carton 16, folder 11, Eldridge-Cleaver Papers, Bancroft Library, University of California, Berkeley.
32 Confidential memorandum, FBI Director to Secret Service, June 28, 1968, carton 21, folder 27, Eldridge Cleaver Papers, Bancroft Library, University of California, Berkeley.
33 Kathleen Cleaver, "Memories of Love and War," 333.
34 California Department of Corrections, "Parole Report, June 14, 1968," Kathleen Cleaver Archive, private collection.
35 Stew Albert, *Who the Hell Is Stew Albert?* (Pasadena, CA: Red Hen Press, 2004), 106.
36 California Department of Corrections, "Parole Report, June 14, 1968," Kathleen Cleaver Archive, private collection.
37 Eldridge Cleaver, "Barristers Club Speech," carton 2, folder 74, Eldridge Cleaver Papers, Bancroft Library, University of California, Berkeley.
38 California Department of Corrections, "Parole Report, June 14, 1968," Kathleen Cleaver Archive, private collection.
39 Cleaver, "Barristers Club Speech."
40 California Department of Corrections, "Parole Report, June 14, 1968," Kathleen Cleaver Archive, private collection.
41 Bloom and Martin, *Black Against Empire*, 125.
42 Eldridge Cleaver, "Why I Am Running for President," carton 2, folder 39, Eldridge Cleaver Papers, University of California, Berkeley.
43 Rout, *Eldridge Cleaver*, 87.
44 "Rafferty Warns on Cleaver Talks," *New York Times*, October 6, 1968, 34.
45 Lawrence Davies, "Berkeley Campus Faces Tense Week," *New York Times*, October 6, 1968, 35.
46 Bloom and Martin, *Black Against Empire*, 136–138.
47 Brown, "The Minister of Information Raps," 75.

48 Eldridge Cleaver, "Berkeley Lecture," October 15, 1968, carton 2, folder 77, Eldridge Cleaver Papers, Bancroft Library, University of California, Berkeley.
49 Lawrence Davies, "Cleaver Derides Reagan and 3 Candidates in Lecture at Stanford," *New York Times*, October 3, 1968, 22.
50 Eldridge Cleaver, "Sacramento State College Speech," October 2, 1968, carton 24, folder 17, Eldridge Cleaver Papers, Bancroft Library, University of California, Berkeley.
51 Rout, *Eldridge Cleaver*, 83.
52 Donald Cox, *Just Another Nigger: My Life in the Black Panther Party* (Berkeley, CA: Heyday, 2019), 74; Hilliard and Cole, *This Side of Glory*, 127.
53 Eldridge Cleaver, "A Word to Students," *The University and Revolution*, edited by Gary Weaver and James Weaver (Englewood Cliffs, NJ: Prentice Hall, 1969), 153.
54 Memorandum, SAC Sacramento to FBI Director, "Counterintelligence Program," December 2, 1968, carton 24, folder 17, Eldridge Cleaver Papers, Bancroft Library, University of California, Berkeley.
55 Memorandum, SAC San Francisco to FBI Director, November 15, 1968, carton 24, folder 17, Eldridge Cleaver Papers, Bancroft Library, University of California, Berkeley.
56 Memorandum, SAC New York to FBI Director, "Counterintelligence Program," October 22, 1968, carton 24, folder 16, Eldridge Cleaver Papers, Bancroft Library, University of California, Berkeley.
57 California Department of Corrections, "Parole Report, June 14, 1968," Kathleen Cleaver Archive, private collection.
58 Cleaver, *Soul on Fire,* 141.
59 Cleaver, "Slow Boat to Cuba," 28.
60 Earl Caldwell, "Cleaver Is Sought as Coast Fugitive for Defying Order," *New York Times*, November 28, 1968, 1
61 Eldridge Cleaver, "The Transformation of Eldridge Cleaver, a Treatment," Kathleen Cleaver Archive, private collection, 1.
62 Cleaver, 4.

CHAPTER 11: CUBA

1 Philip Foner, *The Spanish-Cuban-American War and the Birth of American Imperialism,* vol. 1, *1895–1898* (New York, International Publishers, 1963), 47.
2 Matt Childs, *The 1812 Aponte Rebellion in Cuba and the Struggle Against Atlantic Slavery* (Chapel Hill, University of North Carolina Press, 2006), 4.
3 Cleaver, "Slow Boat to Cuba," 18.
4 Cleaver, 1.
5 Associated Press, "Cleaver Is Reported Restricted in Havana Luxury Apartment," *New York Times*, June 1, 1969, 50.
6 Cleaver, "My Autobiography," 13.
7 Eldridge Cleaver, *Target Zero: A Life in Writing* (New York, Palgrave Macmillan, 2006), 242.
8 Cleaver, "My Autobiography," 17.
9 Kathleen Cleaver, "Back to Africa: The Evolution of the International Section of the Black Panther Party (1969–1972)," in *The Black Panther Party Reconsidered*, ed. Charles E. Jones (Baltimore, MD: Black Class Press, 1998), 217.
10 Eldridge Cleaver, "Tapes from Cuba," n.d., tape 362, side A, Kathleen Cleaver Archive, private collection.
11 Cleaver, "My Autobiography," 17.
12 Mark Sawyer, *Racial Politics in Post-Revolutionary Cuba* (Cambridge: Cambridge University Press, 2006), 65-67.
13 Teishan A. Latner, "Take Me to Havana! Airline Hijacking, U.S.-Cuba Relations, and Political Protest in Late Sixties America," *Diplomatic History* 39, no. 1 (2015): 16.
14 Cleaver, *Target Zero*, 247
15 Cleaver, *Target Zero*, 248

16 Cleaver, "Cuba Journal," 1.
17 Cleaver, "Cuba Journal," 3.
18 Cleaver, "My Autobiography," 17.
19 Memorandum, G. C. Moore to W. C. Sullivan, "Counterintelligence Program," August 21, 1968, carton 25, folder 5, Eldridge Cleaver Papers, Bancroft Library, University of California, Berkeley; Memorandum, G. C. Moore to W. C. Sullivan, "Counterintelligence Program, August 21, 1968," carton 25, folder 7, Eldridge Cleaver Papers, Bancroft Library, University of California, Berkeley.

CHAPTER 12: ALGERIA

1 Kathleen Cleaver, "Memories of Love and War," draft 1, 1.
2 Kathleen Cleaver, 1.
3 Eldridge Cleaver, "My Autobiography," 13.
4 Kathleen Cleaver, "Memories of Love and War," draft 2, 1.
5 Kathleen Cleaver, 11.
6 Kathleen Cleaver, in discussion with the author, April 17, 2018.
7 Eldridge Cleaver to Cyrilly Abels, June 13, 1969, carton 3, folder 2, Eldridge Cleaver Papers, Bancroft Library, University of California, Berkeley.
8 Cyrilly Abels to Eldridge Cleaver, June 19, 1969, carton 3, folder 2, Eldridge Cleaver Papers, Bancroft Library, University of California, Berkeley.
9 Elaine Mokhtefi, *Algiers, Third World Capital* (London: Verso, 2018), 87.
10 Mokhtefi, 90.
11 Ministere de L'Information to Mr. and Mrs. Cleaver, June 11, 1969, carton 4, folder 18, Eldridge Cleaver Papers, Bancroft Library, University of California, Berkeley.
12 Mokhtefi, *Algiers*, 89.
13 Lockwood, *Conversation with Eldridge Cleaver*, 118.
14 Charles. E. Jones, ed., *The Black Panther Party [Reconsidered]* (Baltimore, MD: Black Classic Press, 2005), 212.
15 Bloom and Martin, *Black Against Empire,* 316.
16 Malloy, *Out of Oakland*, 145.
17 Kathleen Cleaver, "Memories of Love and War," 42.
18 Kathleen Cleaver, "Memories of Love and War," draft 1, 50.
19 Nathan Hare, "A Report on the Pan-African Cultural Festival," *Black Scholar* 1, no. 1 (November 1969): 6.
20 Eldridge Cleaver, "An Open Letter to Stokely," *Black Panther,* August 16, 1969, 32.
21 Malloy, *Out of Oakland*, 156.
22 Malloy, 145.
23 Eldridge Cleaver, "Ministry of Information Release to B.P.P." August 8, 1969, box 1, folder 17, Eldridge Cleaver Collection, Cushing Archive, Texas A&M.
24 Kathleen Cleaver to Eldridge Cleaver, May 11, 1970, box 1, folder 1, Eldridge Cleaver Papers, Bancroft Library, University of California, Berkeley.
25 Kathleen Cleaver to Eldridge Cleaver, August 23, 1969, carton 5, folder 27, Eldridge Cleaver Papers, Bancroft Library, University of California, Berkeley.
26 Kathleen Cleaver to Eldridge Cleaver, n.d, box 1, folder 1, Eldridge Cleaver Papers, Bancroft Library, University of California, Berkeley.
27 Anonymous to Frank Taylor, November 19, 1969, carton 3, folder 12, Eldridge Cleaver Papers, Bancroft Library, University of California, Berkeley.
28 Kathleen Cleaver, "Memories of Love and War," 82.
29 Eldridge Cleaver to Cyrilly Abels, September 2, 1969, carton 3, folder 9, Eldridge Cleaver Papers, Bancroft Library, University of California, Berkeley.
30 Cyrilly Abels to Eldridge Cleaver, August 25, 1969, carton 3, folder 9, Eldridge Cleaver-Papers, Bancroft Library, University of California, Berkeley.
31 Cyrilly Abels to Eldridge Cleaver, October 20, 1969, Kathleen Cleaver Collection, private collection.

32 Eldridge Cleaver to Max Geismar, December 31, 1969, Lani Kask Archive, private collection.
33 Judy Tzu-Chun Wu, *Radicals on the Road: Internationalism, Orientalism, and Feminism During the Vietnam Era* (Ithaca, NY: Cornell University Press, 2013), 142.
34 Eldridge Cleaver, foreword to *Juche: The Speeches and Writings of Kim Il Sung* by Kim Il Sung, ed. Li Yuk-Sa (New York: Grossman Publishers), 1972.
35 Korean Journalists' Union to Eldridge Cleaver, August 1, 1969, Kathleen Cleaver Archive, private collection.
36 Eldridge Cleaver to David Hilliard, September 5, 1969, box 1, folder 9, Eldridge Cleaver Collection, Cushing Archive, Texas A&M.
37 Eldridge Cleaver, "Radio Program," carton 5, folder 7, Eldridge Cleaver Papers, Bancroft Library, University of California, Berkeley.
38 Eldridge Cleaver, "Solidarity of the Peoples Until Victory or Death," carton 4, folder 4, Eldridge Cleaver Papers, Bancroft Library, University of California, Berkeley.
39 Eldridge Cleaver, "Revolutionary Spirit of Comrade Kim Il Sung," box 1, folder 18, Eldridge Cleaver Collection, Cushing Archive, Texas A&M.
40 Malloy, *Out of Oakland*, 154.
41 Eldridge Cleaver, "Revolutionary Spirit of Comrade Kim Il Sung," September 28, 1969, Kathleen Cleaver Archive, private collection.
42 Eldridge Cleaver to Kathleen Cleaver, September 11, 1969, Kathleen Cleaver Archive, private collection.
43 Eldridge Cleaver to Kathleen Cleaver, September 13, 1969, Kathleen Cleaver Archive, private collection.
44 Kathleen Cleaver to Eldridge Cleaver, May 11, 1970, box 1, folder 1, Eldridge Cleaver Papers, Bancroft Library, University of California, Berkeley.
45 Kathleen Cleaver, "Memories of Love and War," 13, Kathleen Cleaver Archive, private collection.
46 Cox, *Just Another Nigger*, 153.
47 Elaine Mokhtefi, in discussion with the author, October 26, 2018.
48 Don Cox, interview by PBS for *The Black Panthers: Vanguard of the Revolution*, Kathleen Cleaver Archive, private collection.
49 Kathleen Cleaver, journal, April 16, 1970, Kathleen Cleaver Archive, private collection.
50 William Eagleton to Arthur Lowrie, Officer in Charge, December 2, 1969, National Archives and Records Administration, College Park, MD, EO 13526, section 3.3.
51 Charles Geary, "The Persecution of the Black Panther Party," in *The Black Panthers Speak*, ed. Philip S. Foner (Cambridge, MA: De Capo Press, 1995), 257–258.
52 SAC San Francisco to FBI Director, March 3, 1970, teletype, carton 24, folder 1, Eldridge Cleaver Papers, Bancroft Library, University of California, Berkeley.
53 SAC SF to FBI Director, "Connie Matthews to David Hilliard," April 20, 1970, carton 24, folder 1, Eldridge Cleaver Papers, Bancroft Library, University of California, Berkeley.
54 SAC San Francisco to FBI Director, March 26, 1970, teletype, Kathleen Cleaver Archive, private collection.
55 Cyrilly Abels to Eldridge Cleaver, April 25, 1970, carton 3, folder 16, Eldridge Cleaver Papers, Bancroft Library, University of California, Berkeley.
56 Cyrilly Abels to Barney Drefus, April 27, 1970, carton 3, folder 16, Eldridge Cleaver Papers, Bancroft Library, University of California, Berkeley.
57 Kathleen Cleaver to Eldridge Cleaver, May 11, 1970, box 1, folder 1, Eldridge Cleaver Papers, Bancroft Library, University of California, Berkeley.
58 Kathleen Cleaver to Eldridge Cleaver, May 12, 1970, box 1, folder 1, Eldridge Cleaver Papers, Bancroft Library, University of California, Berkeley.
59 Kathleen Cleaver to Eldridge Cleaver, June 12, 1970, Kathleen Cleaver Archive, private collection.
60 Randy (Rappaport) Ross, in discussion with the author, May 14, 2018.
61 (Rappaport) Ross.
62 Wu, *Radicals on the Road*, 144, 165.

63 Kathleen Cleaver, "Back to Africa," 234; Wu, *Radicals on the Road*, 147.
64 Alex Hing, in discussion with the author, March 15, 2019.
65 Elaine Brown, "Hidden Traitor," Newton Foundation Records, collection M864, box 48, Stanford University, 24.
66 (Rappaport) Ross, discussion.

CHAPTER 13: THE INTERNATIONAL SECTION OF THE BLACK PANTHER PARTY

1 Michael Zwerin, "Revolutionary Bust," *Village Voice*, February 4, 1971.
2 Memorandum, Department of State, National Archives and Records Administration, College Park, MD, EO 13526, section 3.3.
3 Eldridge Cleaver, "Cleaver from Algiers," January 12, 1971, box 59, folder 1, Huey Newton Papers, Stanford University.
4 Eldridge Cleaver, interview by Charles Jones.
5 Bloom and Martin, *Black Against Empire*, 184–187.
6 FBI Director to SAC New York, July 22, 1969, carton 24, folder 1, Eldridge Cleaver Papers, Bancroft Library, University of California, Berkeley.
7 SAC New York to FBI Director, October 7, 1970, carton 24, folder 3, Eldridge Cleaver Papers, Bancroft Library, University of California, Berkeley.
8 SAC New York to FBI Director, October 19, 1970, carton 16, folder 16, Eldridge Cleaver Papers, Bancroft Library, University of California, Berkeley.
9 SAC Los Angeles to FBI Director, December 3, 1970, carton 26, folder 4, Eldridge Cleaver Papers, Bancroft Library, University of California, Berkeley.
10 Eldridge Cleaver to Huey Newton, December 20, 1970, Kathleen Cleaver Archive, private collection.
11 FBI Director to SACs Atlanta, Boston, Chicago, Detroit, New York, San Francisco, Washington, airtel, December 31, 1970, carton 26, folder 4, Eldridge Cleaver Papers, Bancroft Library, University of California, Berkeley.
12 FBI, Anonymous to Huey Newton, Kathleen Cleaver Archive, private collection.
13 FBI Director to SACs Boston and San Francisco, airtel, January 18, 1971, carton 24, folder 1, Eldridge Cleaver Papers, Bancroft Library, University of California, Berkeley.
14 Select Committee to Study Governmental Operations.
15 SAC San Francisco to FBI Director, airtel, February 25, 1971, carton 24, folder 1, Eldridge Cleaver Papers, Bancroft Library, University of California, Berkeley.
16 Huey Newton, "On the Purge of Geronimo from the Black Panther Party," *Black Panther*, January 23 1971, 7.
17 SAC New York to FBI Director, "Urgent," January 27, 1971, Kathleen Cleaver Archive, private collection.
18 SAC San Francisco to FBI Director, airtel, January 27, 1971, Kathleen Cleaver Archive, private collection.
19 G. C. Moore to C. D. Brennan, January 29, 1971, carton 26, folder 5, Eldridge Cleaver Papers, Bancroft Library, University of California, Berkeley.
20 FBI Director to SACs, airtel, February 2, 1971, carton 26, folder 5, Eldridge Cleaver Papers, Bancroft Library, University of California, Berkeley.
21 FBI Director to SACs New York, airtel, February 3, 1971, Kathleen Cleaver Archive, private collection.
22 Eldridge Cleaver to Lumumba, telegram, February 15, 1971, carton 26, folder 5, Eldridge Cleaver Papers, Bancroft Library, University of California, Berkeley.
23 SAC San Francisco to FBI Director, teletype, February 9, 1971, Kathleen Cleaver Archive, private collection.
24 Eldridge Cleaver, tape 157, side A, Kathleen Cleaver Archive, private collection.
25 Elaine Mokhtefi, discussion.
26 San Quentin Black Panthers to Eldridge Cleaver, box 50, folder 3, Huey Newton Papers, Stanford University.

27 Kathleen Cleaver, "Memories of Love and War," 13.
28 Bloom and Martin, *Black Against Empire*, 368–369.
29 SAC New York to FBI Director, March 2, 1971, carton 26, folder 6, Eldridge Cleaver Papers, Bancroft Library, University of California, Berkeley.
30 FBI Director to SAC San Francisco and Chicago, airtel, March 23, 1971, carton 26, folder 7, Eldridge Cleaver Papers, Bancroft Library, University of California, Berkeley.
31 Eldridge Cleaver to Cyrilly Abels, December 7, 1970, carton 4, folder 20, Eldridge Cleaver Papers, Bancroft Library, University of California, Berkeley.
32 Kathleen Cleaver to Cyrilly Abels, February 23, 1971, carton 3, folder 21, Eldridge Cleaver Papers, Bancroft Library, University of California, Berkeley.
33 William Eagleton to Arthur Lowrie, March 17, 1971, National Archives and Records Administration, College Park, MD, EO 13526, section 3.3.
34 William Eagleton, to Arthur Lowrie, December 9, 1970, National Archives and Records Administration, College Park, MD, EO 13526, section 3.3.
35 Kathleen Cleaver to Frank Taylor, June 25, 1971, Kathleen Cleaver Archive, private collection.
36 Daniel Moses to Cyrilly Abels, June 7, 1971, Kathleen Cleaver Archive, private collection.
37 Malloy, *Out of Oakland*, 193–197.
38 Eldridge Cleaver, "Towards a People's Army," October 1, 1971," in RPCN 1, no. 7, carton 2, folder 32, Eldridge Cleaver Papers, Bancroft Library, University of California, Berkeley.
39 Bloom and Martin, *Black Against Empire*, 387-389.
40 Malloy, *Out of Oakland*, 11–12, 225.
41 Denise Oliver-Velez, in discussion with the author, May 15, 2018.
42 Eldridge Cleaver, "After Malcolm," in *Revolution in the Congo* (London: Revolutionary Peoples' Communication Network, 1971), 9.
43 Oliver-Velez, discussion.
44 Kathleen Cleaver, "Memories of Love and War," 652.
45 Kathleen Cleaver, 641–42.
46 Cyrilly Abels to Eldridge Cleaver, "Letter, undated," Eldridge Cleaver Papers, Carton 3, Folder 21, Bancroft Library, University of California, Berkeley.
47 Eldridge Cleaver, "In Defense of Air-Craft Expropriations," July 14, 1972, Revolutionary People's Communications Network, Black Panther Archive, Centre des Archives Diplomatiques de Nantes.
48 Kathleen Cleaver to Fredrika Teer, June 10, 1972, Kathleen Cleaver Archive, private collection.
49 Brendan I. Koerner, *The Skies Belong to Us* (New York: Broadway, 2013), 194.
50 Eldridge Cleaver to Houari Boumediene, "An Open Letter," August 2, 1972, Black Panther Archive, Centre des Archives Diplomatiques de Nantes.
51 Melvin McNair, Jean McNair, Larry Burgess, Joyce Burgess, and George Brown to President Boumediene, August 8, 1972, Black Panther Collection, Centre des Archives Diplomatiques de Nantes.
52 Kathleen Cleaver, "Second Meeting with C. Salah," August 16, 1972, Kathleen Cleaver Archive, private collection.
53 Koerner, *Skies Belong to Us*, 201.
54 Eldridge Cleaver to Reggie Major, December 15, 1972, Kathleen Cleaver Archive, private collection.
55 Kathleen Cleaver to Gayle, December 13, 1972, Kathleen Cleaver Archive, private collection.
56 Allen Davis to George Lane, December 27, 1972, National Archives and Records Administration, College Park, MD, EO 13526, section 3.3.
57 Mokhtefi, *Algiers*, 179.

CHAPTER 14: PARIS

1 "Richard" to "Mercedes," January 7, 1973, box 1, folder 2, Eldridge Cleaver Papers, Bancroft Library, University of California, Berkeley.

2 James Clarity, "Cleaver Seeks Political Asylum in France: Notes on People," *New York Times*, April 4, 1973, 39.
3 Eldridge Cleaver to Monsieur le Premier Ministre, undated, Kathleen Cleaver Archive, private collection.
4 "France Rejects Request from Cleaver for Asylum," *New York Times*, May 20, 1973, 17.
5 Eldridge Cleaver to Louis, February 21, 1974, Kathleen Cleaver Archive, private collection.
6 Cleaver, *Soul on Fire*, 186.
7 Kathleen Cleaver, in discussion with the author, April 17, 2017.
8 Kathleen Cleaver to Cyrilly Abels, April 20, 1974, Kathleen Cleaver Archive, private collection.
9 Kathleen Cleaver to Cyrilly Abels, July 25, 1974, Kathleen Cleaver Archive, private collection.
10 "Stacy" to "Marie," April 9, 1973, Kathleen Cleaver Archive, private collection.
11 Peter Hyun to Eldridge Cleaver, n.d., Kathleen Cleaver Archive, private collection.
12 Peter Hyun to Eldridge Cleaver, April 8, 1974, Kathleen Cleaver Archive, private collection.
13 Eldridge Cleaver to Peter Huyn, April 15, 1974, Kathleen Cleaver Archive, private collection.
14 Eldridge Cleaver to Kathleen Cleaver, May 2, 1975, Kathleen Cleaver Archive, private collection.
15 Cleaver, "My Autobiography," 25.
16 Kathleen Cleaver to Eldridge Cleaver, January 26, 1975, box 1, folder 3, Eldridge Cleaver Papers, Bancroft Library, University of California, Berkeley.
17 Cleaver, "My Autobiography," 35.
18 Cleaver, 37.
19 Kathleen Cleaver to Eldridge Cleaver, July 10, 1975, box 1, folder 3, Eldridge Cleaver Papers, Bancroft Library, University of California, Berkeley.
20 Correspondence to Eldridge Cleaver from unknown sender (illegible name), May 18, 1975, Kathleen Cleaver Archive, private collection.
21 Cleaver, *Soul on Fire*, 210.
22 Carl Salans to Brent Scowcroft, May 5, 1975, box 6, folder "Cleaver, Eldridge," Kissinger-Scowcroft West Wing Office Files, Gerald Ford Presidential Library, Ann Arbor, Michigan.
23 Cleaver, "My Autobiography," 39.
24 Eldridge Cleaver to Kathleen Cleaver, April 11, 1975, Kathleen Cleaver Archive, private collection.
25 Kathleen Cleaver to Eldridge Cleaver, April 15, 1975, box 1, folder 1, Eldridge Cleaver Papers, Bancroft Library, University of California, Berkeley.
26 Kathleen Cleaver to Eldridge Cleaver, May 19, 1975, box 1, folder 1, Eldridge Cleaver Papers, Bancroft Library, University of California, Berkeley.
27 Eldridge Cleaver, interview by Joseph Duffy and Arch Davis, 1982, carton 13, folder 73, Eldridge Cleaver Papers, Bancroft Library, University of California, Berkeley.
28 Eldridge Cleaver, "Origin of Pants," carton 11, folder 16, Eldridge Cleaver Papers, Bancroft Library, University of California, Berkeley.
29 Eldridge Cleaver to Kathleen Cleaver, June 16, 1975, Kathleen Cleaver Archive, private collection.
30 Eldridge Cleaver to Kathleen Cleaver, June 17, 1975, Kathleen Cleaver Archive, private collection.
31 Eldridge Cleaver to Henry Louis Gates, June 18, 1975, Kathleen Cleaver Archive, private collection.
32 Mary Blume, "Eldridge Cleaver as Rebellious Pants Designer," *International Herald Tribune*, August 14, 1975.

33 "Can You See Eldridge Cleaver in Sexy Pants?" *Sun-Reporter,* August 30, 1975, 13.
34 "Cleaver Faces Arrest on Return Today," *Los Angeles Times,* November 18, 1975, A1.
35 Eldridge Cleaver, "Why I Left the U.S. and Why I Am Returning," *New York Times,* November 18, 1975, 37.
36 Lettijane Levine, "Cleaver's Born-Again Menswear," *Los Angeles View,* January 11, 1978, F1.
37 Eldridge Cleaver, "My Autobiography," 39.
38 John F. Burns, "Cleaver Seized on Return Here After 7 Years Exile," *New York Times,* November 19, 1975, 20.
39 Eldridge Cleaver to Cher Revy, December 13, 1975, Kathleen Cleaver Archive, private collection.

CHAPTER 15: BORN AGAIN

1 Cleaver to Cher Revy.
2 Eldridge Cleaver to Carole Roussopulos, December 30, 1975, Kathleen Cleaver Archive, private collection.
3 Cleaver to Cher Revy.
4 "Notes on People: Speeding Legislators Snared," *New York Times,* December 18, 1975, 55.
5 Eldridge Cleaver to Cher Revy, December 30, 1975, Kathleen Cleaver Archive, private collection.
6 Eldridge Cleaver, "Worst Moment," Kathleen Cleaver Archive, private collection.
7 Cleaver, "My Autobiography," 43.
8 "Eldridge Cleaver Tour: Report from East Coast Region," Eldridge Cleaver Papers, carton 14, folder 5, Bancroft Library, University of California, Berkeley.
9 Cleaver, "My Autobiography," 42.
10 Cleaver, *Soul on Fire,* 224.
11 Steven Miller, *The Age of Evangelicalism: America's Born-Again Years* (New York: Oxford, 2014).
12 Kendrick Oliver, "How to be (the Author of) *Born Again*: Charles Colson and the Writing of Conversion in the Age of Evangelicalism," *Religions* 5, no. 3 (2014): 886-911.
13 Cleaver, *Soul on Fire,* 211.
14 Laura Nadworay to Eldridge Cleaver, January 1, 1976, carton 6, folder 10, Eldridge Cleaver Papers, Bancroft Library, University of California, Berkeley.
15 Letters to Cleaver, carton 7, folder 12, Eldridge Cleaver Papers, Bancroft Library, University of California, Berkeley.
16 Pat Boone to Eldridge Cleaver, September 30, 1976, carton 5, folder 67, Eldridge Cleaver Papers, Bancroft Library, University of California, Berkeley.
17 Eldridge Cleaver to Ellen Wright, August 2, 1976, carton 6, folder 10, Eldridge Cleaver Papers, Bancroft Library, University of California, Berkeley.
18 Eldridge Cleaver to Carole Roussopoulos, July 24, 1976, Kathleen Cleaver Archive, private collection.
19 Eldridge Cleaver, *Meet the Press,* August 29, 1976, carton 6, folder 17, Eldridge Cleaver Papers, Bancroft Library, University of California, Berkeley, transcript.
20 Henry Mitchell, "Eldridge Cleaver at Exile's End," *Washington Post,* August 31, 1976, B1.
21 Arthur DeMoss to Eldridge Cleaver, June 17, 1977, carton 7, folder 43, Eldridge Cleaver Papers, Bancroft Library, University of California, Berkeley.
22 Charles Colson to Eldridge Cleaver, May 12, 1977, carton 7, folder 41, Eldridge Cleaver Papers, Bancroft Library, University of California, Berkeley.
23 Marvin X, *Eldridge Cleaver: My Friend, the Devil* (Baton Rouge, LA: Black Bird Press, 2009), 49.
24 Marvin Jackmon, in discussion with the author, August 27, 2017.
25 Eldridge Cleaver, "Eldridge Cleaver Crusades Contract," carton 7, folder 7, Eldridge Cleaver Papers, Bancroft Library, University of California, Berkeley.

26 Billy Zeoli and Al Hartley to Eldridge Cleaver, December 16, 1977, carton 11, folder 4, Eldridge Cleaver Papers, Bancroft Library, University of California, Berkeley.
27 Oliver-Velez, discussion.
28 Jackmon, discussion.
29 June Kelly, "Cleaver Gets Mixed Reception at WSP," *Ader News*, November 14, 1977.
30 Anarchist Party of Canada, press release, n.d., carton 12, folder 12, Eldridge Cleaver Papers, Bancroft Library, University of California, Berkeley.
31 Ahmad Cleaver, in discussion with the author, April 2, 2018.
32 Ahmad Cleaver.
33 "Eldridge Cleaver Designs Pants 'For Men Only,'" *Jet*, September 21, 1978, 23.
34 Rout, *Eldridge Cleaver*, 226–227.
35 "Former Black Panther Leader EC Has New Outlook—in Shades of Gray," *Chicago Tribune*, October 3, 1978, section 2, 2.
36 Richard Gilman, "Review of *Soul on Fire*, by Eldridge Cleaver," *New Republic*, January 20, 1979, 458.
37 Eldridge and Kathleen Cleaver to "To Whom It May Concern," September 28, 1972, Kathleen Cleaver Archive, private collection.
38 *Axelrod v. Cleaver*, "Judgement by Court Against Defendant Eldridge Cleaver After Default," February 7, 1979 (Superior Court of California County of San Francisco), Kathleen Cleaver Archive, private collection.
39 Eldridge Cleaver, mass mailing, June 6, 1979, carton 11, folder 12, Eldridge Cleaver Papers, Bancroft Library, University of California, Berkeley.
40 "Cleaver Plan to Build Religious Facility Reported," *Los Angeles Times*, June 7, 1979, E8.
41 "Born-Again Cleaver Buys Nevada Land," *San Francisco Examiner*, June 7, 1979, 45.
42 X, *My Friend, the Devil*, 83.
43 Joseph Duffy and Arch Davis, interview with Eldridge Cleaver, Eldridge Cleaver Papers, carton 13, folder 73, Bancroft Library, University of California, Berkeley.
44 X, *My Friend, the Devil*, 84–85.
45 "Eldridge Cleaver Given Probation for 1968 Assault," *New York Times*, January 3, 1980, A10.
46 Eldridge Cleaver to Mrs. DeMoss, April 20, 1981, carton 13, folder 21, Eldridge Cleaver Papers, Bancroft Library, University of California, Berkeley.
47 Eldridge Cleaver, "Articles of Incorporation of the 4th of July Commemoration Institute," carton 13, folder 62, Eldridge Cleaver Papers, Bancroft Library, University of California, Berkeley.
48 Eldridge Cleaver, "Preliminary Draft of Purpose and Belief of The 4th of July Movement," carton 13, folder 63, Eldridge Cleaver Papers, Bancroft Library, University of California, Berkeley.
49 Eldridge Cleaver "Fourth of July Movement Launching Plan," carton 13, folder 65, Eldridge Cleaver Papers, Bancroft Library, University of California, Berkeley.
50 Cleaver, "My Autobiography," 48.
51 Cleaver, 50.
52 Cleaver, 52.
53 Newell Bringhurst, "Eldridge Cleaver's Passage through Mormonism," *Journal of Mormon History*, vol. 28.1 (spring 2002): 80-110.
54 Eldridge Cleaver, "Speech to the Century Club," February 25, 1981, carton 13, folder 69, Eldridge Cleaver Papers, Bancroft Library, University of California, Berkeley.
55 Eldridge Cleaver, interview by Ray Briem, *Ray Briem Show*, February 1981, carton 13, folder 71, Eldridge Cleaver Papers, Bancroft Library, University of California, Berkeley, transcript.
56 Cleaver.
57 "Your Colored Girl" to Eldridge Cleaver, September 11, 1980, box 3, folder 17, Eldridge Cleaver Papers, Bancroft Library, University of California, Berkeley.

58 "Cleaver Tells Why He Is a Wife Beater—And More," *Jet*, June 12, 1980, 41.
59 Phyllus Brown, "Kathleen Cleaver Wants Peace, a Balanced Life," *Peninsula Times Tribune*, May 15, 1981.
60 Ahmad Cleaver, in discussion with the author, May 10, 2018.

CHAPTER 16: AMERICA

1 Eldridge Cleaver, "Still a Brother: Eldridge Cleaver's Overture to Huey P. Newton," *Black Male/Female Relationships* 2 (Winter 1981): 43–45.
2 Eldridge Cleaver to Bobby Seale, July 14, 1982, box 3, folder 11, Eldridge Cleaver Papers, Bancroft Library, University of California, Berkeley.
3 Collegiate Association for the Research of Principles, "Goals," carton 14, folder 9, Eldridge Cleaver Papers, Bancroft Library, University of California, Berkeley.
4 Katherine Ellison, "Eldridge Cleaver Squares Off Against 'Cesspool' of the Left," *Mercury News*, March 3, 1984, A-7.
5 Hilda Bryant, "Cleaver Turns to the Right," *Seattle Post-Intelligencer*, May 29, 1981.
6 "Vietnam Memorial Site of Rallies on US Latin Policy," *Los Angeles Times*, July 3, 1983, A18.
7 "Cleaver Slugs Heckler Before Speech," *San Francisco Examiner*, May 20, 1982, 28.
8 "Eldridge Cleaver Tour: Report from East Coast Region," carton 14, folder 5, Eldridge Cleaver Papers, Bancroft Library, University of California, Berkeley.
9 Eldridge Cleaver to Odd Inge, September 18, 1984, carton 14, folder 1, Eldridge Cleaver Papers, Bancroft Library, University of California, Berkeley.
10 Beth Hughes, "Eldridge Cleaver Seeks Mayor's Seat, Born-Again Panther Party," *San Francisco Examiner*, January 24, 1983, 16.
11 Eldridge Cleaver to the Allison Group, carton 14, folder 20, Eldridge Cleaver Papers, Bancroft Library, University of California, Berkeley.
12 Dudley Pierson, "Former Black Panther Sounds Like Reagan," *Lansing State Journal*, October 20, 1982.
13 "Can Cleaver Beat Dellums?" *Inside Washington*, January 21, 1984, 5.
14 Paul Rabner, "Ex-Rated Politics: The Campaign of Eldridge Cleaver," *Express*, February 10, 1984, 3.
15 Eldridge Cleaver, "Open Letter Cleaver to Jesse Jackson," *National Review*, Feb 10, 1984, 33.
16 Thomas D. Elias, "Berkeley Providing Fall's Best Election Theater," *Placerville Mountain Democrat*, October 26, 1984, 4.
17 "Cleaver Is Arrested After Picketing Home," *San Ana Orange County Register*, October 21, 1984, 392.
18 Eldridge Cleaver, "The Rose Garden" (unpublished manuscript, November 2, 1987), Kathleen Cleaver Archive, private collection.
19 Ulrike Langer, "Cleaver Steps Up Fight for Rights of Disabled," *Oregonian*, September 24, 1994, D11.
20 Larry Peterson, "A Radically Changed Eldridge Cleaver Returns to OC Friday," *Santa Ana Orange County Register*, February 20, 1986.
21 Rick Shaughnessy, "Senate Race Fireworks Spark GOP Convention," *San Diego Union Tribune*, March 10, 1986, A3.
22 Phillip Trounstine, "New GOP is Full of Fight—Often With One Another," *Mercury News*, 1B.
23 Marvin X, *My Friend, the Devil*, 121.
24 Eldridge Cleaver, "Dan White, Welcome Here," January 9, 1985, carton 1, folder 69, Eldridge Cleaver Papers, Bancroft Library, University of California, Berkeley.
25 "Cleaver: Treasure Island Hides Jewel Fortune," *San Jose Mercury News*, September 25, 1987, 12B.
26 "Cleaver Calls Drug Arrest an 'Ambush,'" *San Jose Mercury News*, October 5, 1987, 1E.
27 "Life in America," *Miami Herald*, October 26, 1987, 2A.

28 Harriet Chang, "Eldridge Cleaver Arrested in Oakland," *San Francisco Chronicle*, February 12, 1988, B8.
29 "Cleaver Gets Probation in House Burglary," *San Jose Mercury News*, June 29, 1988, 3B.
30 Laura Kurtzman, "Cleaver Launches Recycling War," *San Jose Mercury News*, October 2, 1989, 1B.
31 Eldridge Cleaver to Lani Kask, May 26, 1997, Lani Cask Archive, private collection.
32 Eldridge Cleaver, "The Alters of Satan: A Pro-Children Song," Kathleen Cleaver Archive, private collection.
33 Eldridge Cleaver to Carole Roussopoulos, December 4, 1990, Kathleen Cleaver Archive, private collection.
34 "Cleaver Arraigned in Rock Cocaine Case—Former Panther Spokesman Held in Oakland," *San Francisco Chronicle*, June 5, 1992, A26.
35 "Cleaver Arrested on Cocaine Charge," *Washington Times*, June 5, 1992, A2.
36 Janice Wells, "Cleaver Has Brain Surgery After Arrest in Berkeley," *San Francisco Chronicle*, March 2, 1994, A13.
37 Jennifer Skordas, "Cleaver Did It: From Panthers to Mormonism Cleaver Lives His Life as He Calls It," *Salt Lake Tribune*, February 15, 1995, B1.
38 Eldridge Cleaver, "Biographical Sketch of and by Eldridge Cleaver," December 24, 1994. Kathleen Cleaver Archive, private collection.
39 Tim Tesconi, "Cleaver Leads Vigil in Santa Rosa for Churches," *Santa Rosa Press Democrat*, July 1, 1996, B1.
40 Eldridge Cleaver, "A State of Creation Address: Earth's Soul on Ice," April 18, 1998, Kathleen Cleaver Archive, private collection.
41 Eldridge Cleaver to Lani Kask, January 1998, Lani Kask Archive, private collection.
42 Eldridge Cleaver to Sandra, April 4, 1998, Kathleen Cleaver Archive, private collection.
43 Eldridge Cleaver, "The Overview," Kathleen Cleaver Archive, private collection.
44 Eldridge Cleaver, "Resolution," January 8, 1998, Kathleen Cleaver Archive, private collection.
45 Eldridge Cleaver, "Police Departments," Kathleen Cleaver Archive, private collection.
46 Eldridge Cleaver, e-mail message to Bobby Seale, March 23, 1998, Kathleen Cleaver Archive, private collection.
47 Eldridge Cleaver, "Police Departments," Kathleen Cleaver Archive, private collection.
48 Ahmad Cleaver, e-mail message to Eldridge Cleaver, April 13, 1998, Kathleen Cleaver Archive, private collection.
49 Eldridge Cleaver to Karen Koekler, October 2, 1997, Kathleen Cleaver Archive, private collection.
50 Eldridge Cleaver to Riley Koekler, October 2, 1997, Kathleen Cleaver Archive, private collection.
51 Joju Cleaver, e-mail message to Eldridge Cleaver, April 13, 1998, Kathleen Cleaver Archive, private collection.
52 Joju Cleaver, e-mail message to Eldridge Cleaver, April 20, 1998, Kathleen Cleaver Archive, private collection.
53 Loretta Green, "Cleaver Speech Turned Out to Be Prophetic," *San Jose Mercury News*, May 22, 1998, 1B.
54 Ahmad Cleaver, in discussion with the author, April 2, 2018.
55 County of Los Angeles Department of Health Services, "Death Certificate for Eldridge Cleaver, May 6, 1998," Kathleen Cleaver Archive, private collection.
56 Larry Gerber, "Panthers, preachers honor Cleaver," *San Francisco Examiner*, May 10, 1998, 60
57 Bobby Seale, "Eldridge 'The Rage' Cleaver," n.d., Kathleen Cleaver Archive, private collection.
58 "Former '60s Black Panther Party Leader Mourned at Area Service," May 10, 1998, 97.
59 Eldridge Cleaver, interview by Lani Kask, 1997, Lani Kask Collection, private collection.

INDEX